ARATA
THE LEGEND

4

We are Man, born of Heaven and Earth,
Moon and Sun and everything under them.

Eyes, Ears, Nose, Tongue, Body, Mind...

Purity will pierce evil and
open up the world of darkness.

All life will be reborn and invigorated.

Appear now.

STORY & ART BY
Yuu Watase

Arata THE LEGEND

CHARACTERS

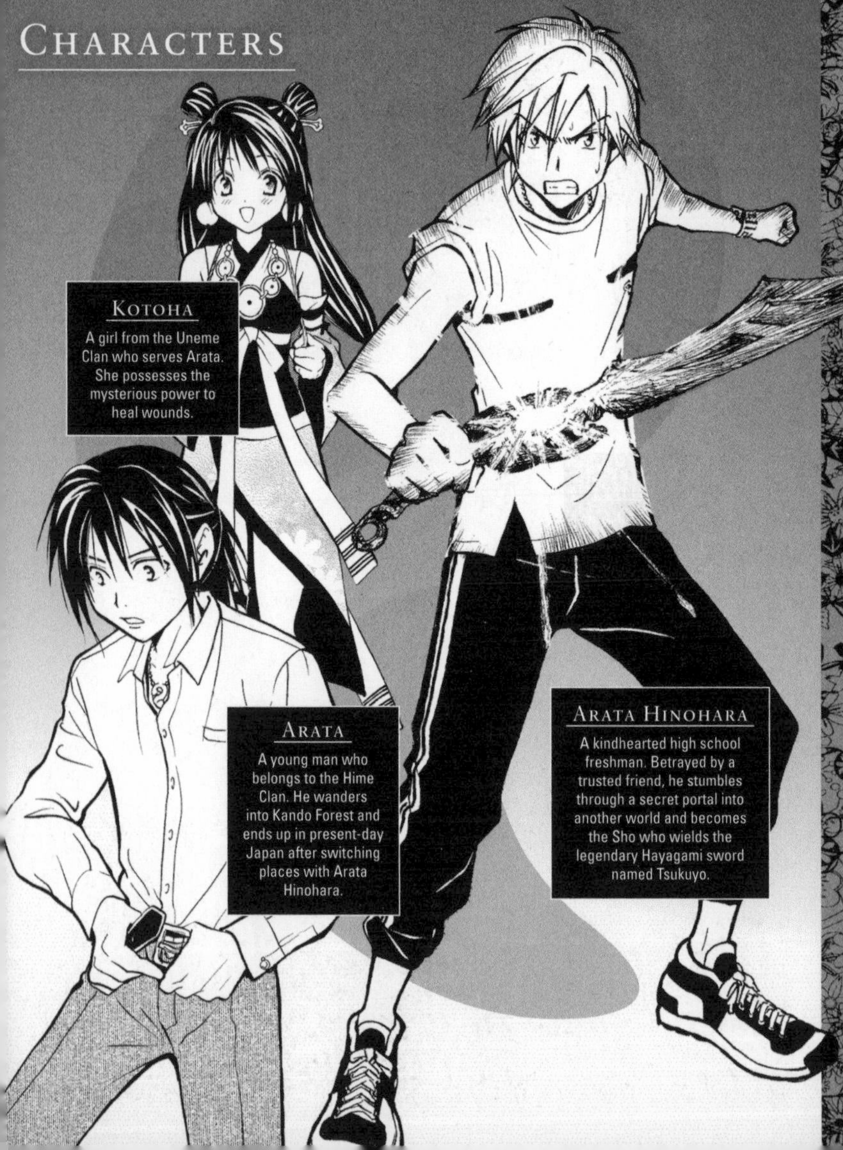

KOTOHA
A girl from the Uneme Clan who serves Arata. She possesses the mysterious power to heal wounds.

ARATA HINOHARA
A kindhearted high school freshman. Betrayed by a trusted friend, he stumbles through a secret portal into another world and becomes the Sho who wields the legendary Hayagami sword named Tsukuyo.

ARATA
A young man who belongs to the Hime Clan. He wanders into Kando Forest and ends up in present-day Japan after switching places with Arata Hinohara.

Kannagi

One of the Twelve Shinsho. He has a Hayagami called "Homura."

Akachi

One of the Twelve Shinsho who rules the Great Land. He took Kannagi's Hayagami Homura from him.

Kanate

He joins the journey after meeting Arata on the prison island of Gatoya.

Present Day

Suguru Nishijima

The first friend Arata makes in high school. Suguru betrays Arata at Kadowaki's request.

Kadowaki

Arata Hinohara's classmate since middle school. Kadowaki targets Arata to bully.

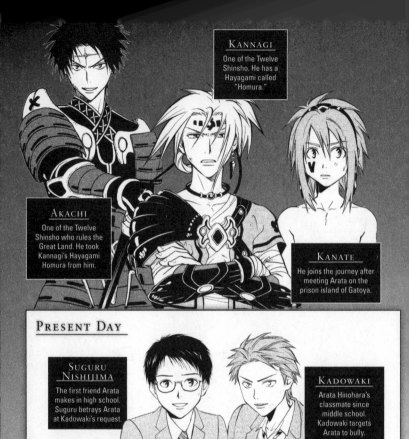

The Story Thus Far

Betrayed by his best friend, Arata Hinohara—a high school student in present-day Japan—wanders through a portal into another world where he and his companions journey onward to deliver a Hayagami sword to Princess Kikuri.

What awaits them in Kannagi's domain is a rebellion led by Akachi, one of the Twelve Shinsho. Akachi forces Kannagi's vassal Ohika to submit to him. Furthermore, he takes possession of Homura, Kannagi's Hayagami sword, thereby setting off a battle for the throne. Arata fears that this will cost countless innocent lives, but then he discovers that his Hayagami is the legendary Tsukuyo. He vows to change the world without submitting to anyone or forcing anyone to submit to him, and yet...

4
Arata
THE LEGEND

COO 908 9000

FPT   £7·99

22·3·13

CONTENTS

CHAPTER 28
PAIN OF THE HEART

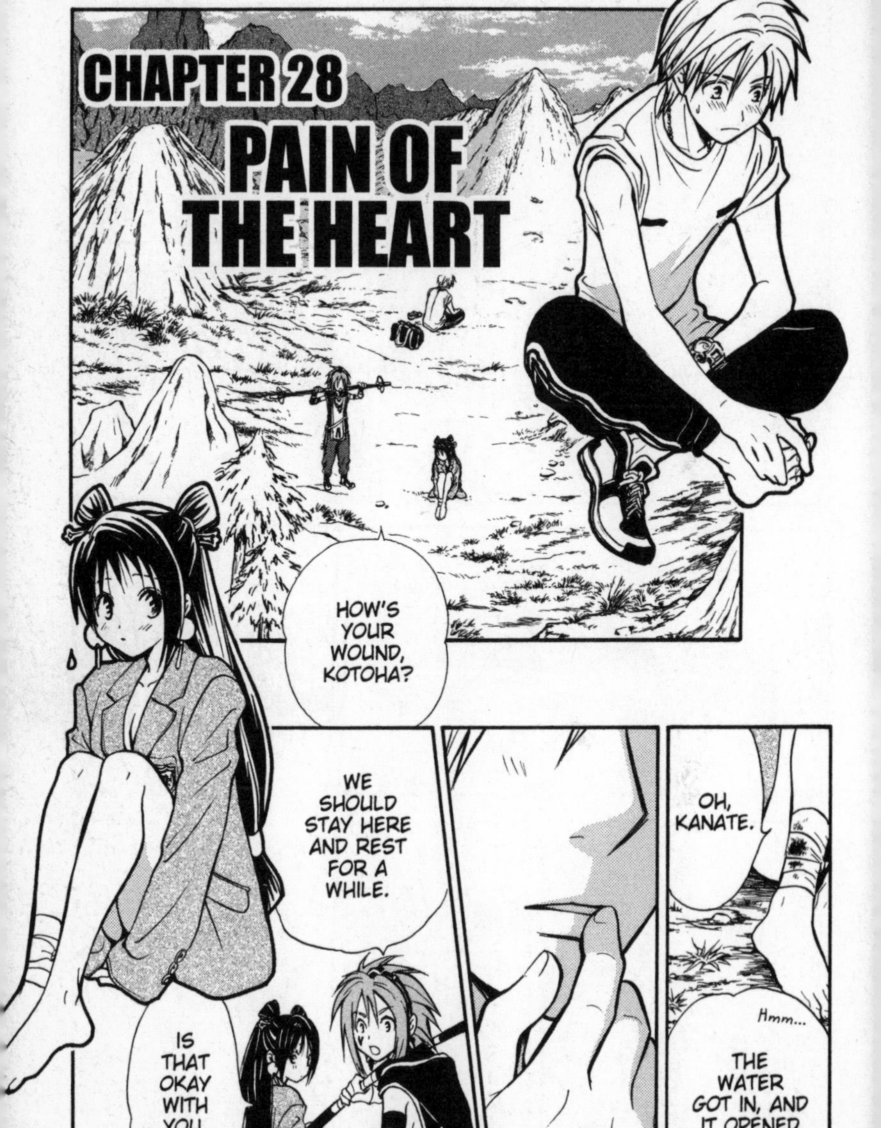
HOW'S YOUR WOUND, KOTOHA?
OH, KANATE.
Hmm...
THE WATER GOT IN, AND IT OPENED UP AGAIN.
WE SHOULD STAY HERE AND REST FOR A WHILE.
IS THAT OKAY WITH YOU, ARATA?

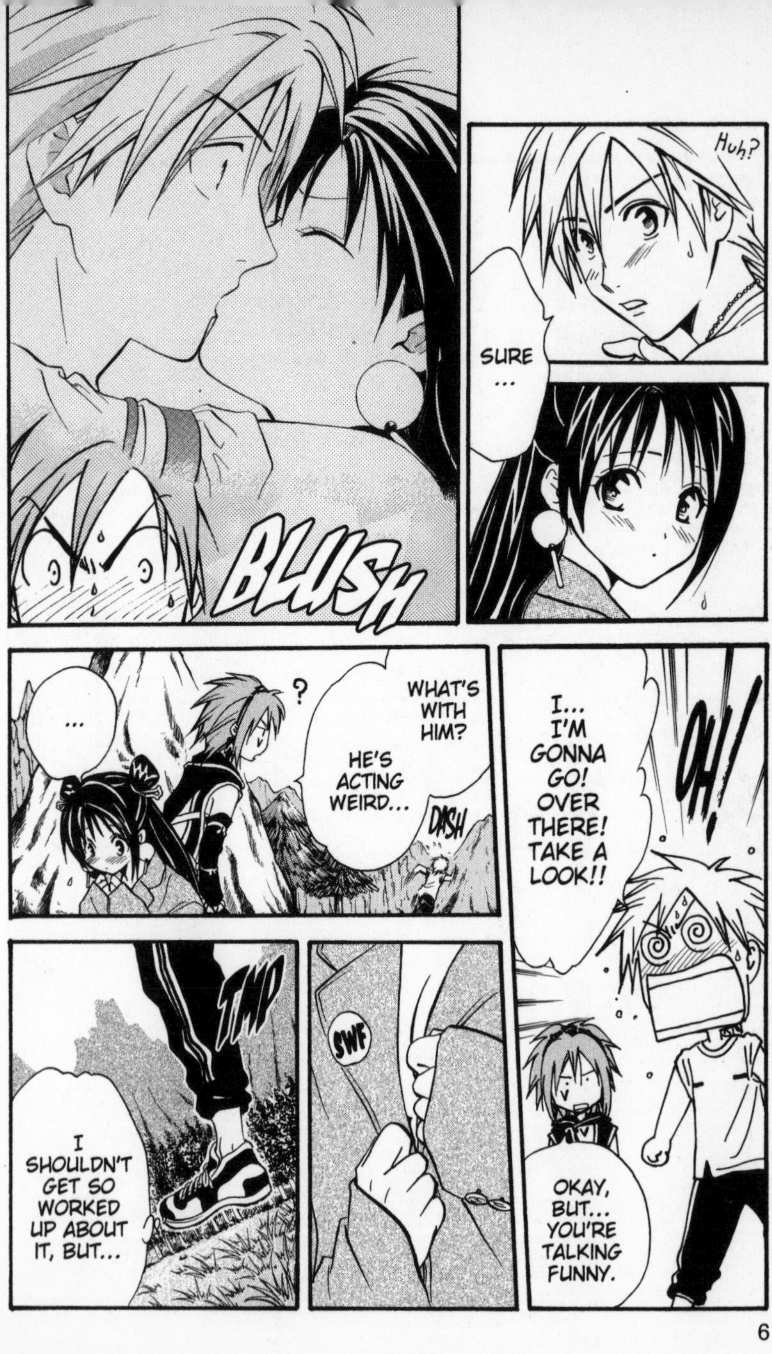
Huh?
SURE ...
BLUSH
OH!
I... I'M GONNA GO! OVER THERE! TAKE A LOOK!!
OKAY, BUT... YOU'RE TALKING FUNNY.
WHAT'S WITH HIM?
HE'S ACTING WEIRD...
?
...
DASH
SWF
TMP
I SHOULDN'T GET SO WORKED UP ABOUT IT, BUT...

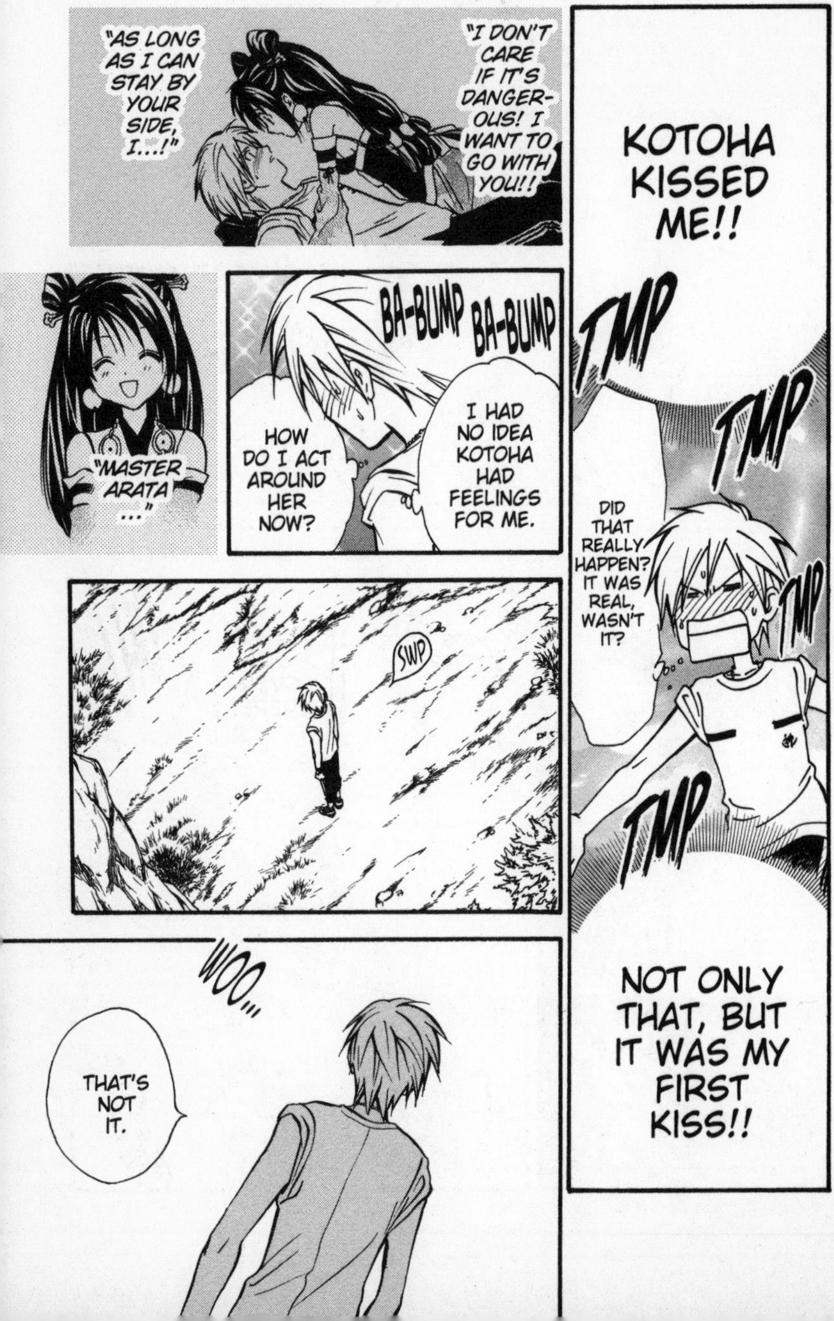
KOTOHA KISSED ME!!
TMP
TMP
DID THAT REALLY HAPPEN? IT WAS REAL, WASN'T IT?
TMP
TMP
NOT ONLY THAT, BUT IT WAS MY FIRST KISS!!
"I DON'T CARE IF IT'S DANGER-OUS! I WANT TO GO WITH YOU!!
"AS LONG AS I CAN STAY BY YOUR SIDE, I...!"
BA-BUMP BA-BUMP
I HAD NO IDEA KOTOHA HAD FEELINGS FOR ME.
HOW DO I ACT AROUND HER NOW?
"MASTER ARATA..."
SWP
WOO...
THAT'S NOT IT.

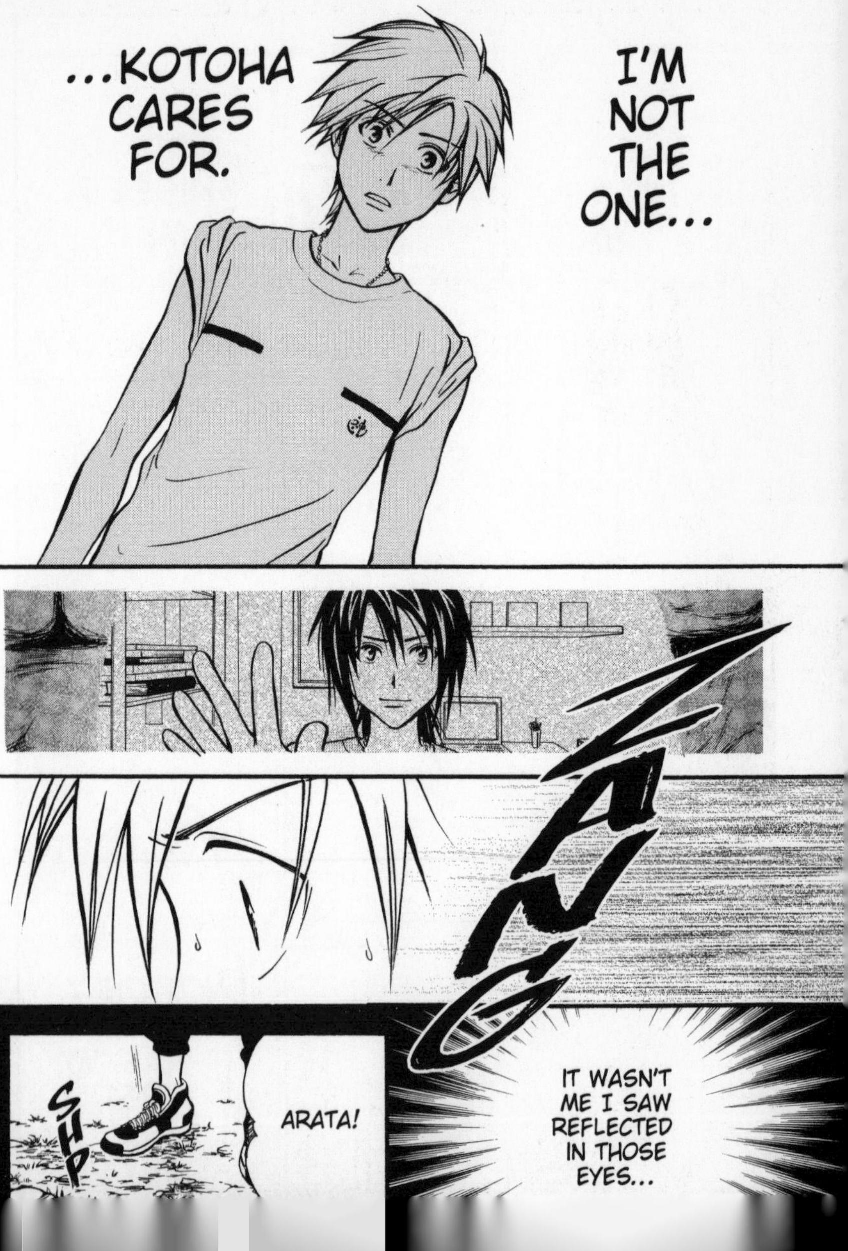
I'M NOT THE ONE...
...KOTOHA CARES FOR.
ZANG
IT WASN'T ME I SAW REFLECTED IN THOSE EYES...
ARATA!
SHP

YOU'RE BACK ALREADY?
OOPS! I MADE A U-TURN WITHOUT REALIZING IT!!
TWITCH
AH... MASTER ARATA...
DASH
GEEZ, WHAT'S UP WITH HIM?
Is he going crazy or some-thing?
THAT'S RIGHT.
ALL SHE SEES IS "MASTER ARATA."
EVERYONE IN THIS WORLD THINKS I'M THE OTHER ARATA.
SO THAT MEANS KOTOHA'S HAD THESE FEELINGS FOR ARATA FOR A LONG TIME NOW...
...AND ALL HER PENT-UP EMOTIONS LED TO THAT KISS.

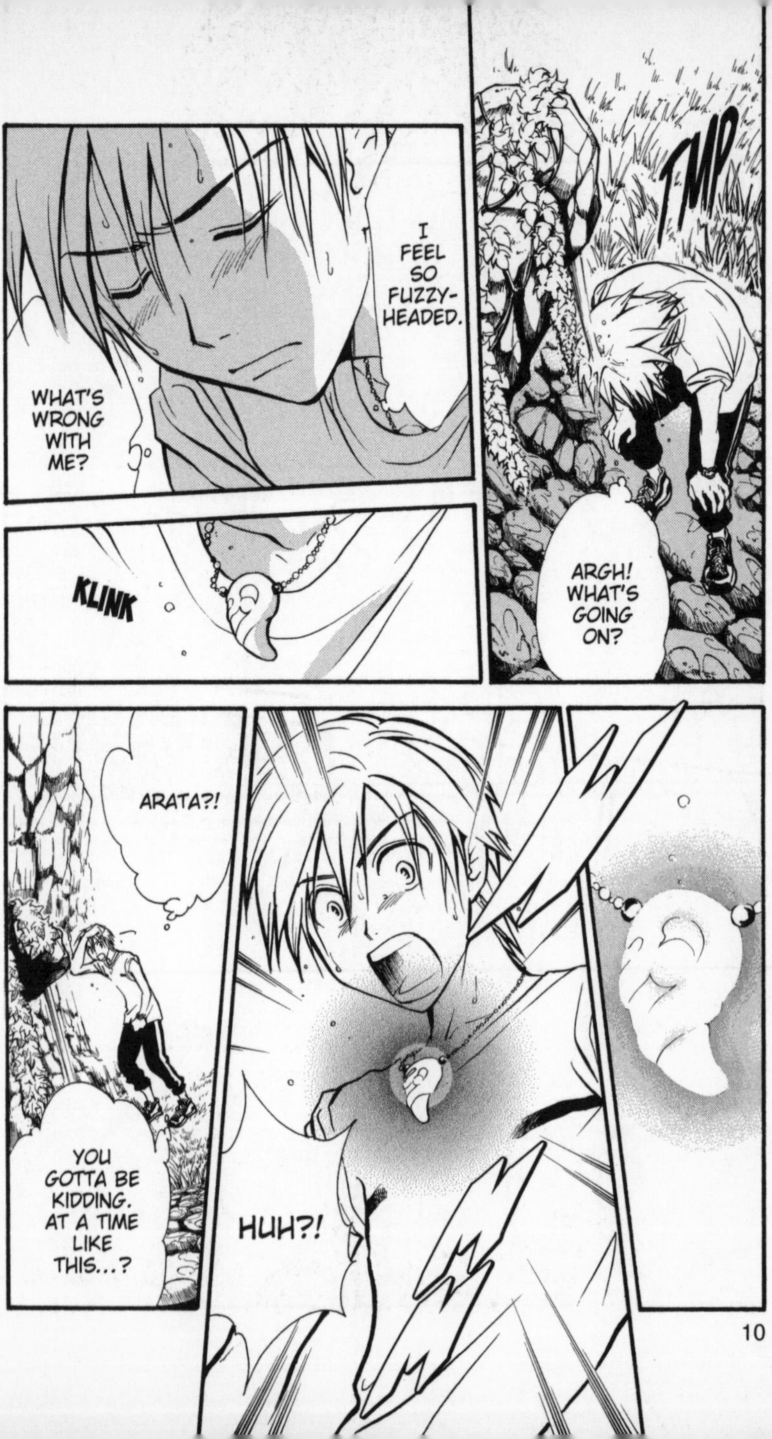
TMP
ARGH! WHAT'S GOING ON?
I FEEL SO FUZZY-HEADED.
WHAT'S WRONG WITH ME?
KLINK
HUH?!
ARATA?!
YOU GOTTA BE KIDDING. AT A TIME LIKE THIS...?

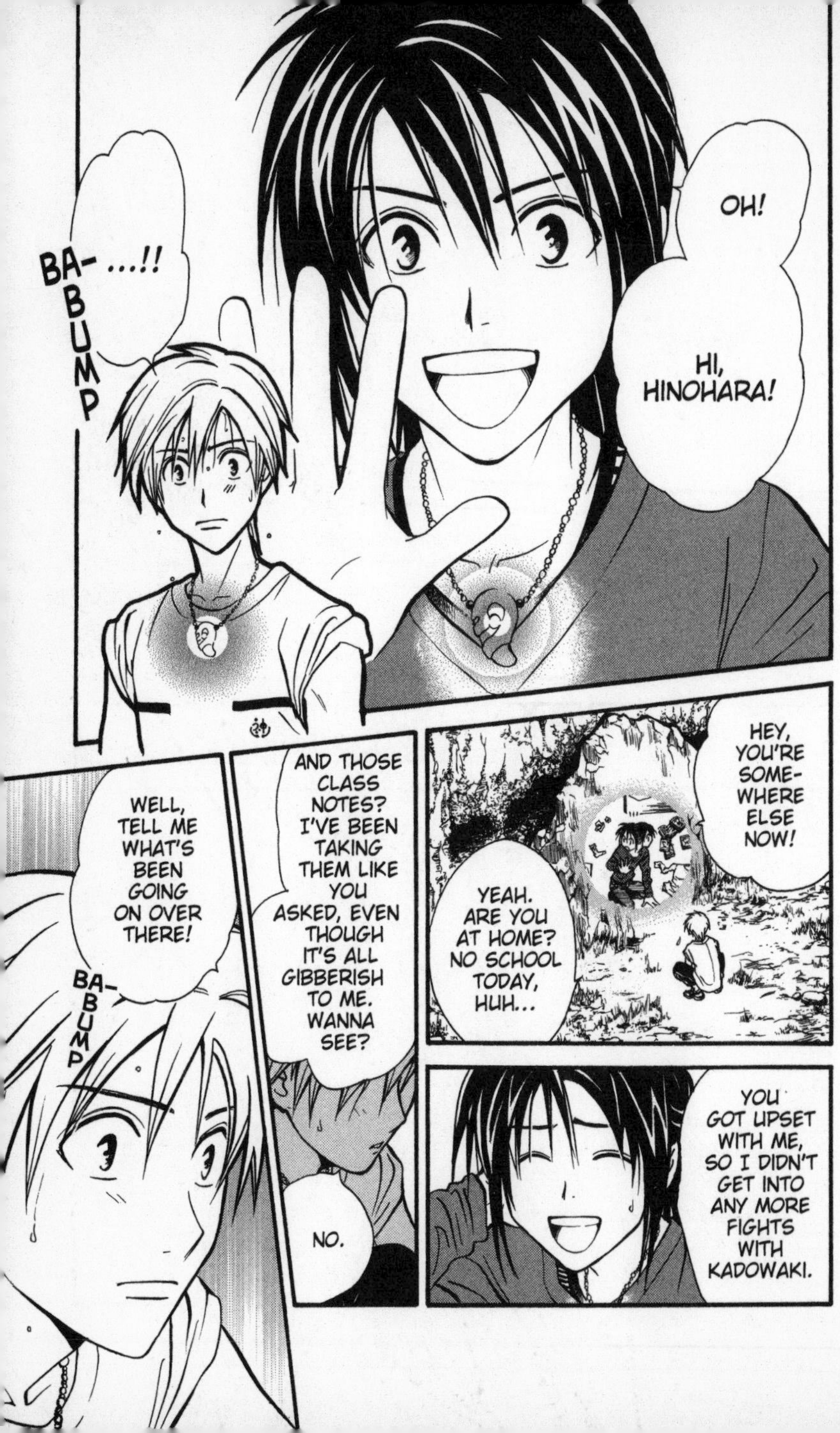
OH!
HI, HINOHARA!
...!!
BA-BUMP
HEY, YOU'RE SOME-WHERE ELSE NOW!
YEAH. ARE YOU AT HOME? NO SCHOOL TODAY, HUH...
YOU GOT UPSET WITH ME, SO I DIDN'T GET INTO ANY MORE FIGHTS WITH KADOWAKI.
AND THOSE CLASS NOTES? I'VE BEEN TAKING THEM LIKE YOU ASKED, EVEN THOUGH IT'S ALL GIBBERISH TO ME. WANNA SEE?
NO.
WELL, TELL ME WHAT'S BEEN GOING ON OVER THERE!
BA-BUMP

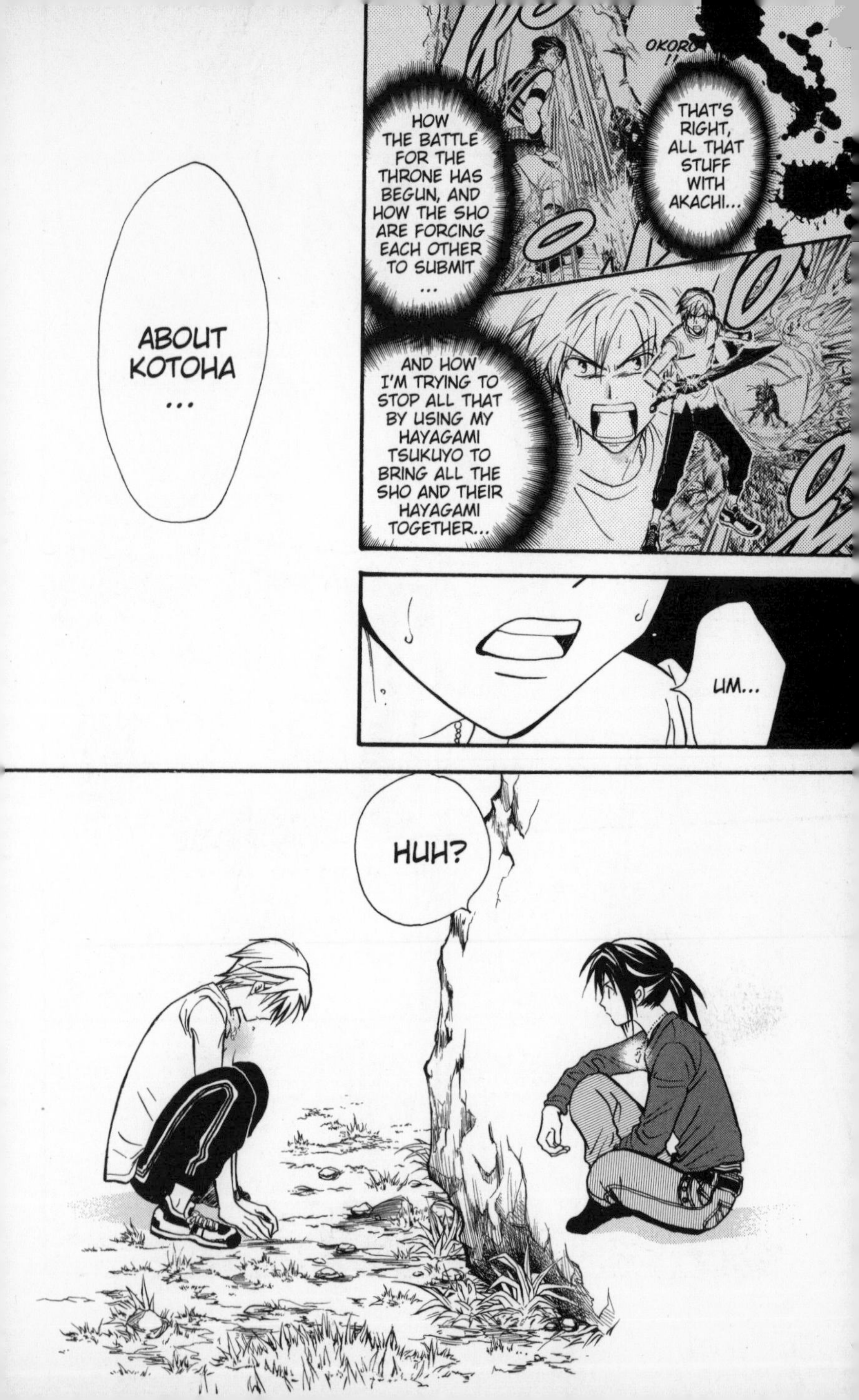
OKORO!!
THAT'S RIGHT, ALL THAT STUFF WITH AKACHI...
HOW THE BATTLE FOR THE THRONE HAS BEGUN, AND HOW THE SHO ARE FORCING EACH OTHER TO SUBMIT...
AND HOW I'M TRYING TO STOP ALL THAT BY USING MY HAYAGAMI TSUKUYO TO BRING ALL THE SHO AND THEIR HAYAGAMI TOGETHER...
UM...
ABOUT KOTOHA...
HUH?

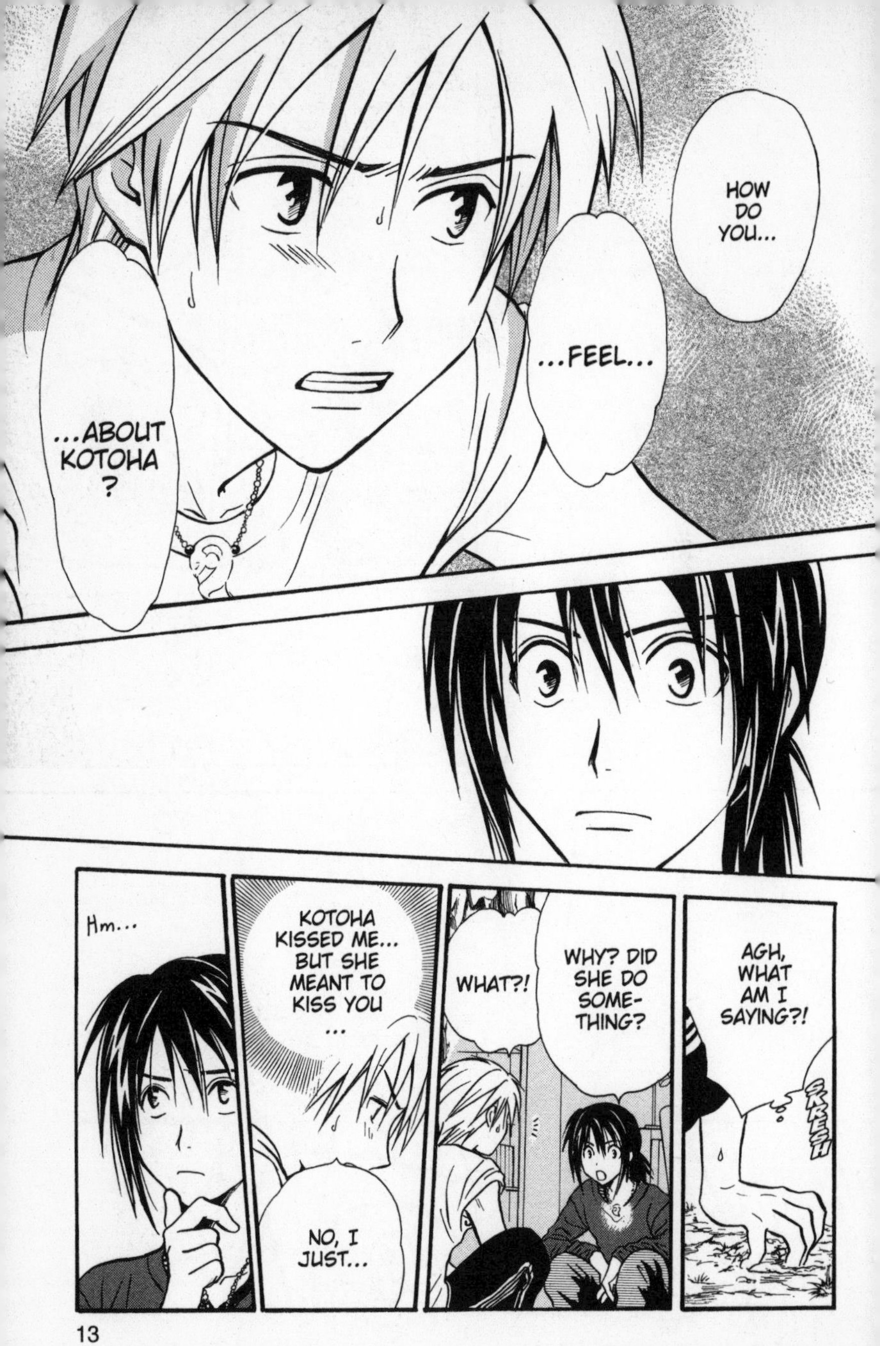
HOW DO YOU...
...FEEL...
...ABOUT KOTOHA?
AGH, WHAT AM I SAYING?!
SKRESH
WHY? DID SHE DO SOME-THING?
WHAT?!
KOTOHA KISSED ME... BUT SHE MEANT TO KISS YOU ...
NO, I JUST...
Hm...

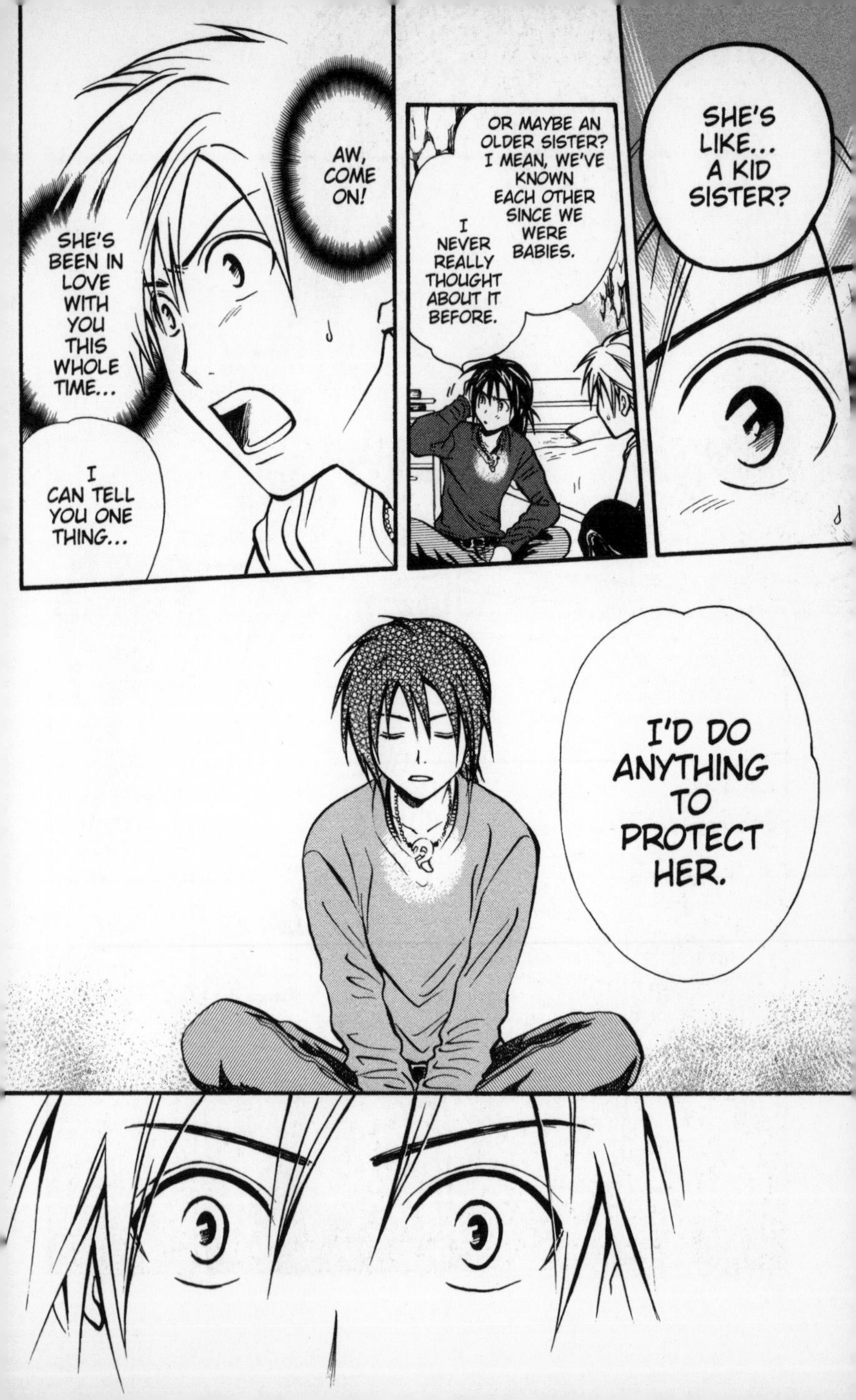
SHE'S LIKE... A KID SISTER?
OR MAYBE AN OLDER SISTER? I MEAN, WE'VE KNOWN EACH OTHER SINCE WE WERE BABIES.
I NEVER REALLY THOUGHT ABOUT IT BEFORE.
AW, COME ON!
SHE'S BEEN IN LOVE WITH YOU THIS WHOLE TIME...
I CAN TELL YOU ONE THING...
I'D DO ANYTHING TO PROTECT HER.

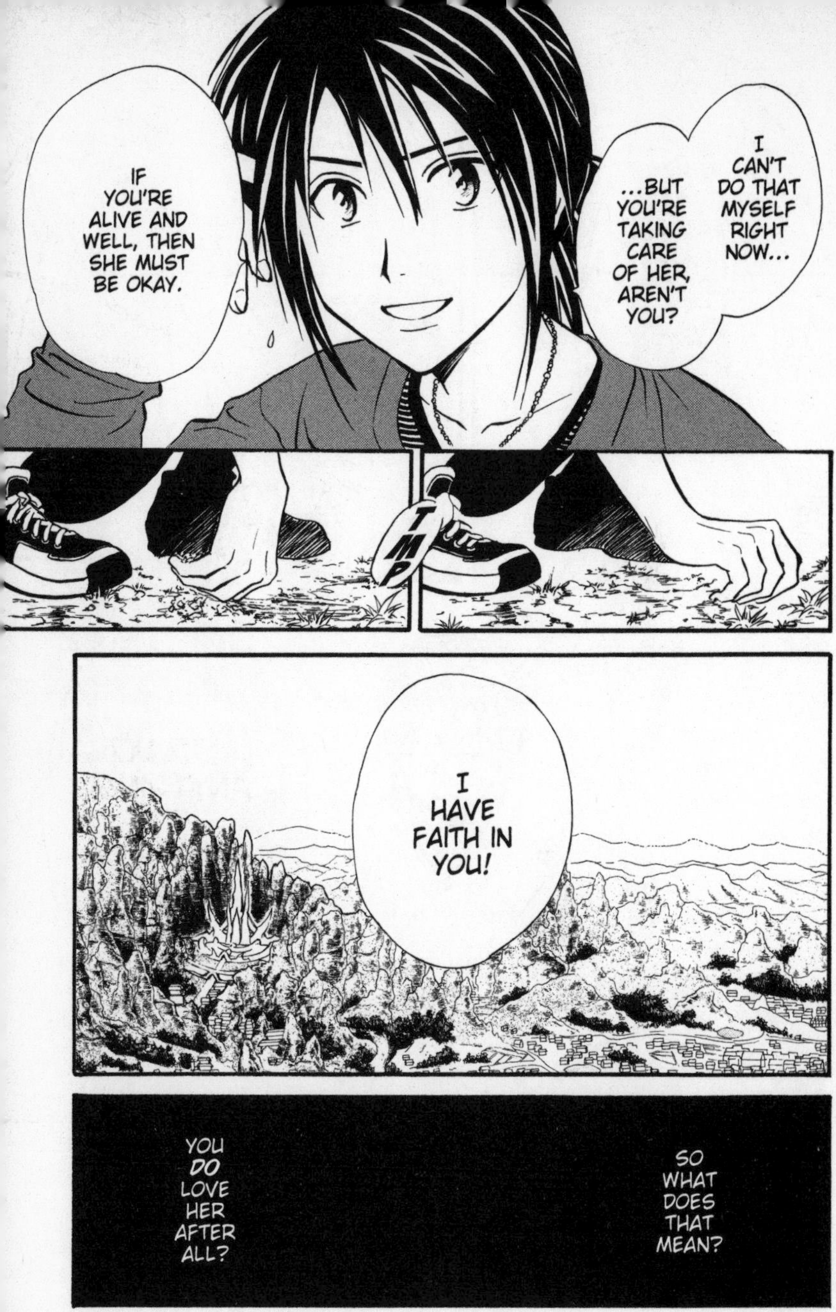
I CAN'T DO THAT MYSELF RIGHT NOW...
...BUT YOU'RE TAKING CARE OF HER, AREN'T YOU?
IF YOU'RE ALIVE AND WELL, THEN SHE MUST BE OKAY.
TMP
I HAVE FAITH IN YOU!
SO WHAT DOES THAT MEAN?
YOU *DO* LOVE HER AFTER ALL?

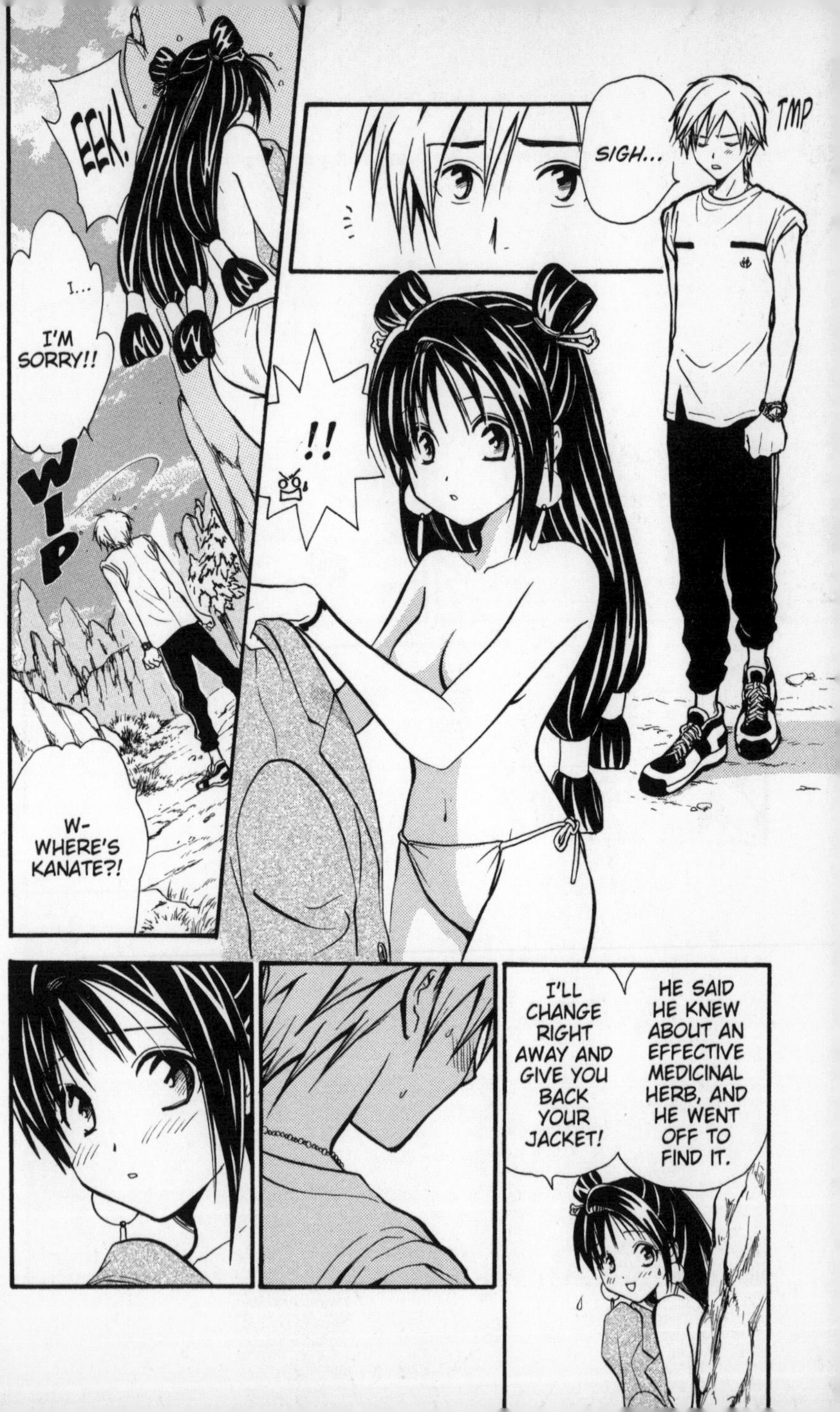

SIGH...
TMP
!!
EEK!
I...
I'M SORRY!!
WIP
W- WHERE'S KANATE?!
HE SAID HE KNEW ABOUT AN EFFECTIVE MEDICINAL HERB, AND HE WENT OFF TO FIND IT.
I'LL CHANGE RIGHT AWAY AND GIVE YOU BACK YOUR JACKET!

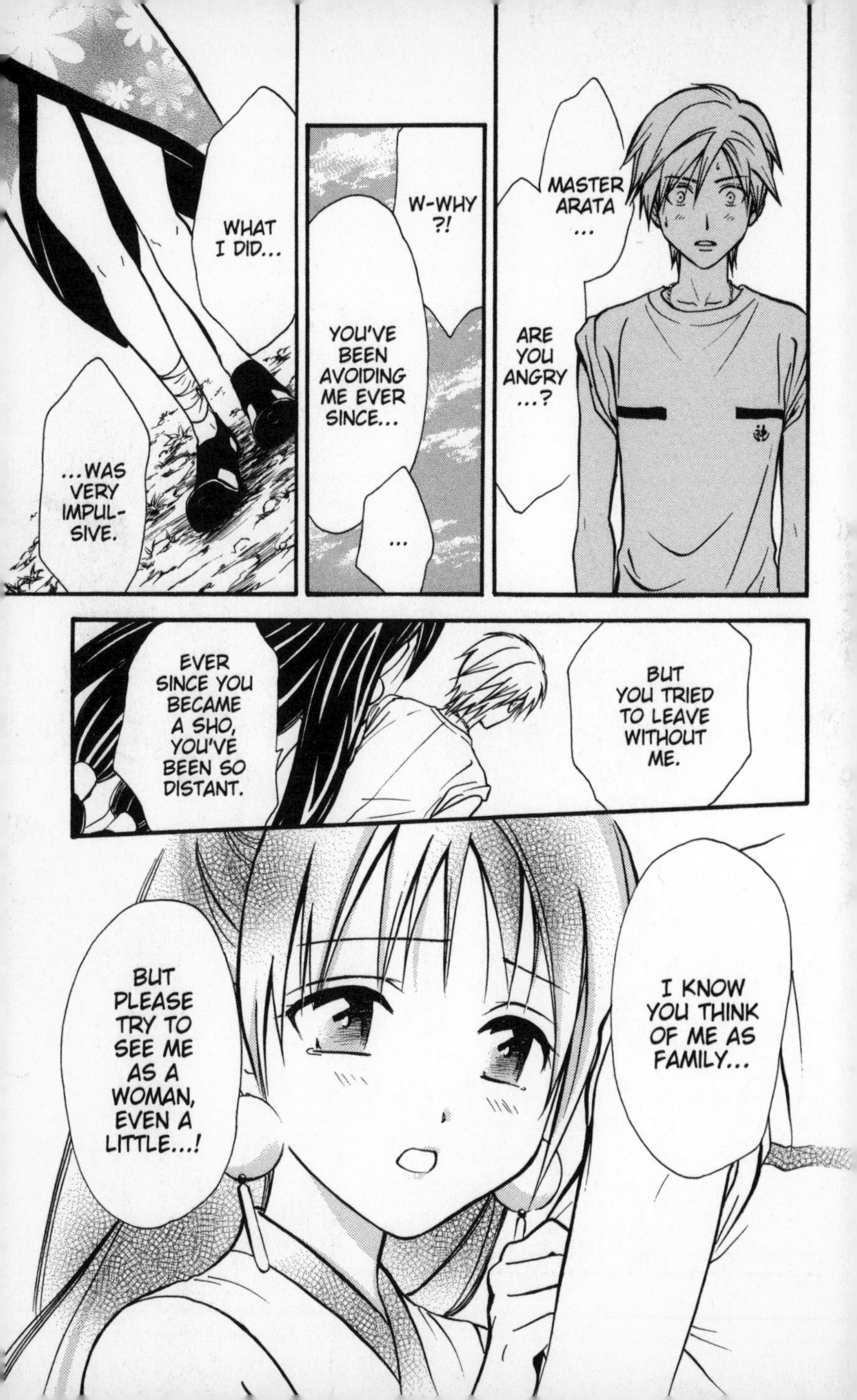
MASTER ARATA ...
ARE YOU ANGRY ...?
W-WHY ?!
YOU'VE BEEN AVOIDING ME EVER SINCE...
...
WHAT I DID...
...WAS VERY IMPUL-SIVE.
BUT YOU TRIED TO LEAVE WITHOUT ME.
EVER SINCE YOU BECAME A SHO, YOU'VE BEEN SO DISTANT.
I KNOW YOU THINK OF ME AS FAMILY...
BUT PLEASE TRY TO SEE ME AS A WOMAN, EVEN A LITTLE...!

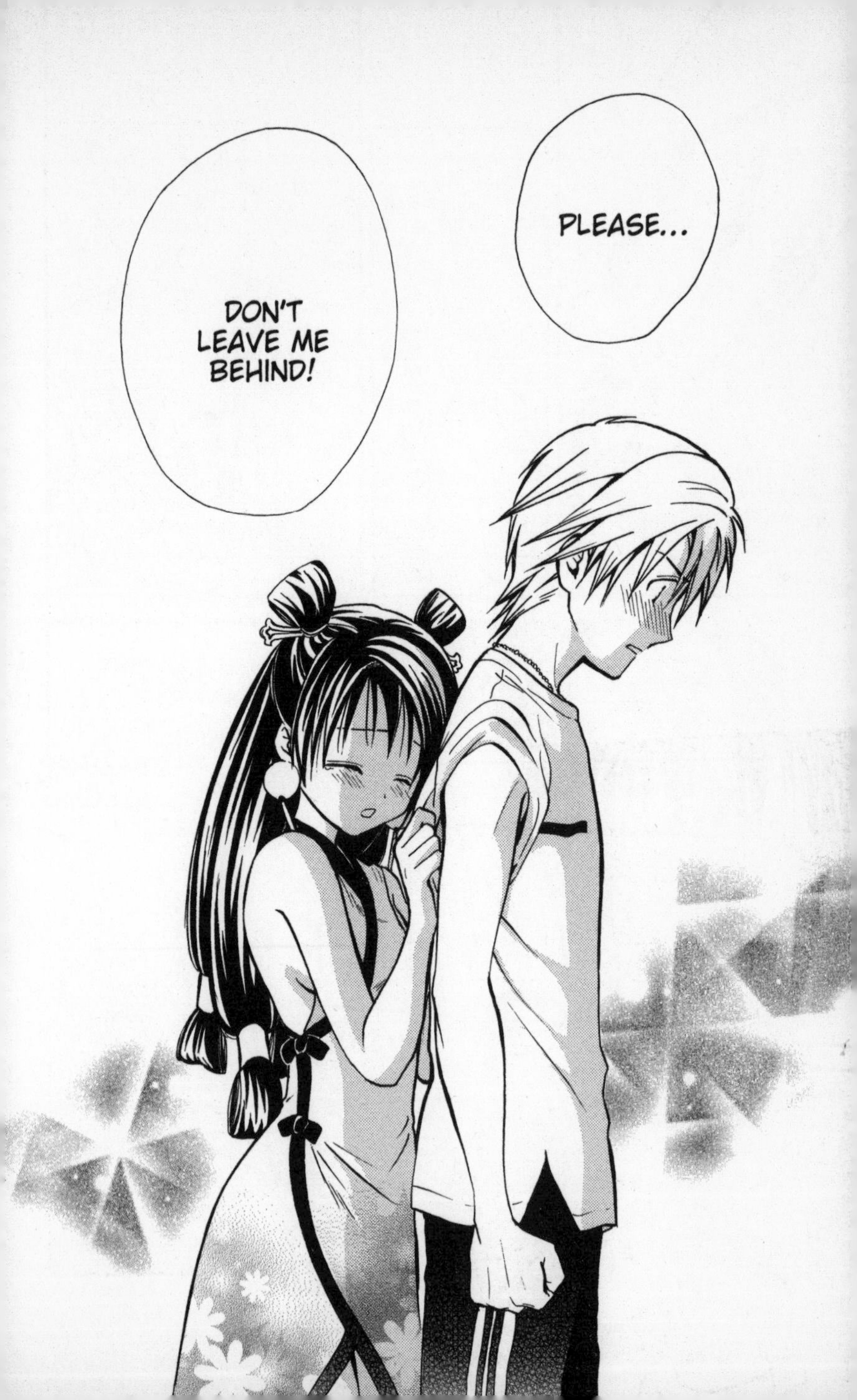
PLEASE...
DON'T LEAVE ME BEHIND!

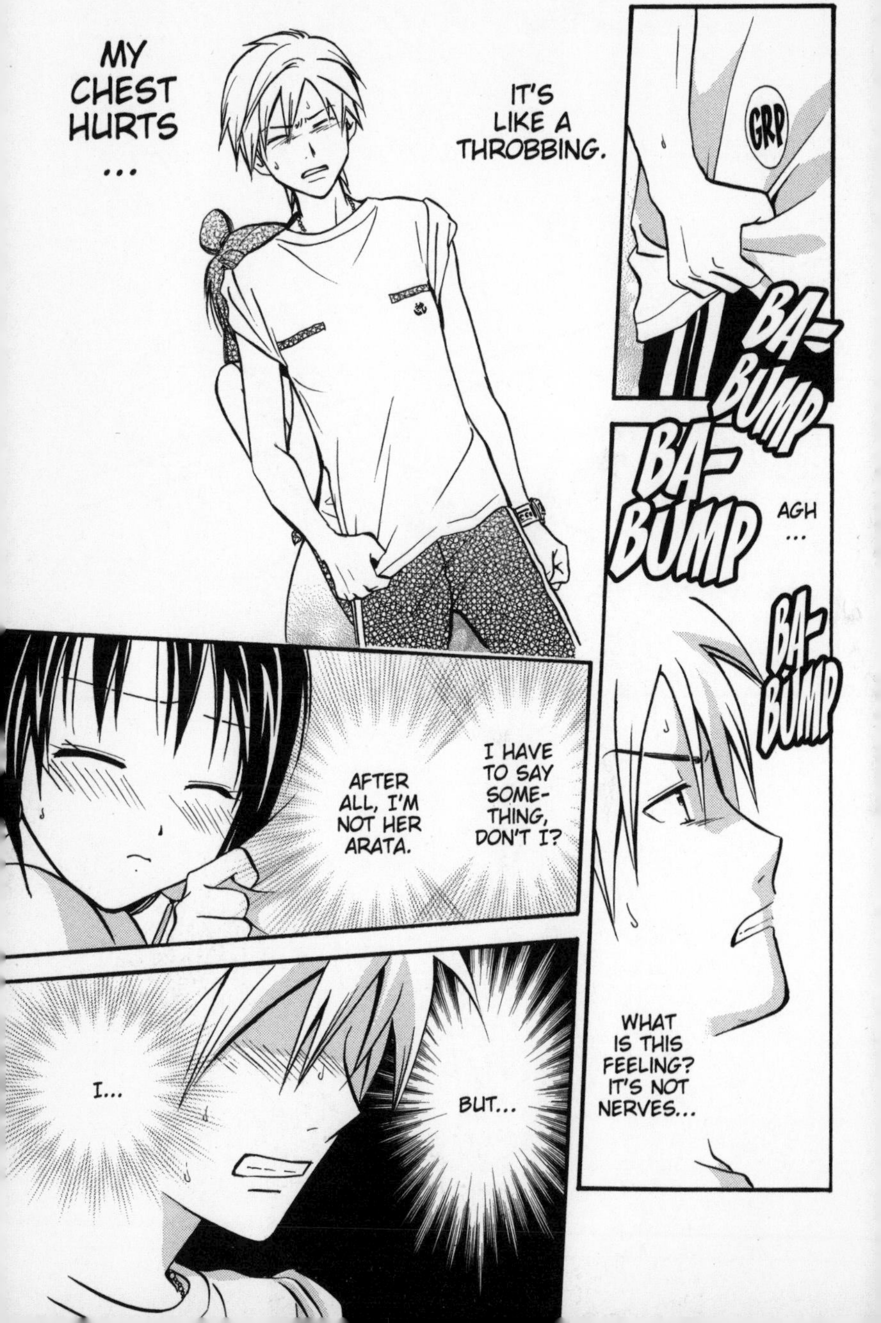
GRP
BA-BUMP
IT'S LIKE A THROBBING.
MY CHEST HURTS ...
BA-BUMP
AGH ...
BA-BUMP
WHAT IS THIS FEELING? IT'S NOT NERVES...
I HAVE TO SAY SOME-THING, DON'T I?
AFTER ALL, I'M NOT HER ARATA.
BUT...
I...

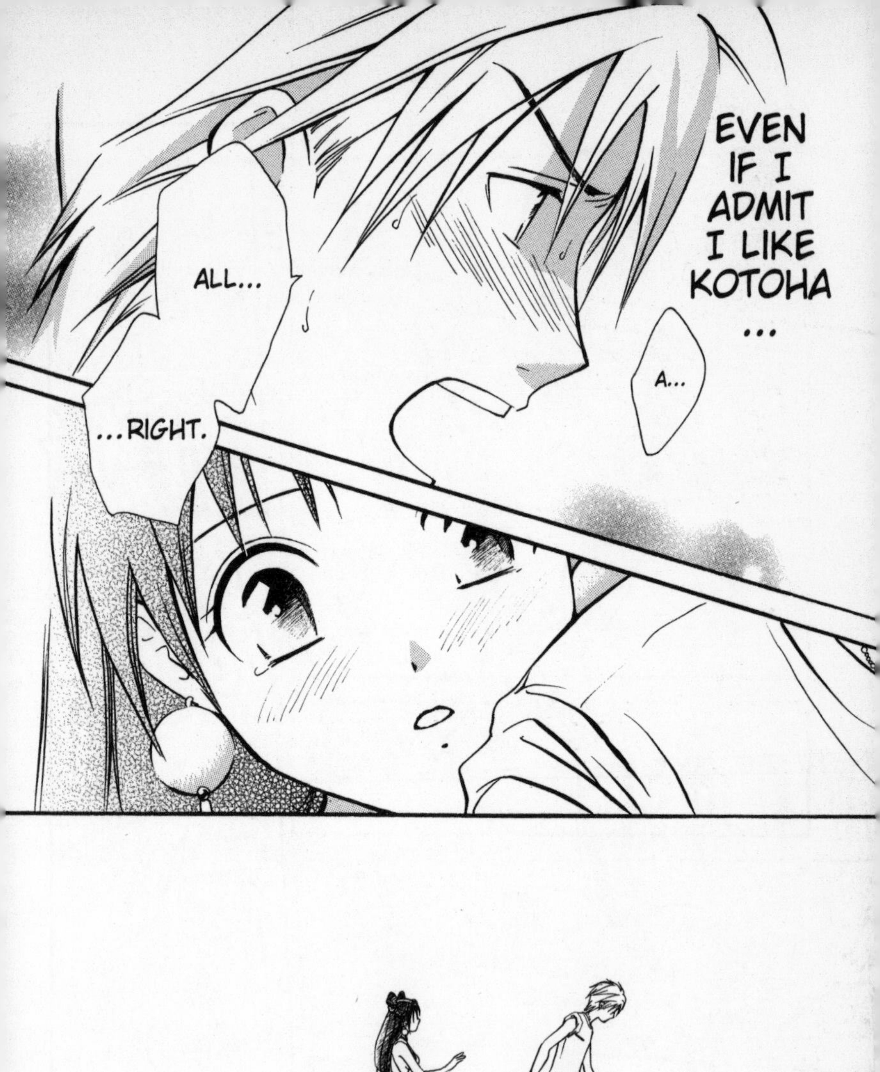
EVEN IF I ADMIT I LIKE KOTOHA ...
A...
ALL...
...RIGHT.

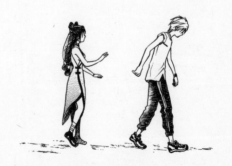

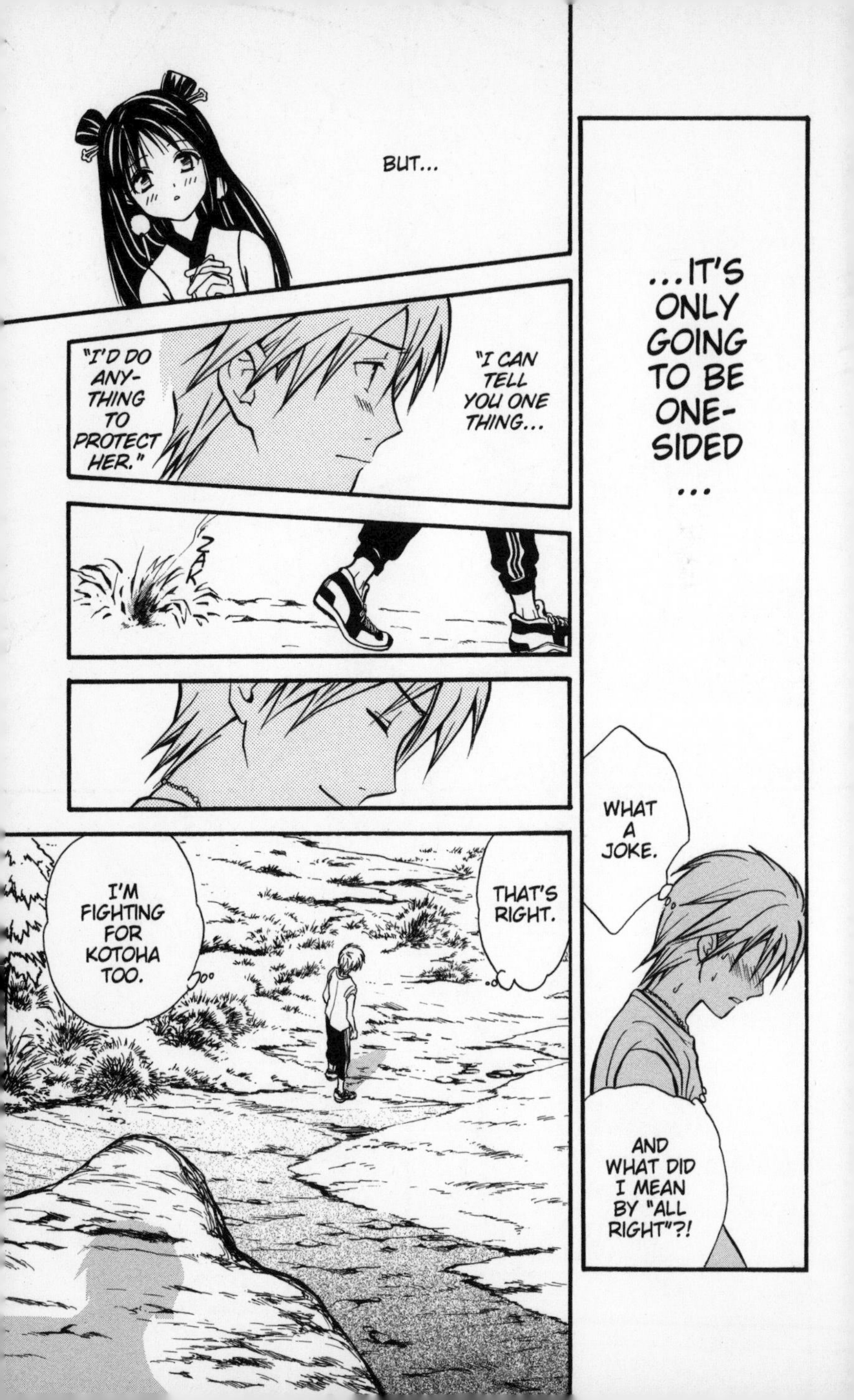
...IT'S ONLY GOING TO BE ONE-SIDED...
WHAT A JOKE.
AND WHAT DID I MEAN BY "ALL RIGHT"?!
BUT...
"I CAN TELL YOU ONE THING...
"I'D DO ANY-THING TO PROTECT HER."
ZAK
THAT'S RIGHT.
I'M FIGHTING FOR KOTOHA TOO.

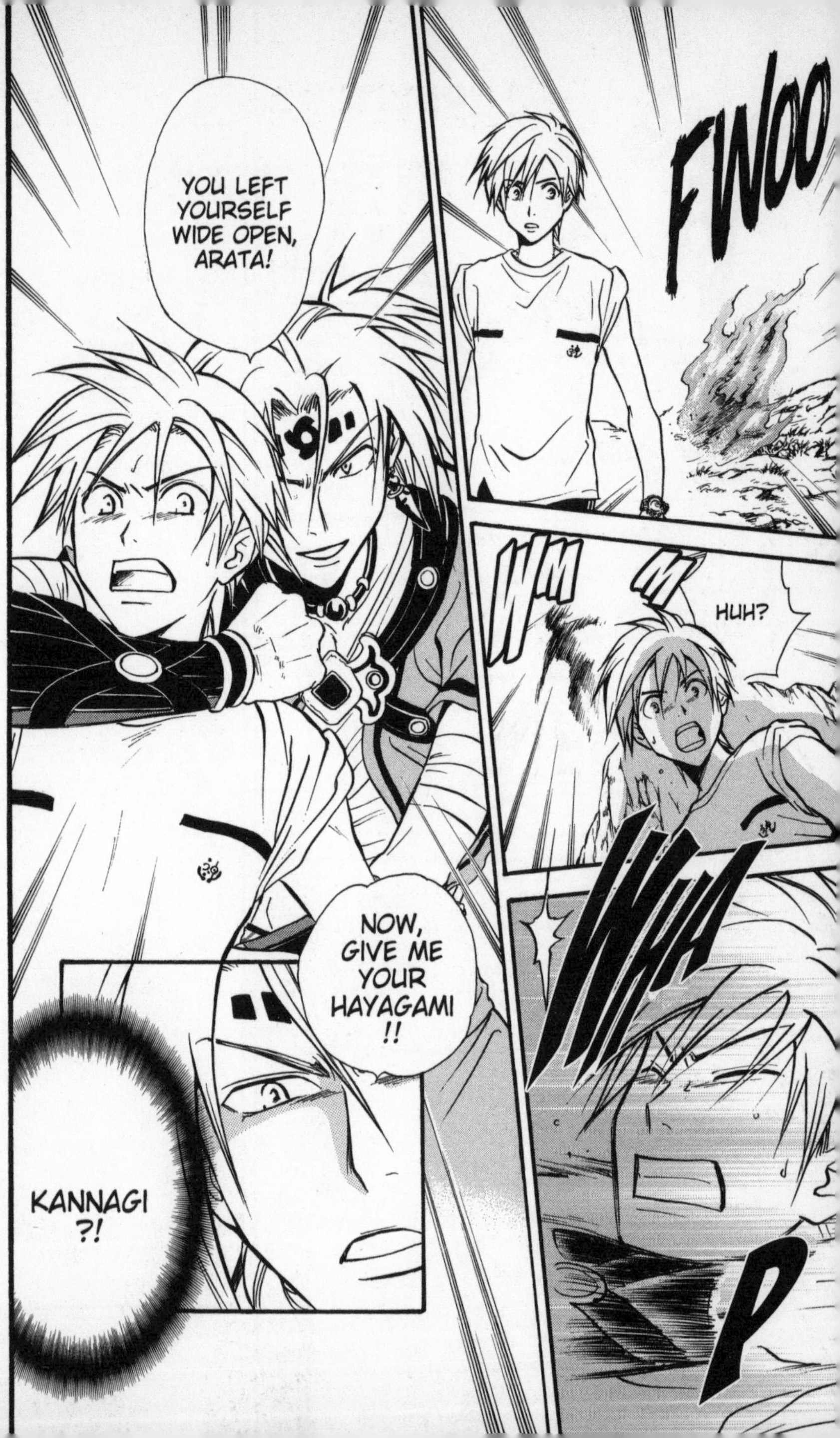
FWOO
WMMM
HUH?
WHAP
YOU LEFT YOURSELF WIDE OPEN, ARATA!
NOW, GIVE ME YOUR HAYAGAMI!!
KANNAGI?!

CHAPTER 29
WITHIN THE FLAMES

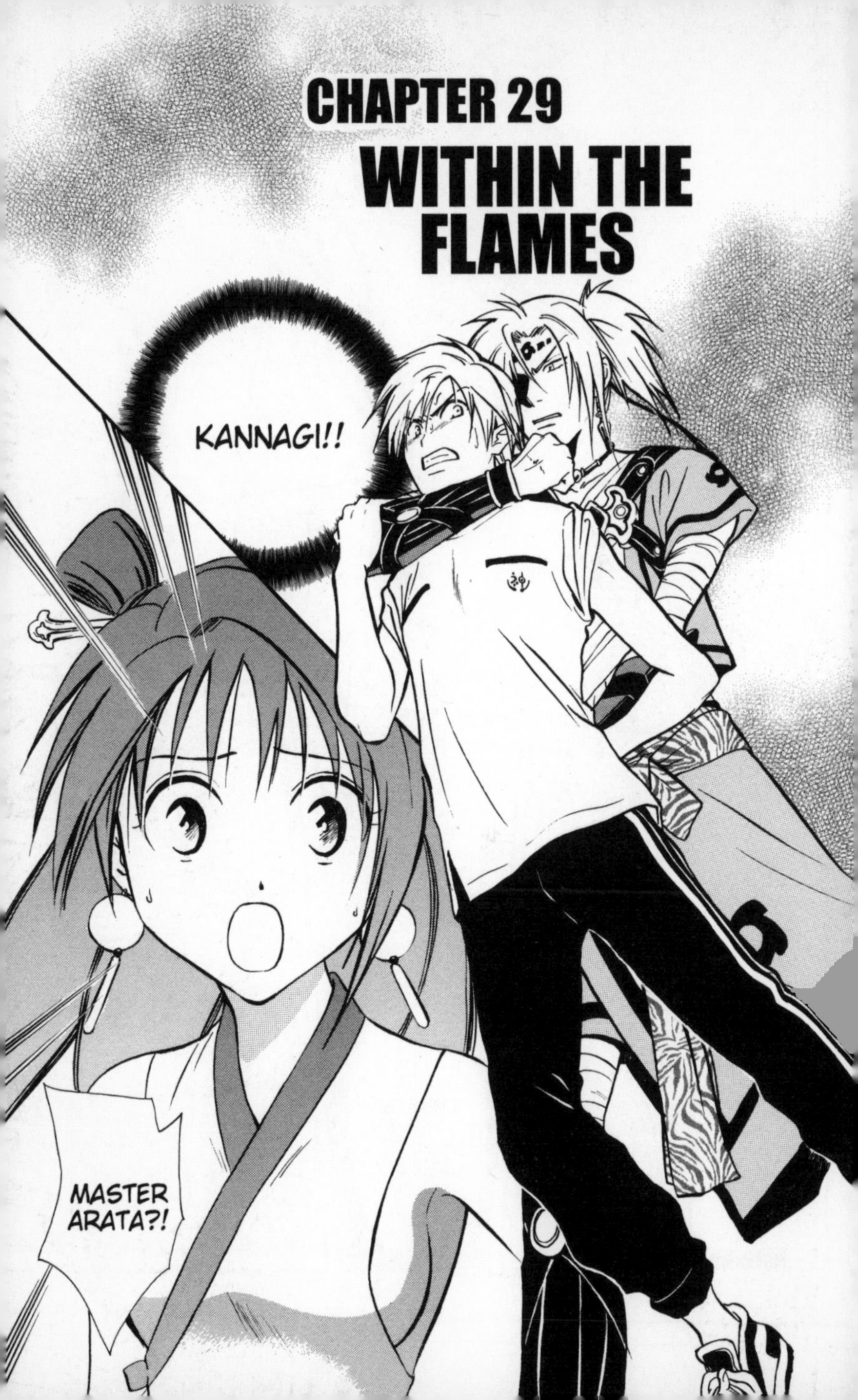
KANNAGI!!
MASTER ARATA?!

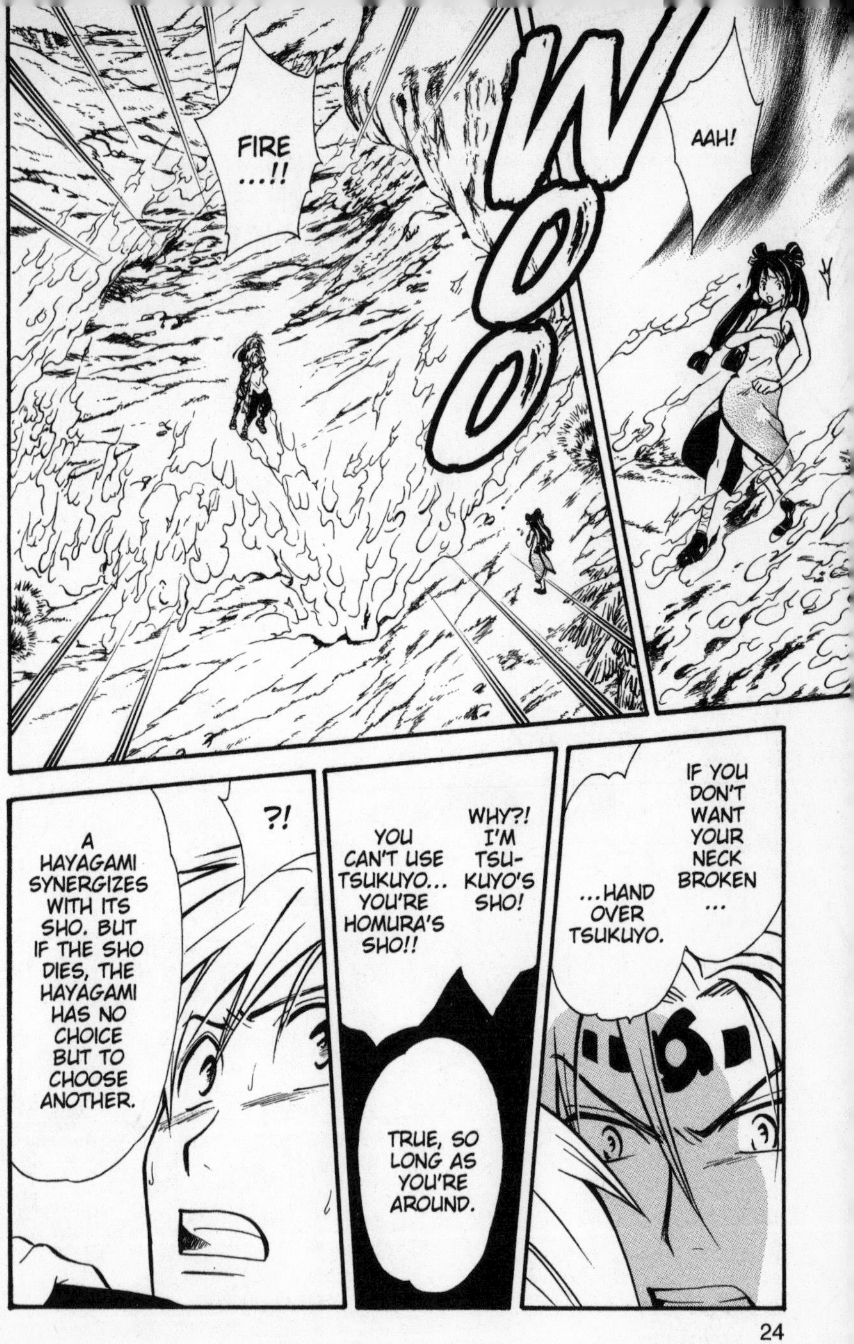
AAH!
WOOO
FIRE ...!!
IF YOU DON'T WANT YOUR NECK BROKEN ...
...HAND OVER TSUKUYO.
WHY?! I'M TSU-KUYO'S SHO!
YOU CAN'T USE TSUKUYO... YOU'RE HOMURA'S SHO!!
TRUE, SO LONG AS YOU'RE AROUND.
?!
A HAYAGAMI SYNERGIZES WITH ITS SHO. BUT IF THE SHO DIES, THE HAYAGAMI HAS NO CHOICE BUT TO CHOOSE ANOTHER.

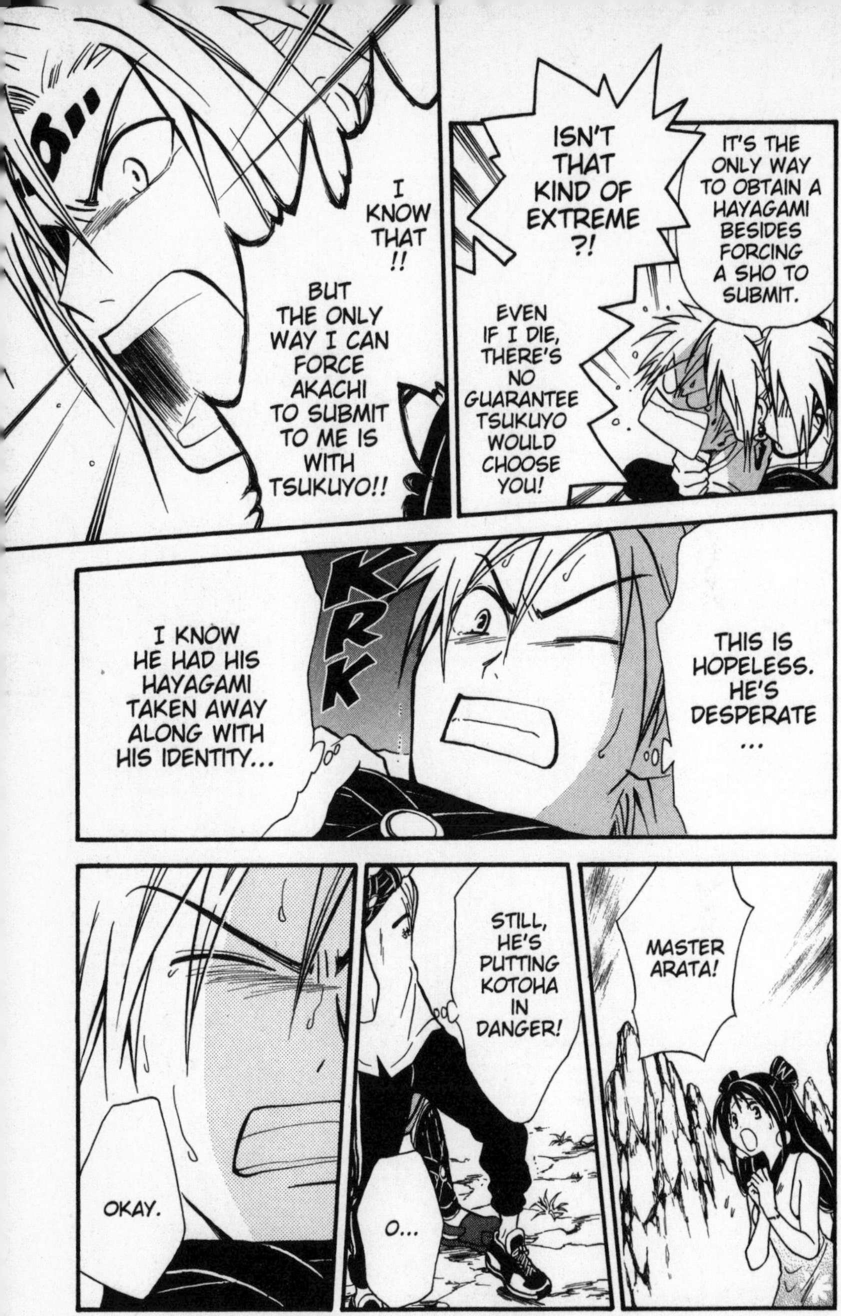
IT'S THE ONLY WAY TO OBTAIN A HAYAGAMI BESIDES FORCING A SHO TO SUBMIT.
ISN'T THAT KIND OF EXTREME ?!
EVEN IF I DIE, THERE'S NO GUARANTEE TSUKUYO WOULD CHOOSE YOU!
I KNOW THAT !!
BUT THE ONLY WAY I CAN FORCE AKACHI TO SUBMIT TO ME IS WITH TSUKUYO!!
THIS IS HOPELESS. HE'S DESPERATE ...
KRK
I KNOW HE HAD HIS HAYAGAMI TAKEN AWAY ALONG WITH HIS IDENTITY...
MASTER ARATA!
STILL, HE'S PUTTING KOTOHA IN DANGER!
O...
OKAY.

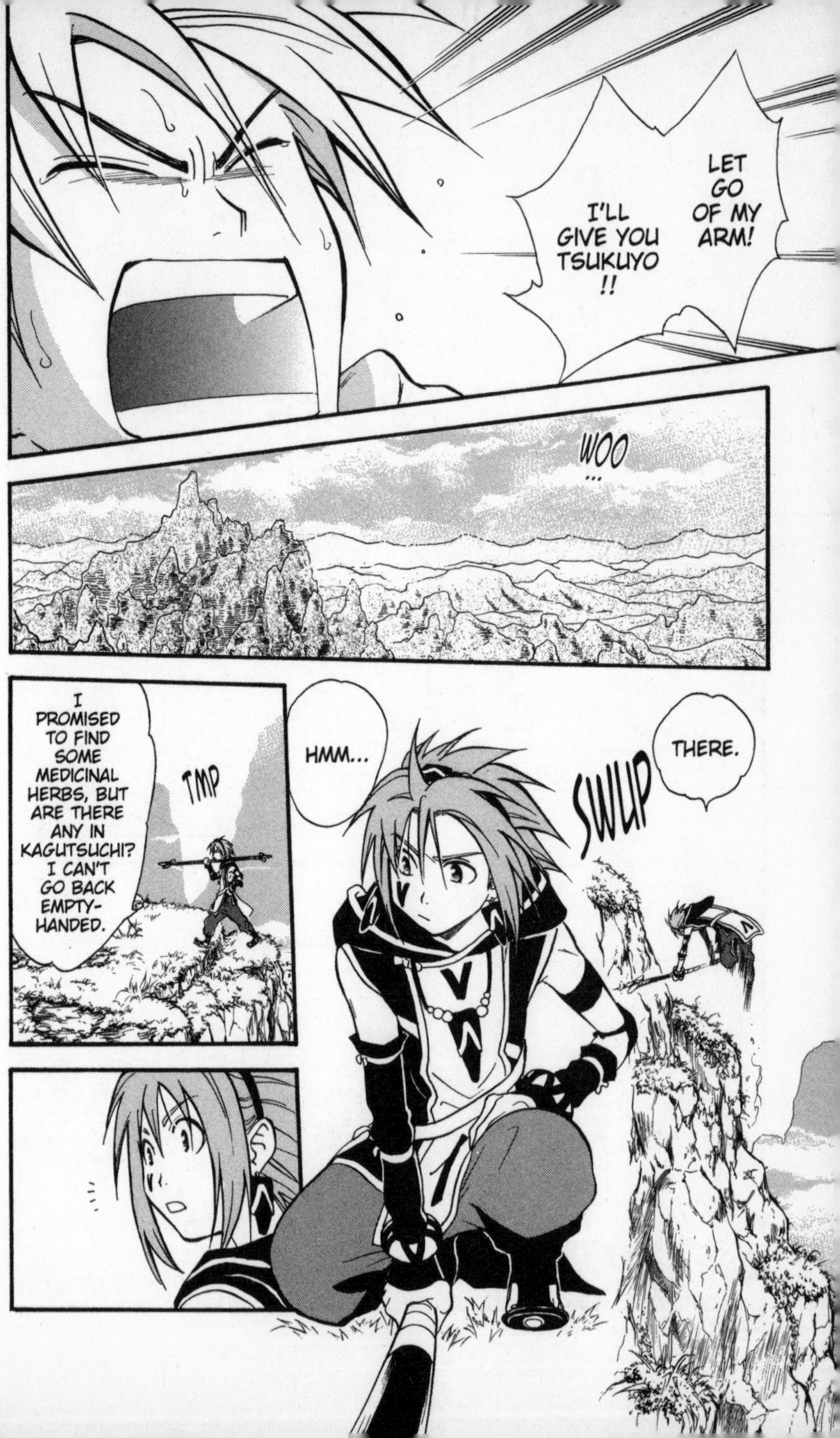

LET GO OF MY ARM!
I'LL GIVE YOU TSUKUYO!!
WOO...
THERE.
SWUP
HMM...
I PROMISED TO FIND SOME MEDICINAL HERBS, BUT ARE THERE ANY IN KAGUTSUCHI? I CAN'T GO BACK EMPTY-HANDED.
TMP

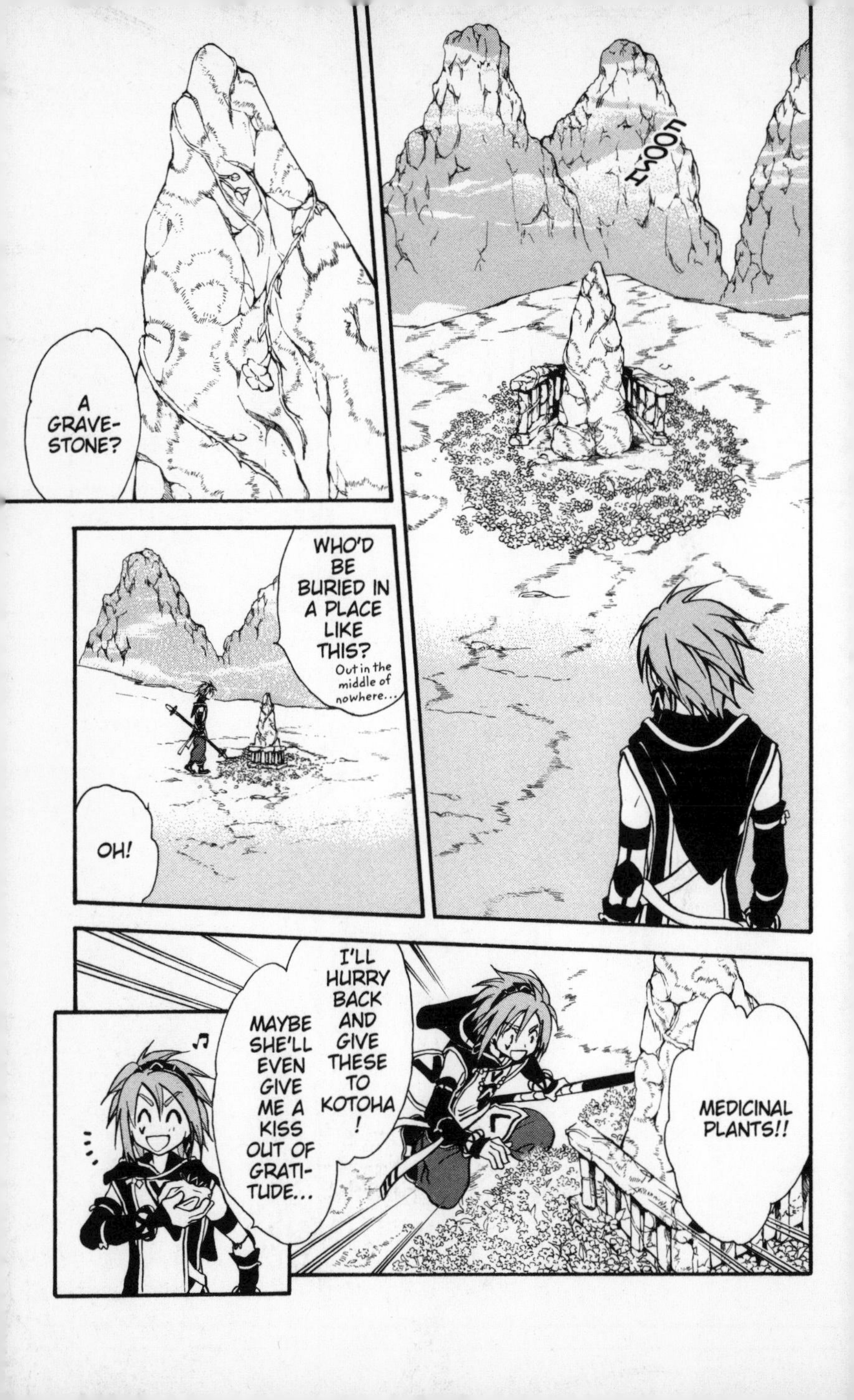
WOOSH
A GRAVE-STONE?
WHO'D BE BURIED IN A PLACE LIKE THIS?
Out in the middle of nowhere...
OH!
MEDICINAL PLANTS!!
I'LL HURRY BACK AND GIVE THESE TO KOTOHA!
MAYBE SHE'LL EVEN GIVE ME A KISS OUT OF GRATI-TUDE...

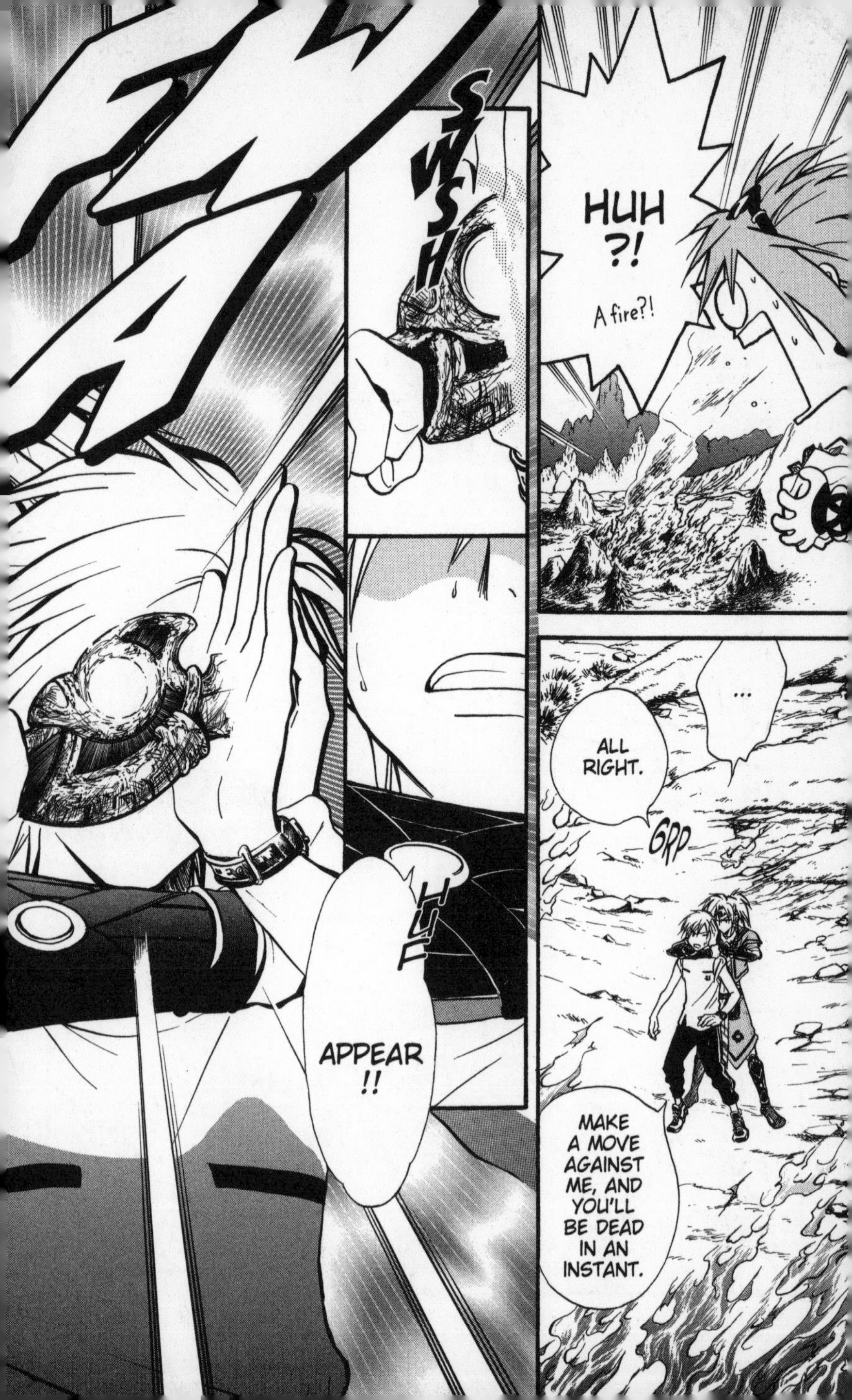
HUH ?!
A fire?!
...
ALL RIGHT.
GRP
MAKE A MOVE AGAINST ME, AND YOU'LL BE DEAD IN AN INSTANT.
SWISH
APPEAR !!

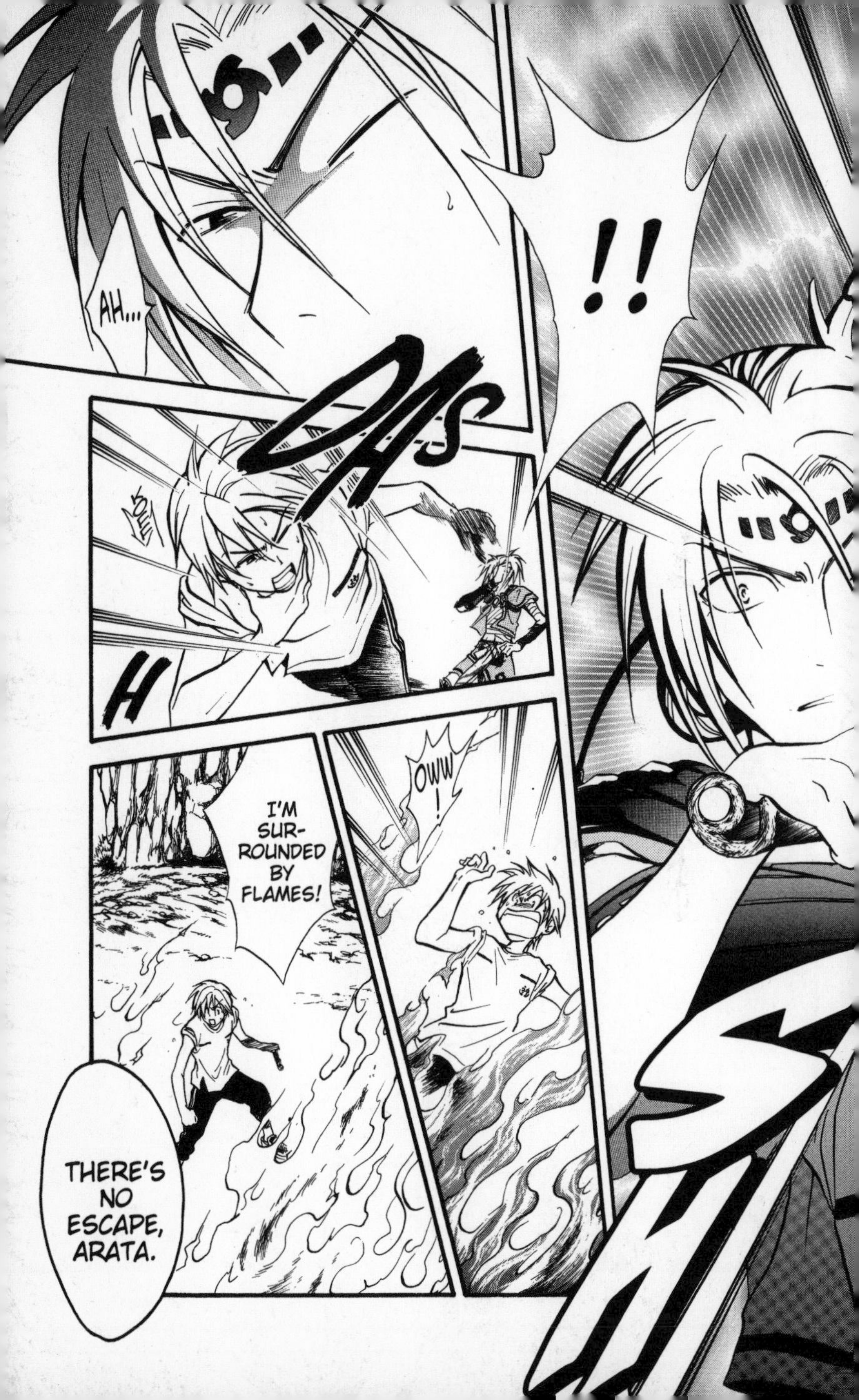

AH...
!!
DASH
OWW!
I'M SUR-ROUNDED BY FLAMES!
THERE'S NO ESCAPE, ARATA.

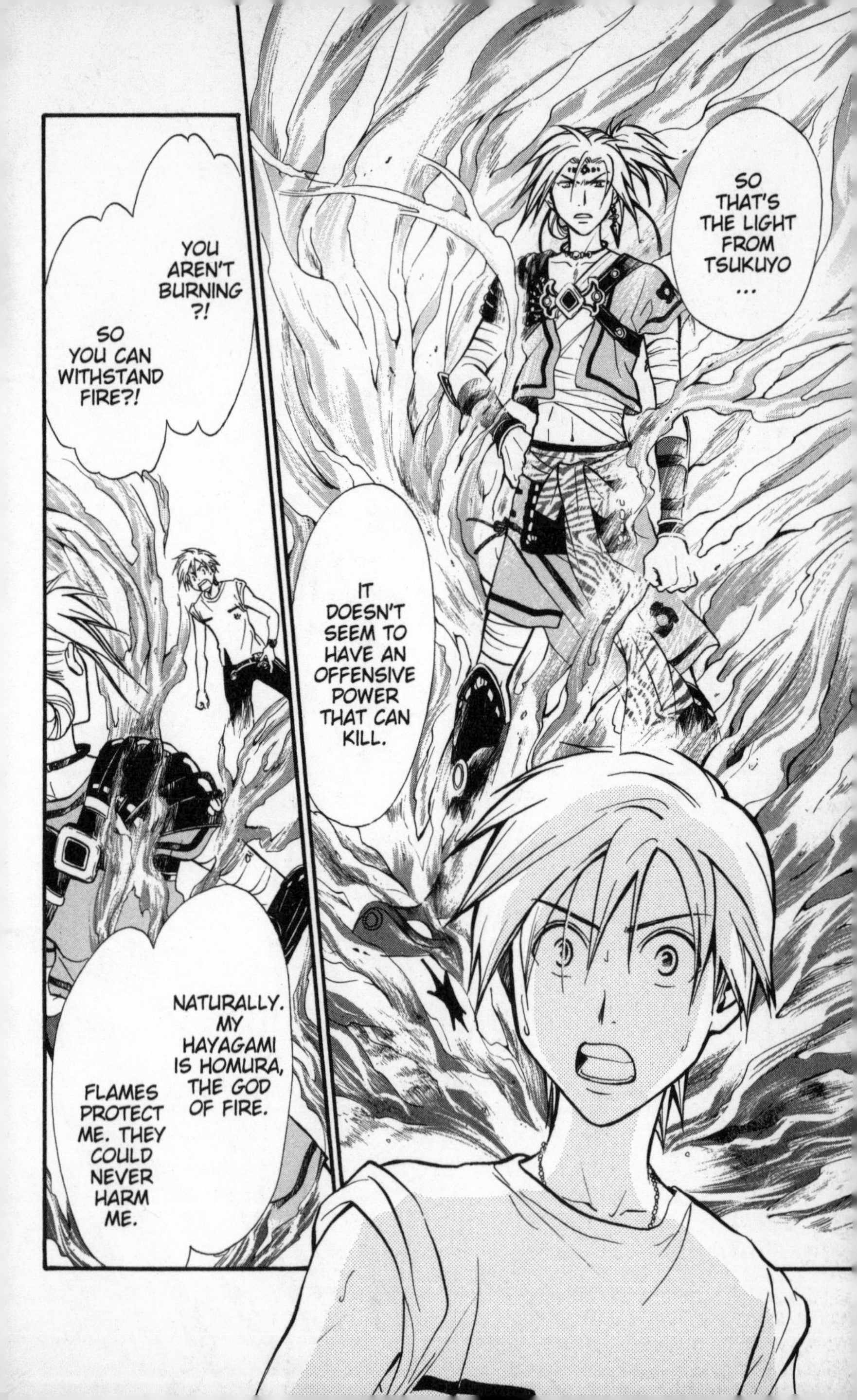
SO THAT'S THE LIGHT FROM TSUKUYO ...
IT DOESN'T SEEM TO HAVE AN OFFENSIVE POWER THAT CAN KILL.
YOU AREN'T BURNING ?!
SO YOU CAN WITHSTAND FIRE?!
NATURALLY. MY HAYAGAMI IS HOMURA, THE GOD OF FIRE.
FLAMES PROTECT ME. THEY COULD NEVER HARM ME.

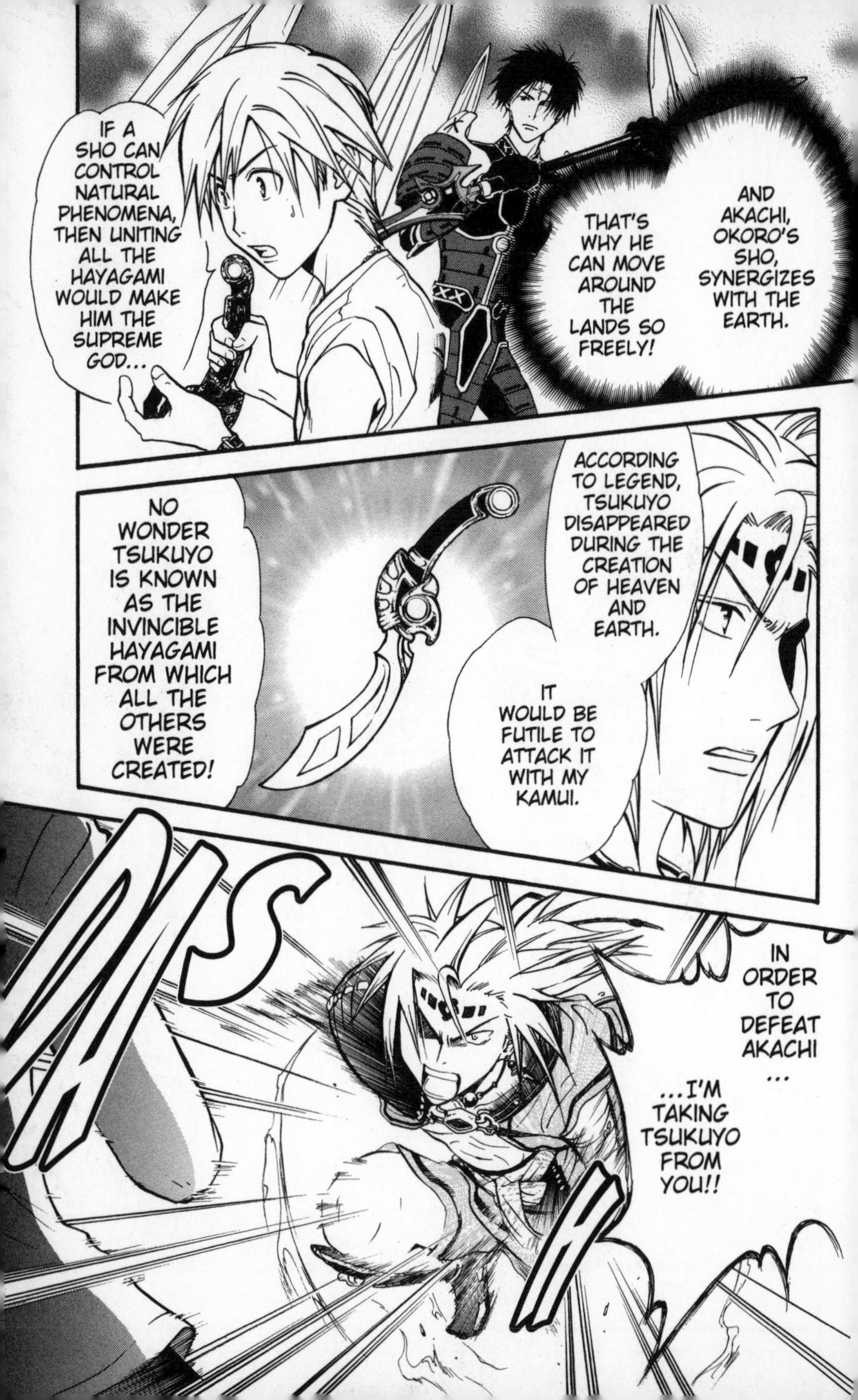
AND AKACHI, OKORO'S SHO, SYNERGIZES WITH THE EARTH.
THAT'S WHY HE CAN MOVE AROUND THE LANDS SO FREELY!
IF A SHO CAN CONTROL NATURAL PHENOMENA, THEN UNITING ALL THE HAYAGAMI WOULD MAKE HIM THE SUPREME GOD...
ACCORDING TO LEGEND, TSUKUYO DISAPPEARED DURING THE CREATION OF HEAVEN AND EARTH.
IT WOULD BE FUTILE TO ATTACK IT WITH MY KAMUI.
NO WONDER TSUKUYO IS KNOWN AS THE INVINCIBLE HAYAGAMI FROM WHICH ALL THE OTHERS WERE CREATED!
IN ORDER TO DEFEAT AKACHI...
...I'M TAKING TSUKUYO FROM YOU!!
DASH

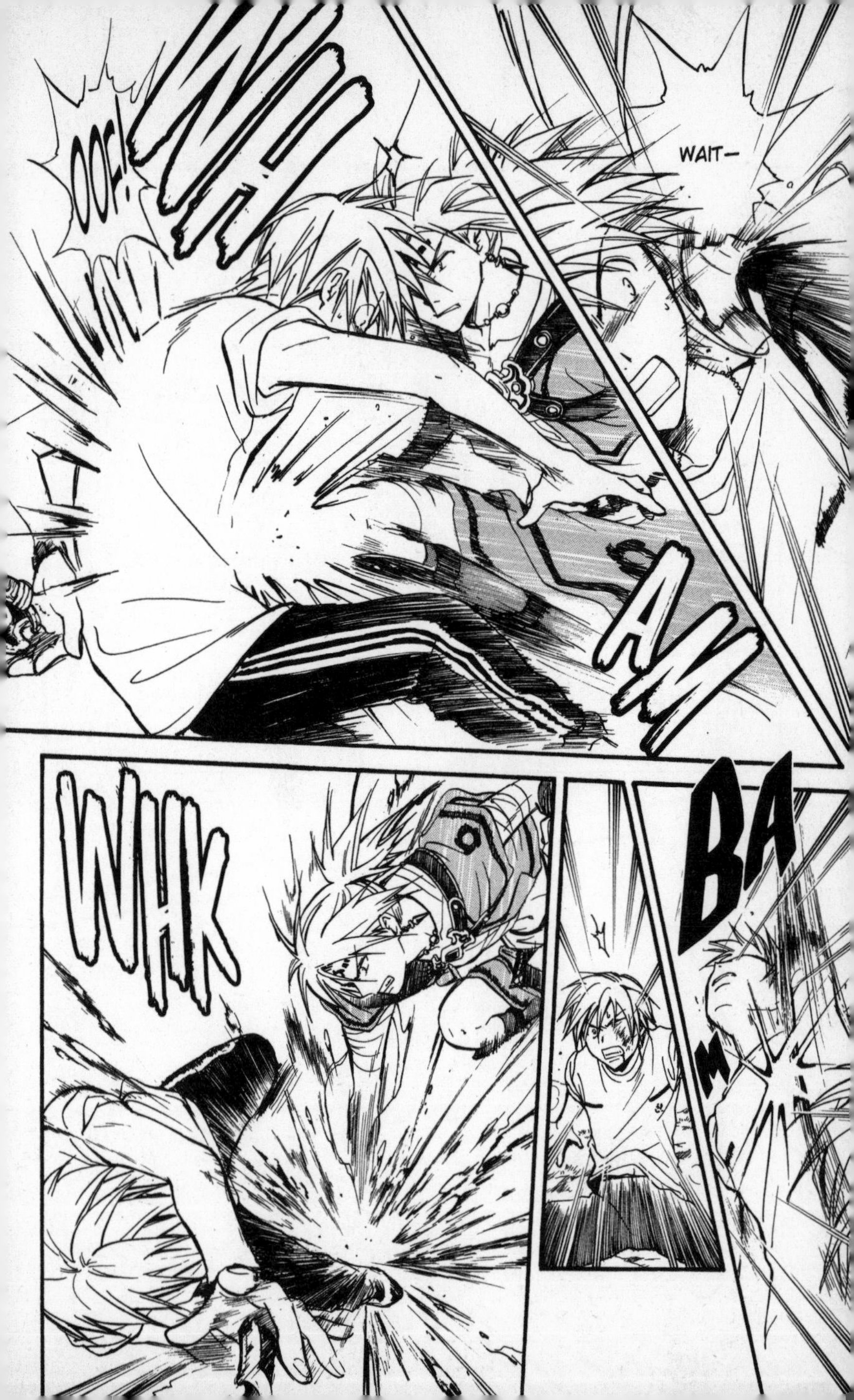
WAIT—
OOF!
BAM
WHK

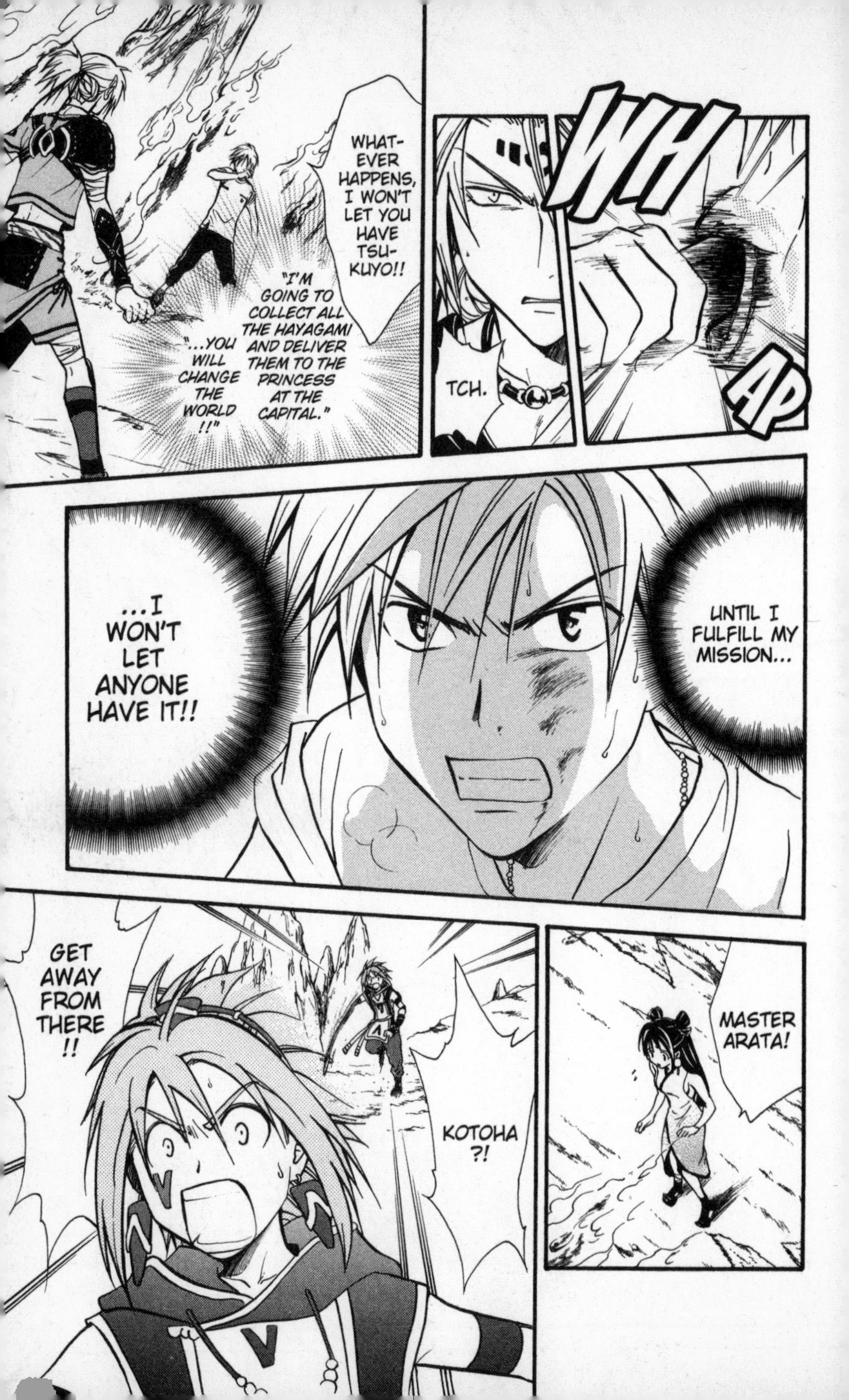
WHAP
TCH.
WHATEVER HAPPENS, I WON'T LET YOU HAVE TSUKUYO!!
"I'M GOING TO COLLECT ALL THE HAYAGAMI AND DELIVER THEM TO THE PRINCESS AT THE CAPITAL."
"...YOU WILL CHANGE THE WORLD!!"
UNTIL I FULFILL MY MISSION...
...I WON'T LET ANYONE HAVE IT!!
MASTER ARATA!
KOTOHA?!
GET AWAY FROM THERE!!

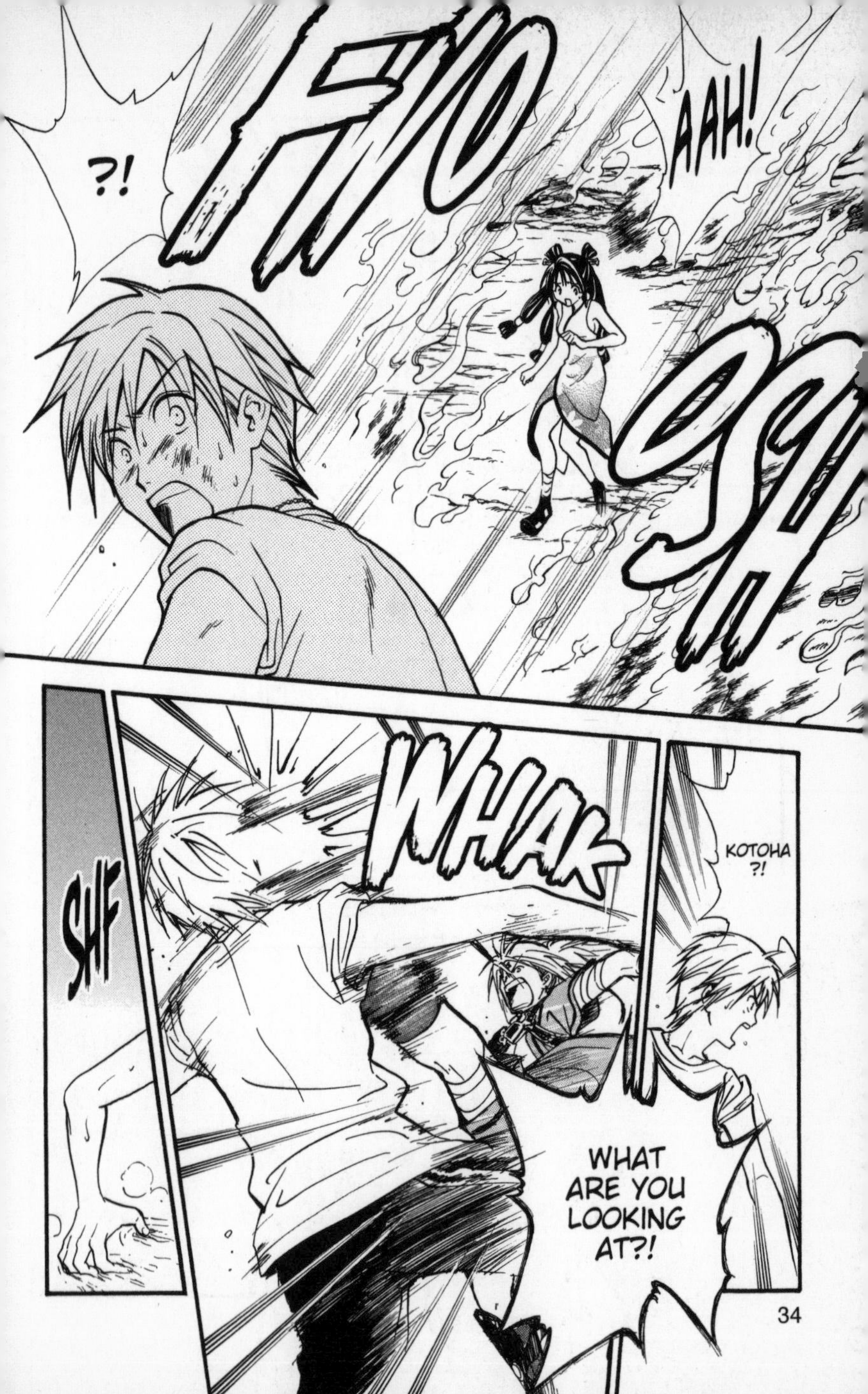
AAH!
FWOOSH
?!
KOTOHA ?!
WHAK
WHAT ARE YOU LOOKING AT?!
SHF

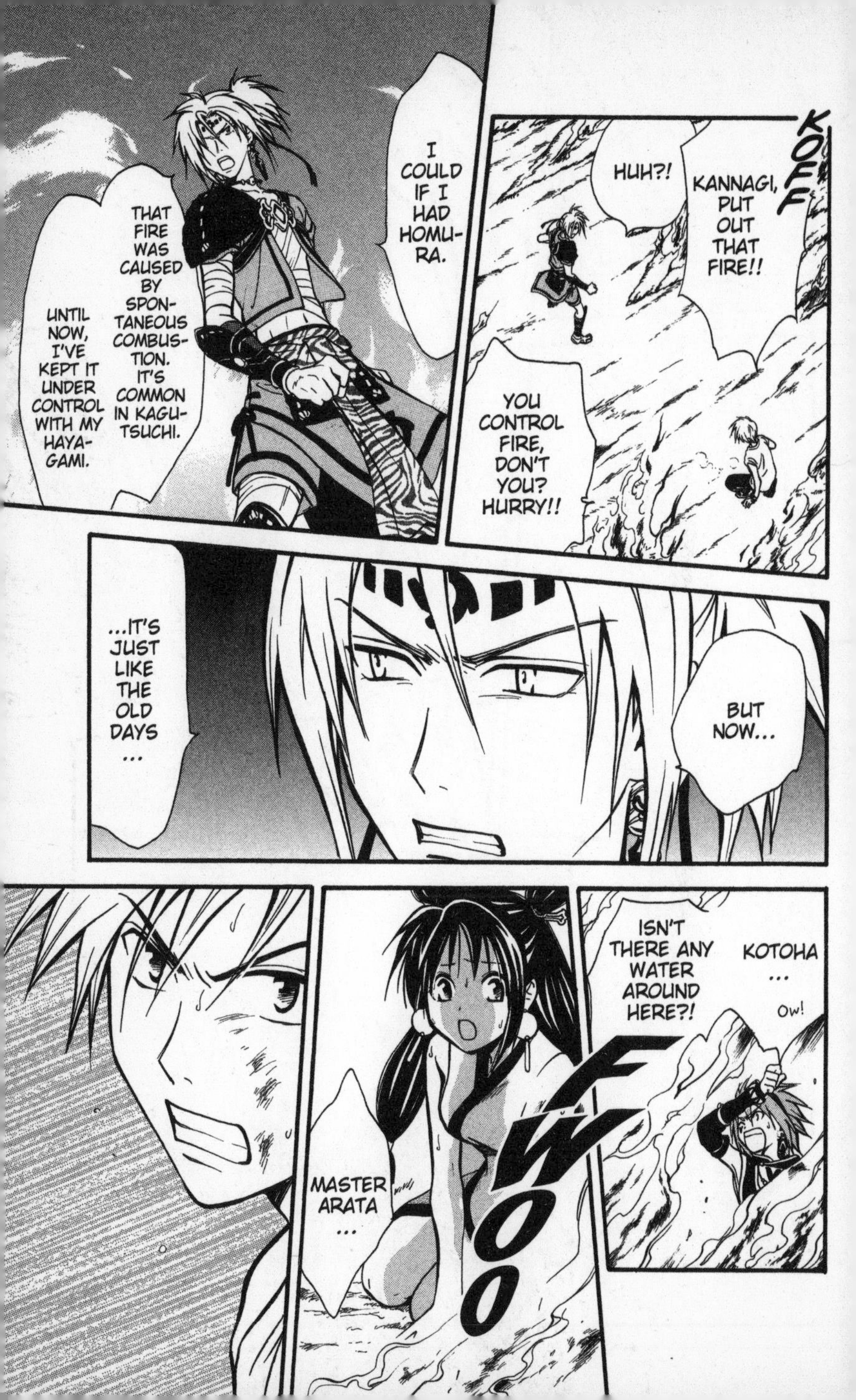
KOFF
KANNAGI, PUT OUT THAT FIRE!!
HUH?!
YOU CONTROL FIRE, DON'T YOU? HURRY!!
I COULD IF I HAD HOMURA.
THAT FIRE WAS CAUSED BY SPONTANEOUS COMBUSTION. IT'S COMMON IN KAGUTSUCHI.
UNTIL NOW, I'VE KEPT IT UNDER CONTROL WITH MY HAYAGAMI.
BUT NOW...
...IT'S JUST LIKE THE OLD DAYS...
KOTOHA...
OW!
ISN'T THERE ANY WATER AROUND HERE?!
FWOOO
MASTER ARATA...

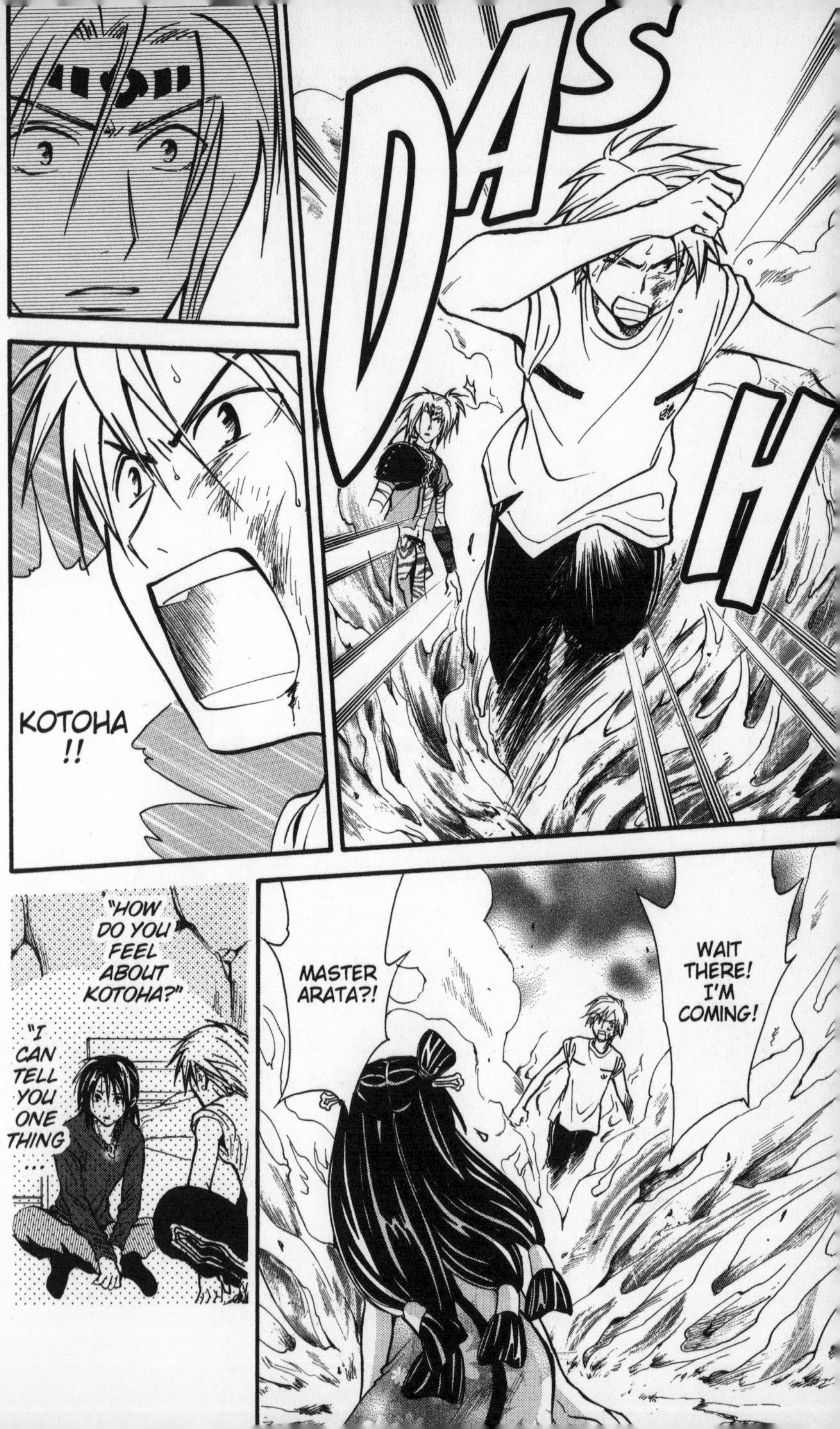
DASH
KOTOHA!!
WAIT THERE! I'M COMING!
MASTER ARATA?!
"HOW DO YOU FEEL ABOUT KOTOHA?"
"I CAN TELL YOU ONE THING..."

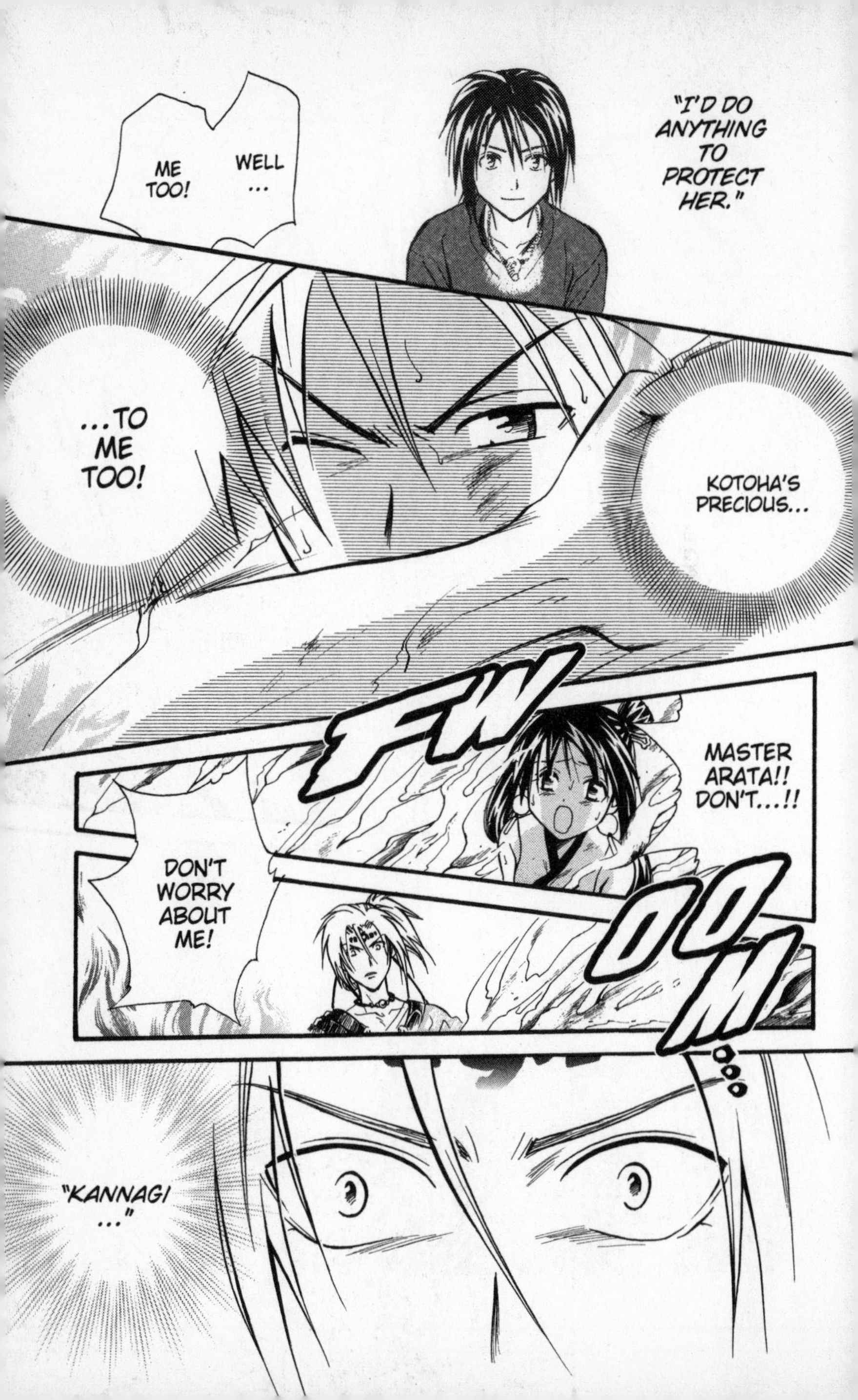
"I'D DO ANYTHING TO PROTECT HER."
WELL ...
ME TOO!
KOTOHA'S PRECIOUS...
...TO ME TOO!
MASTER ARATA!! DON'T...!!
FW
OOM
DON'T WORRY ABOUT ME!
"KANNAGI ..."

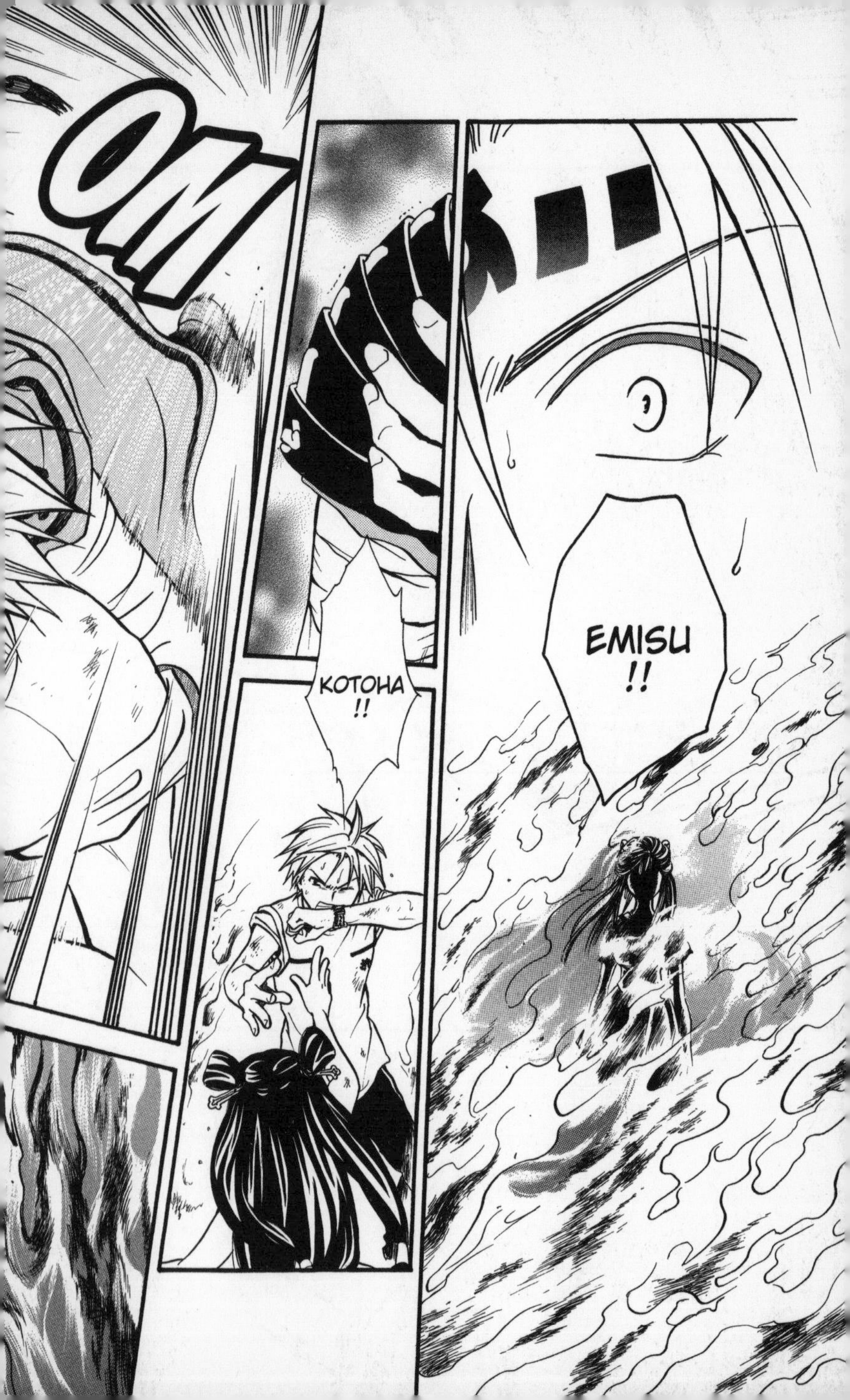
EMISU !!
KOTOHA !!

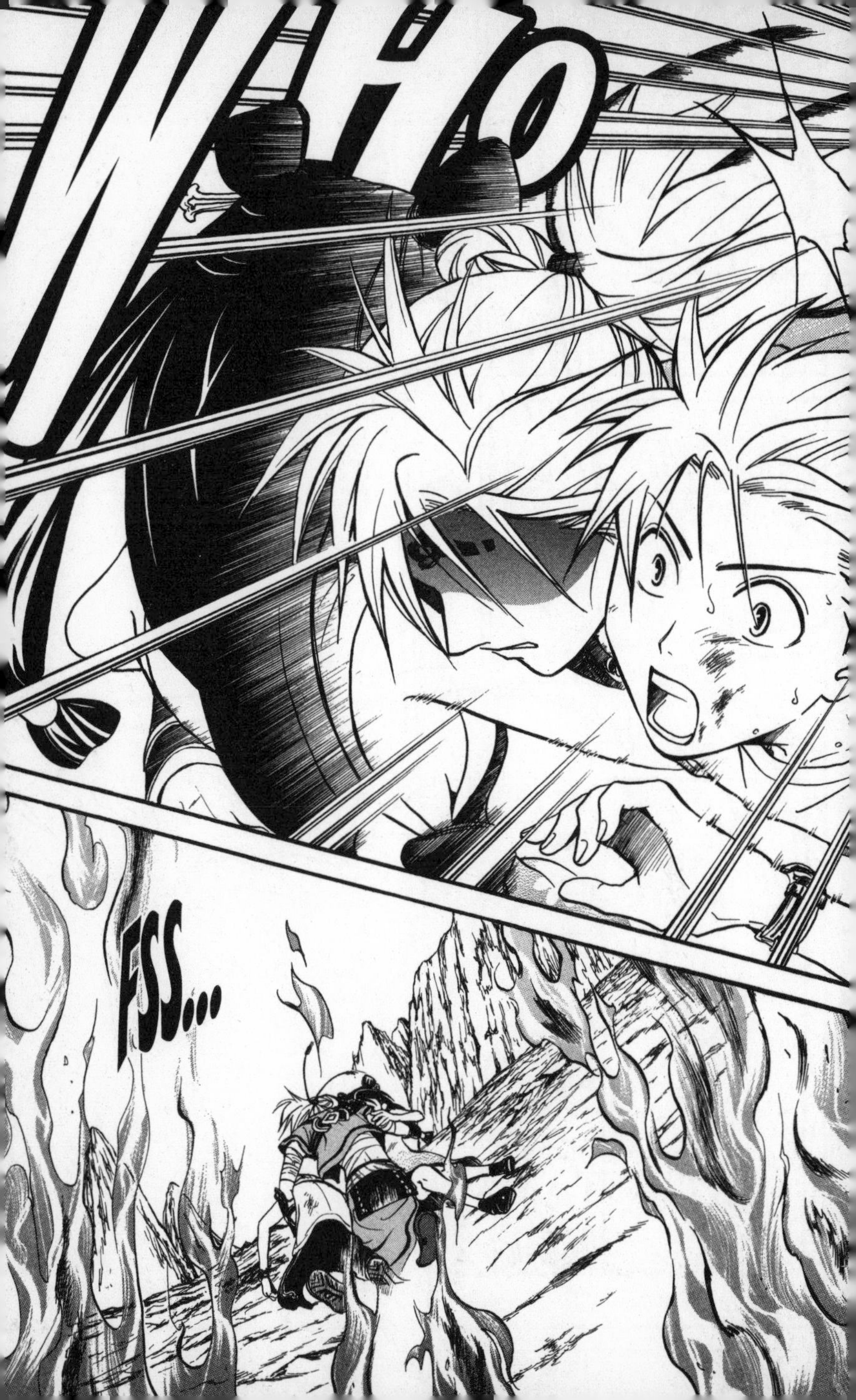
WHO
FSS...

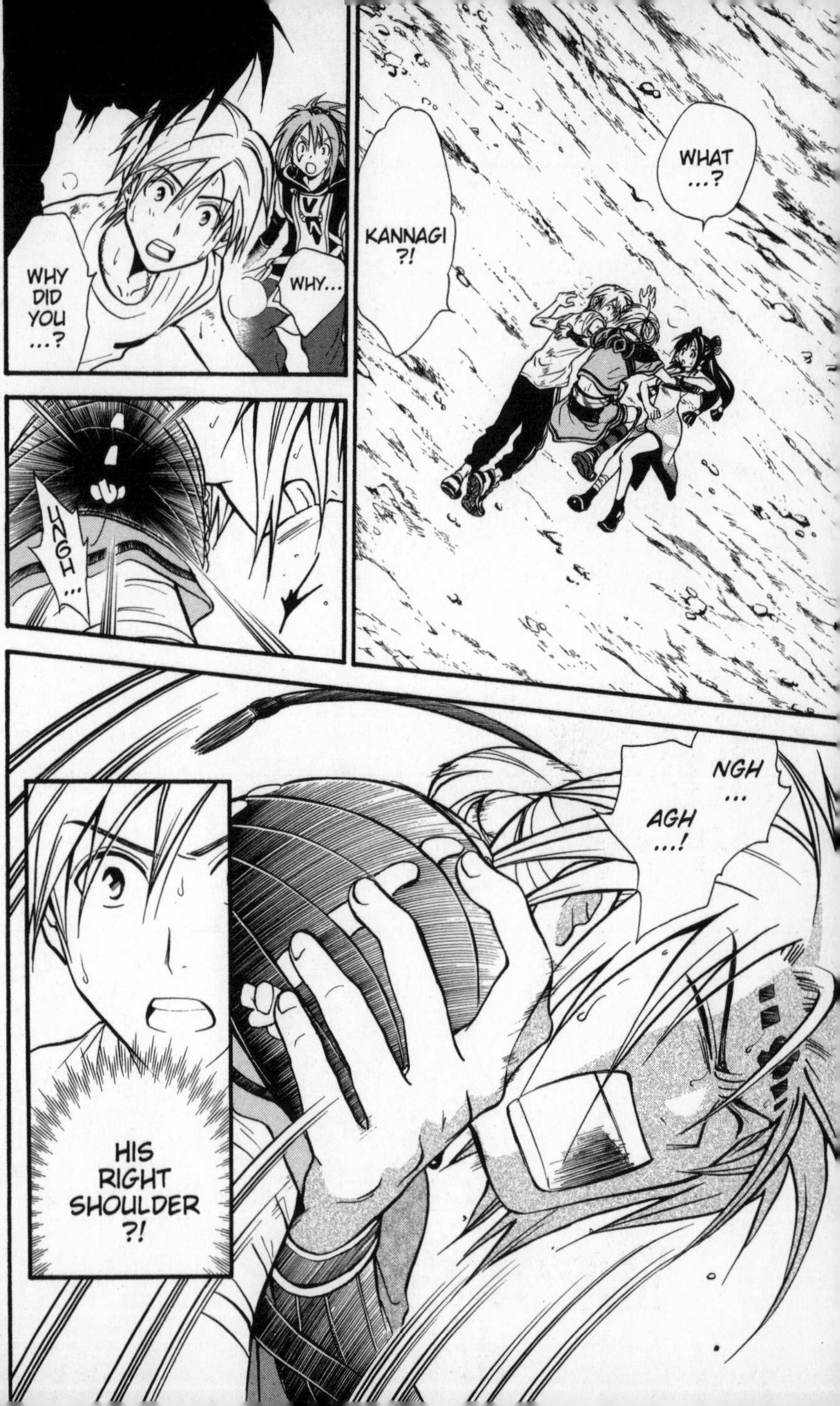
WHAT ...?
KANNAGI ?!
WHY...
WHY DID YOU ...?
UNGH ...
NGH ...
AGH ...!
HIS RIGHT SHOULDER ?!

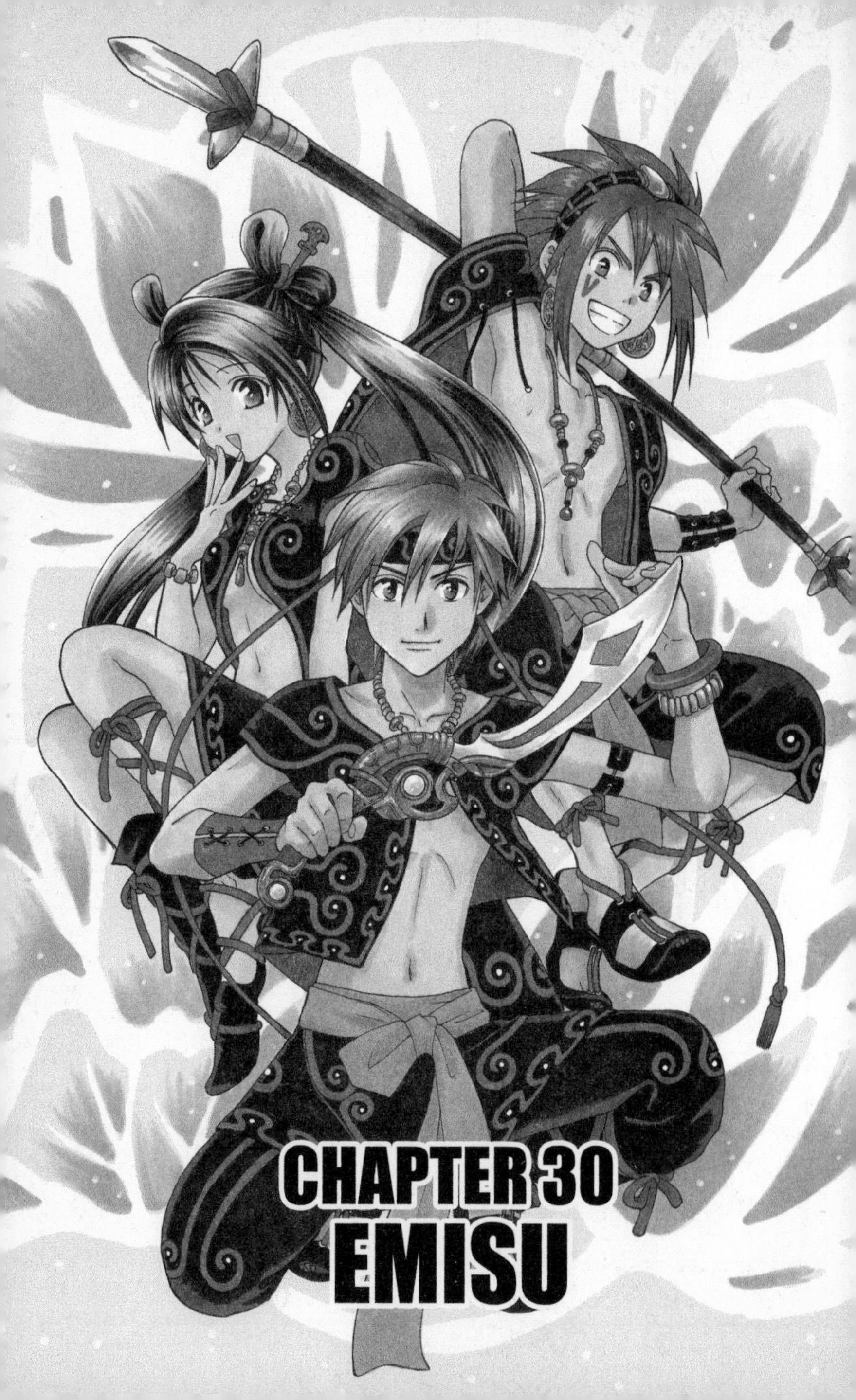
CHAPTER 30
EMISU

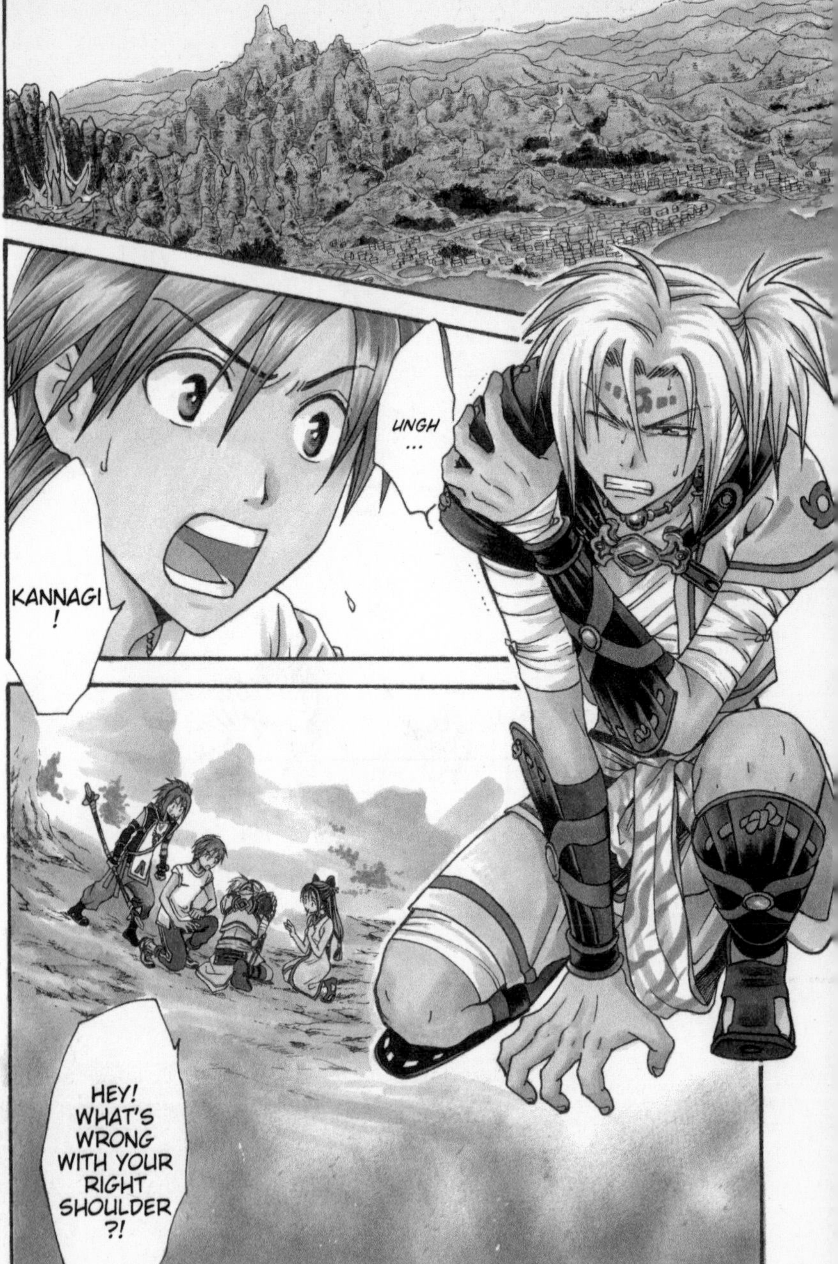
UNGH...
KANNAGI!
HEY! WHAT'S WRONG WITH YOUR RIGHT SHOULDER?!

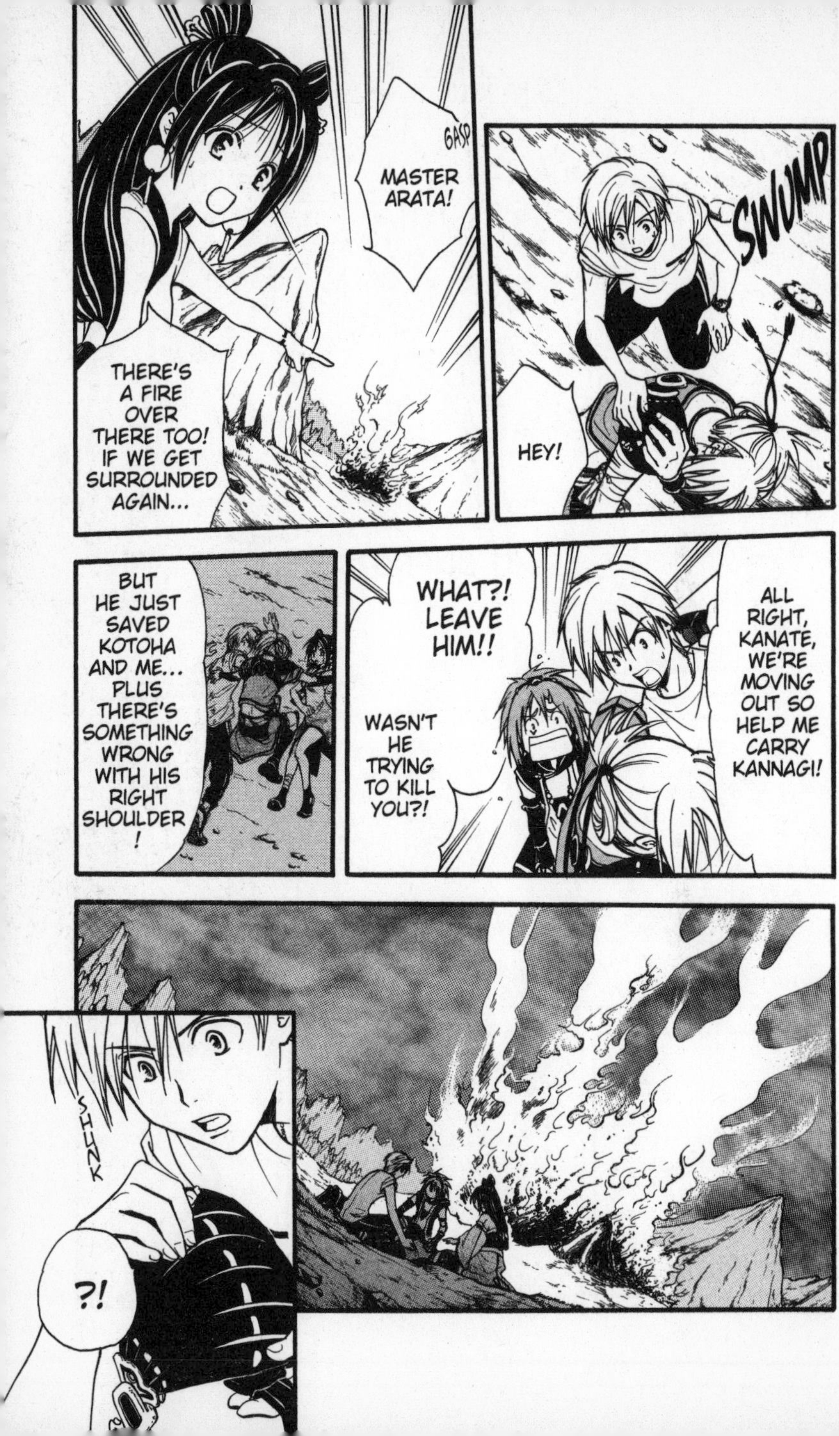
SWUMP
HEY!
GASP
MASTER ARATA!
THERE'S A FIRE OVER THERE TOO! IF WE GET SURROUNDED AGAIN...
ALL RIGHT, KANATE, WE'RE MOVING OUT SO HELP ME CARRY KANNAGI!
WHAT?! LEAVE HIM!!
WASN'T HE TRYING TO KILL YOU?!
BUT HE JUST SAVED KOTOHA AND ME... PLUS THERE'S SOMETHING WRONG WITH HIS RIGHT SHOULDER!
SHUNK
?!

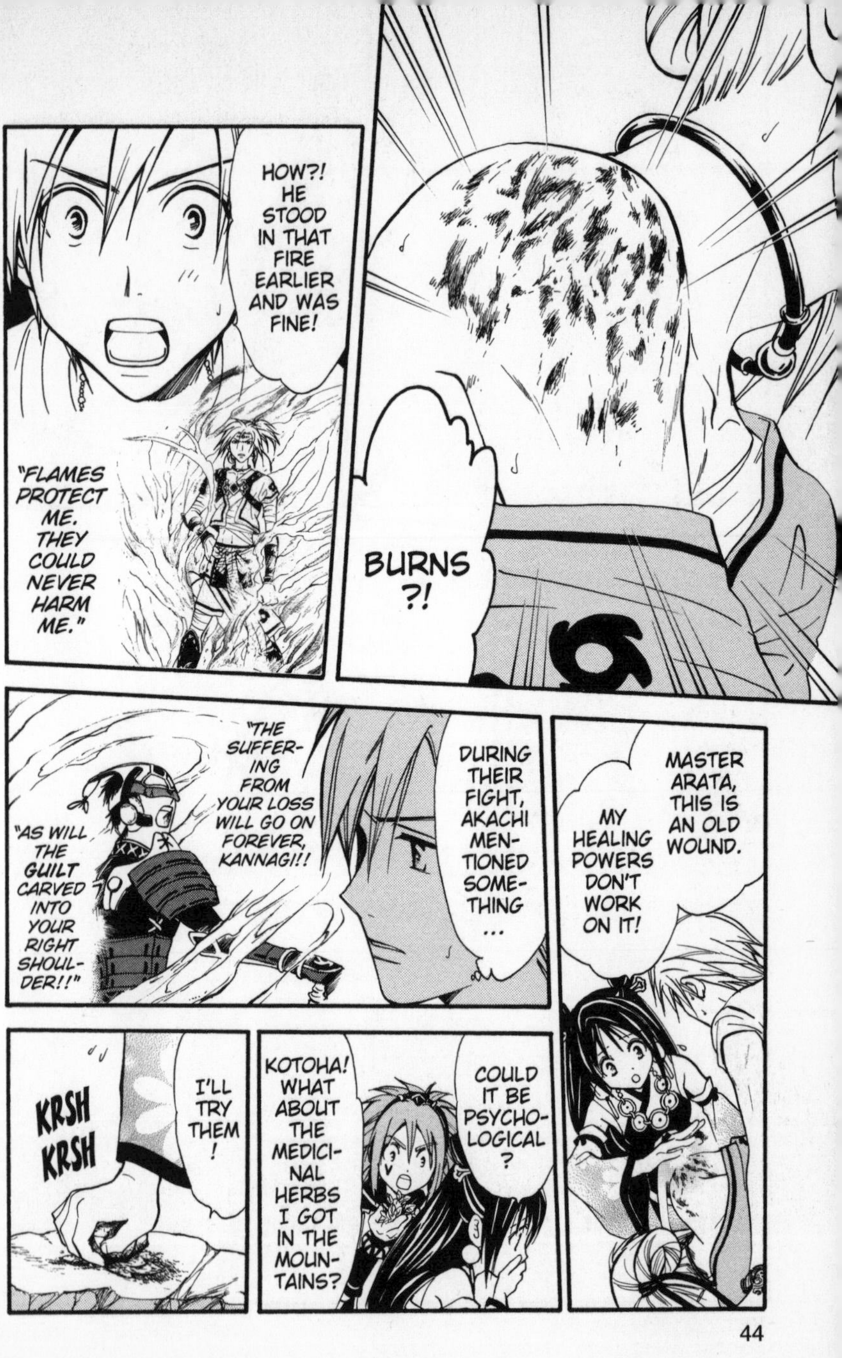
BURNS ?!
HOW?! HE STOOD IN THAT FIRE EARLIER AND WAS FINE!
"FLAMES PROTECT ME. THEY COULD NEVER HARM ME."
MASTER ARATA, THIS IS AN OLD WOUND.
MY HEALING POWERS DON'T WORK ON IT!
DURING THEIR FIGHT, AKACHI MENTIONED SOMETHING...
"THE SUFFERING FROM YOUR LOSS WILL GO ON FOREVER, KANNAGI!!
"AS WILL THE GUILT CARVED INTO YOUR RIGHT SHOULDER!!"
COULD IT BE PSYCHOLOGICAL?
KOTOHA! WHAT ABOUT THE MEDICINAL HERBS I GOT IN THE MOUNTAINS?
I'LL TRY THEM!
KRSH KRSH

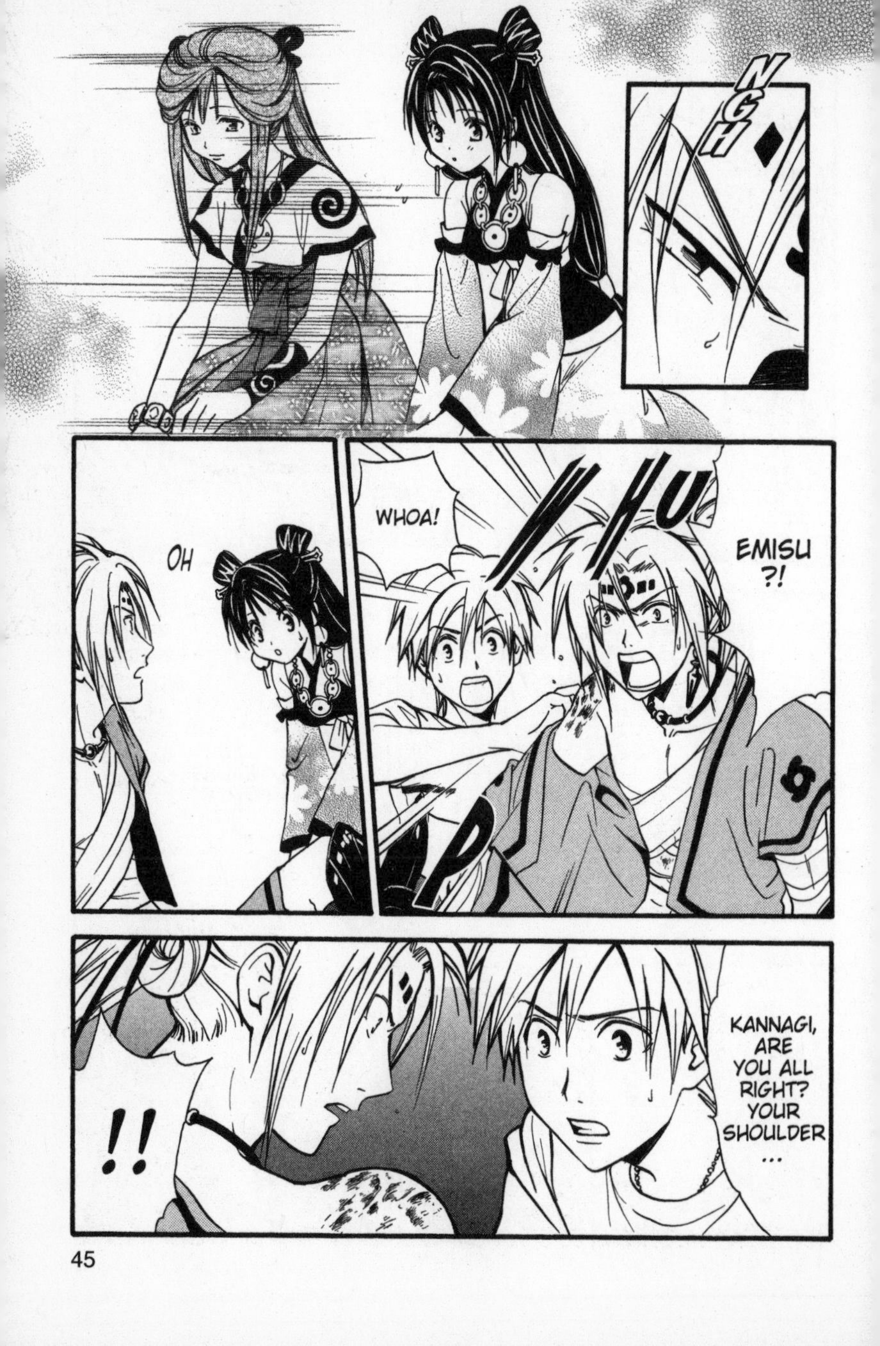
NGH
EMISU ?!
WHOA!
OH
KANNAGI, ARE YOU ALL RIGHT? YOUR SHOULDER ...
!!

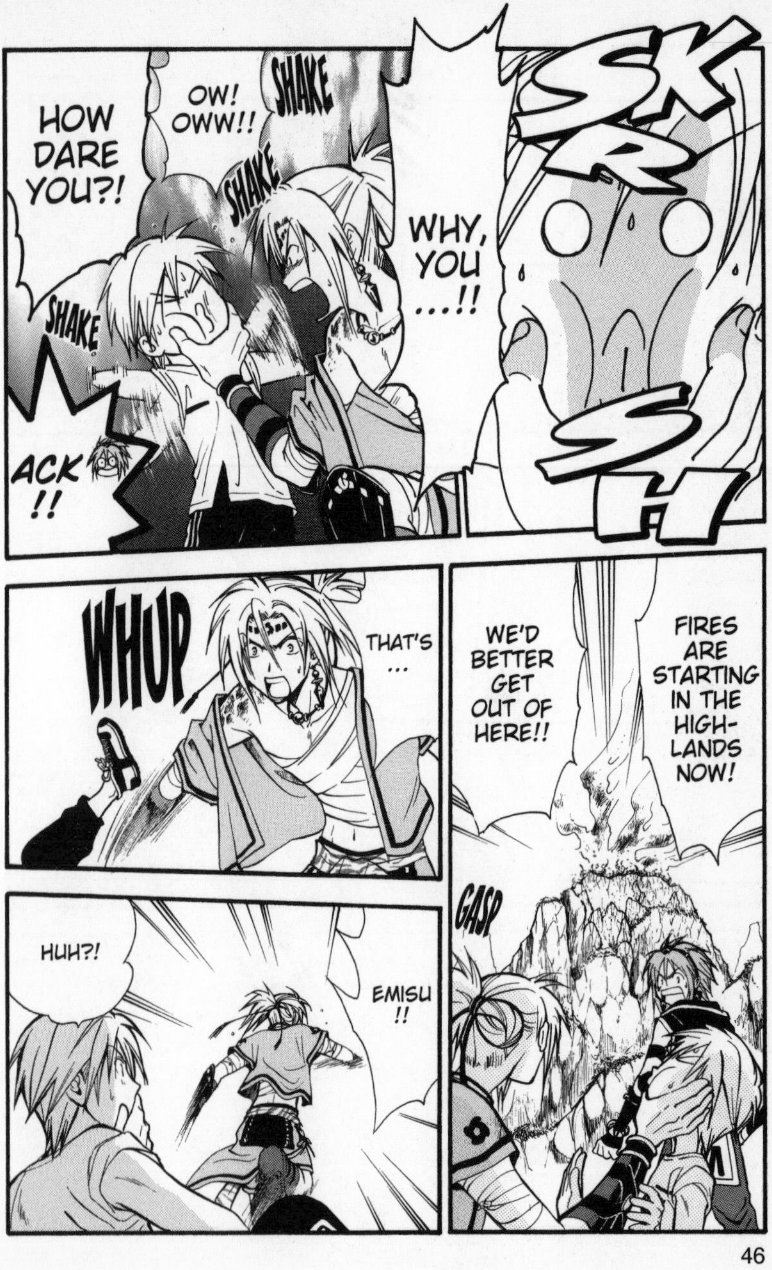
SKR
SSH
WHY, YOU ...!!
SHAKE
OW! OWW!!
HOW DARE YOU?!
SHAKE
SHAKE
ACK!!
FIRES ARE STARTING IN THE HIGH-LANDS NOW!
WE'D BETTER GET OUT OF HERE!!
GASP
THAT'S ...
WHUP
EMISU!!
HUH?!

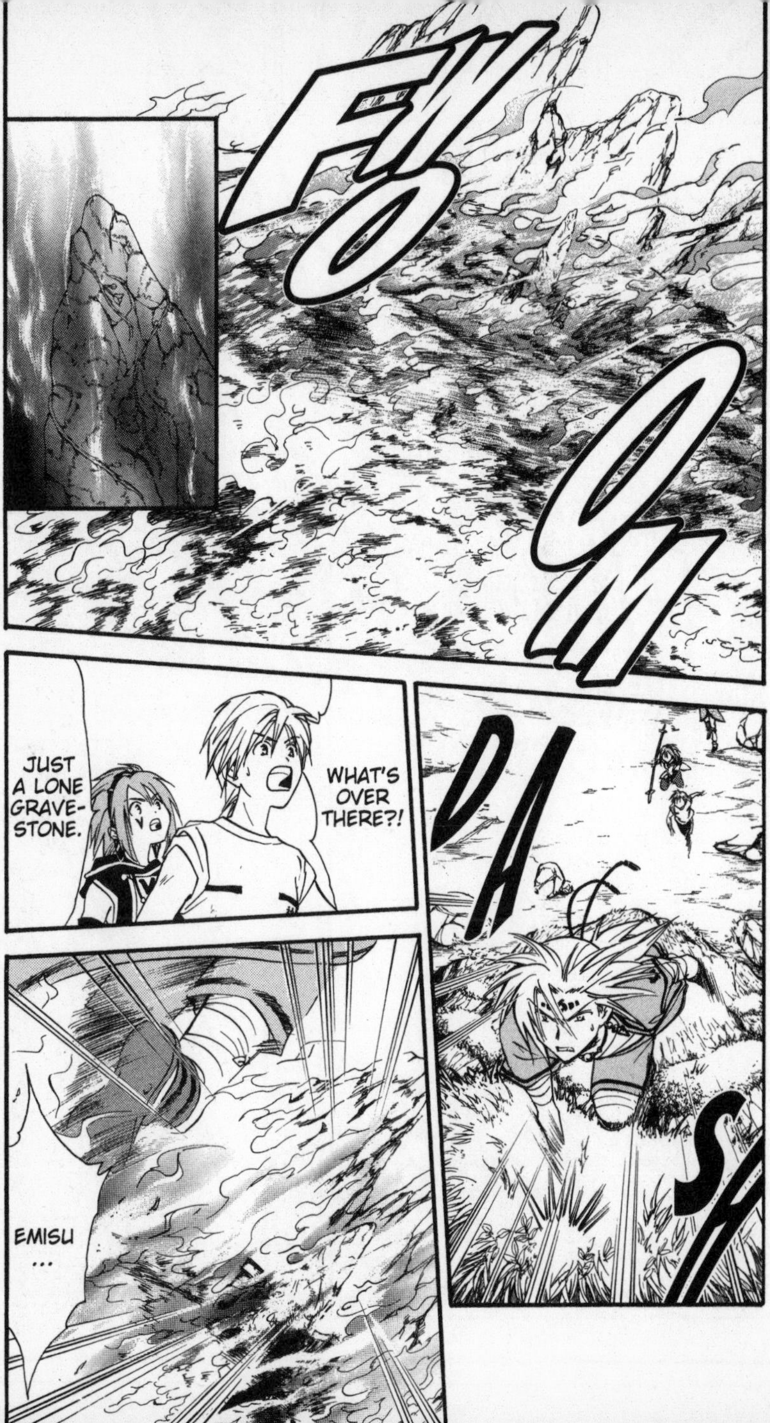
FWOOM
DA
SH
WHAT'S OVER THERE?!
JUST A LONE GRAVE-STONE.
EMISU ...

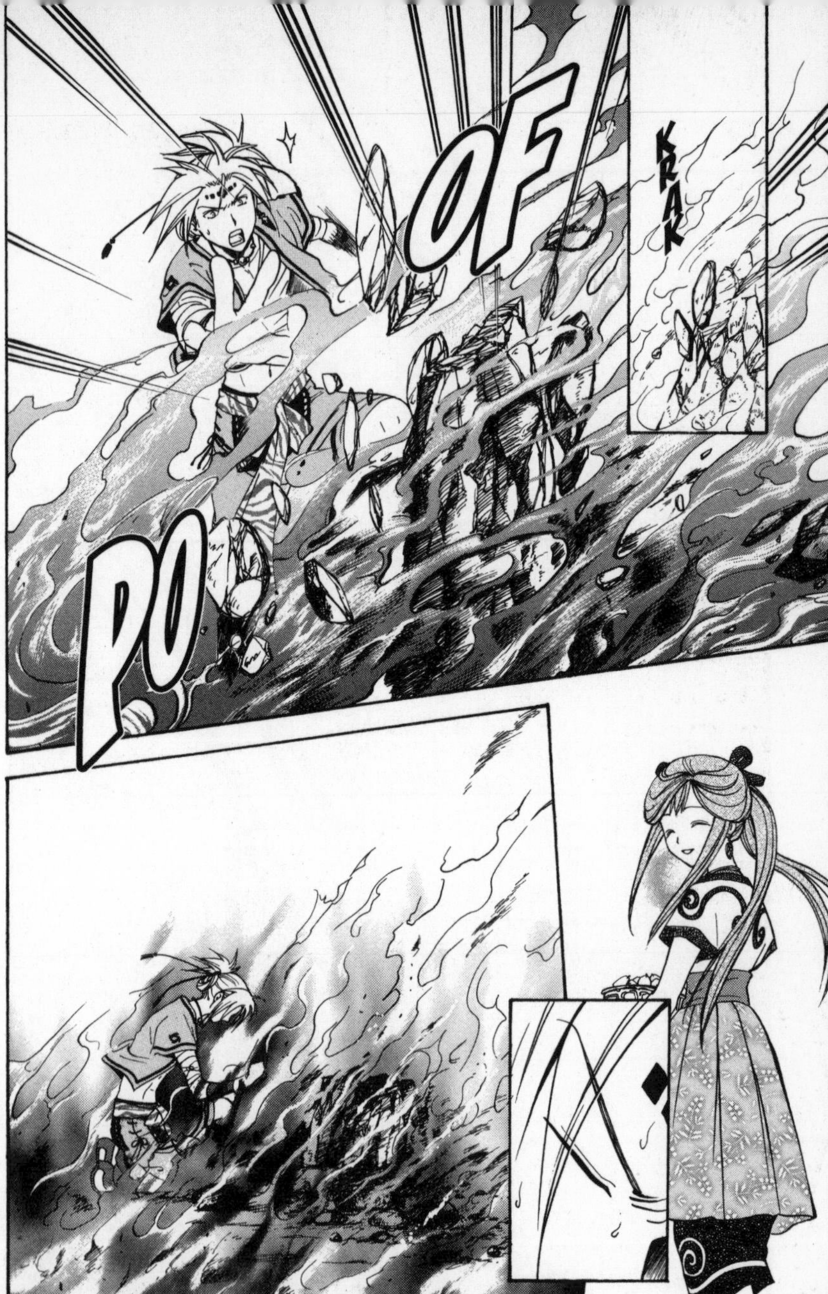
KRAK
PO
OF

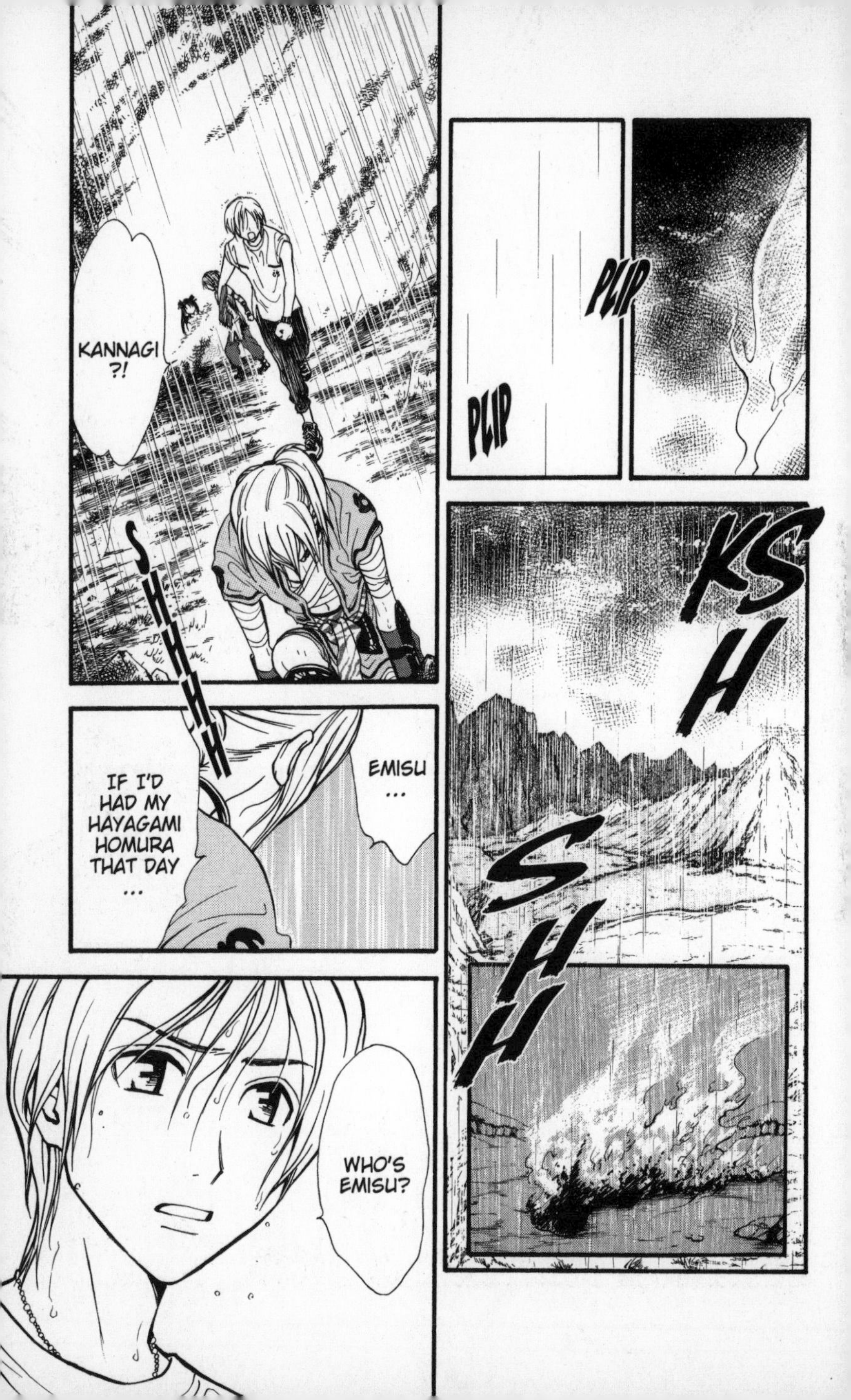
PLIP
PLIP
KSH
SHH
KANNAGI ?!
SHHHHHH
EMISU ...
IF I'D HAD MY HAYAGAMI HOMURA THAT DAY ...
WHO'S EMISU?

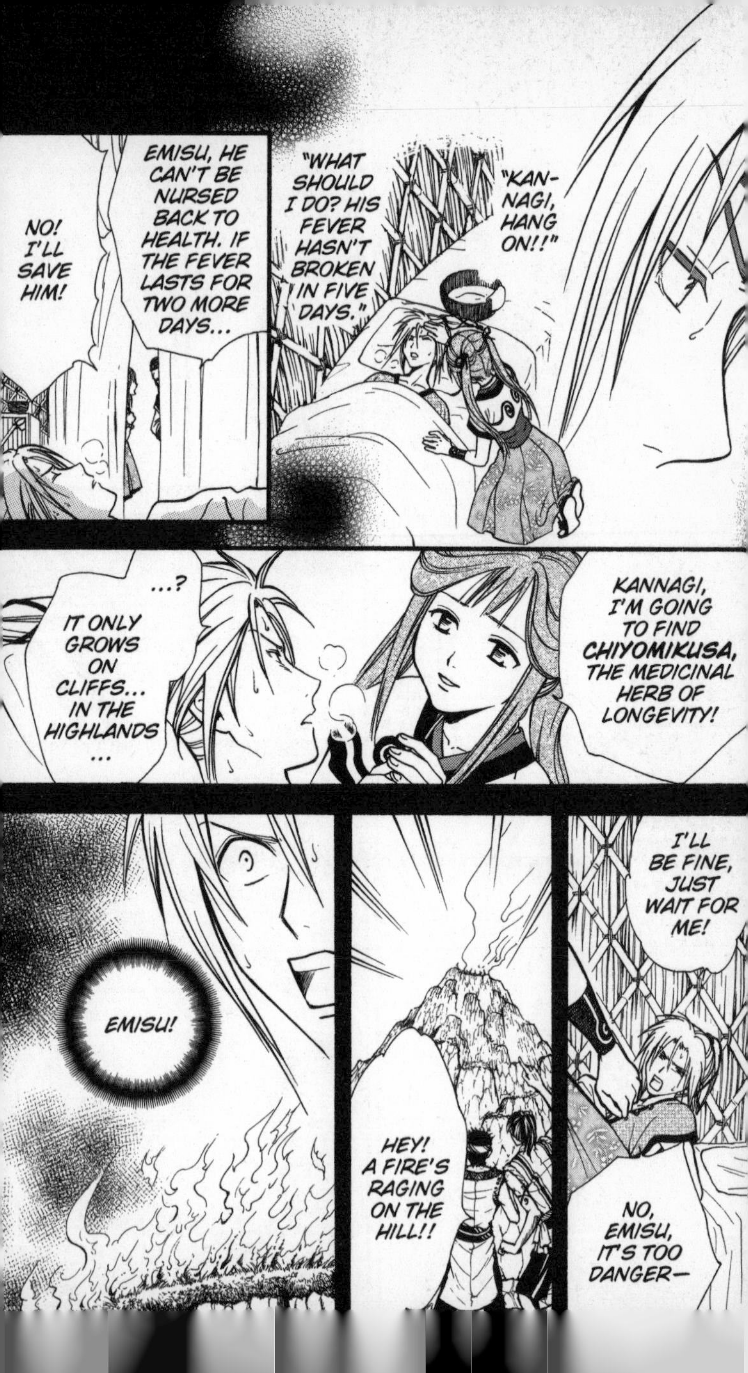
"KAN-NAGI, HANG ON!!"
"WHAT SHOULD I DO? HIS FEVER HASN'T BROKEN IN FIVE DAYS."
EMISU, HE CAN'T BE NURSED BACK TO HEALTH. IF THE FEVER LASTS FOR TWO MORE DAYS...
NO! I'LL SAVE HIM!
KANNAGI, I'M GOING TO FIND CHIYOMIKUSA, THE MEDICINAL HERB OF LONGEVITY!
...?
IT ONLY GROWS ON CLIFFS... IN THE HIGHLANDS ...
I'LL BE FINE, JUST WAIT FOR ME!
NO, EMISU, IT'S TOO DANGER—
HEY! A FIRE'S RAGING ON THE HILL!!
EMISU!

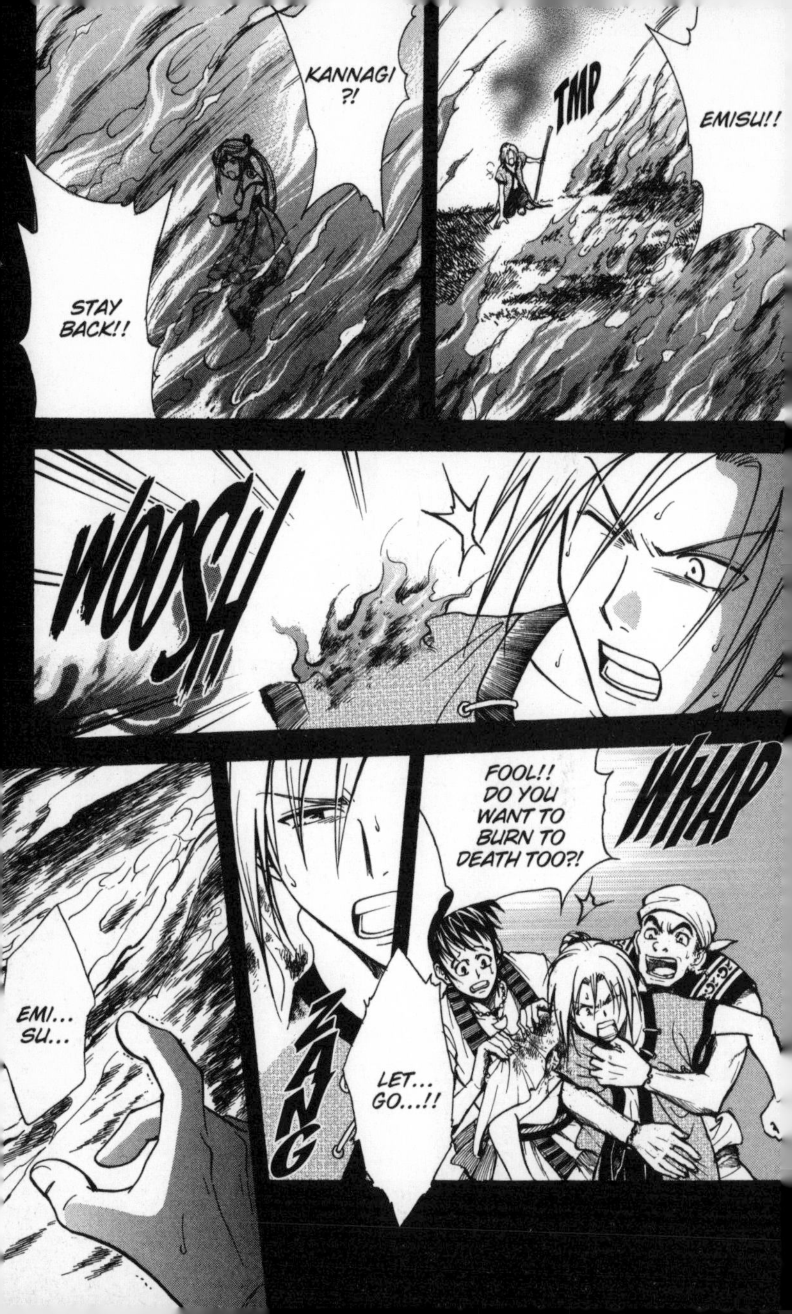
EMISU!!
TMP
KANNAGI ?!
STAY BACK!!
WOOSH
WHAP
FOOL!! DO YOU WANT TO BURN TO DEATH TOO?!
LET... GO...!!
ZANG
EMI... SU...

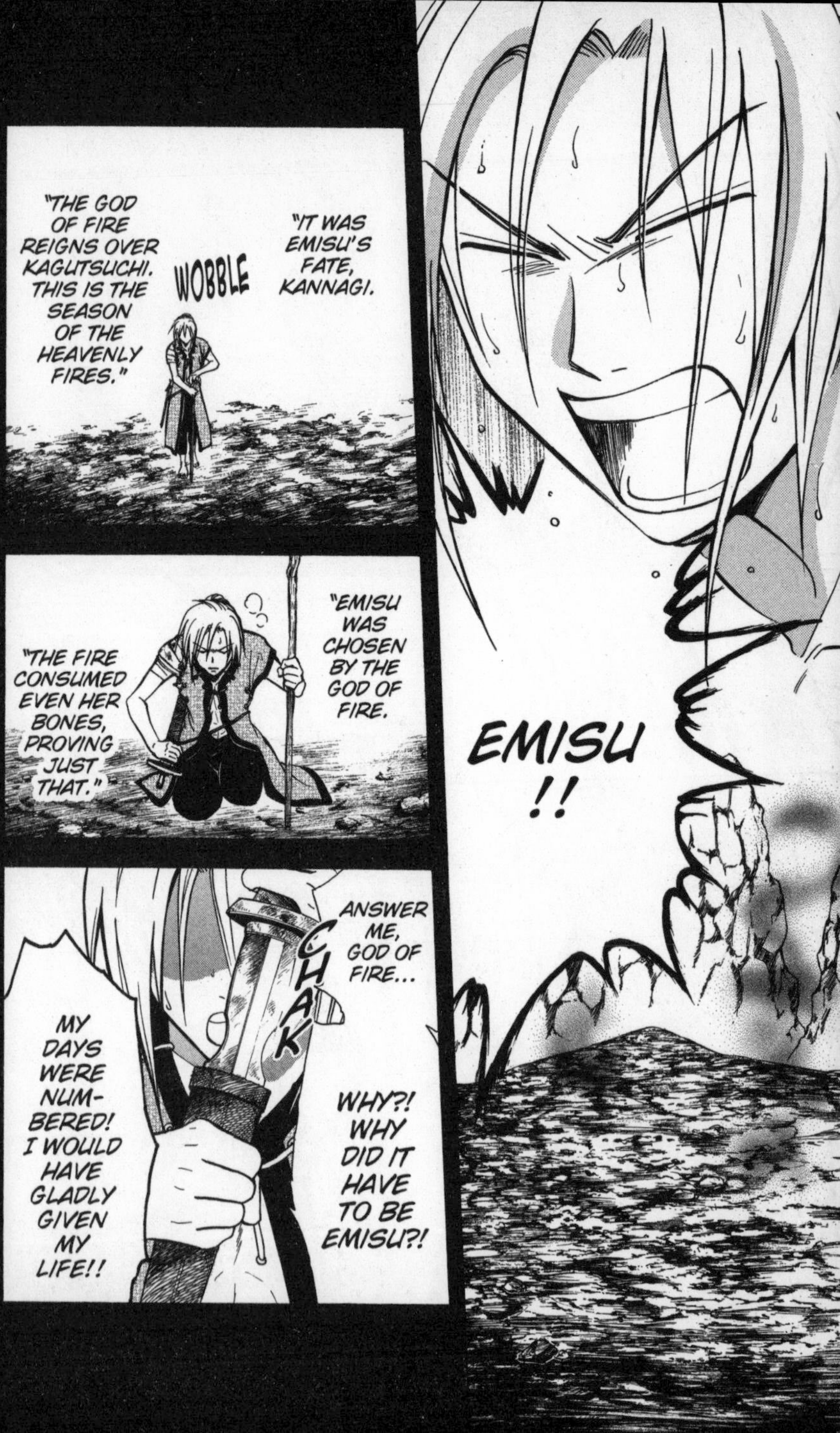
EMISU !!
"IT WAS EMISU'S FATE, KANNAGI.
WOBBLE
"THE GOD OF FIRE REIGNS OVER KAGUTSUCHI. THIS IS THE SEASON OF THE HEAVENLY FIRES."
"EMISU WAS CHOSEN BY THE GOD OF FIRE.
"THE FIRE CONSUMED EVEN HER BONES, PROVING JUST THAT."
ANSWER ME, GOD OF FIRE...
CHAK
WHY?! WHY DID IT HAVE TO BE EMISU?!
MY DAYS WERE NUM-BERED! I WOULD HAVE GLADLY GIVEN MY LIFE!!

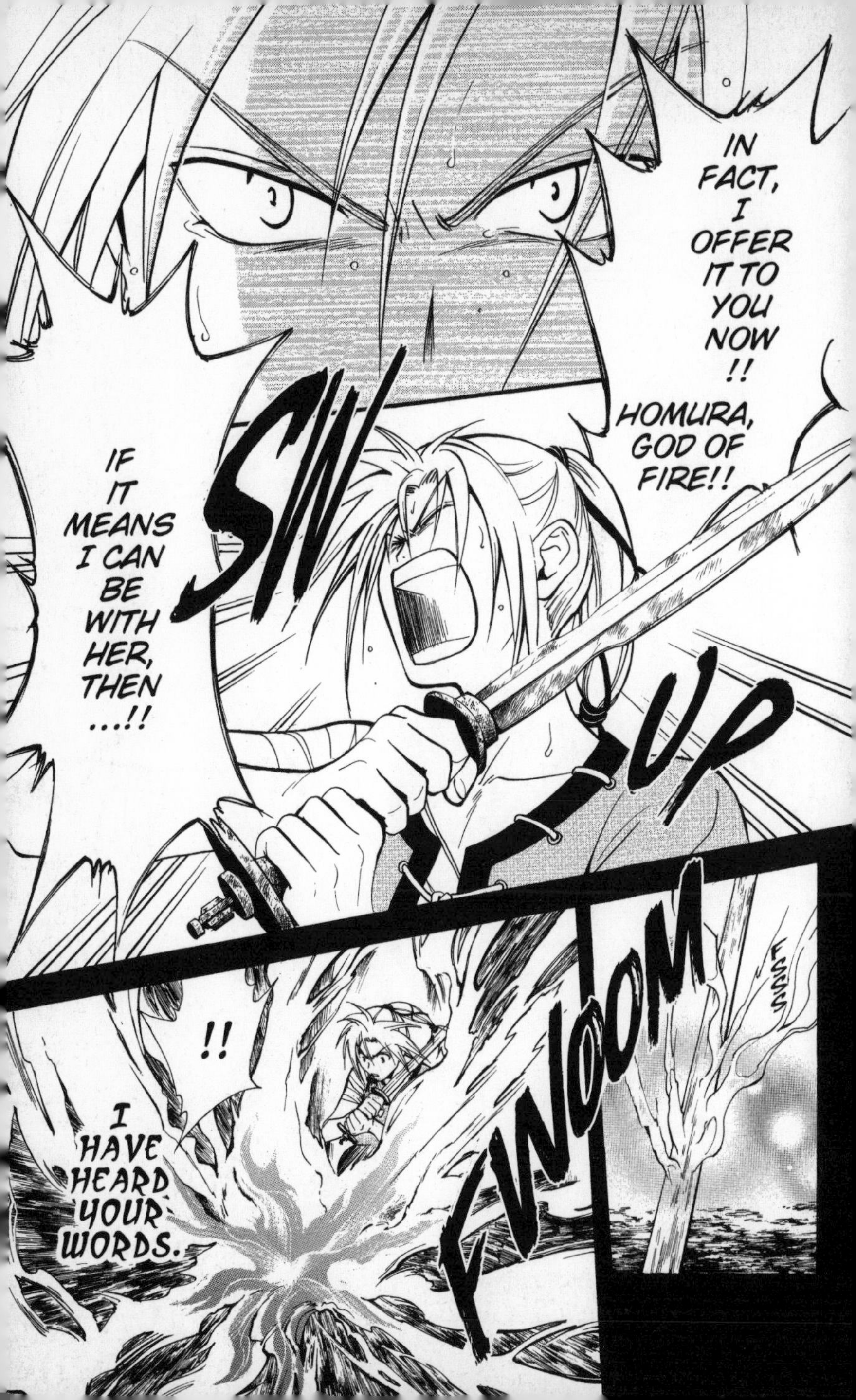
IN FACT, I OFFER IT TO YOU NOW!!
HOMURA, GOD OF FIRE!!
IF IT MEANS I CAN BE WITH HER, THEN...!!
SW
UP
FSSS
FWOOM
!!
I HAVE HEARD YOUR WORDS.

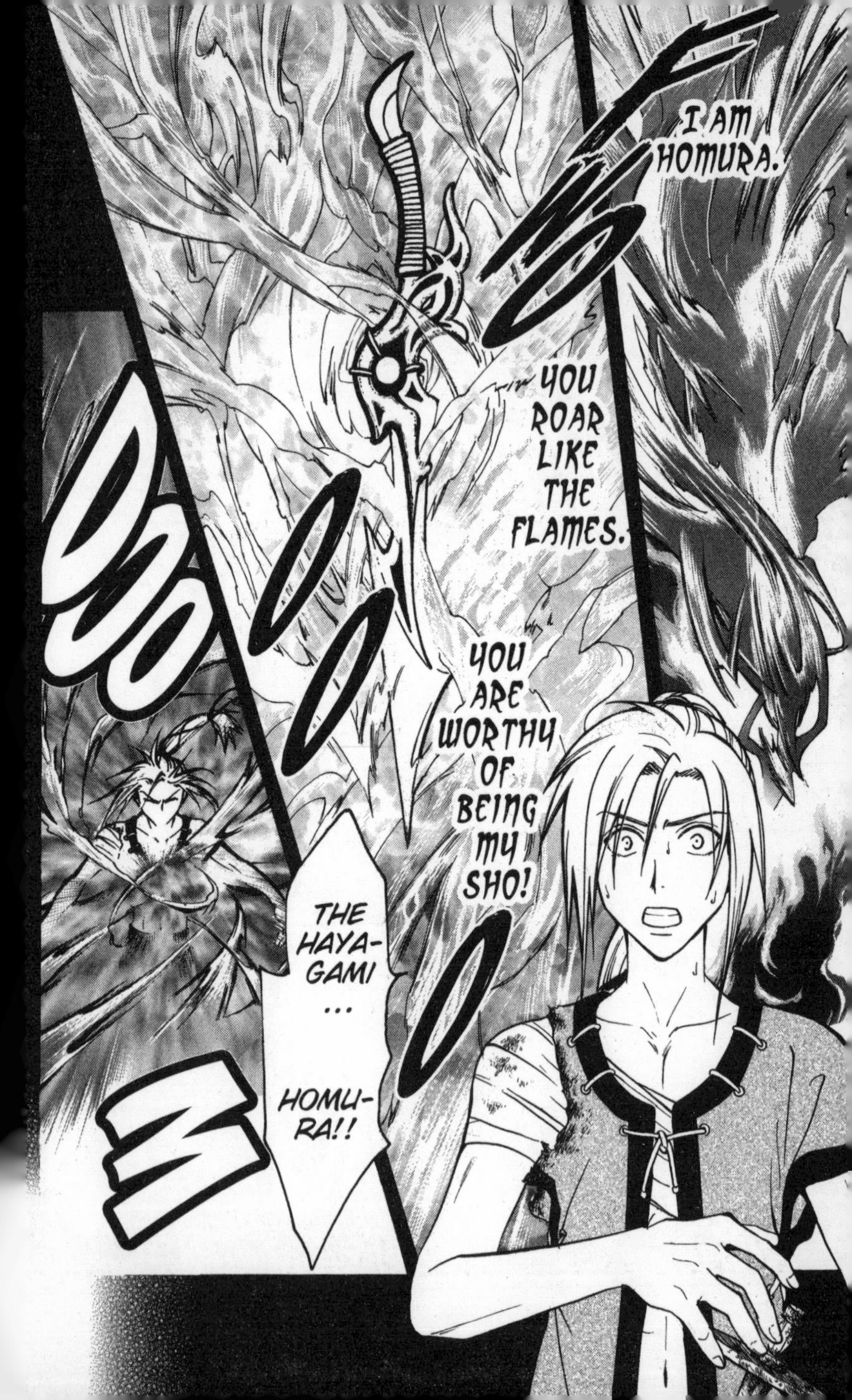
I AM HOMURA.
YOU ROAR LIKE THE FLAMES.
YOU ARE WORTHY OF BEING MY SHO!
THE HAYA-GAMI ...
HOMU-RA!!

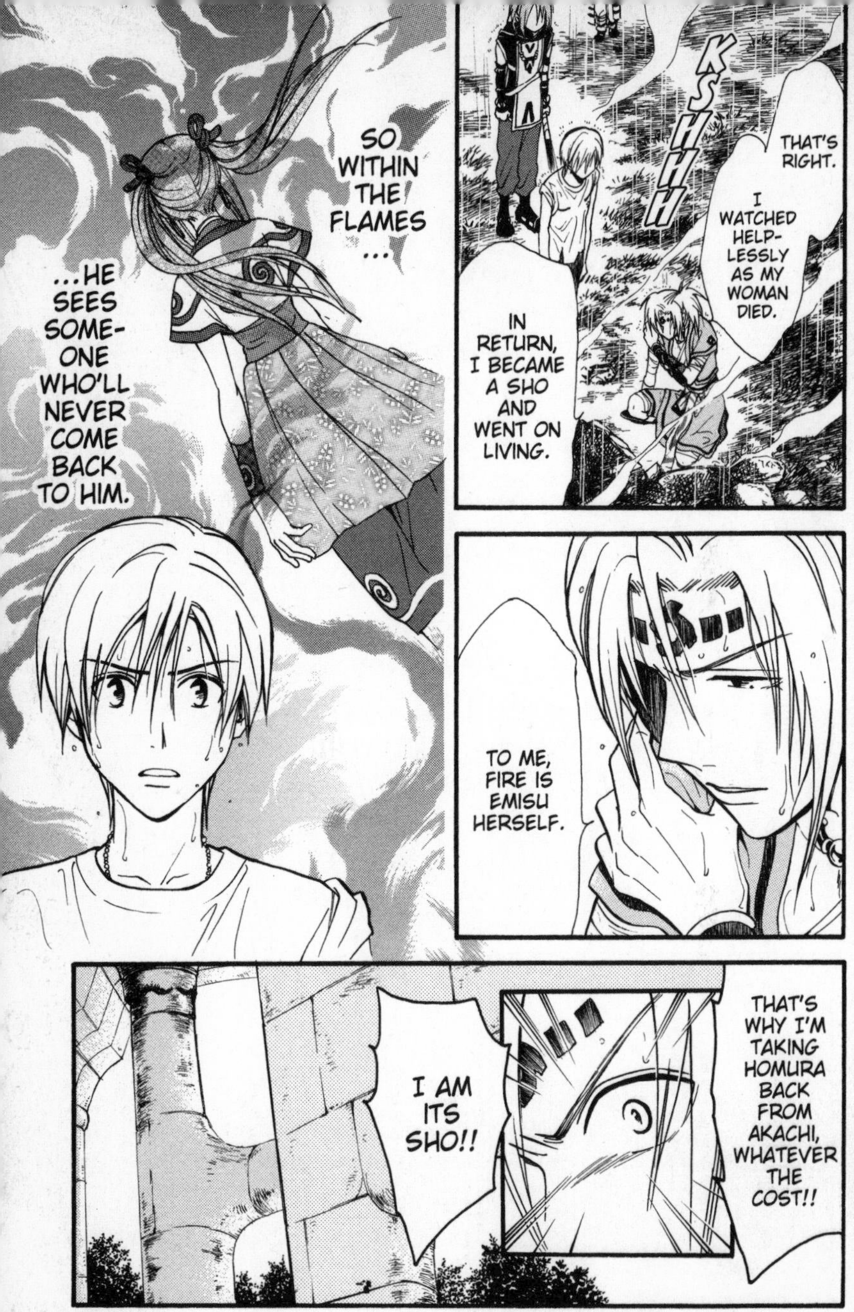
KSHHHH
THAT'S RIGHT.
I WATCHED HELP-LESSLY AS MY WOMAN DIED.
IN RETURN, I BECAME A SHO AND WENT ON LIVING.
TO ME, FIRE IS EMISU HERSELF.
SO WITHIN THE FLAMES...
...HE SEES SOME-ONE WHO'LL NEVER COME BACK TO HIM.
THAT'S WHY I'M TAKING HOMURA BACK FROM AKACHI, WHATEVER THE COST!!
I AM ITS SHO!!

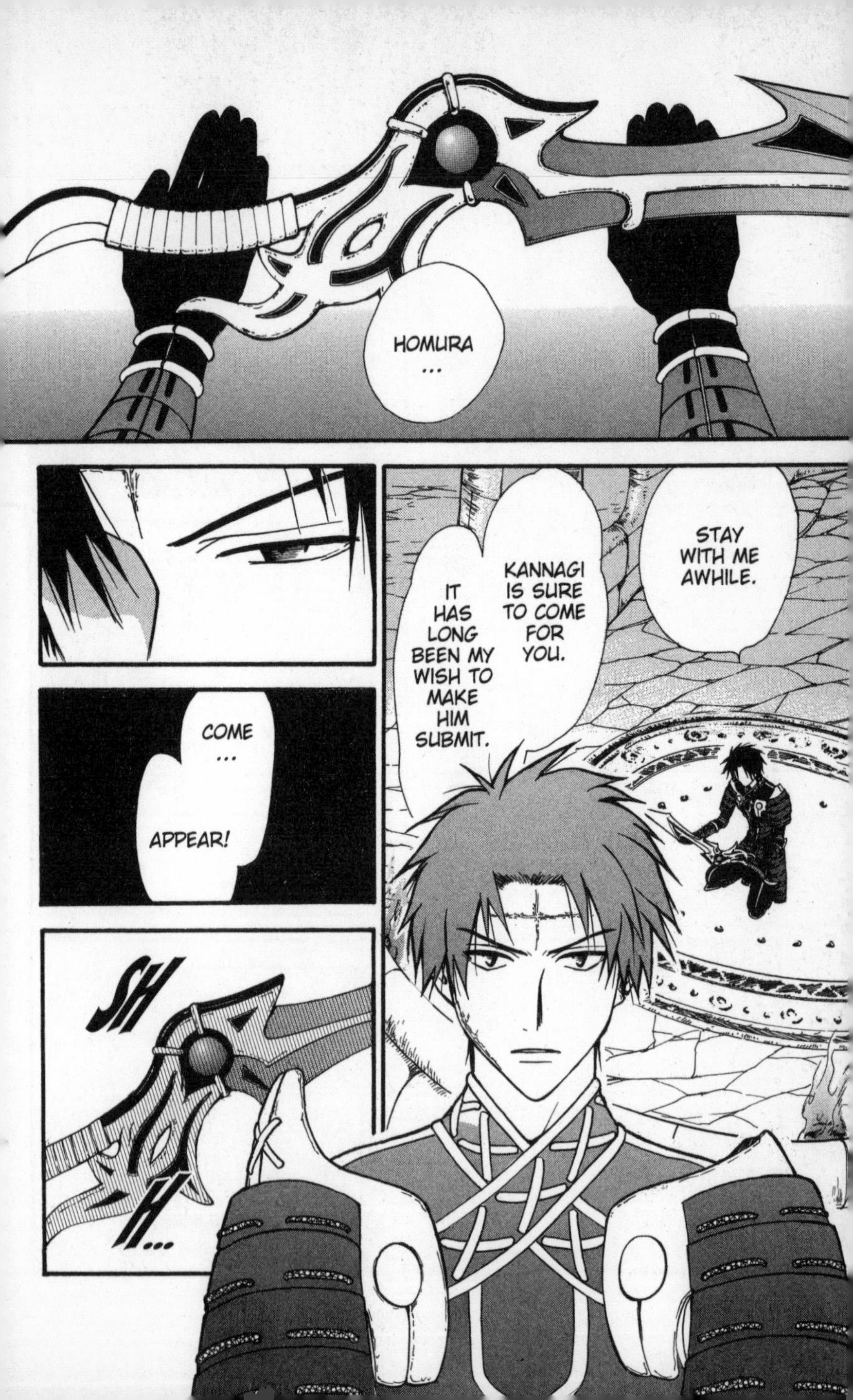
HOMURA ...
STAY WITH ME AWHILE.
KANNAGI IS SURE TO COME FOR YOU.
IT HAS LONG BEEN MY WISH TO MAKE HIM SUBMIT.
COME ...
APPEAR!
SHH...

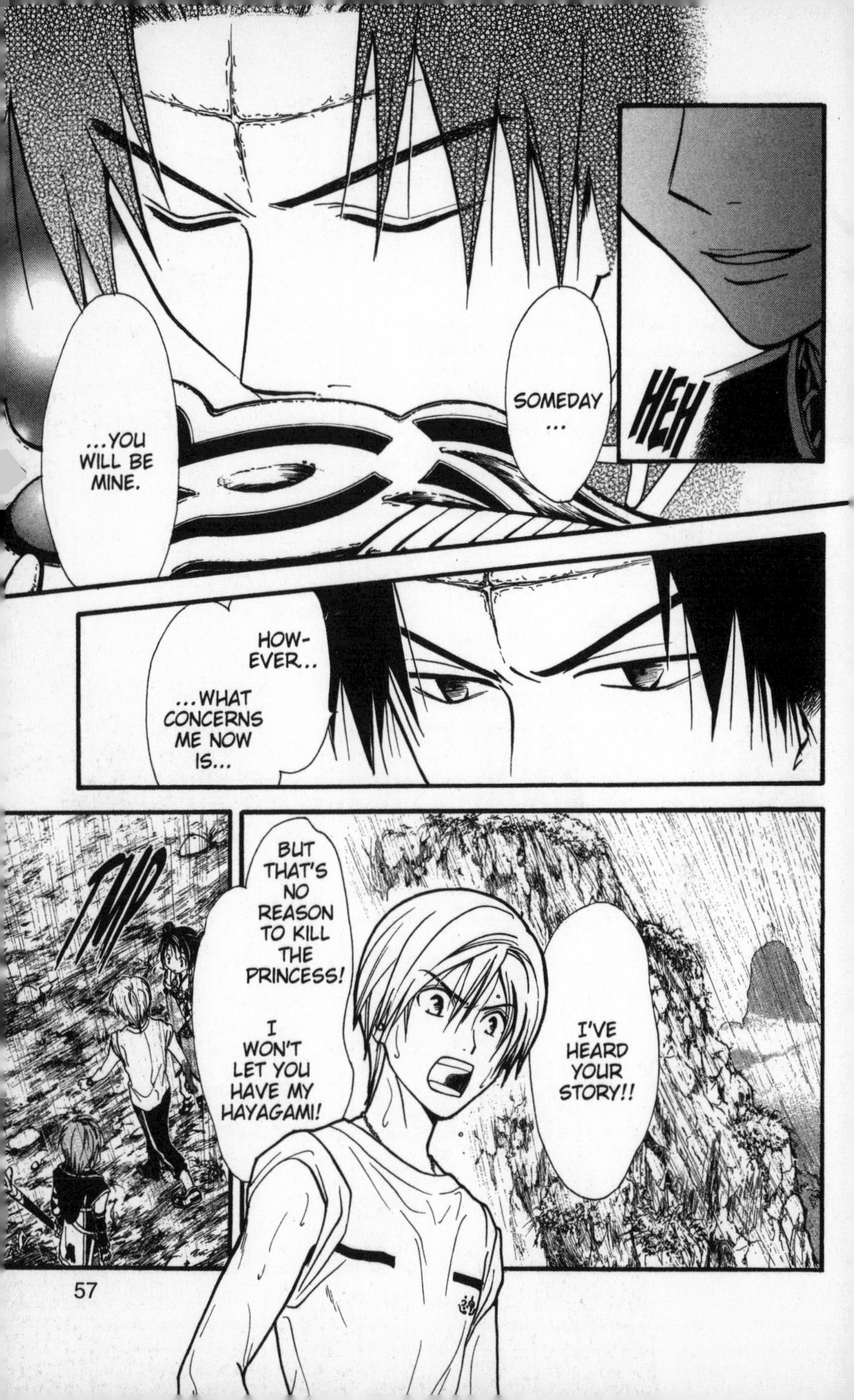
HEH
SOMEDAY...
...YOU WILL BE MINE.
HOW-EVER...
...WHAT CONCERNS ME NOW IS...
I'VE HEARD YOUR STORY!!
BUT THAT'S NO REASON TO KILL THE PRINCESS!
I WON'T LET YOU HAVE MY HAYAGAMI!

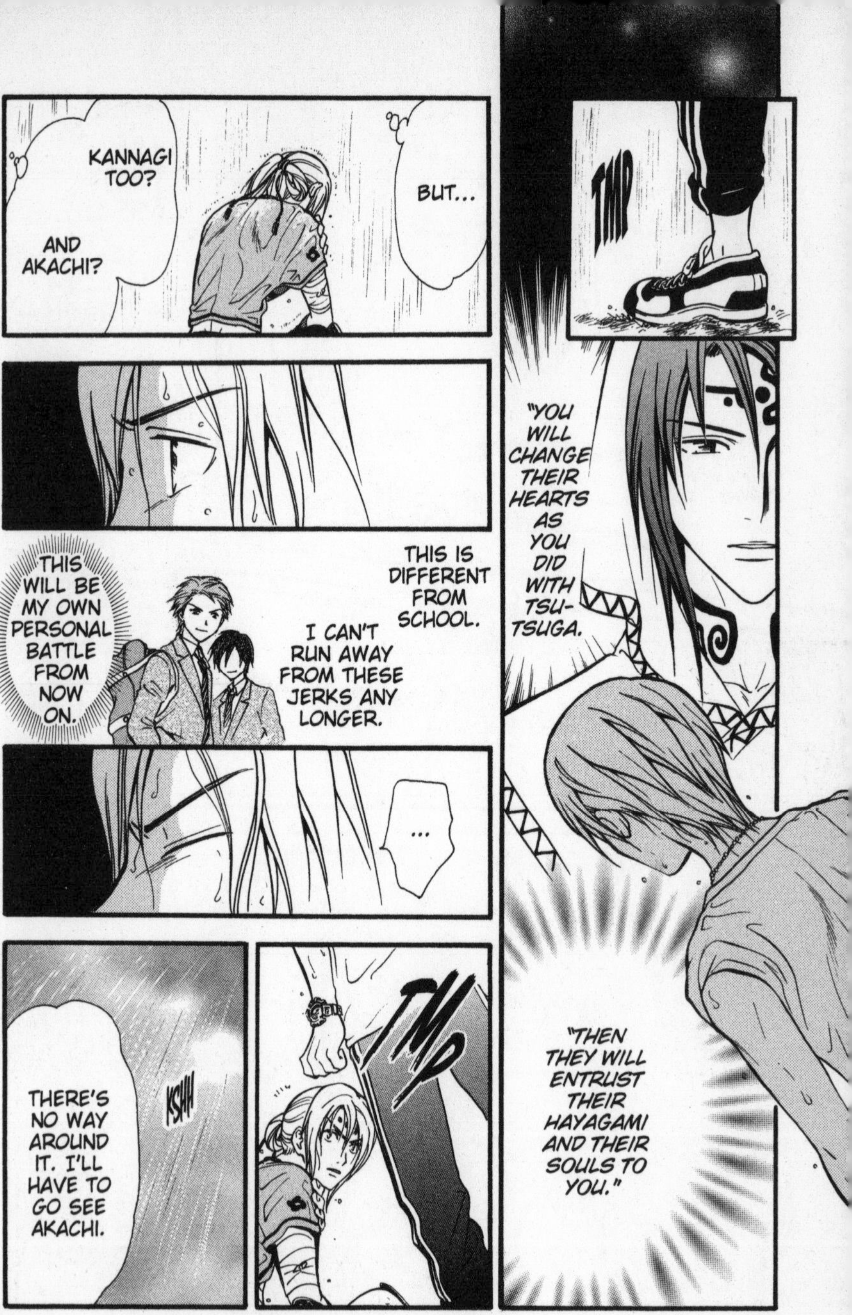

TMP
"YOU WILL CHANGE THEIR HEARTS AS YOU DID WITH TSU-TSUGA.
"THEN THEY WILL ENTRUST THEIR HAYAGAMI AND THEIR SOULS TO YOU."
BUT...
KANNAGI TOO?
AND AKACHI?
THIS IS DIFFERENT FROM SCHOOL.
I CAN'T RUN AWAY FROM THESE JERKS ANY LONGER.
THIS WILL BE MY OWN PERSONAL BATTLE FROM NOW ON.
...
TMP
KSHH
THERE'S NO WAY AROUND IT. I'LL HAVE TO GO SEE AKACHI.

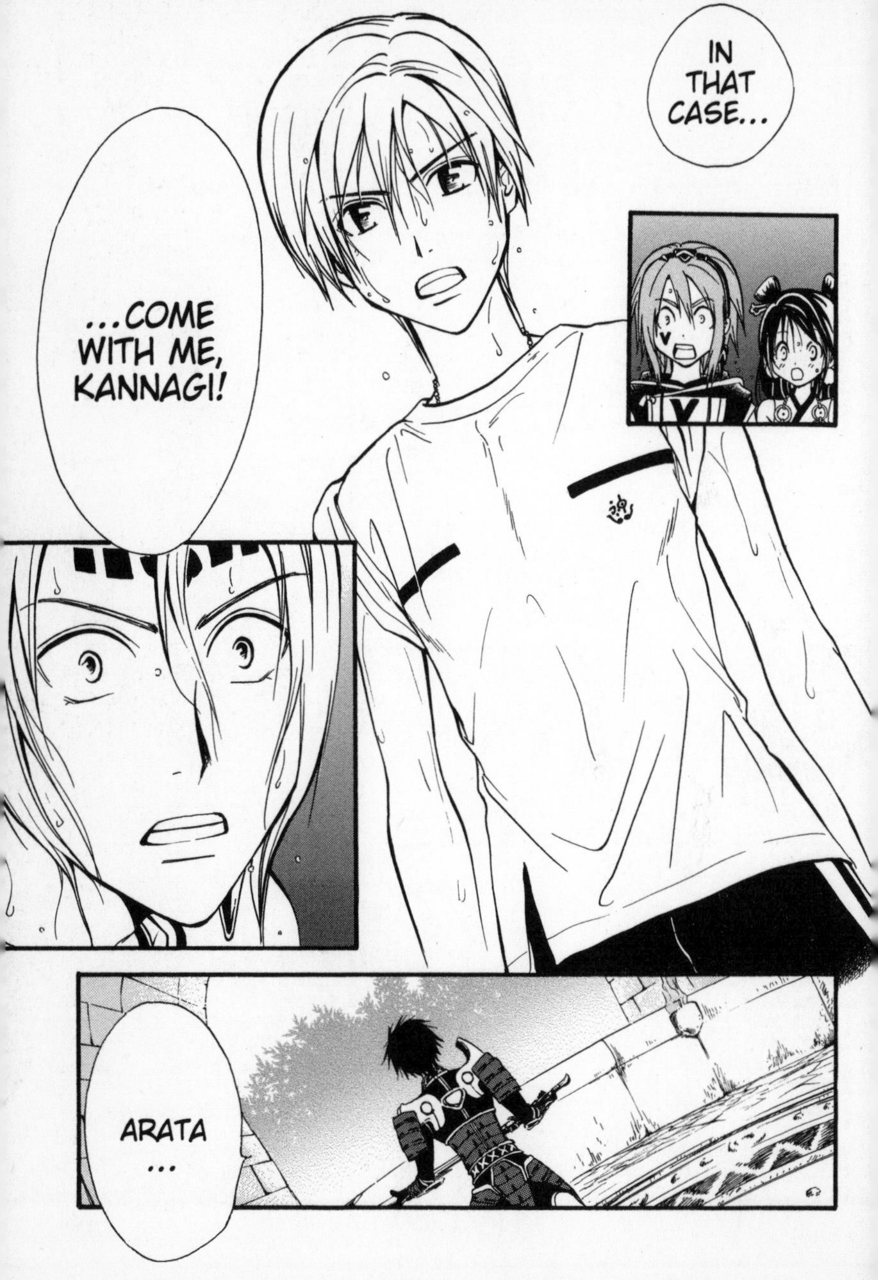
IN THAT CASE...
...COME WITH ME, KANNAGI!
ARATA ...

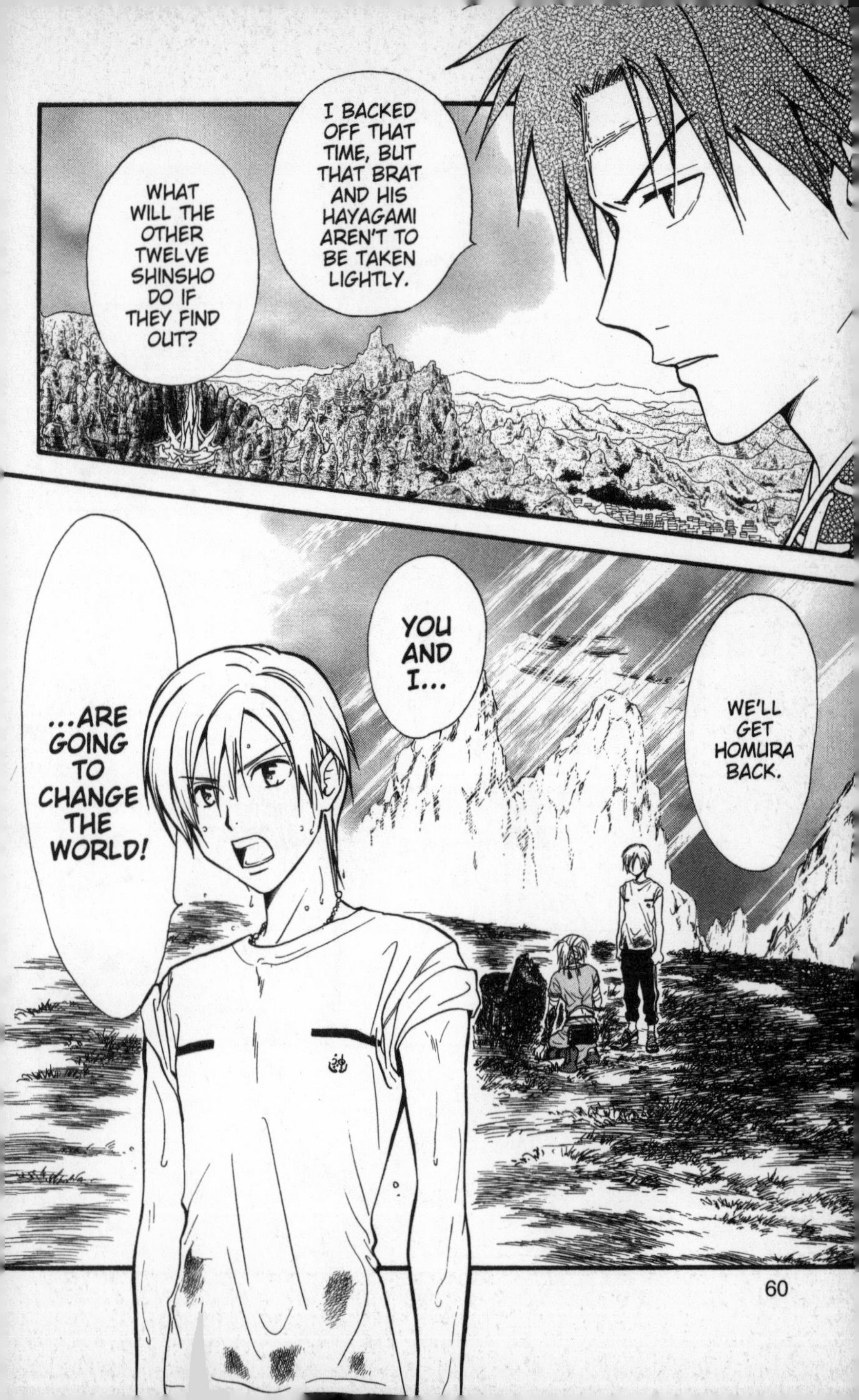

I BACKED OFF THAT TIME, BUT THAT BRAT AND HIS HAYAGAMI AREN'T TO BE TAKEN LIGHTLY.
WHAT WILL THE OTHER TWELVE SHINSHO DO IF THEY FIND OUT?
WE'LL GET HOMURA BACK.
YOU AND I...
...ARE GOING TO CHANGE THE WORLD!

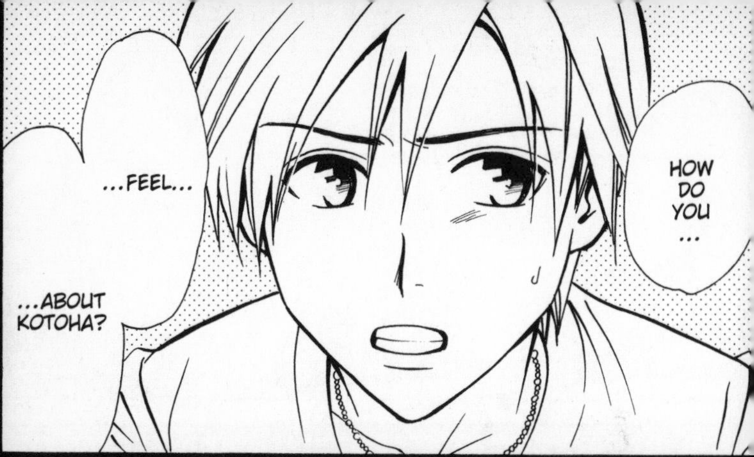
HOW DO YOU ...
...FEEL...
...ABOUT KOTOHA?

CHAPTER 31
KADOWAKI (PART 1)

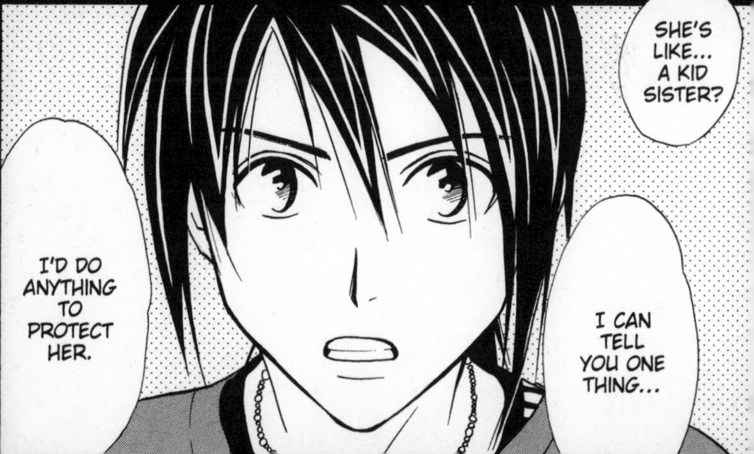
SHE'S LIKE... A KID SISTER?
I CAN TELL YOU ONE THING...
I'D DO ANYTHING TO PROTECT HER.

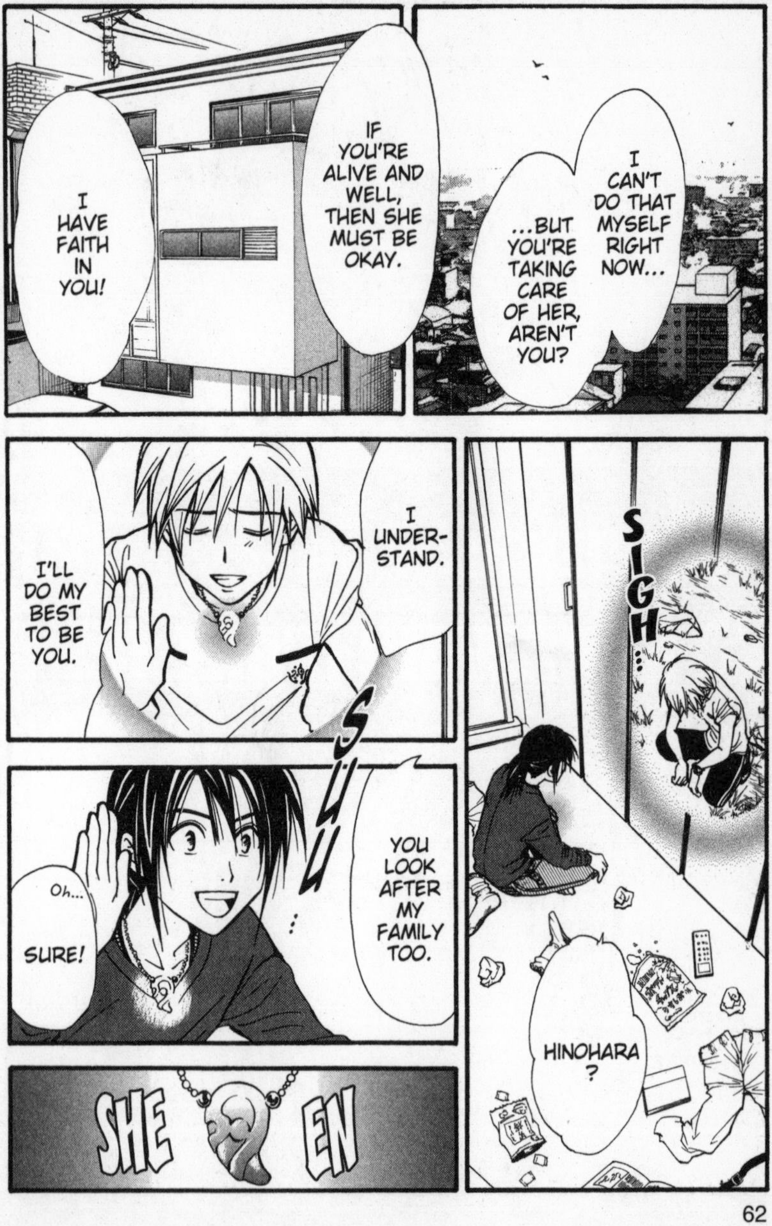
I CAN'T DO THAT MYSELF RIGHT NOW...
...BUT YOU'RE TAKING CARE OF HER, AREN'T YOU?
IF YOU'RE ALIVE AND WELL, THEN SHE MUST BE OKAY.
I HAVE FAITH IN YOU!
SIGH...
HINOHARA?
I UNDER-STAND.
I'LL DO MY BEST TO BE YOU.
SUUU
YOU LOOK AFTER MY FAMILY TOO.
Oh...
SURE!
SHE EN

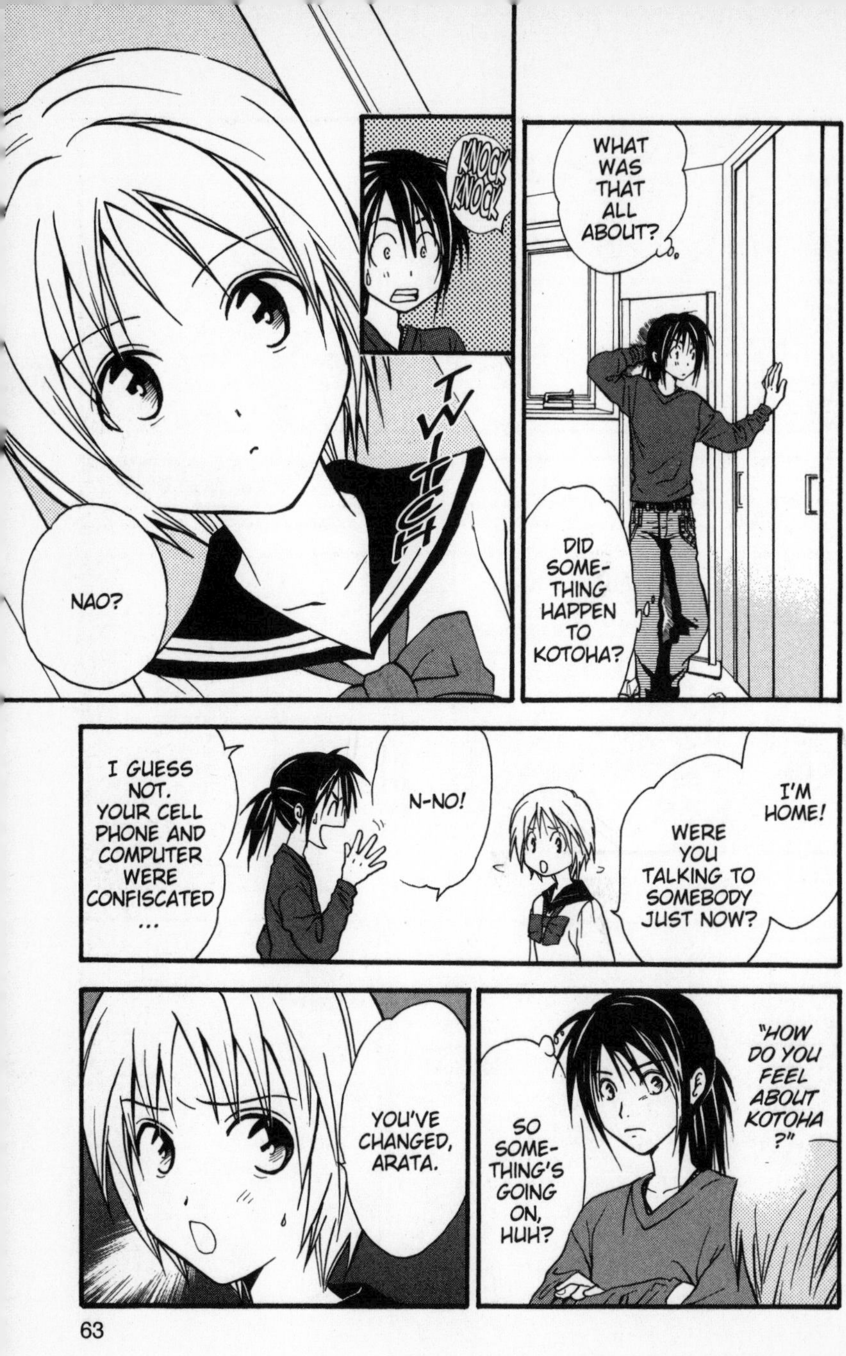
WHAT WAS THAT ALL ABOUT?
DID SOME-THING HAPPEN TO KOTOHA?
KNOCK KNOCK
TWITCH
NAO?
I'M HOME!
WERE YOU TALKING TO SOMEBODY JUST NOW?
N-NO!
I GUESS NOT. YOUR CELL PHONE AND COMPUTER WERE CONFISCATED...
"HOW DO YOU FEEL ABOUT KOTOHA?"
SO SOME-THING'S GOING ON, HUH?
YOU'VE CHANGED, ARATA.

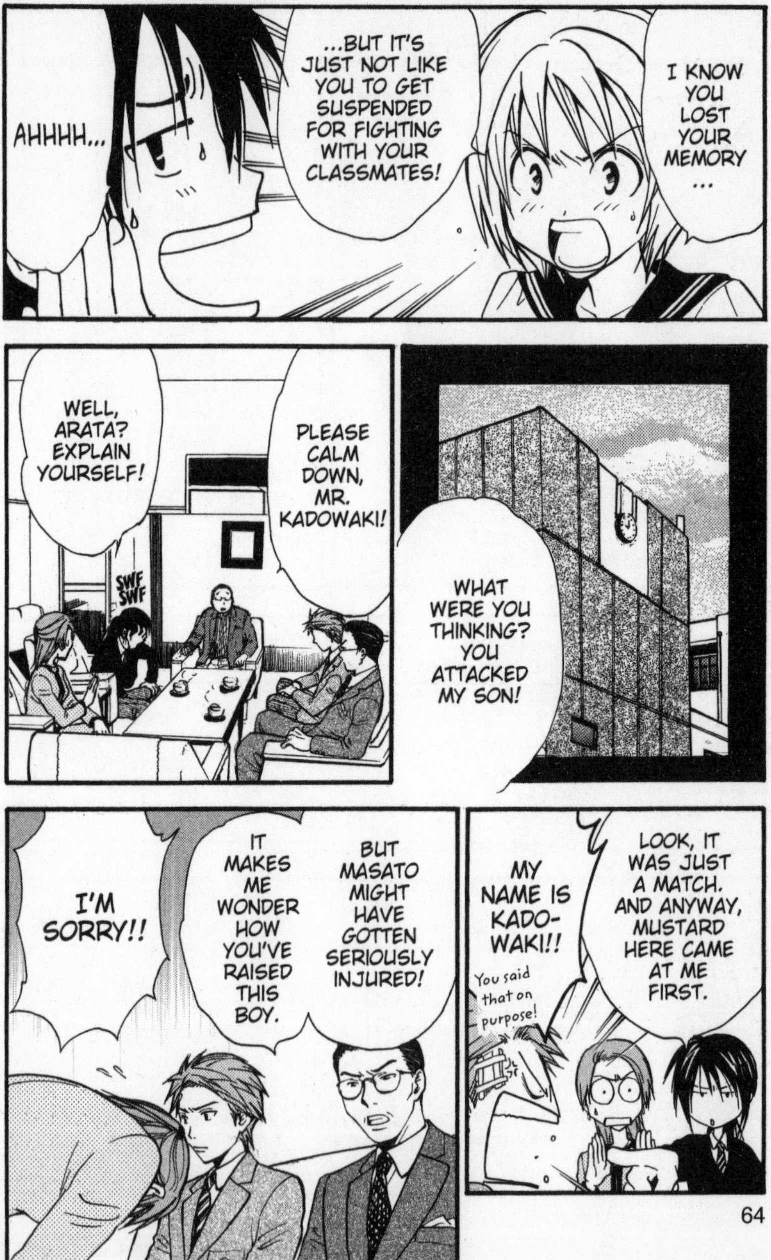
I KNOW YOU LOST YOUR MEMORY ...
...BUT IT'S JUST NOT LIKE YOU TO GET SUSPENDED FOR FIGHTING WITH YOUR CLASSMATES!
AHHHH...
WHAT WERE YOU THINKING? YOU ATTACKED MY SON!
PLEASE CALM DOWN, MR. KADOWAKI!
WELL, ARATA? EXPLAIN YOURSELF!
SWF SWF
LOOK, IT WAS JUST A MATCH. AND ANYWAY, MUSTARD HERE CAME AT ME FIRST.
MY NAME IS KADO-WAKI!!
You said that on purpose!
BUT MASATO MIGHT HAVE GOTTEN SERIOUSLY INJURED!
IT MAKES ME WONDER HOW YOU'VE RAISED THIS BOY.
I'M SORRY!!

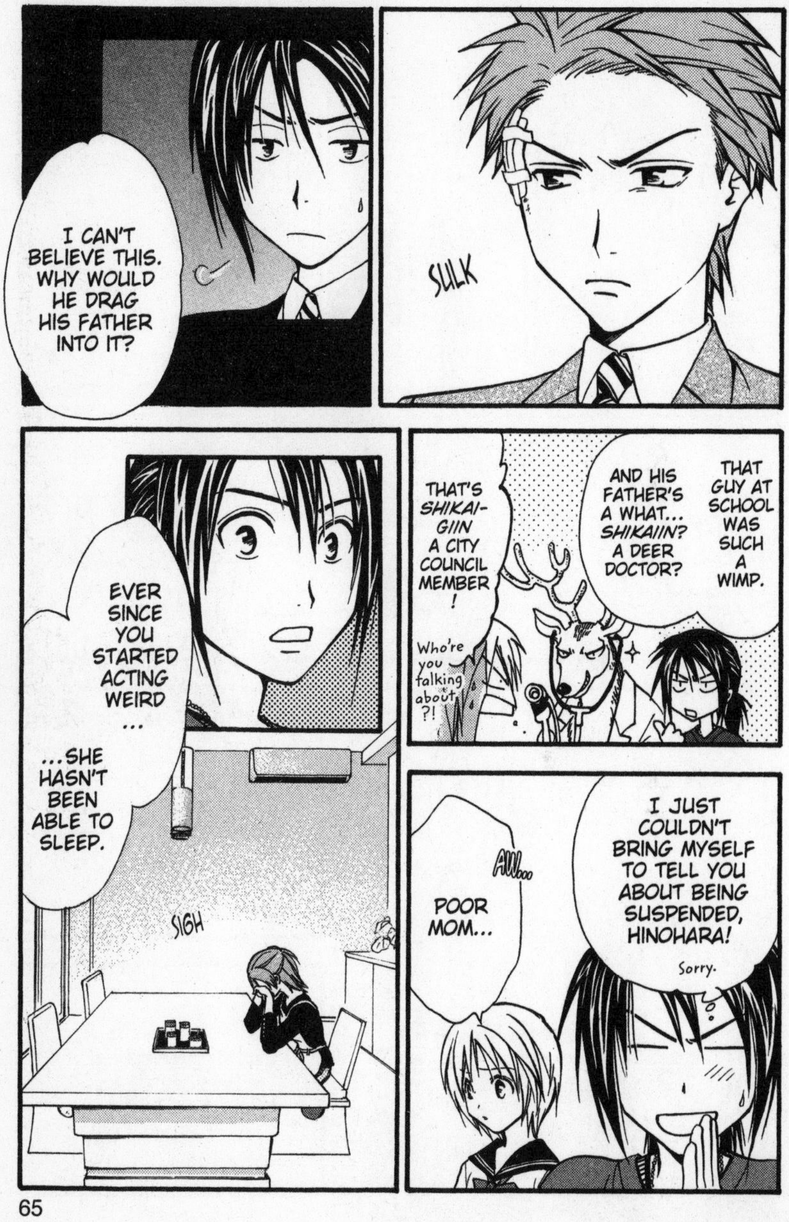
SULK
I CAN'T BELIEVE THIS. WHY WOULD HE DRAG HIS FATHER INTO IT?
THAT GUY AT SCHOOL WAS SUCH A WIMP.
AND HIS FATHER'S A WHAT... *SHIKAIIN*? A DEER DOCTOR?
THAT'S *SHIKAI-GIIN* A CITY COUNCIL MEMBER!
Who're you talking about?!
I JUST COULDN'T BRING MYSELF TO TELL YOU ABOUT BEING SUSPENDED, HINOHARA!
Sorry.
AW...
POOR MOM...
EVER SINCE YOU STARTED ACTING WEIRD...
...SHE HASN'T BEEN ABLE TO SLEEP.
SIGH

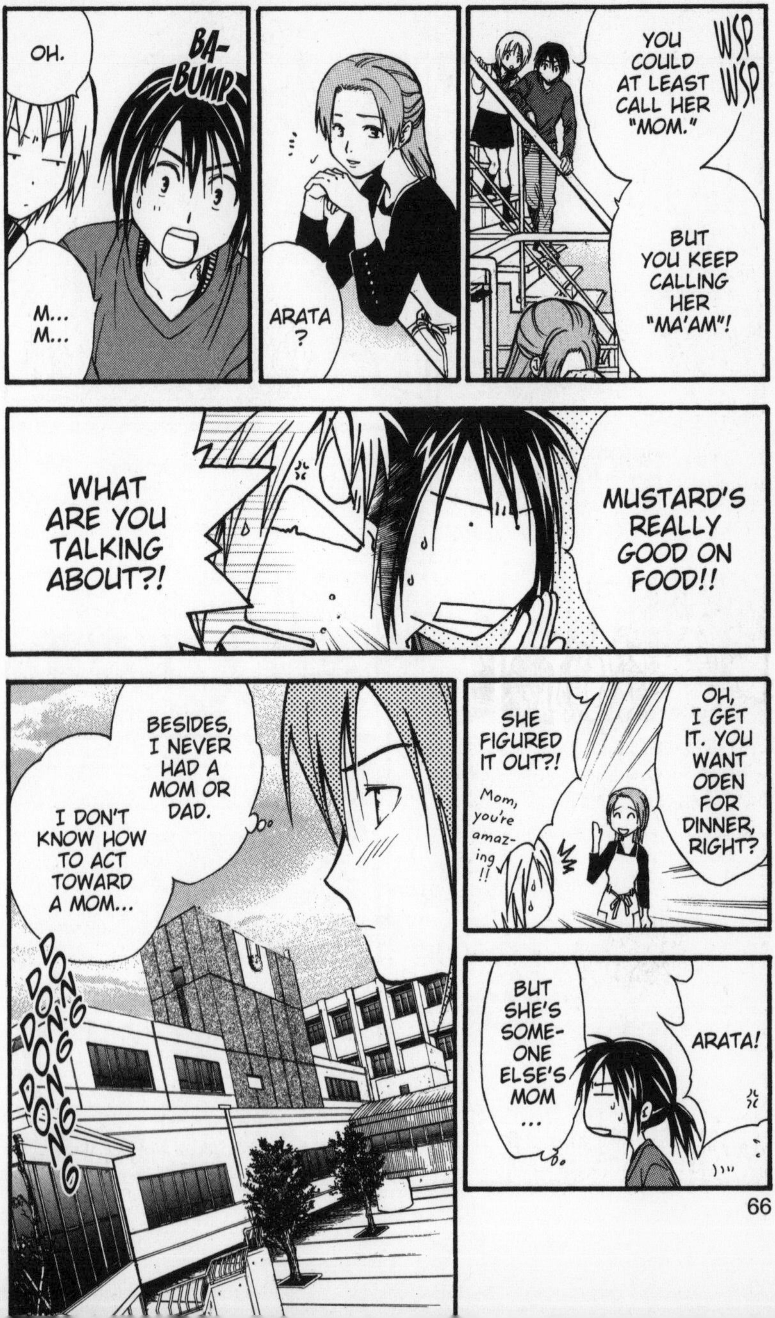
WSP WSP
YOU COULD AT LEAST CALL HER "MOM."
BUT YOU KEEP CALLING HER "MA'AM"!
ARATA ?
BA-BUMP
OH.
M... M...
MUSTARD'S REALLY GOOD ON FOOD!!
WHAT ARE YOU TALKING ABOUT?!
OH, I GET IT. YOU WANT ODEN FOR DINNER, RIGHT?
SHE FIGURED IT OUT?!
Mom, you're amaz-ing!!
ARATA!
BUT SHE'S SOME-ONE ELSE'S MOM ...
BESIDES, I NEVER HAD A MOM OR DAD.
I DON'T KNOW HOW TO ACT TOWARD A MOM...
DONG DONG DONG DONG

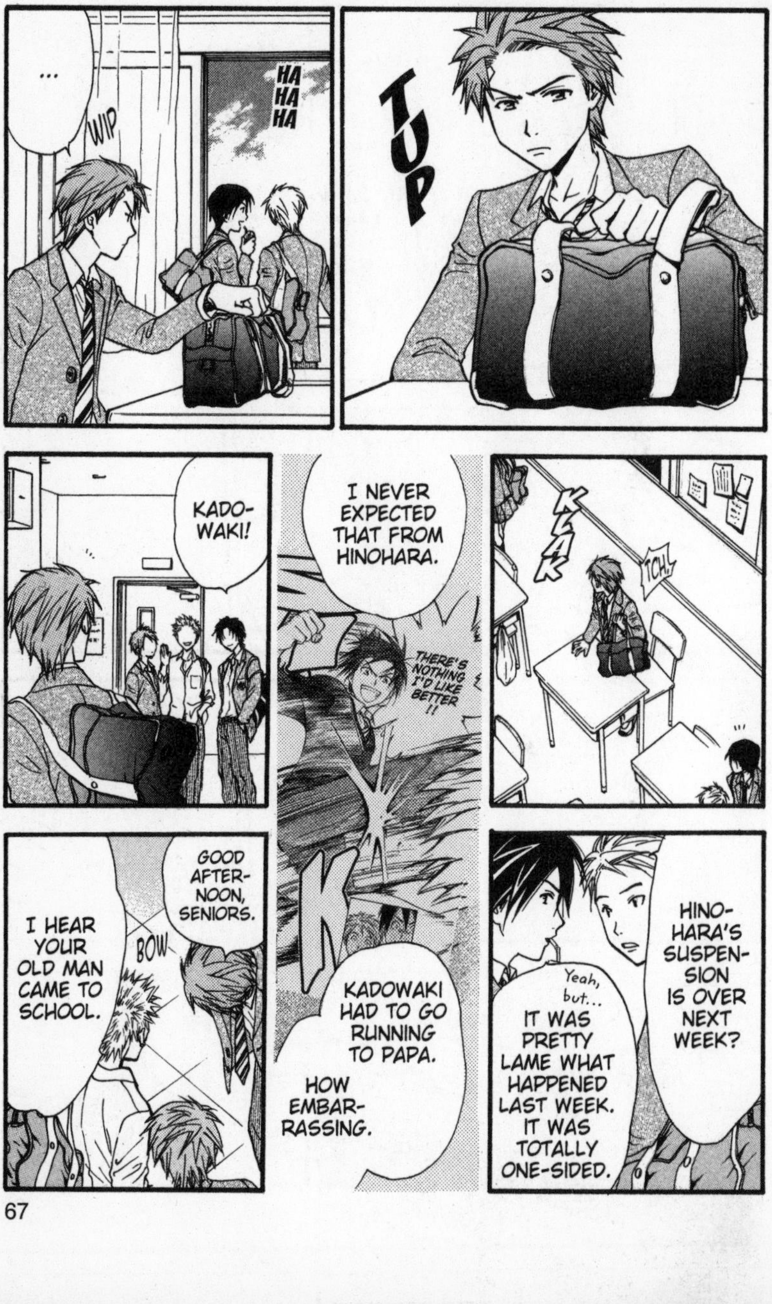
TUP
...
WIP
HA HA HA
KLAK
TCH!
HINO-HARA'S SUSPENSION IS OVER NEXT WEEK?
Yeah, but...
IT WAS PRETTY LAME WHAT HAPPENED LAST WEEK. IT WAS TOTALLY ONE-SIDED.
I NEVER EXPECTED THAT FROM HINOHARA.
THERE'S NOTHING I'D LIKE BETTER!!
K
KADOWAKI HAD TO GO RUNNING TO PAPA.
HOW EMBARRASSING.
KADO-WAKI!
GOOD AFTER-NOON, SENIORS.
BOW
I HEAR YOUR OLD MAN CAME TO SCHOOL.

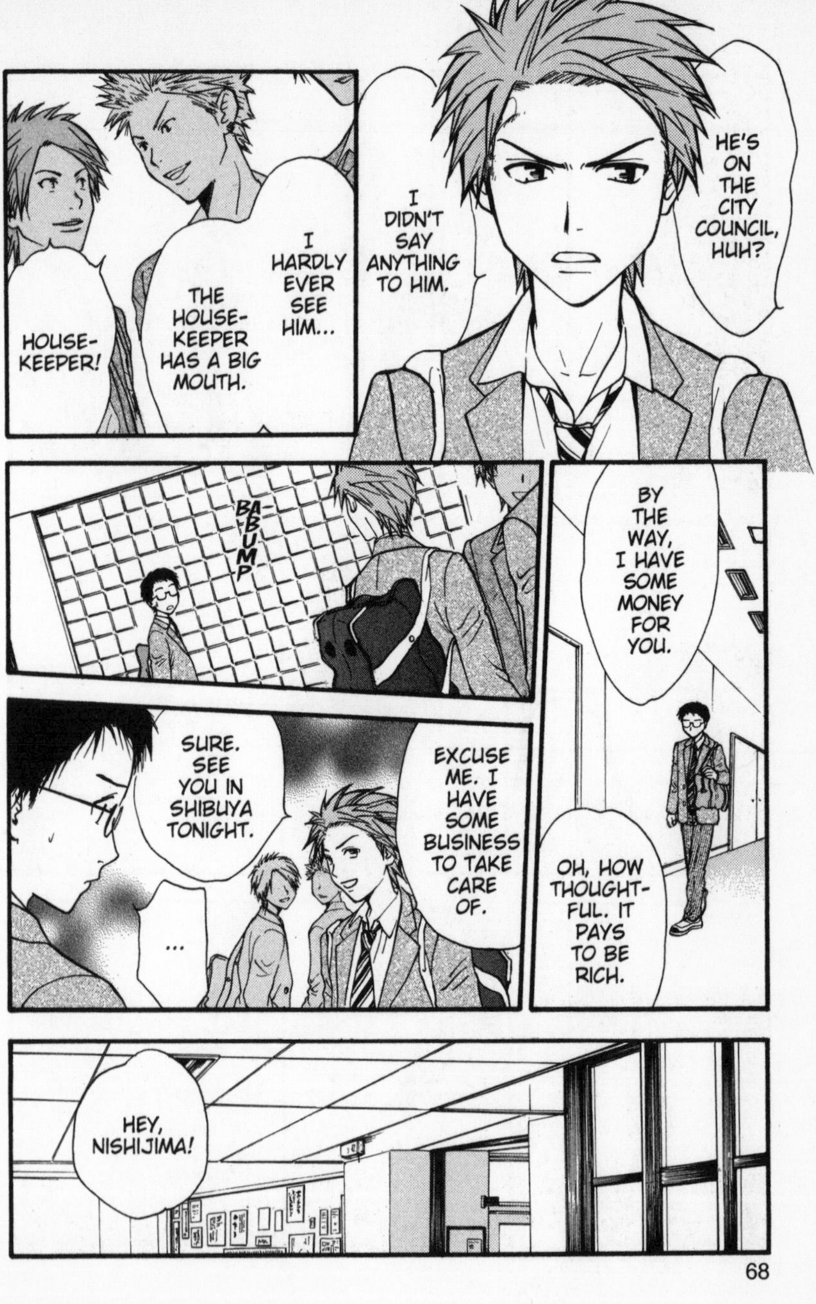
HE'S ON THE CITY COUNCIL, HUH?
I DIDN'T SAY ANYTHING TO HIM.
I HARDLY EVER SEE HIM...
THE HOUSEKEEPER HAS A BIG MOUTH.
HOUSEKEEPER!
BY THE WAY, I HAVE SOME MONEY FOR YOU.
OH, HOW THOUGHTFUL. IT PAYS TO BE RICH.
BA-BUMP
EXCUSE ME. I HAVE SOME BUSINESS TO TAKE CARE OF.
SURE. SEE YOU IN SHIBUYA TONIGHT.
...
HEY, NISHIJIMA!

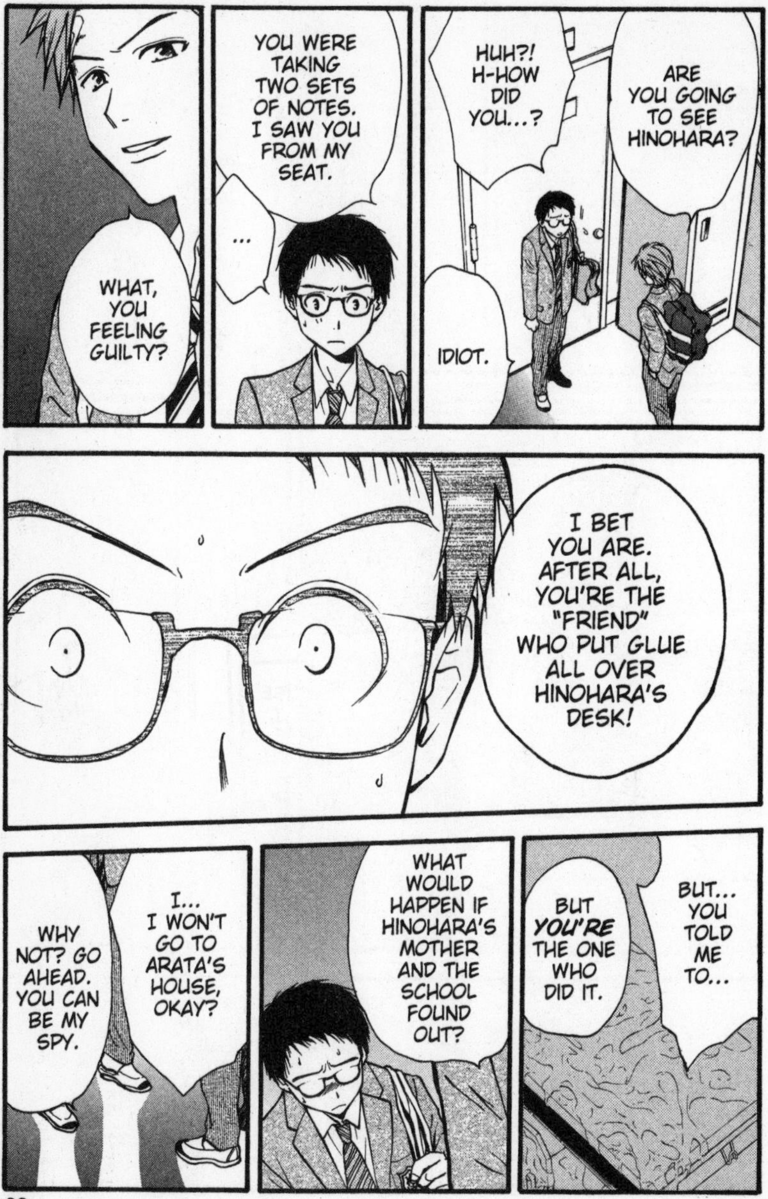
ARE YOU GOING TO SEE HINOHARA?
HUH?! H-HOW DID YOU...?
IDIOT.
YOU WERE TAKING TWO SETS OF NOTES. I SAW YOU FROM MY SEAT.
...
WHAT, YOU FEELING GUILTY?
I BET YOU ARE. AFTER ALL, YOU'RE THE "FRIEND" WHO PUT GLUE ALL OVER HINOHARA'S DESK!
BUT... YOU TOLD ME TO...
BUT *YOU'RE* THE ONE WHO DID IT.
WHAT WOULD HAPPEN IF HINOHARA'S MOTHER AND THE SCHOOL FOUND OUT?
I... I WON'T GO TO ARATA'S HOUSE, OKAY?
WHY NOT? GO AHEAD. YOU CAN BE MY SPY.

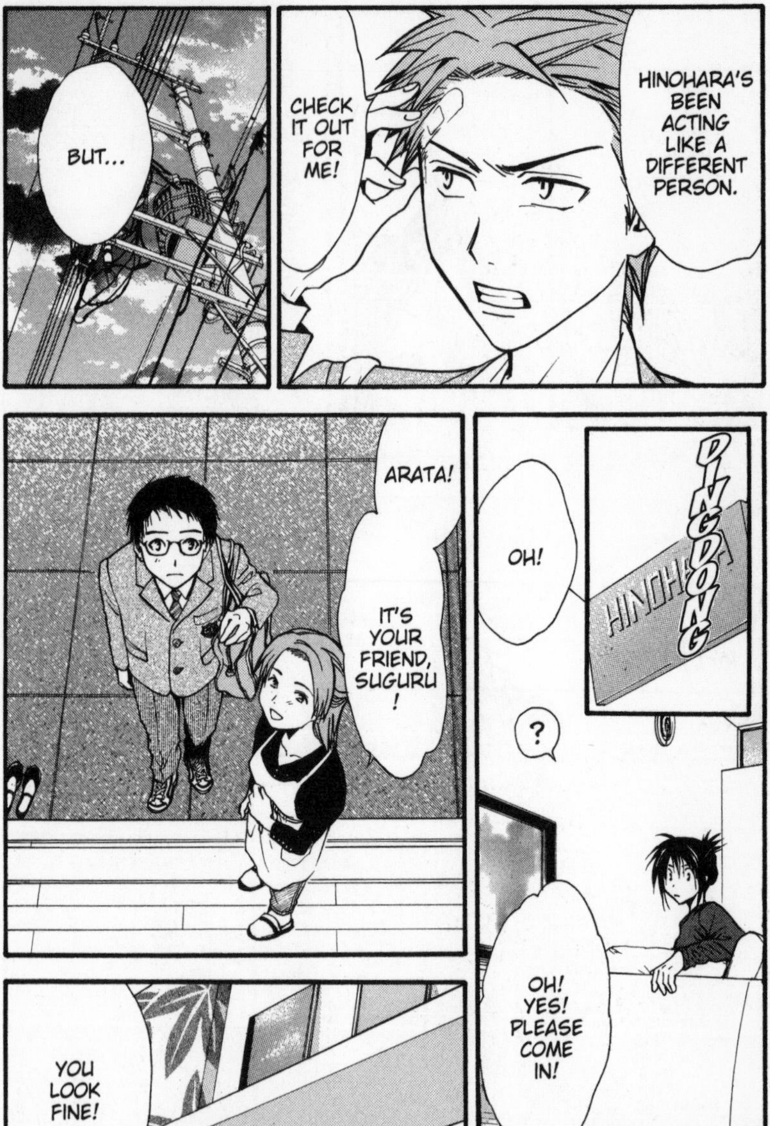
HINOHARA'S BEEN ACTING LIKE A DIFFERENT PERSON.
CHECK IT OUT FOR ME!
BUT...
DING DONG
OH!
?
OH! YES! PLEASE COME IN!
ARATA!
IT'S YOUR FRIEND, SUGURU!
YOU LOOK FINE!

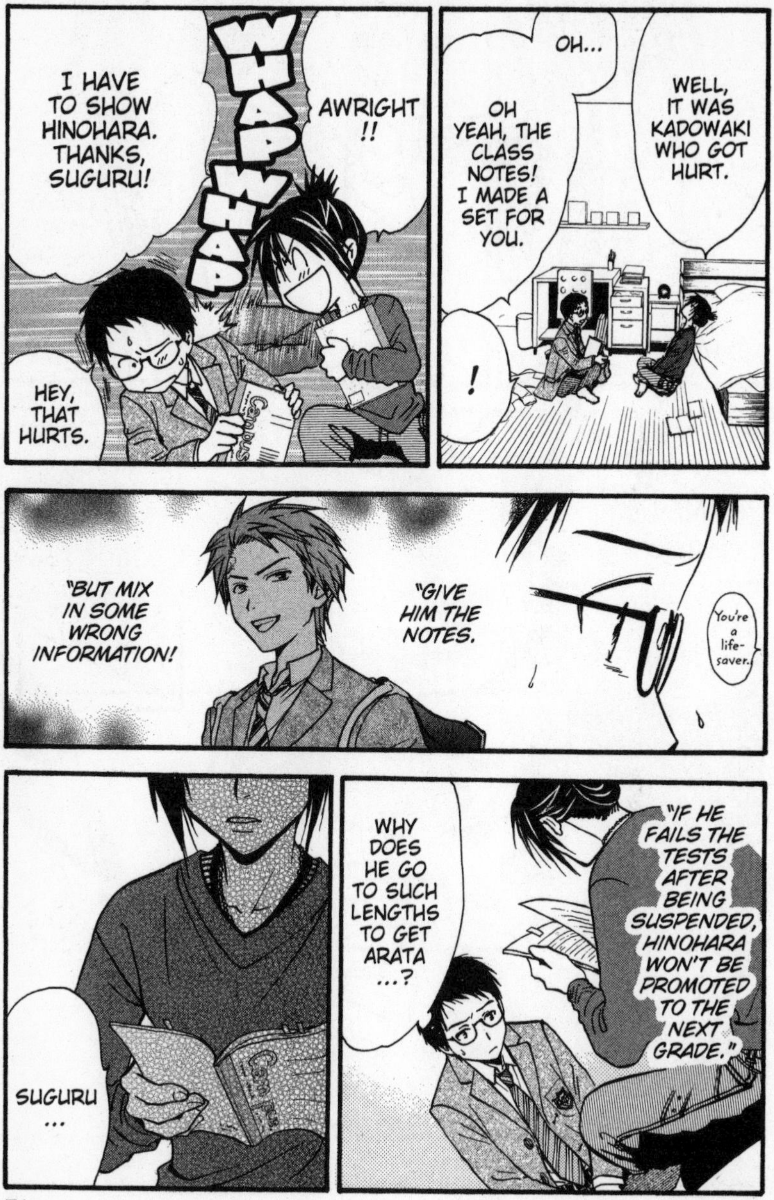
OH...
WELL, IT WAS KADOWAKI WHO GOT HURT.
OH YEAH, THE CLASS NOTES! I MADE A SET FOR YOU.
!
AWRIGHT!!
WHAP WHAP
I HAVE TO SHOW HINOHARA. THANKS, SUGURU!
HEY, THAT HURTS.
You're a life-saver..
"GIVE HIM THE NOTES.
"BUT MIX IN SOME WRONG INFORMATION!
"IF HE FAILS THE TESTS AFTER BEING SUSPENDED, HINOHARA WON'T BE PROMOTED TO THE NEXT GRADE."
WHY DOES HE GO TO SUCH LENGTHS TO GET ARATA...?
SUGURU...

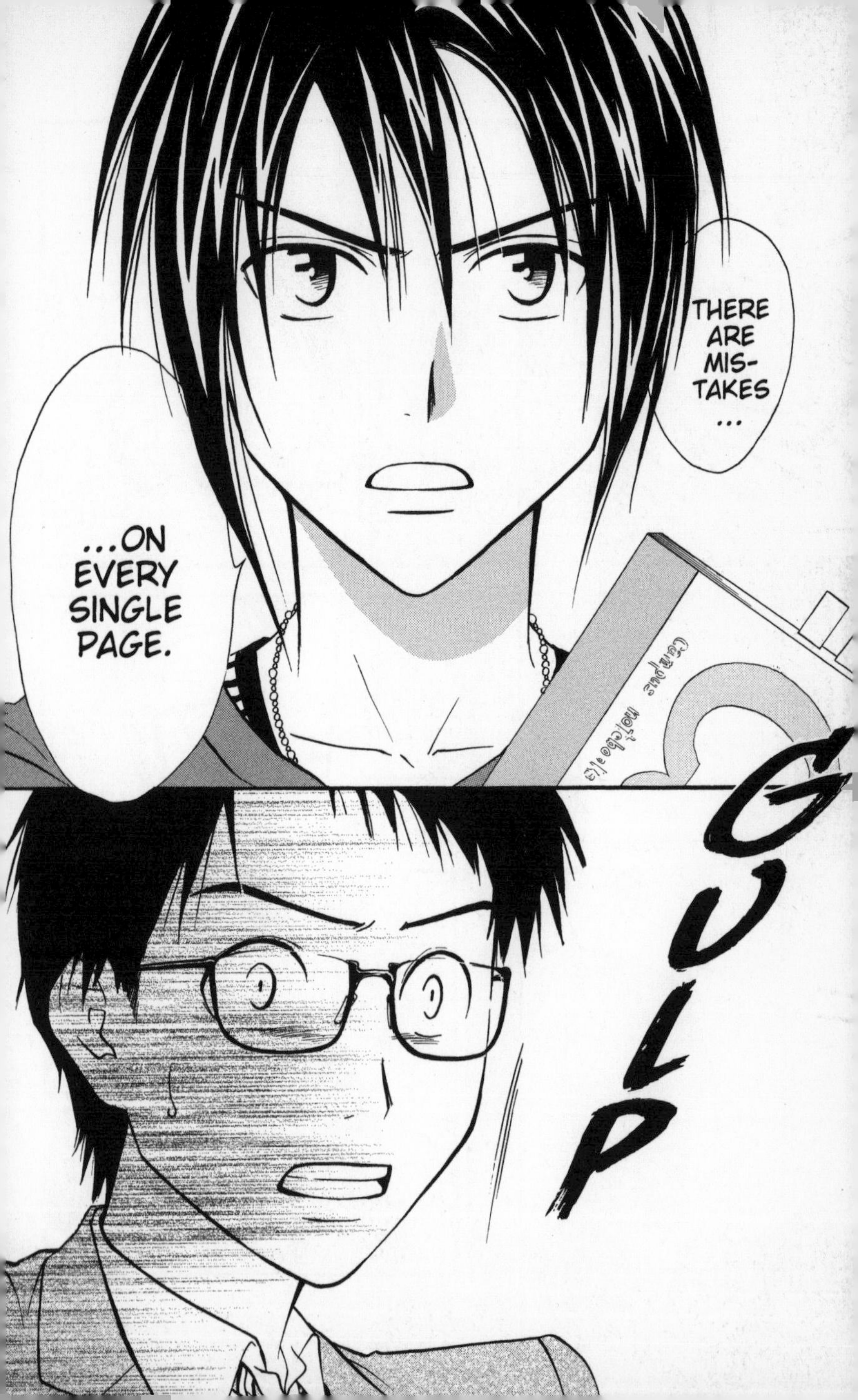
THERE ARE MIS-TAKES ...
...ON EVERY SINGLE PAGE.
GULP

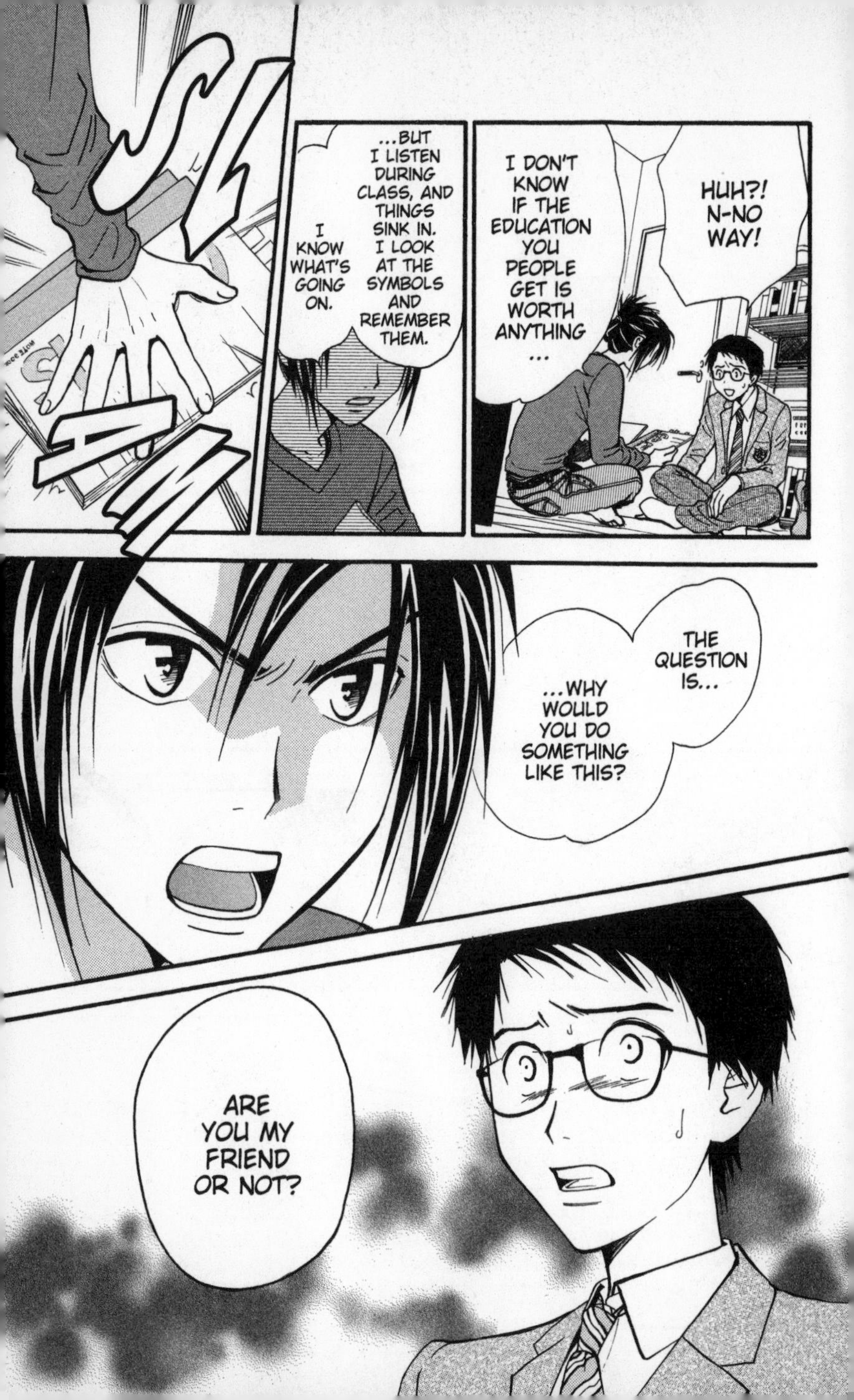
HUH?! N-NO WAY!
I DON'T KNOW IF THE EDUCATION YOU PEOPLE GET IS WORTH ANYTHING...
...BUT I LISTEN DURING CLASS, AND THINGS SINK IN. I LOOK AT THE SYMBOLS AND REMEMBER THEM.
I KNOW WHAT'S GOING ON.
SLAM
THE QUESTION IS...
...WHY WOULD YOU DO SOMETHING LIKE THIS?
ARE YOU MY FRIEND OR NOT?

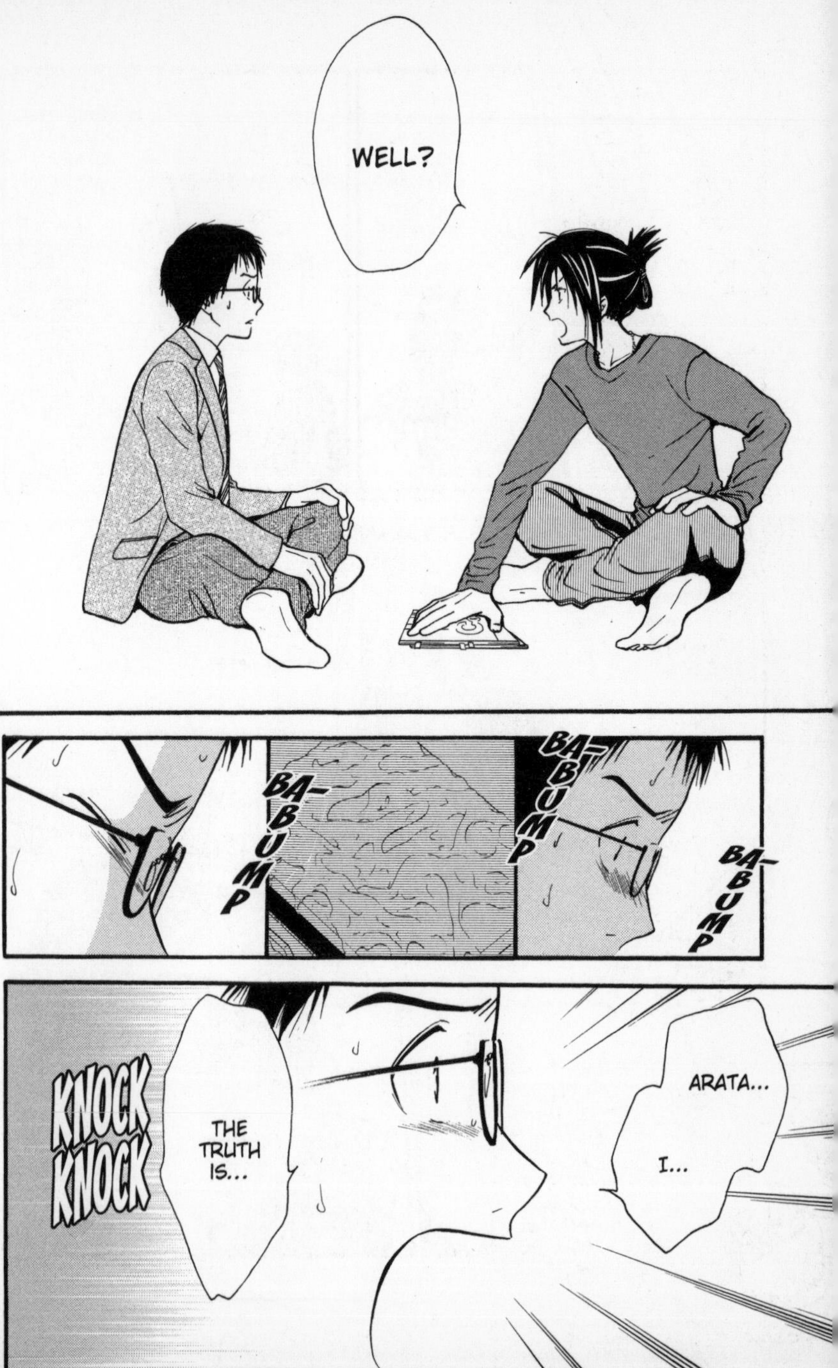
WELL?
BA-BUMP
BA-BUMP
BA-BUMP
ARATA...
I...
THE TRUTH IS...
KNOCK KNOCK

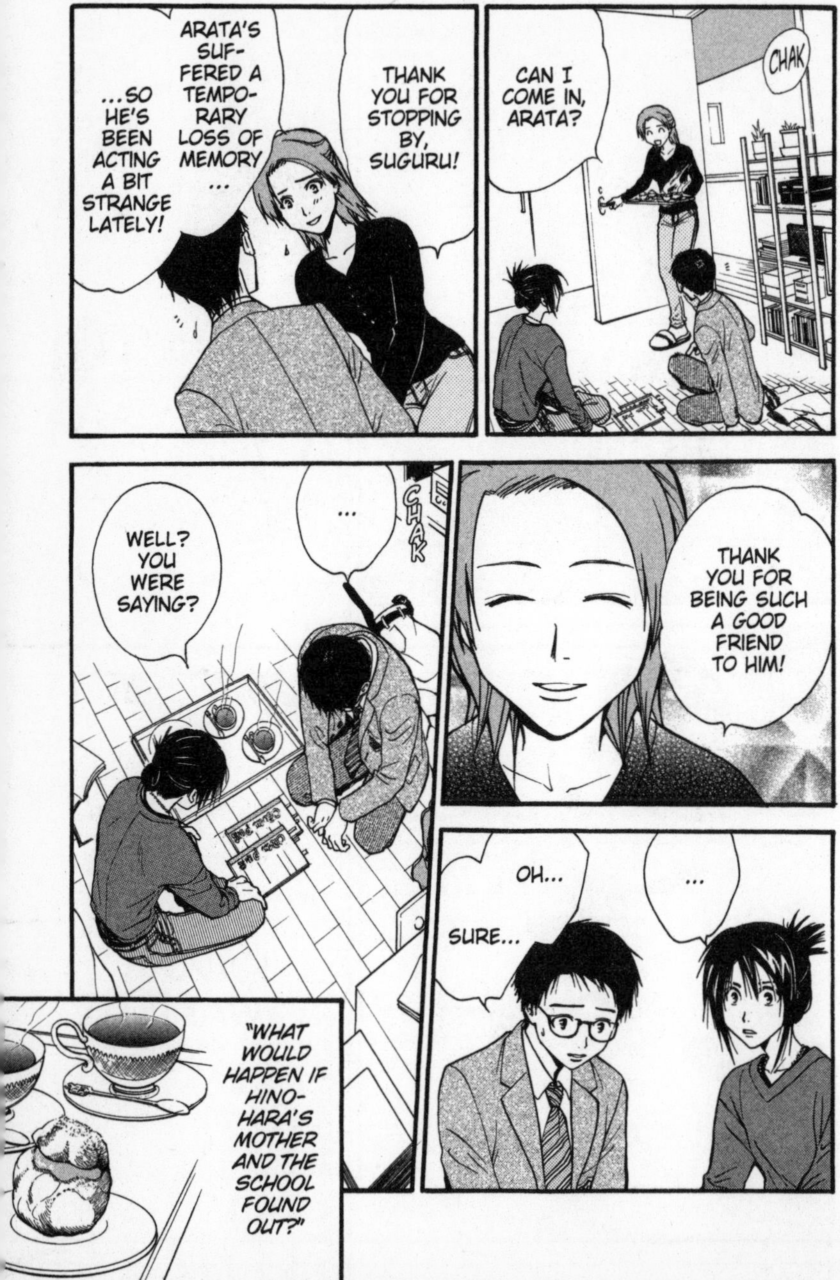
CHAK
CAN I COME IN, ARATA?
THANK YOU FOR STOPPING BY, SUGURU!
ARATA'S SUF-FERED A TEMPO-RARY LOSS OF MEMORY ...
...SO HE'S BEEN ACTING A BIT STRANGE LATELY!
THANK YOU FOR BEING SUCH A GOOD FRIEND TO HIM!
...
OH...
SURE...
CHAK
...
WELL? YOU WERE SAYING?
"WHAT WOULD HAPPEN IF HINO-HARA'S MOTHER AND THE SCHOOL FOUND OUT?"

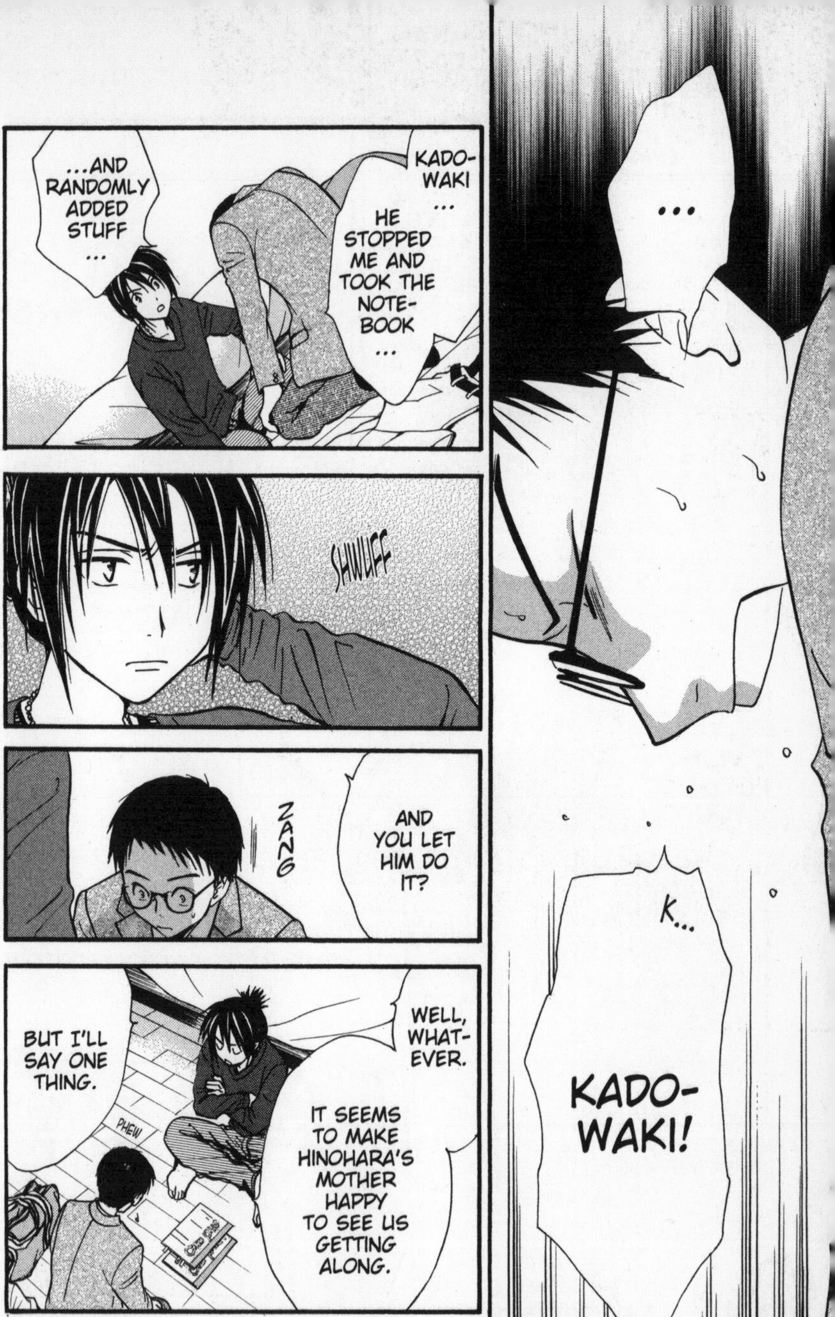
...
K...
KADO-WAKI!
KADO-WAKI ...
HE STOPPED ME AND TOOK THE NOTE-BOOK ...
...AND RANDOMLY ADDED STUFF ...
SHWUFF
AND YOU LET HIM DO IT?
ZANG
WELL, WHAT-EVER.
IT SEEMS TO MAKE HINOHARA'S MOTHER HAPPY TO SEE US GETTING ALONG.
PHEW
BUT I'LL SAY ONE THING.

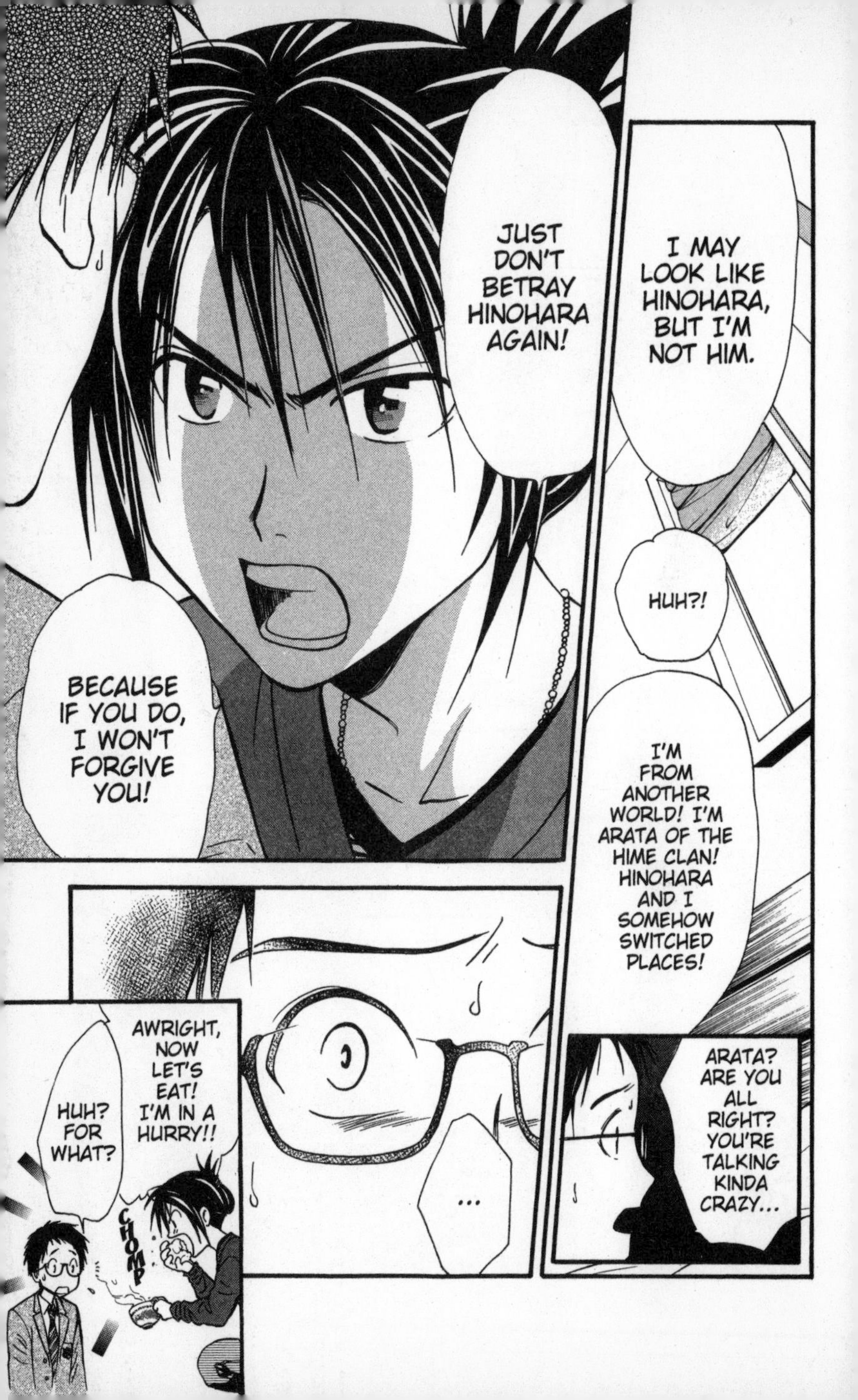
JUST DON'T BETRAY HINOHARA AGAIN!
BECAUSE IF YOU DO, I WON'T FORGIVE YOU!
I MAY LOOK LIKE HINOHARA, BUT I'M NOT HIM.
HUH?!
I'M FROM ANOTHER WORLD! I'M ARATA OF THE HIME CLAN! HINOHARA AND I SOMEHOW SWITCHED PLACES!
ARATA? ARE YOU ALL RIGHT? YOU'RE TALKING KINDA CRAZY...
...
AWRIGHT, NOW LET'S EAT! I'M IN A HURRY!!
HUH? FOR WHAT?
CHOMP

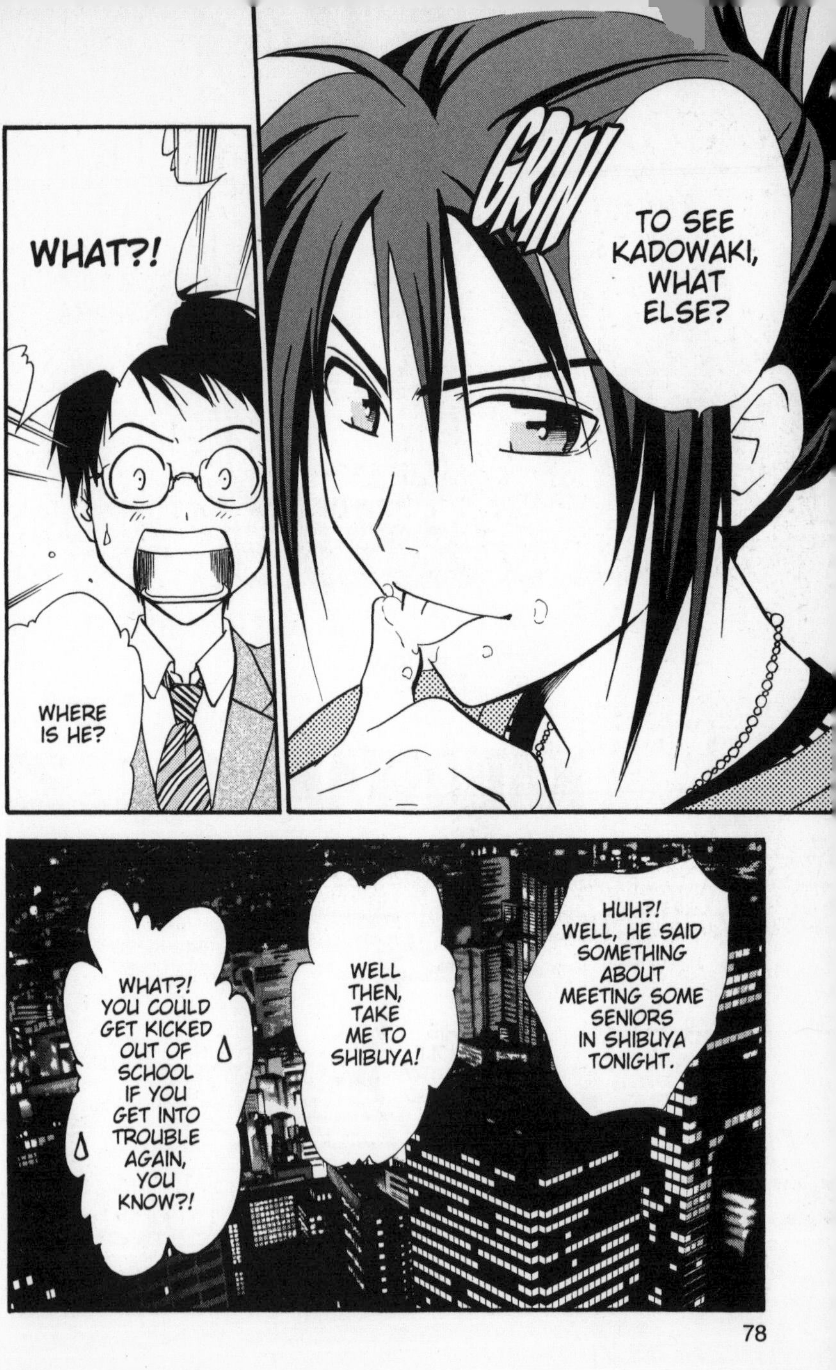
GRIN
TO SEE KADOWAKI, WHAT ELSE?
WHAT?!
WHERE IS HE?
HUH?! WELL, HE SAID SOMETHING ABOUT MEETING SOME SENIORS IN SHIBUYA TONIGHT.
WELL THEN, TAKE ME TO SHIBUYA!
WHAT?! YOU COULD GET KICKED OUT OF SCHOOL IF YOU GET INTO TROUBLE AGAIN, YOU KNOW?!

CHAPTER 32

KADOWAKI (PART 2)

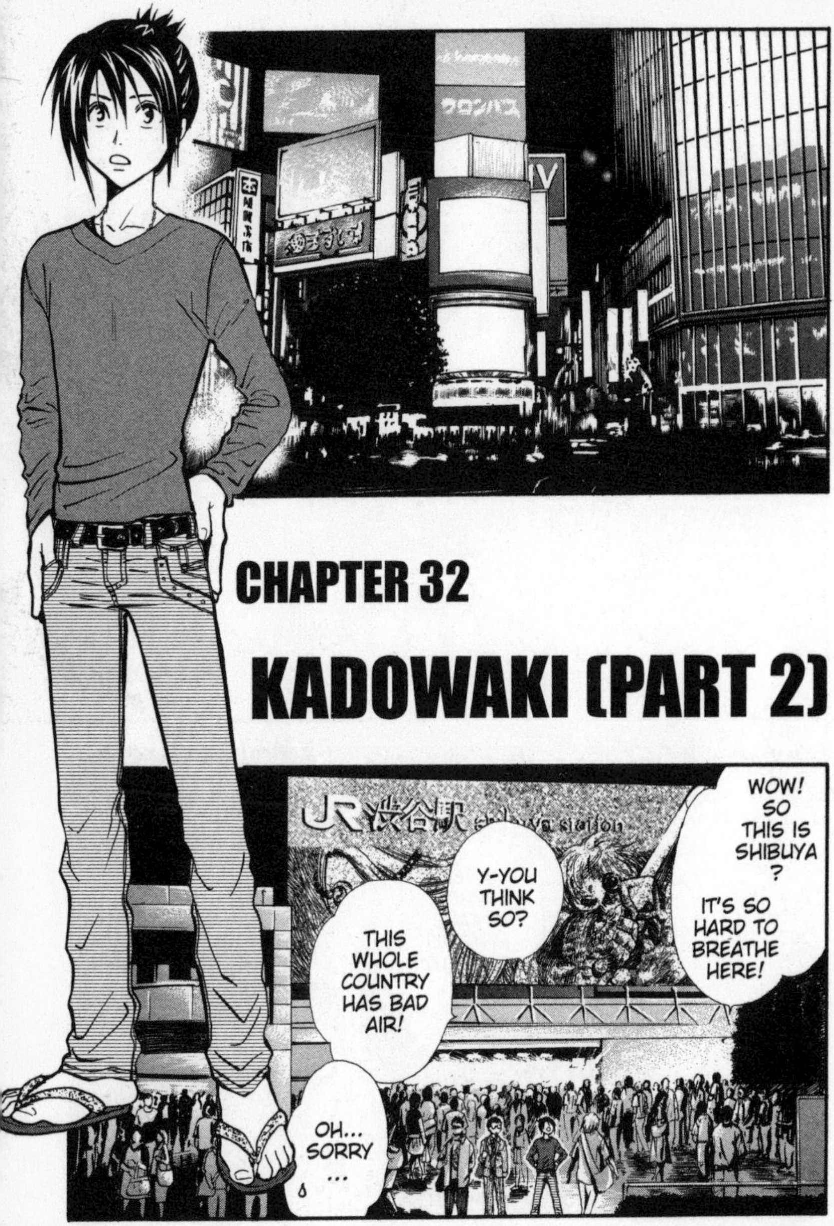
JR 渋谷駅 shibuya station
WOW! SO THIS IS SHIBUYA? IT'S SO HARD TO BREATHE HERE!
Y-YOU THINK SO?
THIS WHOLE COUNTRY HAS BAD AIR!
OH... SORRY ...

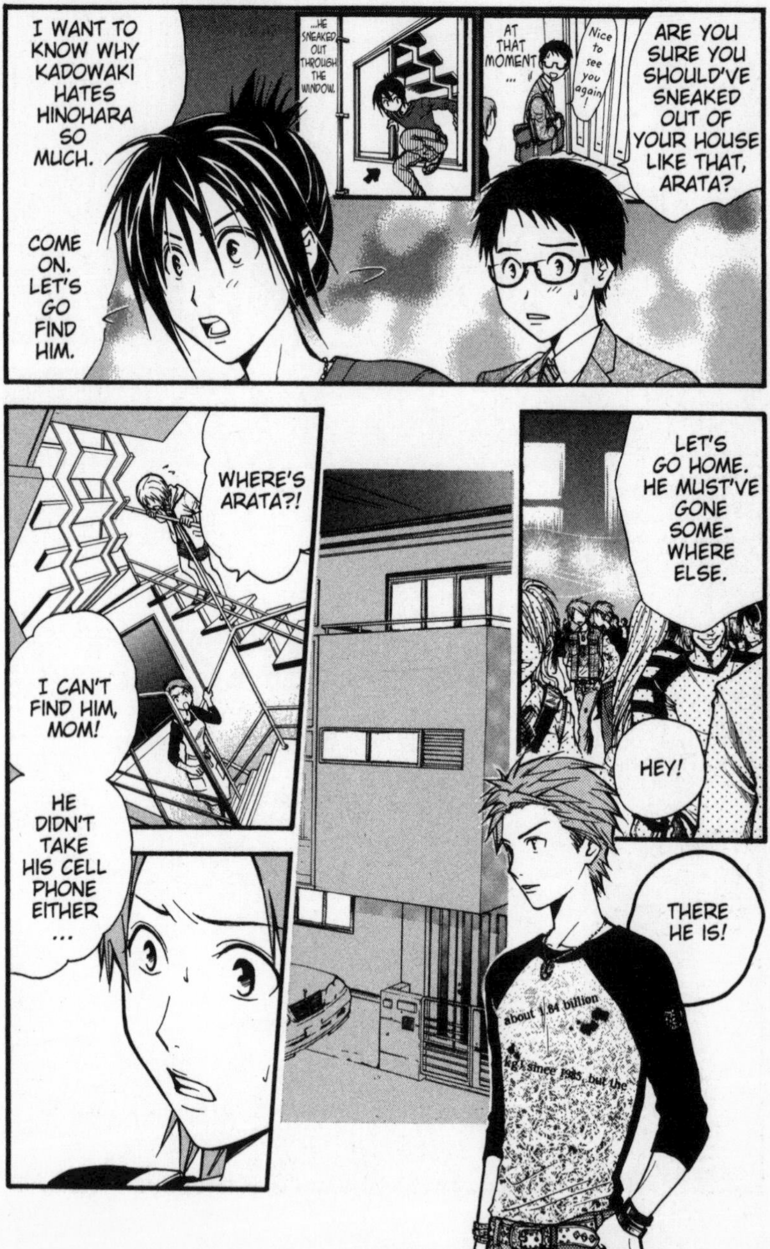
ARE YOU SURE YOU SHOULD'VE SNEAKED OUT OF YOUR HOUSE LIKE THAT, ARATA?
AT THAT MOMENT...
Nice to see you again!
...HE SNEAKED OUT THROUGH THE WINDOW.
I WANT TO KNOW WHY KADOWAKI HATES HINOHARA SO MUCH.
COME ON. LET'S GO FIND HIM.
LET'S GO HOME. HE MUST'VE GONE SOMEWHERE ELSE.
HEY!
THERE HE IS!
about 1.84 billion
WHERE'S ARATA?!
I CAN'T FIND HIM, MOM!
HE DIDN'T TAKE HIS CELL PHONE EITHER...

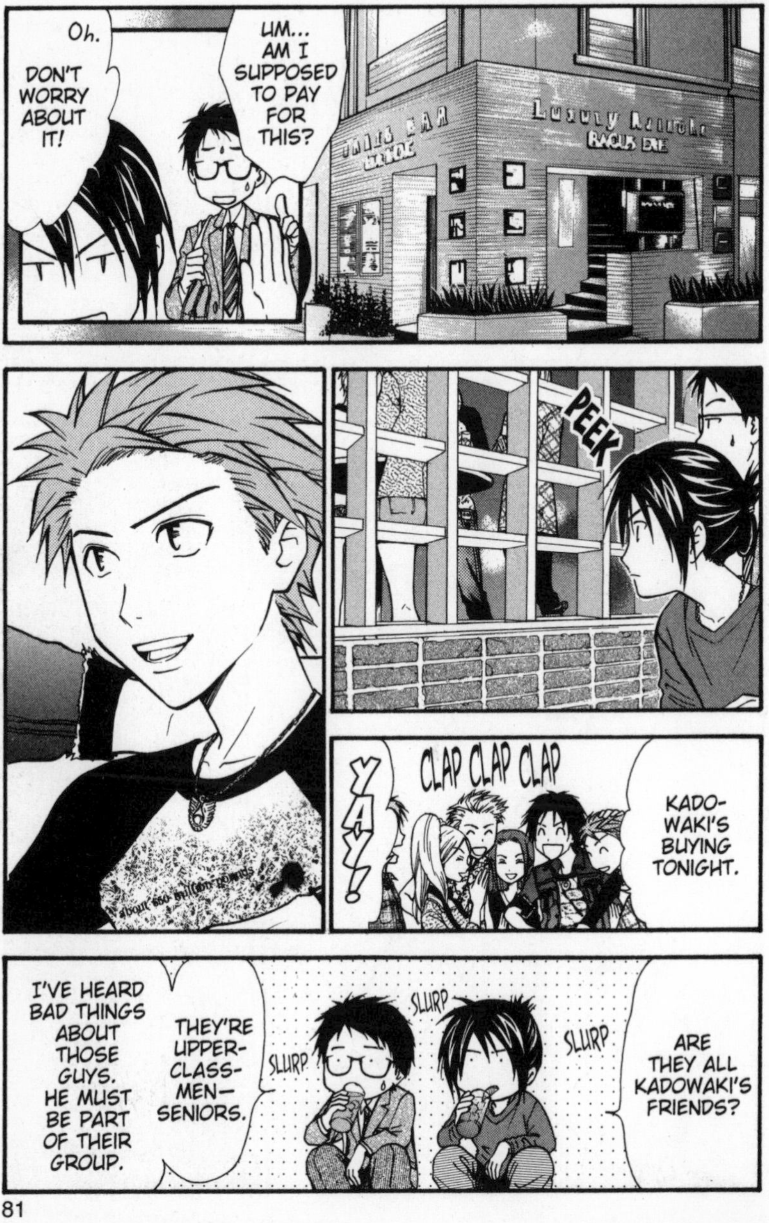
UM... AM I SUPPOSED TO PAY FOR THIS?
Oh.
DON'T WORRY ABOUT IT!
PEEK
KADO-WAKI'S BUYING TONIGHT.
CLAP CLAP CLAP
YAY!
ARE THEY ALL KADOWAKI'S FRIENDS?
SLURP
SLURP
SLURP
THEY'RE UPPER-CLASS-MEN—SENIORS.
I'VE HEARD BAD THINGS ABOUT THOSE GUYS. HE MUST BE PART OF THEIR GROUP.

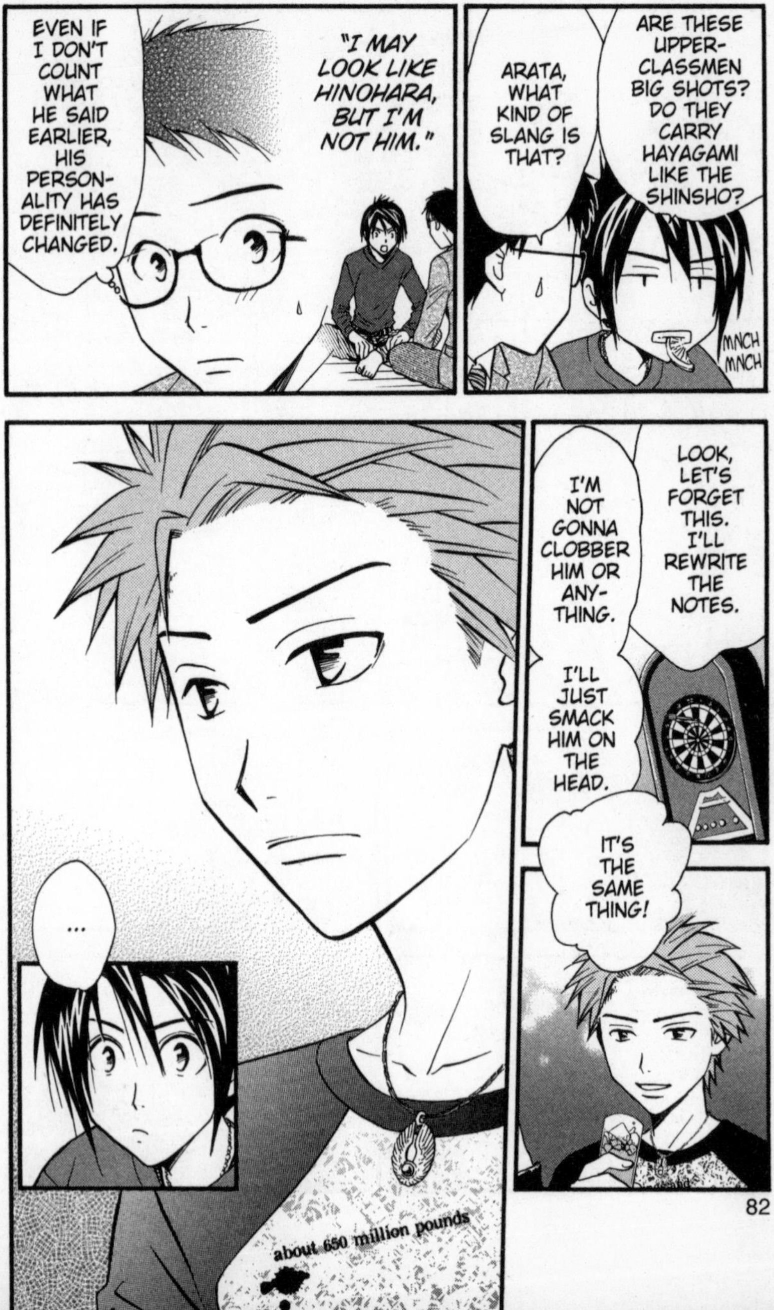
ARE THESE UPPER-CLASSMEN BIG SHOTS? DO THEY CARRY HAYAGAMI LIKE THE SHINSHO?
ARATA, WHAT KIND OF SLANG IS THAT?
MNCH MNCH
"I MAY LOOK LIKE HINOHARA, BUT I'M NOT HIM."
EVEN IF I DON'T COUNT WHAT HE SAID EARLIER, HIS PERSON-ALITY HAS DEFINITELY CHANGED.
LOOK, LET'S FORGET THIS. I'LL REWRITE THE NOTES.
I'M NOT GONNA CLOBBER HIM OR ANY-THING.
I'LL JUST SMACK HIM ON THE HEAD.
IT'S THE SAME THING!
...
about 650 million pounds

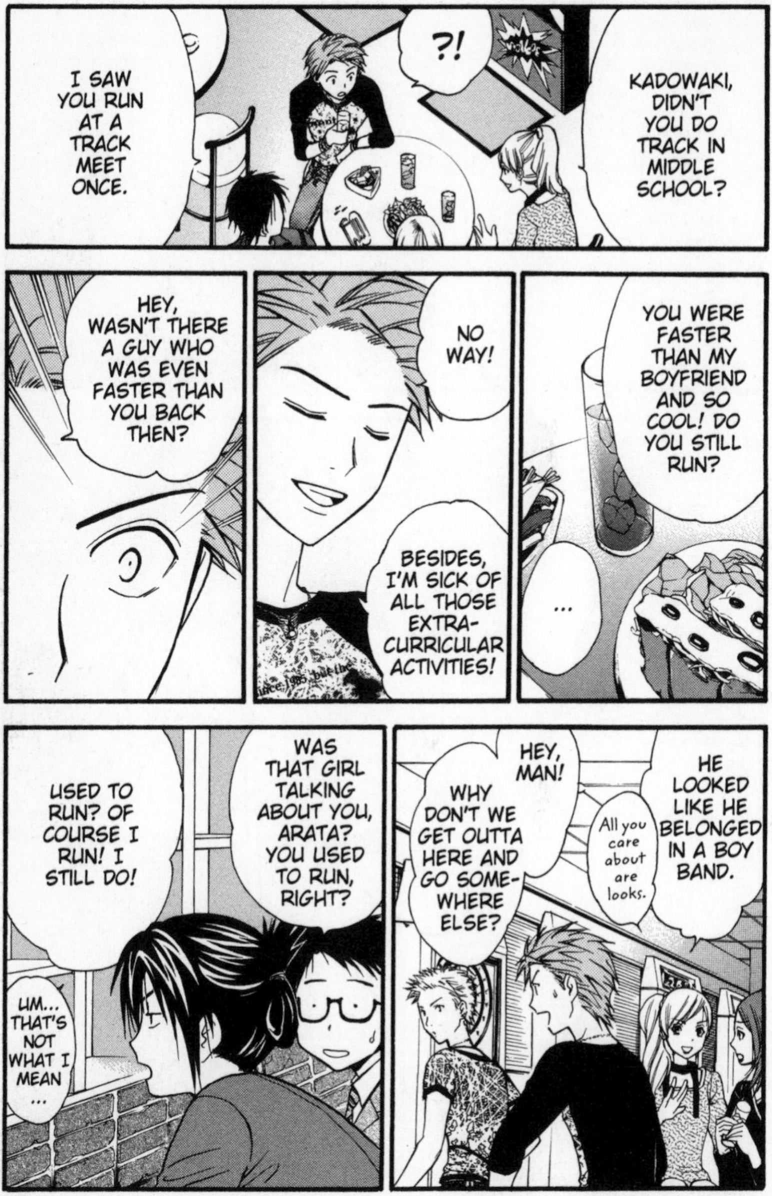
KADOWAKI, DIDN'T YOU DO TRACK IN MIDDLE SCHOOL?
?!
I SAW YOU RUN AT A TRACK MEET ONCE.
YOU WERE FASTER THAN MY BOYFRIEND AND SO COOL! DO YOU STILL RUN?
...
NO WAY!
BESIDES, I'M SICK OF ALL THOSE EXTRA-CURRICULAR ACTIVITIES!
HEY, WASN'T THERE A GUY WHO WAS EVEN FASTER THAN YOU BACK THEN?
HE LOOKED LIKE HE BELONGED IN A BOY BAND.
All you care about are looks.
HEY, MAN!
WHY DON'T WE GET OUTTA HERE AND GO SOME-WHERE ELSE?
WAS THAT GIRL TALKING ABOUT YOU, ARATA? YOU USED TO RUN, RIGHT?
USED TO RUN? OF COURSE I RUN! I STILL DO!
UM... THAT'S NOT WHAT I MEAN ...

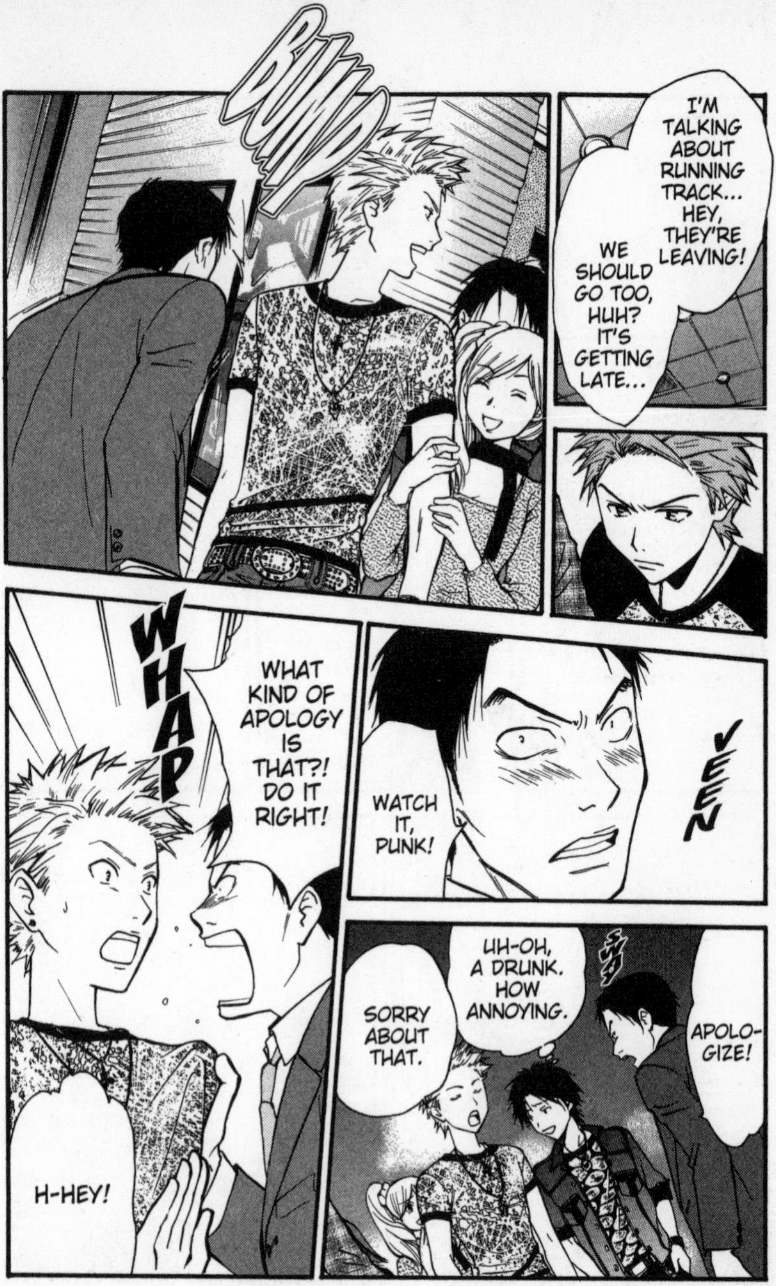
I'M TALKING ABOUT RUNNING TRACK... HEY, THEY'RE LEAVING!
WE SHOULD GO TOO, HUH? IT'S GETTING LATE...
BUMP
VEEN
WATCH IT, PUNK!
APOLO-GIZE!
UH-OH, A DRUNK. HOW ANNOYING.
SORRY ABOUT THAT.
WHAP
WHAT KIND OF APOLOGY IS THAT?! DO IT RIGHT!
H-HEY!

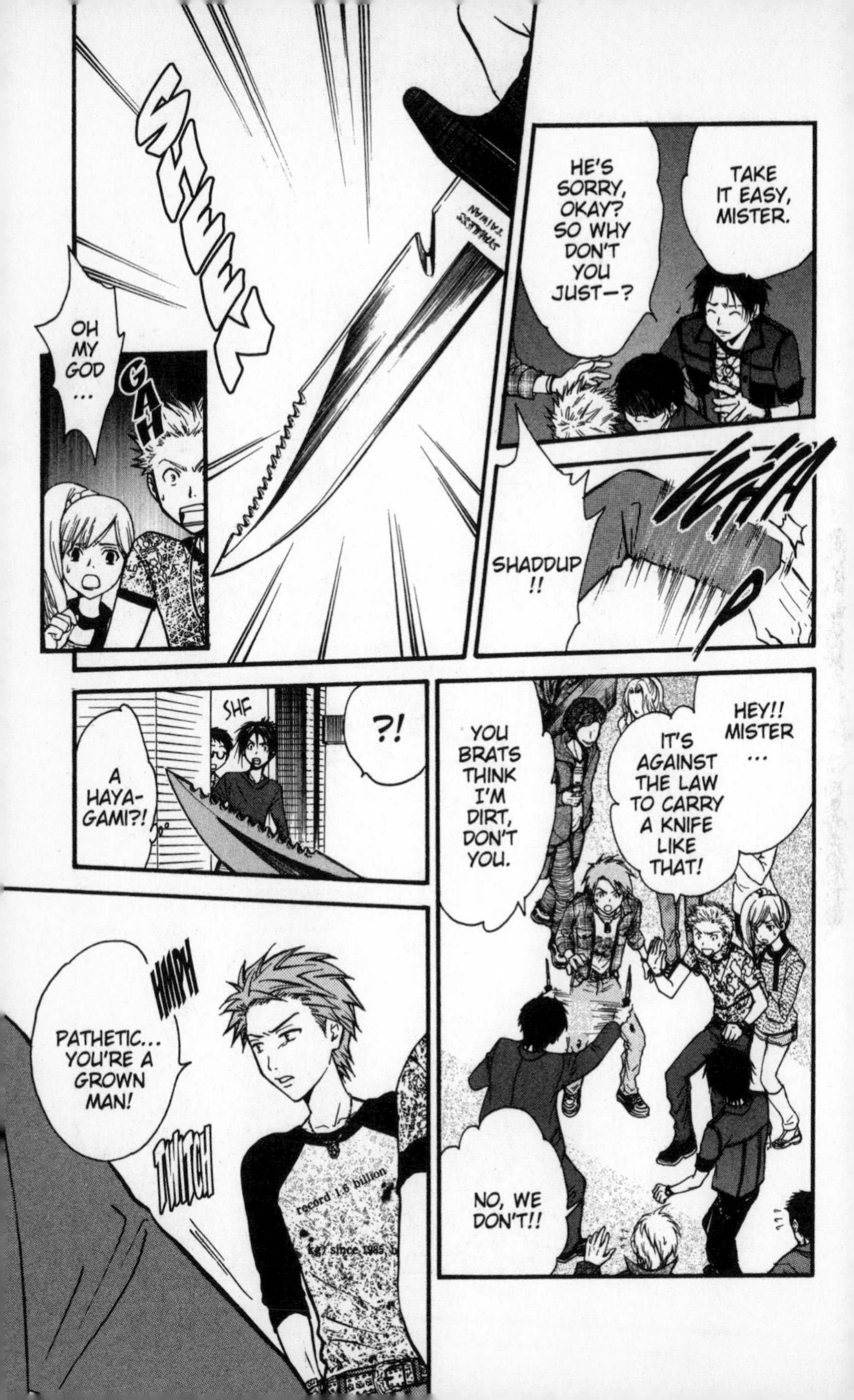
TAKE IT EASY, MISTER.
HE'S SORRY, OKAY? SO WHY DON'T YOU JUST—?
WHAP
SHADDUP!!
SHWING
OH MY GOD...
GAH
HEY!! MISTER...
IT'S AGAINST THE LAW TO CARRY A KNIFE LIKE THAT!
YOU BRATS THINK I'M DIRT, DON'T YOU.
NO, WE DON'T!!
?!
SHF
A HAYA-GAMI?!
HMPH
PATHETIC... YOU'RE A GROWN MAN!
TWITCH

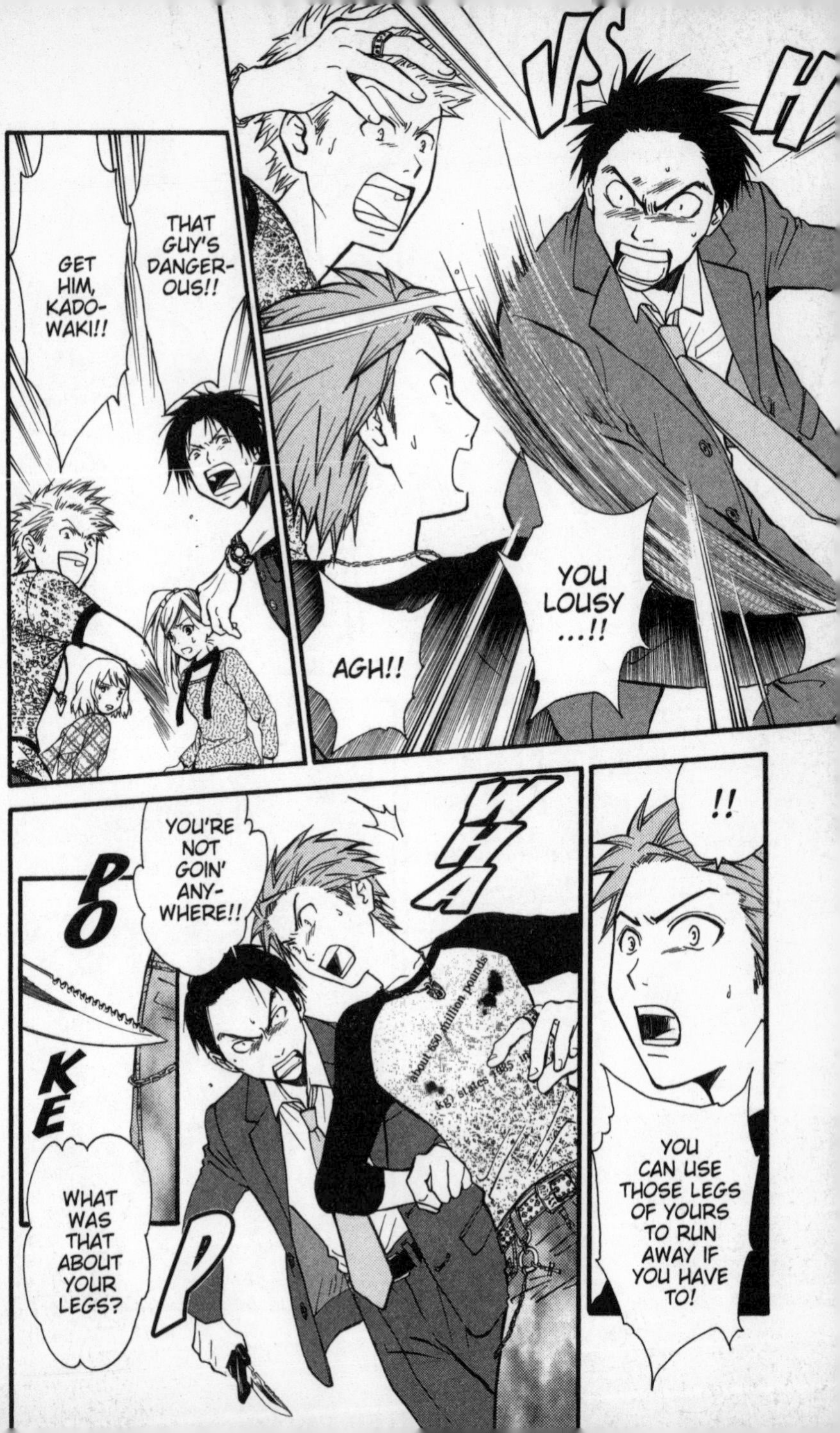
VSH
YOU LOUSY ...!!
AGH!!
THAT GUY'S DANGER-OUS!!
GET HIM, KADO-WAKI!!
!!
YOU CAN USE THOSE LEGS OF YOURS TO RUN AWAY IF YOU HAVE TO!
WHA
YOU'RE NOT GOIN' ANY-WHERE!!
PO
KE
P
WHAT WAS THAT ABOUT YOUR LEGS?

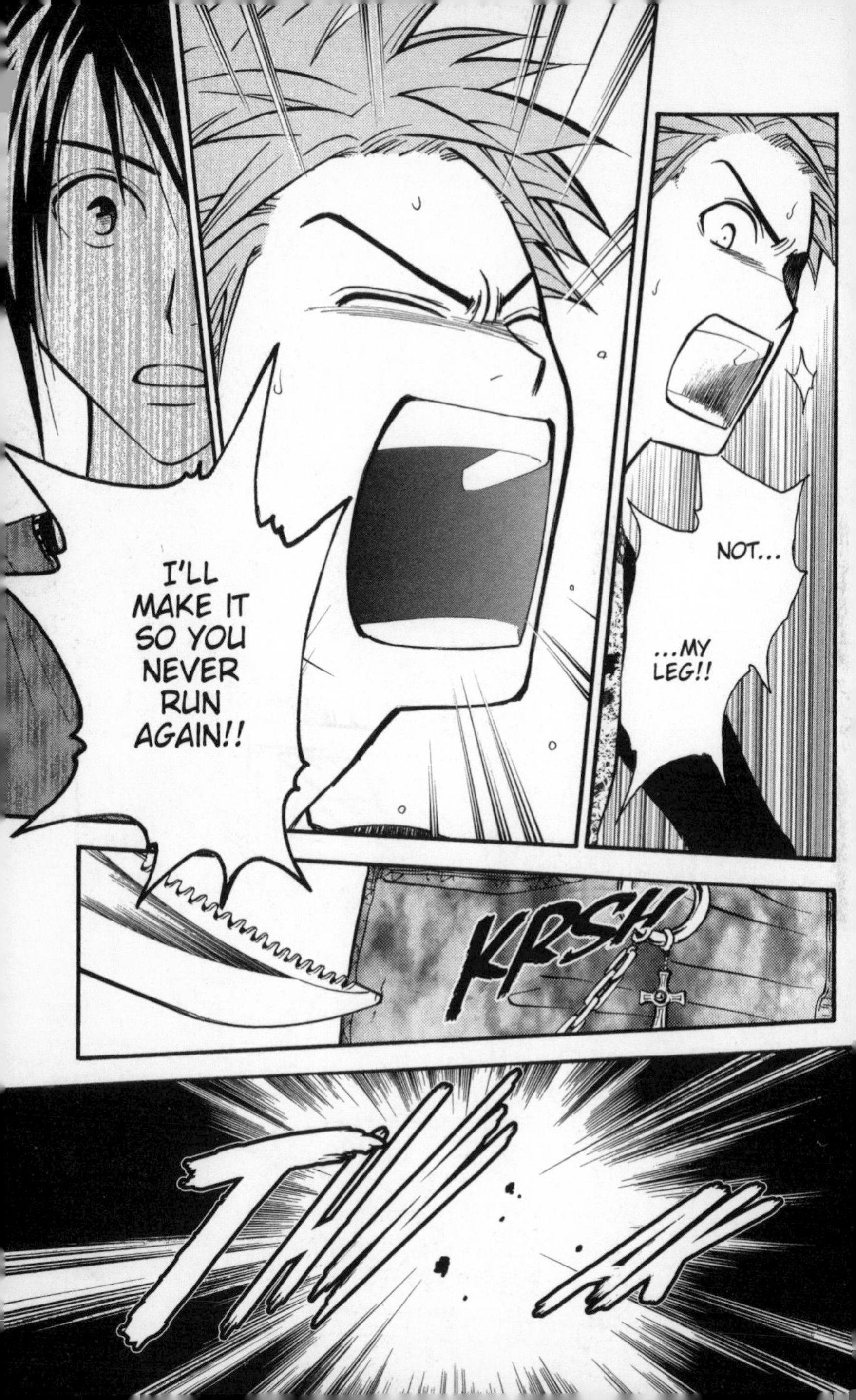
NOT...
...MY LEG!!
I'LL MAKE IT SO YOU NEVER RUN AGAIN!!
KRSH

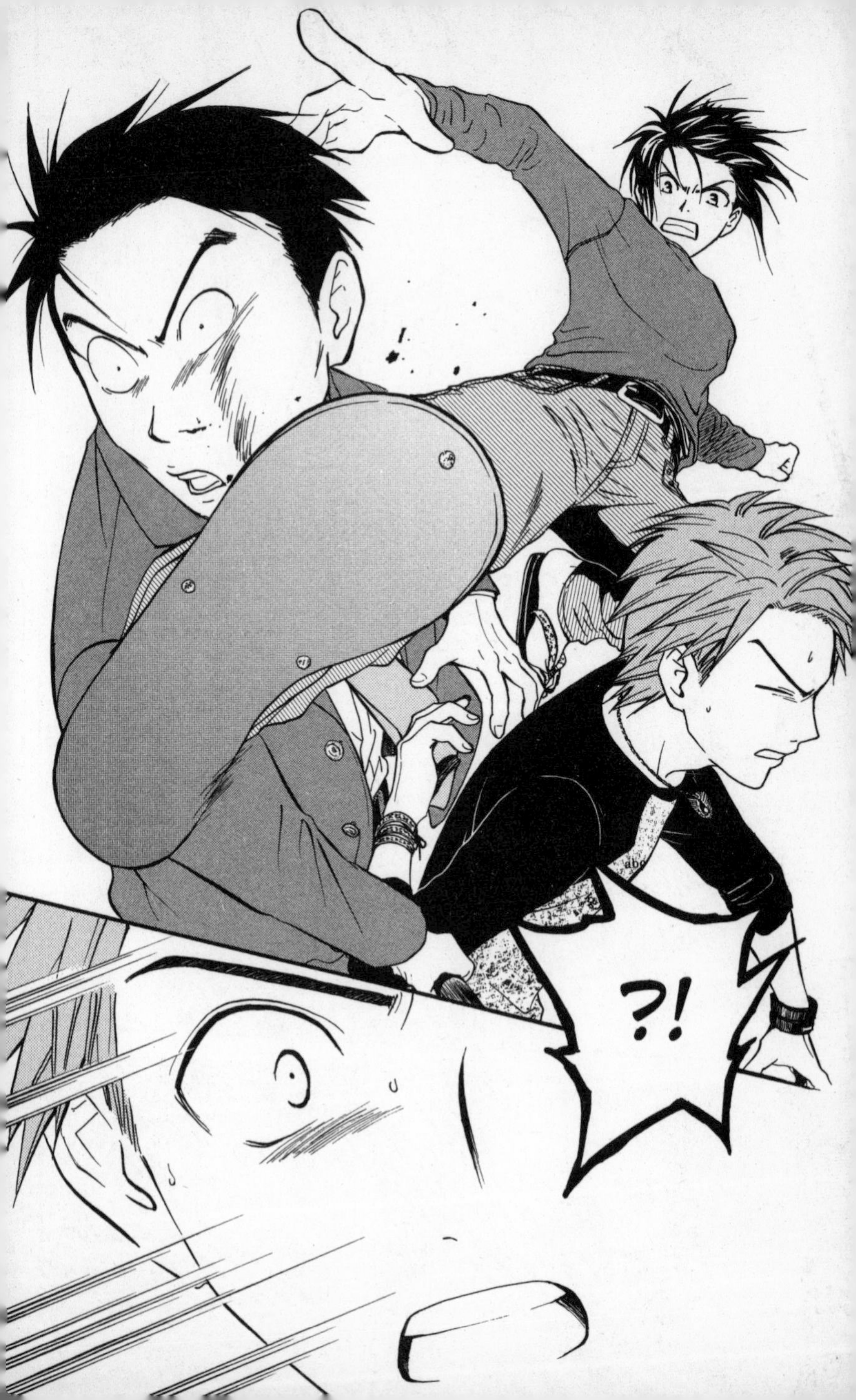
?!

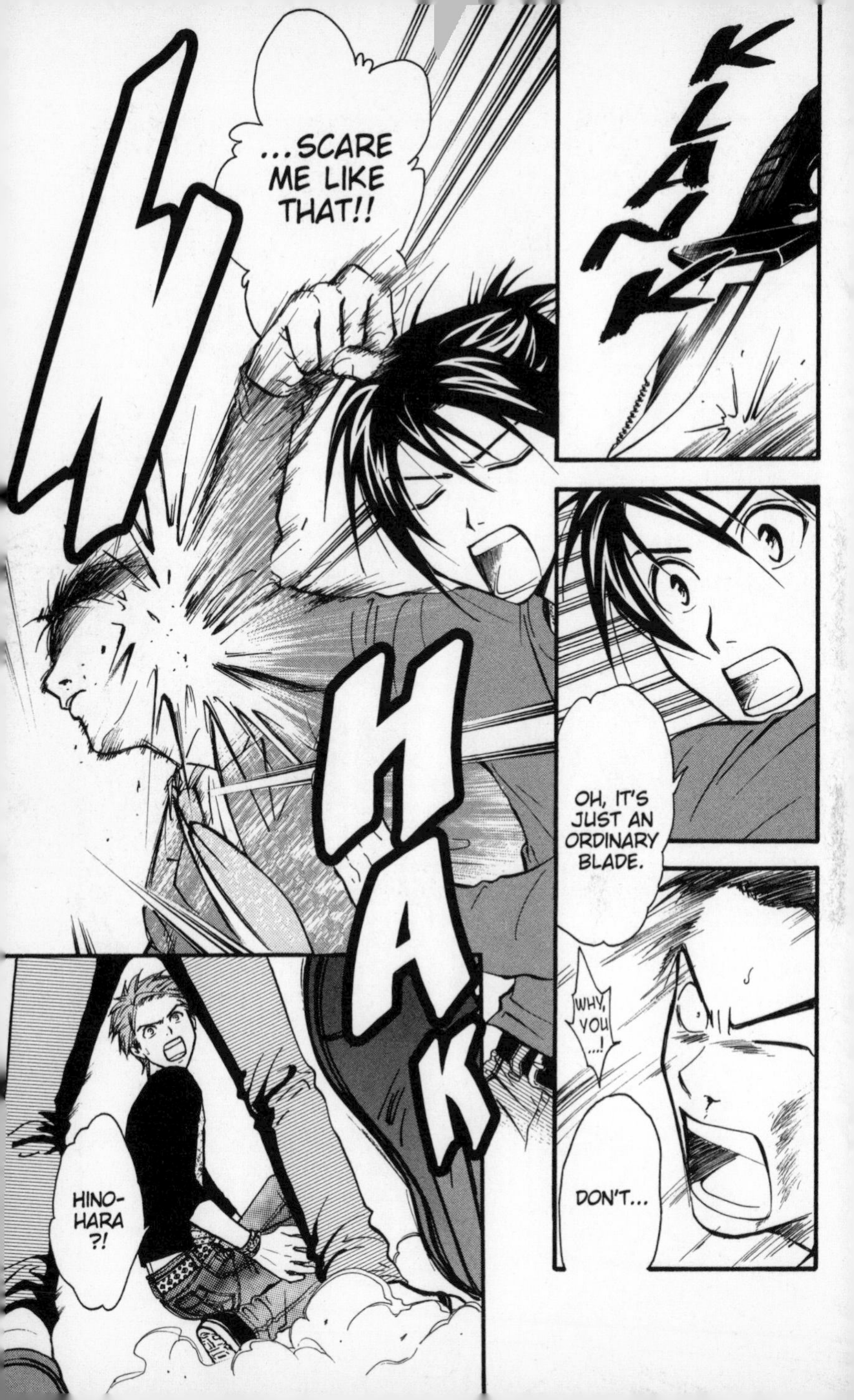
OH, IT'S JUST AN ORDINARY BLADE.
WHY, YOU ...!
DON'T...
...SCARE ME LIKE THAT!!
HINO-HARA ?!

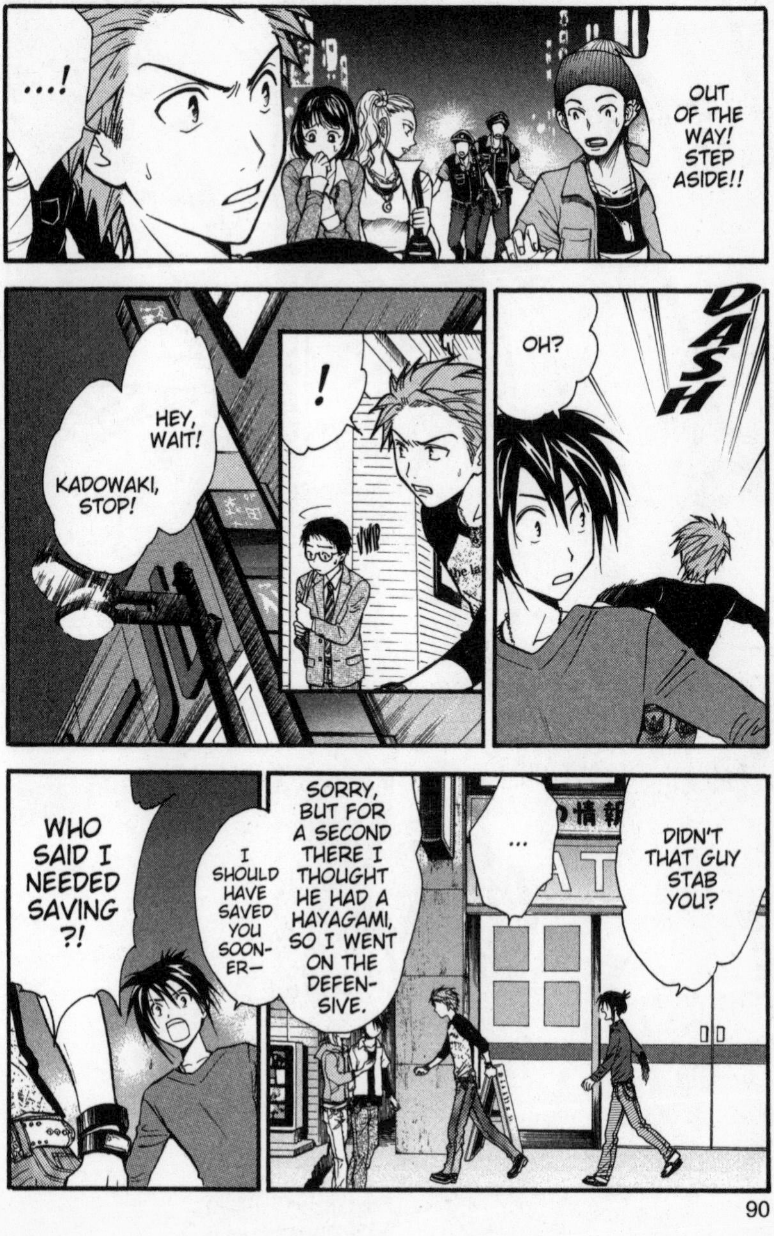
OUT OF THE WAY! STEP ASIDE!!
...!
DASH
OH?
!
HEY, WAIT!
KADOWAKI, STOP!
DIDN'T THAT GUY STAB YOU?
...
SORRY, BUT FOR A SECOND THERE I THOUGHT HE HAD A HAYAGAMI, SO I WENT ON THE DEFENSIVE.
I SHOULD HAVE SAVED YOU SOONER—
WHO SAID I NEEDED SAVING?!

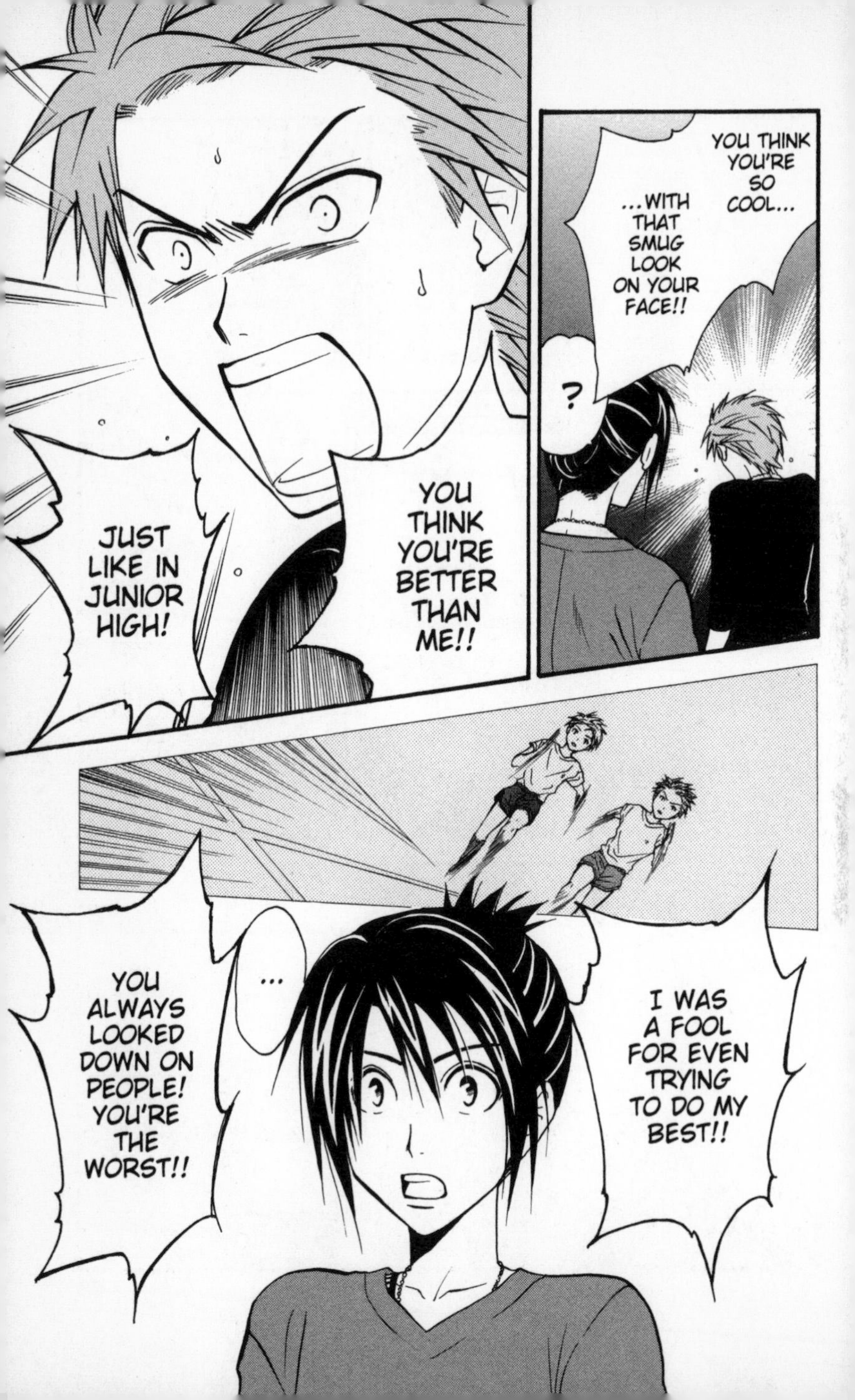
YOU THINK YOU'RE SO COOL...
...WITH THAT SMUG LOOK ON YOUR FACE!!
?
YOU THINK YOU'RE BETTER THAN ME!!
JUST LIKE IN JUNIOR HIGH!
I WAS A FOOL FOR EVEN TRYING TO DO MY BEST!!
...
YOU ALWAYS LOOKED DOWN ON PEOPLE! YOU'RE THE WORST!!

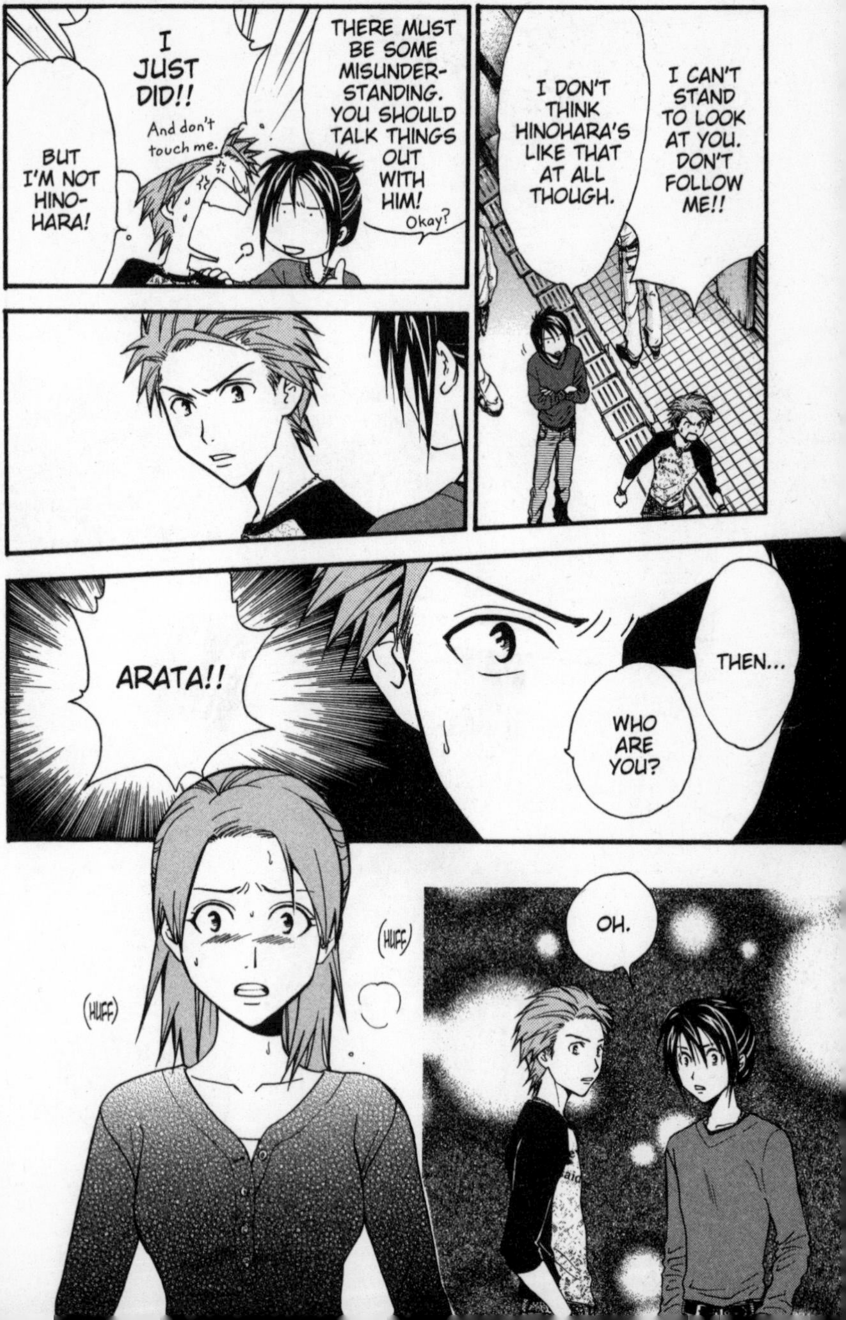
I CAN'T STAND TO LOOK AT YOU. DON'T FOLLOW ME!!
I DON'T THINK HINOHARA'S LIKE THAT AT ALL THOUGH.
THERE MUST BE SOME MISUNDERSTANDING. YOU SHOULD TALK THINGS OUT WITH HIM!
Okay?
I JUST DID!!
And don't touch me.
BUT I'M NOT HINO-HARA!
THEN...
WHO ARE YOU?
ARATA!!
OH.
(HUFF)
(HUFF)

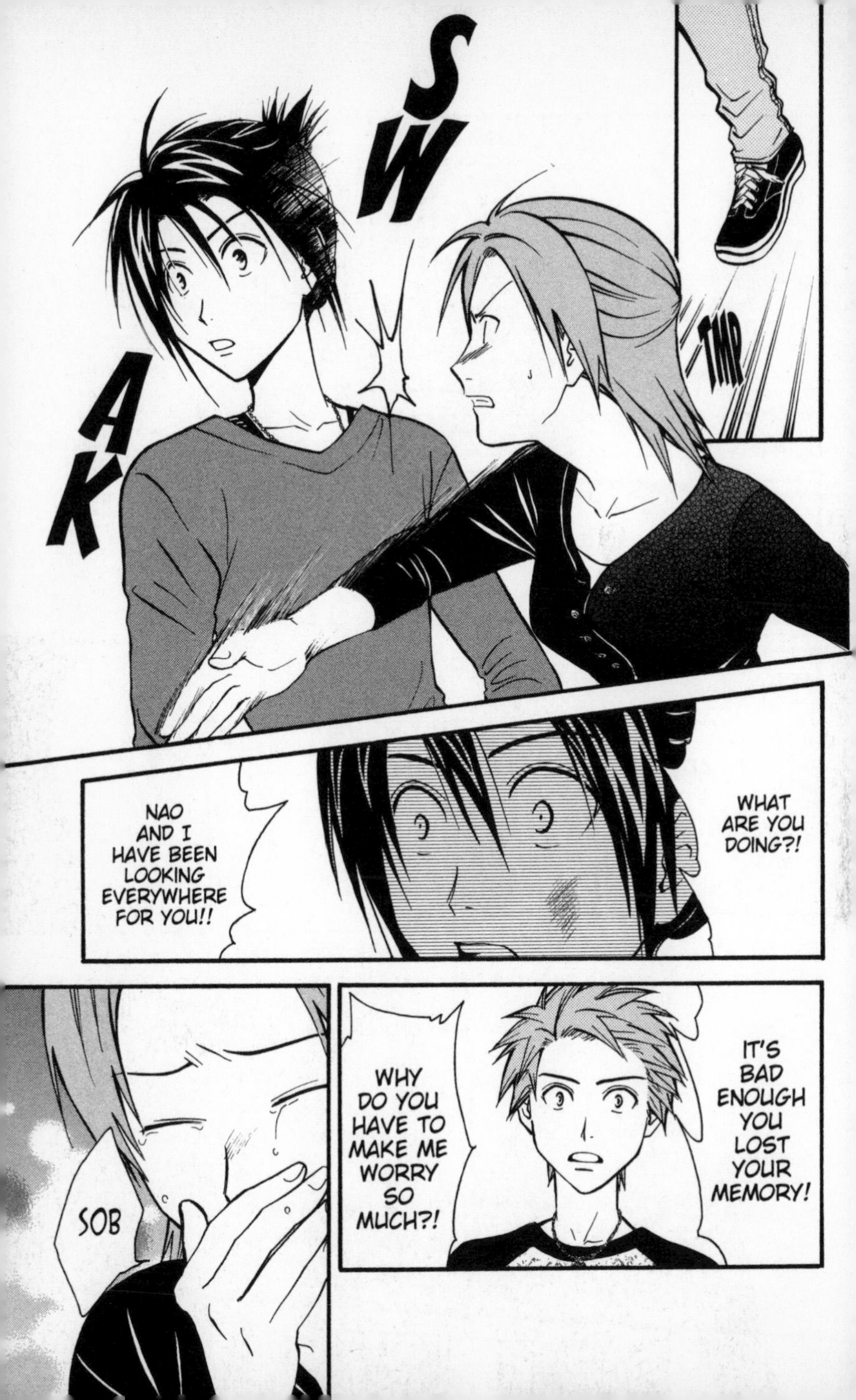
TMP
SWAK
WHAT ARE YOU DOING?!
NAO AND I HAVE BEEN LOOKING EVERYWHERE FOR YOU!!
IT'S BAD ENOUGH YOU LOST YOUR MEMORY!
WHY DO YOU HAVE TO MAKE ME WORRY SO MUCH?!
SOB

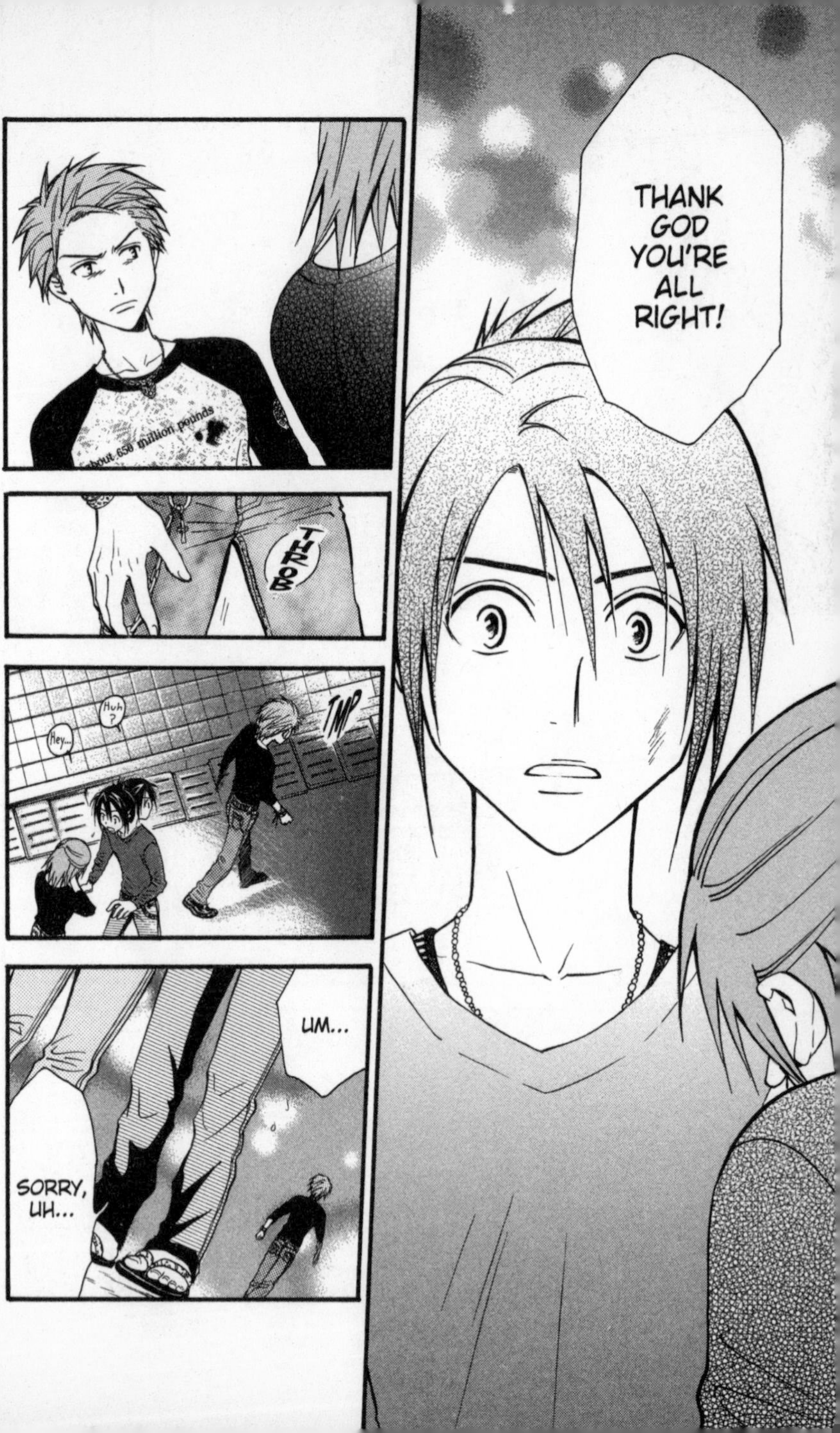
THANK GOD YOU'RE ALL RIGHT!
about 650 million pounds
THROB
TMP
Huh?
Hey...
UM...
SORRY, UH...

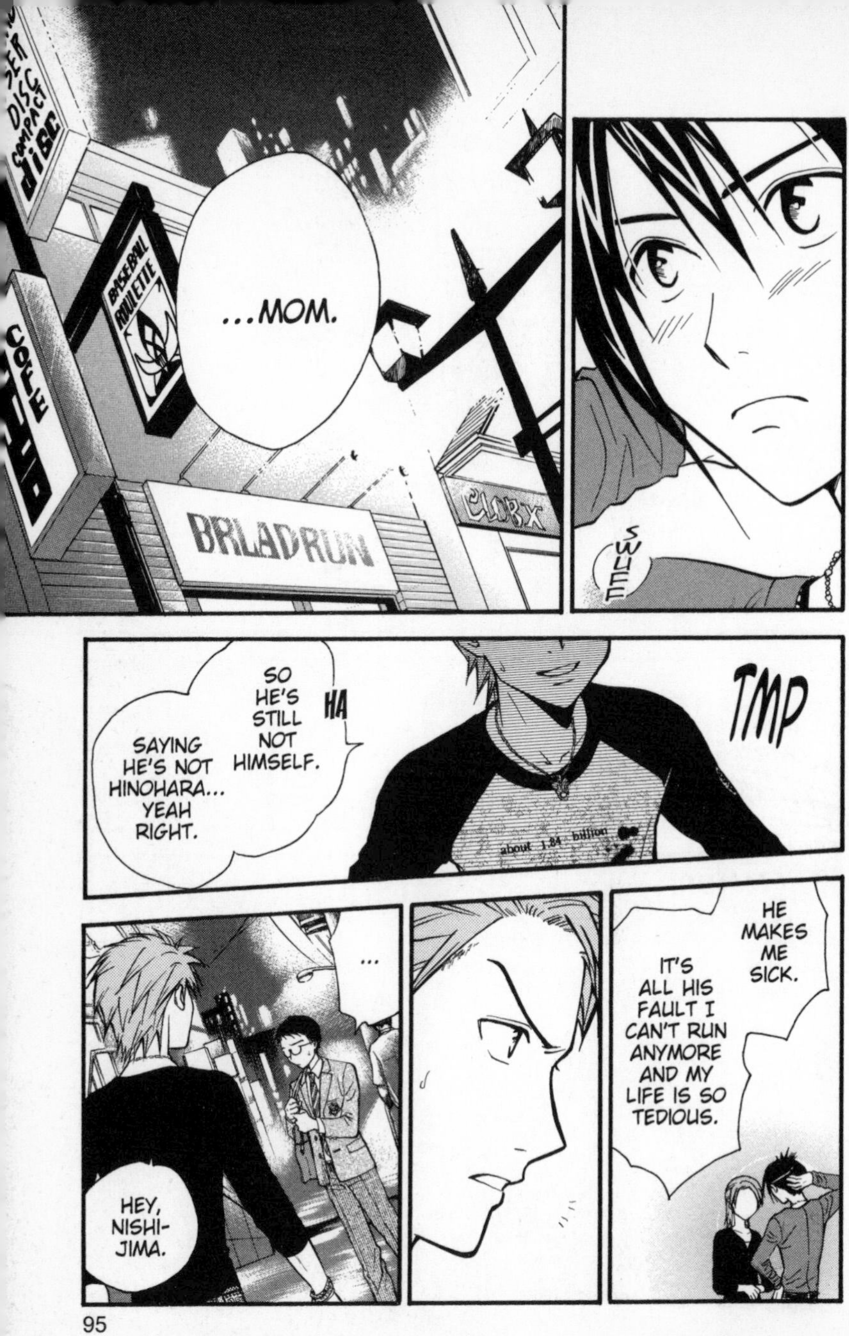
SWUFF
COMPACT disc
BASEBALL ROULETTE
BRLADRUN
...MOM.
TMP
HA
SO HE'S STILL NOT HIMSELF.
SAYING HE'S NOT HINOHARA... YEAH RIGHT.
about 1.84 billion
HE MAKES ME SICK.
IT'S ALL HIS FAULT I CAN'T RUN ANYMORE AND MY LIFE IS SO TEDIOUS.
...
HEY, NISHI-JIMA.

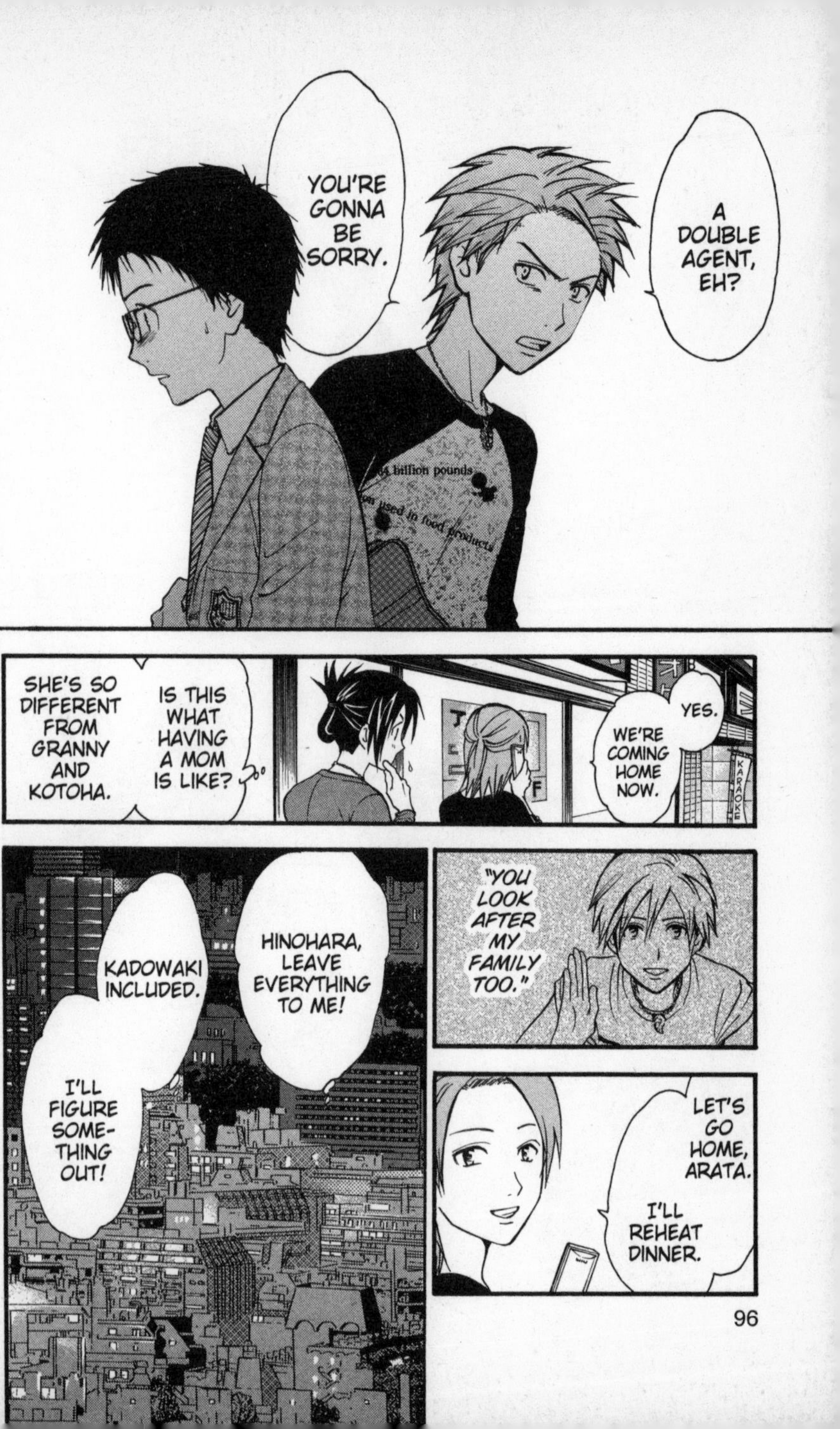
A DOUBLE AGENT, EH?
YOU'RE GONNA BE SORRY.
billion pounds
used in food products
YES.
WE'RE COMING HOME NOW.
KARAOKE
IS THIS WHAT HAVING A MOM IS LIKE?
SHE'S SO DIFFERENT FROM GRANNY AND KOTOHA.
"YOU LOOK AFTER MY FAMILY TOO."
LET'S GO HOME, ARATA.
I'LL REHEAT DINNER.
HINOHARA, LEAVE EVERYTHING TO ME!
KADOWAKI INCLUDED.
I'LL FIGURE SOME-THING OUT!

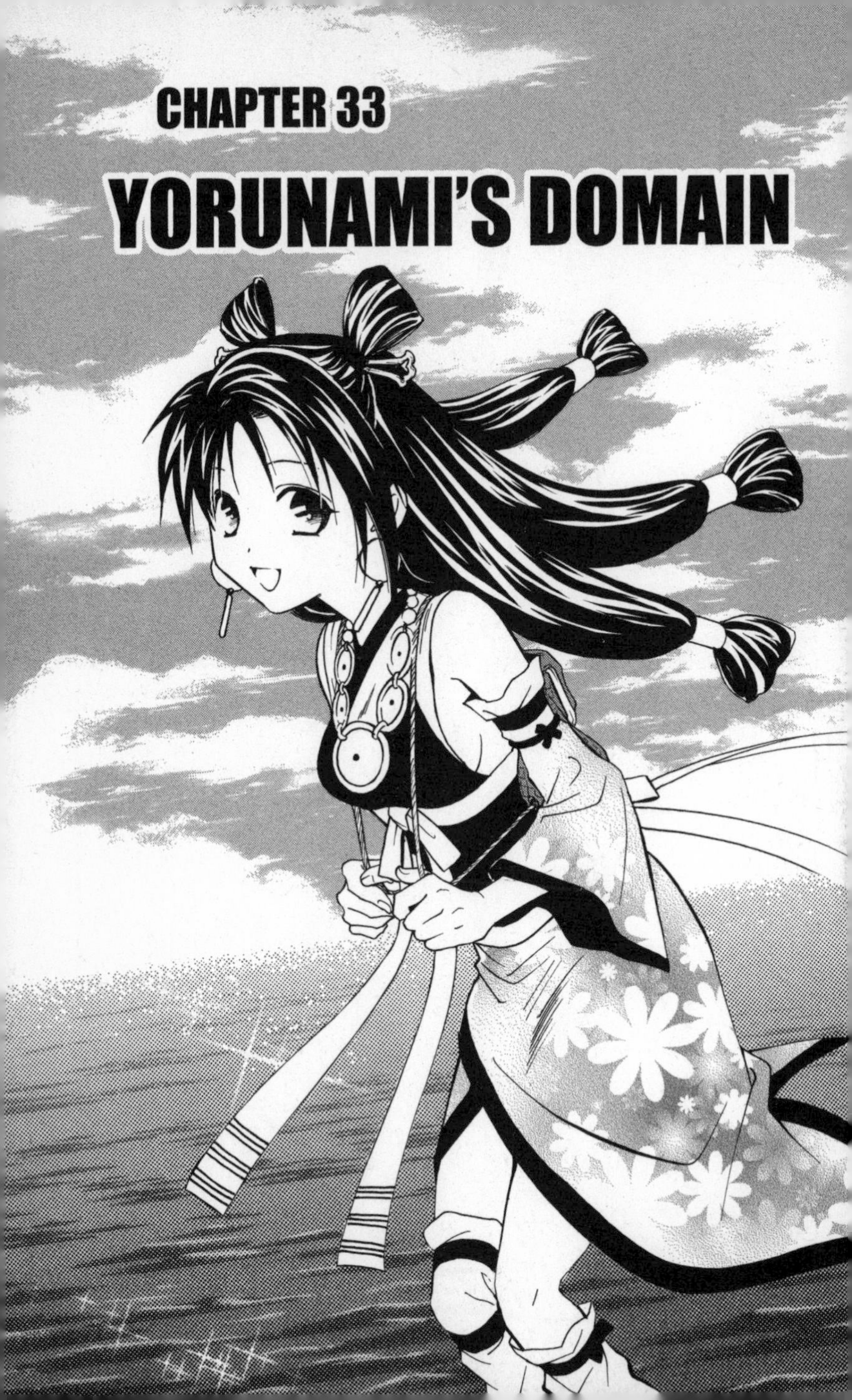
CHAPTER 33
YORUNAMI'S DOMAIN

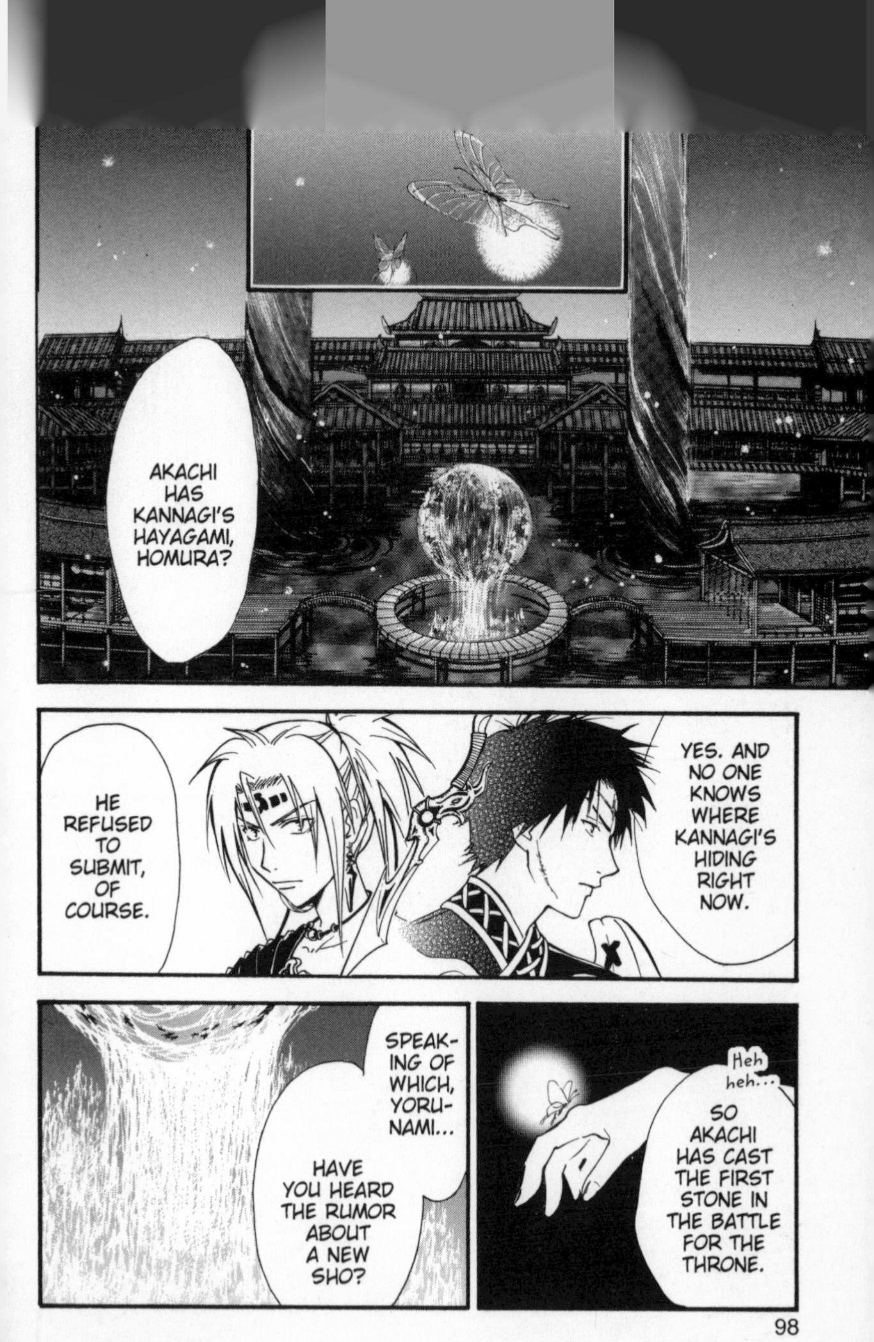
AKACHI HAS KANNAGI'S HAYAGAMI, HOMURA?
YES. AND NO ONE KNOWS WHERE KANNAGI'S HIDING RIGHT NOW.
HE REFUSED TO SUBMIT, OF COURSE.
Heh heh...
SO AKACHI HAS CAST THE FIRST STONE IN THE BATTLE FOR THE THRONE.
SPEAK-ING OF WHICH, YORU-NAMI...
HAVE YOU HEARD THE RUMOR ABOUT A NEW SHO?

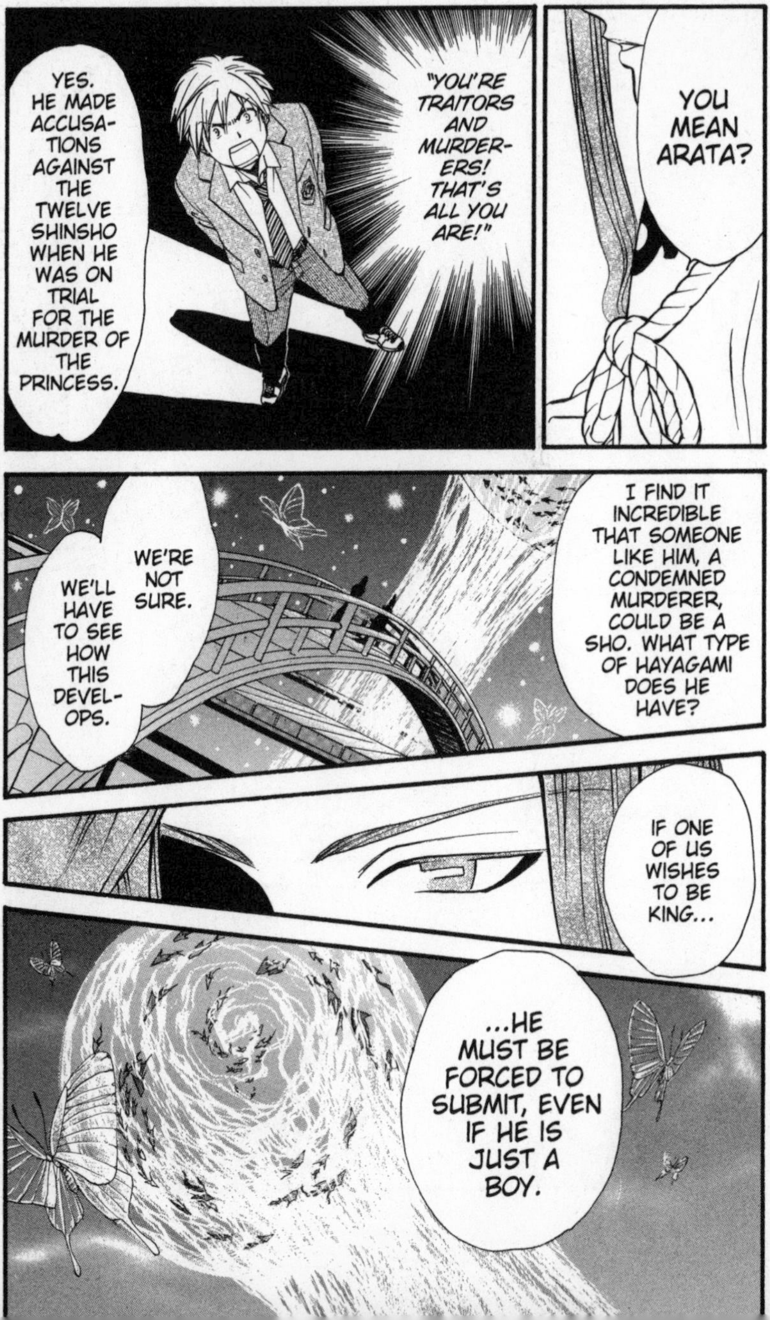
YOU MEAN ARATA?
"YOU'RE TRAITORS AND MURDERERS! THAT'S ALL YOU ARE!"
YES. HE MADE ACCUSATIONS AGAINST THE TWELVE SHINSHO WHEN HE WAS ON TRIAL FOR THE MURDER OF THE PRINCESS.
I FIND IT INCREDIBLE THAT SOMEONE LIKE HIM, A CONDEMNED MURDERER, COULD BE A SHO. WHAT TYPE OF HAYAGAMI DOES HE HAVE?
WE'RE NOT SURE.
WE'LL HAVE TO SEE HOW THIS DEVELOPS.
IF ONE OF US WISHES TO BE KING...
...HE MUST BE FORCED TO SUBMIT, EVEN IF HE IS JUST A BOY.

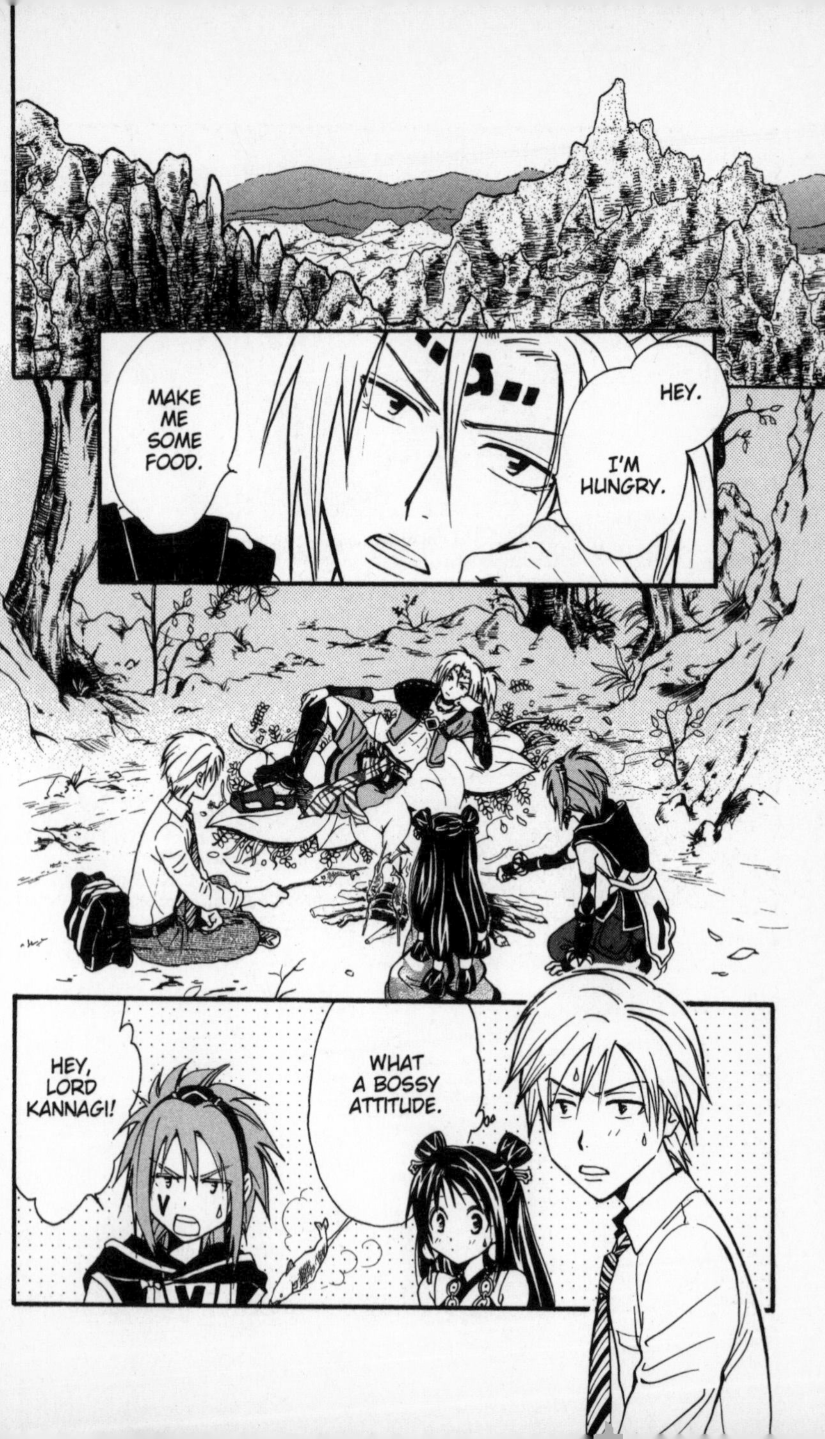
HEY. I'M HUNGRY.
MAKE ME SOME FOOD.
WHAT A BOSSY ATTITUDE.
HEY, LORD KANNAGI!

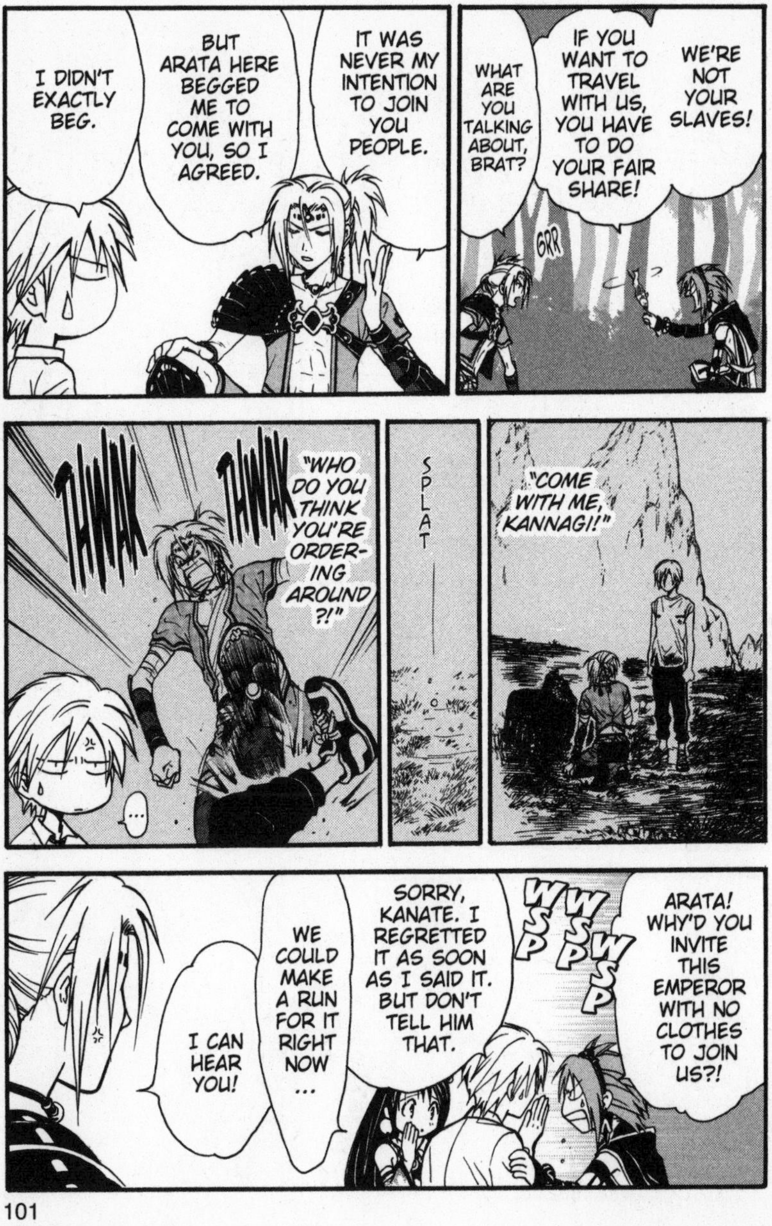
WE'RE NOT YOUR SLAVES!
IF YOU WANT TO TRAVEL WITH US, YOU HAVE TO DO YOUR FAIR SHARE!
WHAT ARE YOU TALKING ABOUT, BRAT?
GRR
IT WAS NEVER MY INTENTION TO JOIN YOU PEOPLE.
BUT ARATA HERE BEGGED ME TO COME WITH YOU, SO I AGREED.
I DIDN'T EXACTLY BEG.
"COME WITH ME, KANNAGI!"
SPLAT
"WHO DO YOU THINK YOU'RE ORDERING AROUND?!"
THWAK
THWAK
...
ARATA! WHY'D YOU INVITE THIS EMPEROR WITH NO CLOTHES TO JOIN US?!
WSP WSP WSP
SORRY, KANATE. I REGRETTED IT AS SOON AS I SAID IT. BUT DON'T TELL HIM THAT.
WE COULD MAKE A RUN FOR IT RIGHT NOW...
I CAN HEAR YOU!

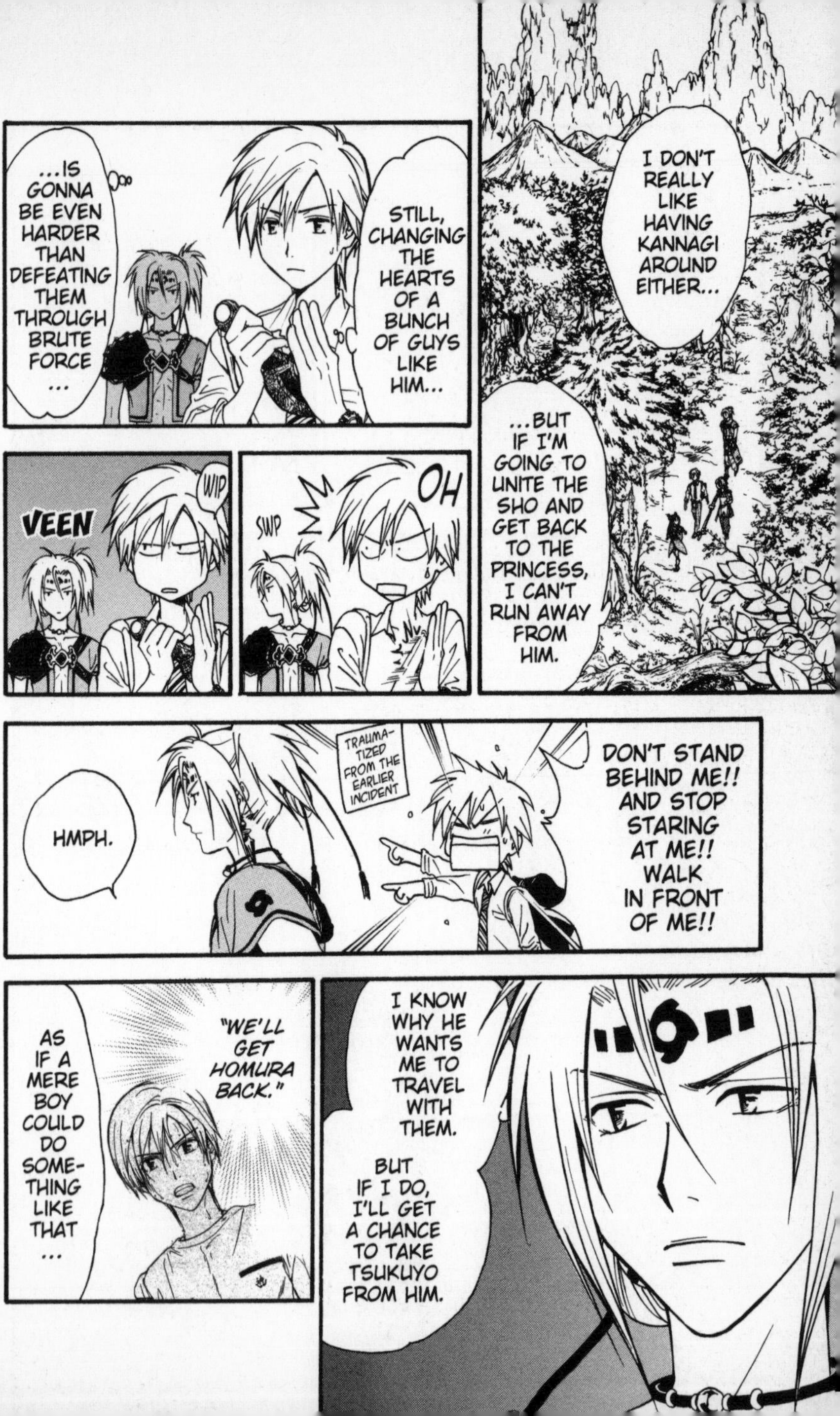
I DON'T REALLY LIKE HAVING KANNAGI AROUND EITHER...
...BUT IF I'M GOING TO UNITE THE SHO AND GET BACK TO THE PRINCESS, I CAN'T RUN AWAY FROM HIM.
STILL, CHANGING THE HEARTS OF A BUNCH OF GUYS LIKE HIM...
...IS GONNA BE EVEN HARDER THAN DEFEATING THEM THROUGH BRUTE FORCE...
OH
SWP
WIP
VEEN
DON'T STAND BEHIND ME!! AND STOP STARING AT ME!! WALK IN FRONT OF ME!!
TRAUMATIZED FROM THE EARLIER INCIDENT
HMPH.
I KNOW WHY HE WANTS ME TO TRAVEL WITH THEM.
BUT IF I DO, I'LL GET A CHANCE TO TAKE TSUKUYO FROM HIM.
"WE'LL GET HOMURA BACK."
AS IF A MERE BOY COULD DO SOMETHING LIKE THAT...

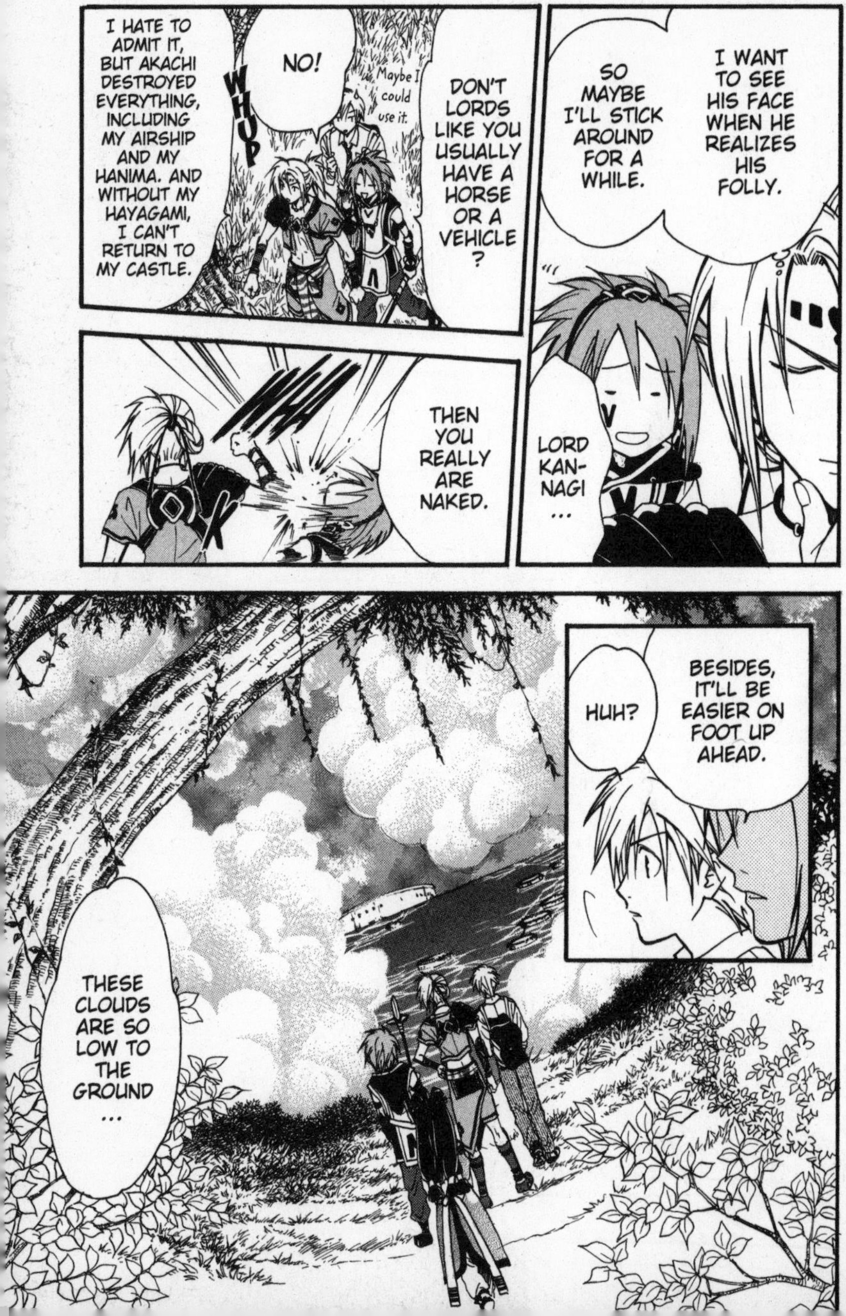
I WANT TO SEE HIS FACE WHEN HE REALIZES HIS FOLLY.
SO MAYBE I'LL STICK AROUND FOR A WHILE.
...
LORD KAN-NAGI ...
DON'T LORDS LIKE YOU USUALLY HAVE A HORSE OR A VEHICLE?
Maybe I could use it.
NO!
WHUP
I HATE TO ADMIT IT, BUT AKACHI DESTROYED EVERYTHING, INCLUDING MY AIRSHIP AND MY HANIMA. AND WITHOUT MY HAYAGAMI, I CAN'T RETURN TO MY CASTLE.
THEN YOU REALLY ARE NAKED.
WHA
BESIDES, IT'LL BE EASIER ON FOOT UP AHEAD.
HUH?
THESE CLOUDS ARE SO LOW TO THE GROUND ...

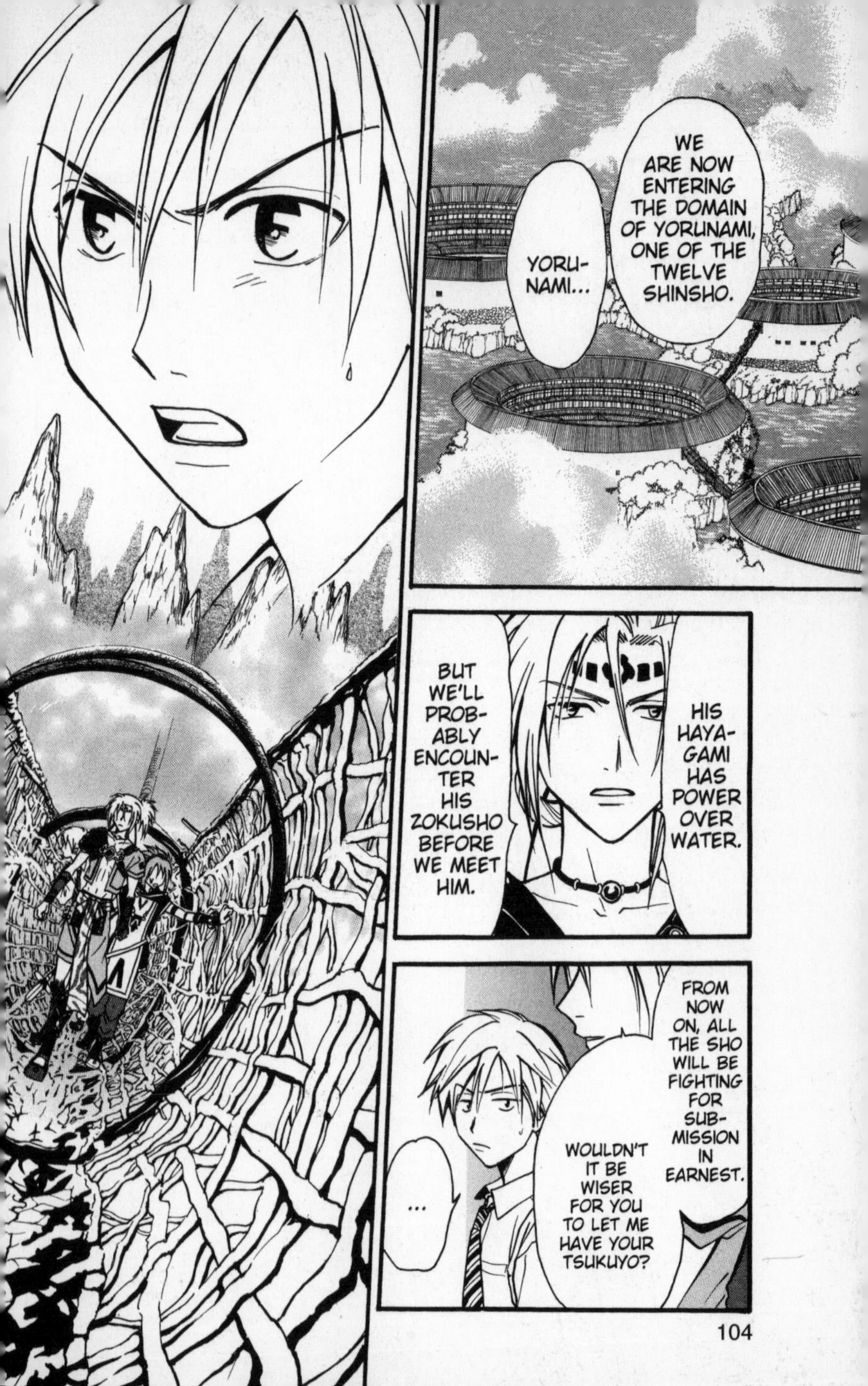
WE ARE NOW ENTERING THE DOMAIN OF YORUNAMI, ONE OF THE TWELVE SHINSHO.
YORU-NAMI...
HIS HAYA-GAMI HAS POWER OVER WATER.
BUT WE'LL PROB-ABLY ENCOUN-TER HIS ZOKUSHO BEFORE WE MEET HIM.
FROM NOW ON, ALL THE SHO WILL BE FIGHTING FOR SUB-MISSION IN EARNEST.
WOULDN'T IT BE WISER FOR YOU TO LET ME HAVE YOUR TSUKUYO?
...

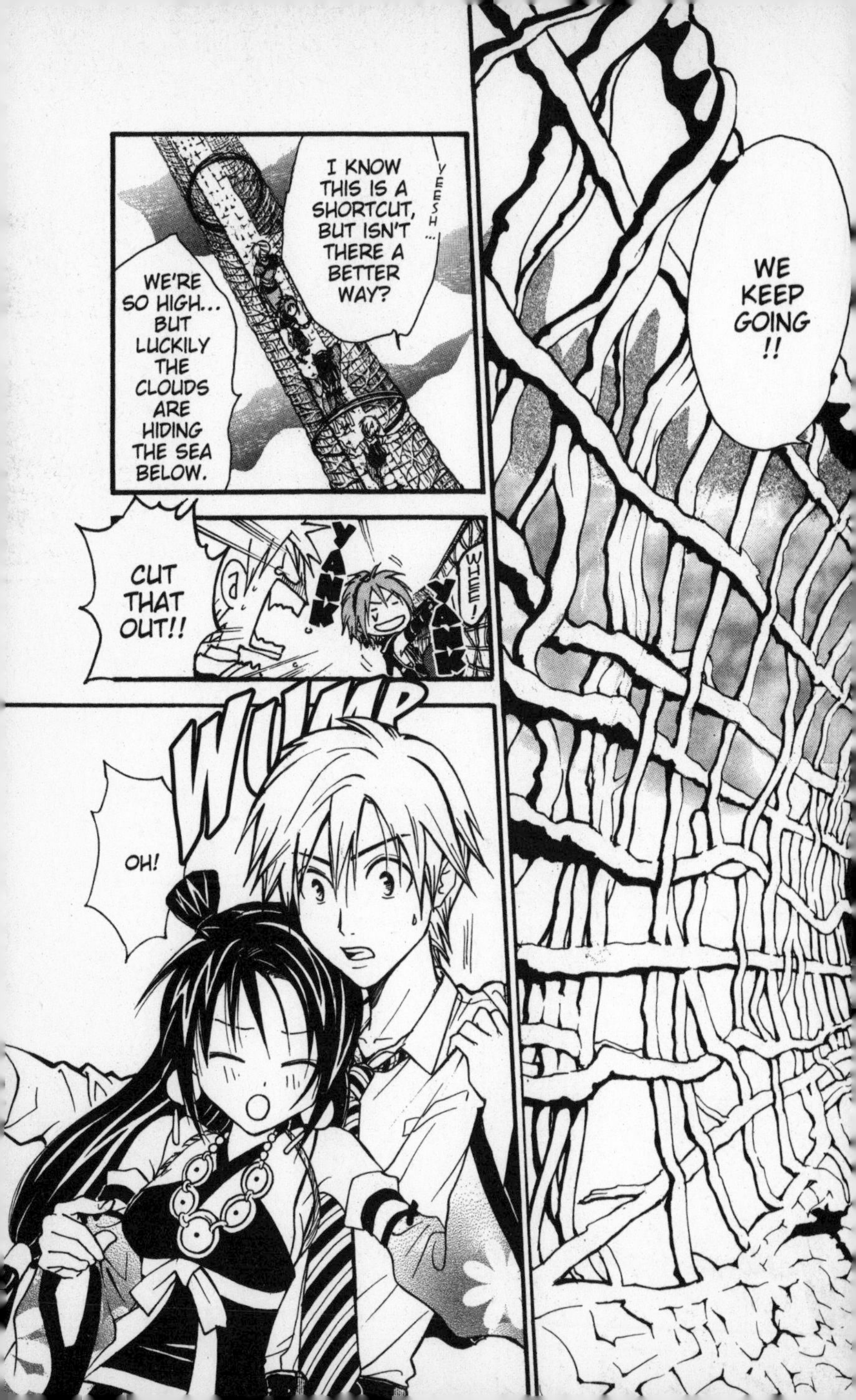
WE KEEP GOING!!
YEESH...
I KNOW THIS IS A SHORTCUT, BUT ISN'T THERE A BETTER WAY?
WE'RE SO HIGH... BUT LUCKILY THE CLOUDS ARE HIDING THE SEA BELOW.
YANK
WHEE!
YANK
CUT THAT OUT!!
WHUMP
OH!

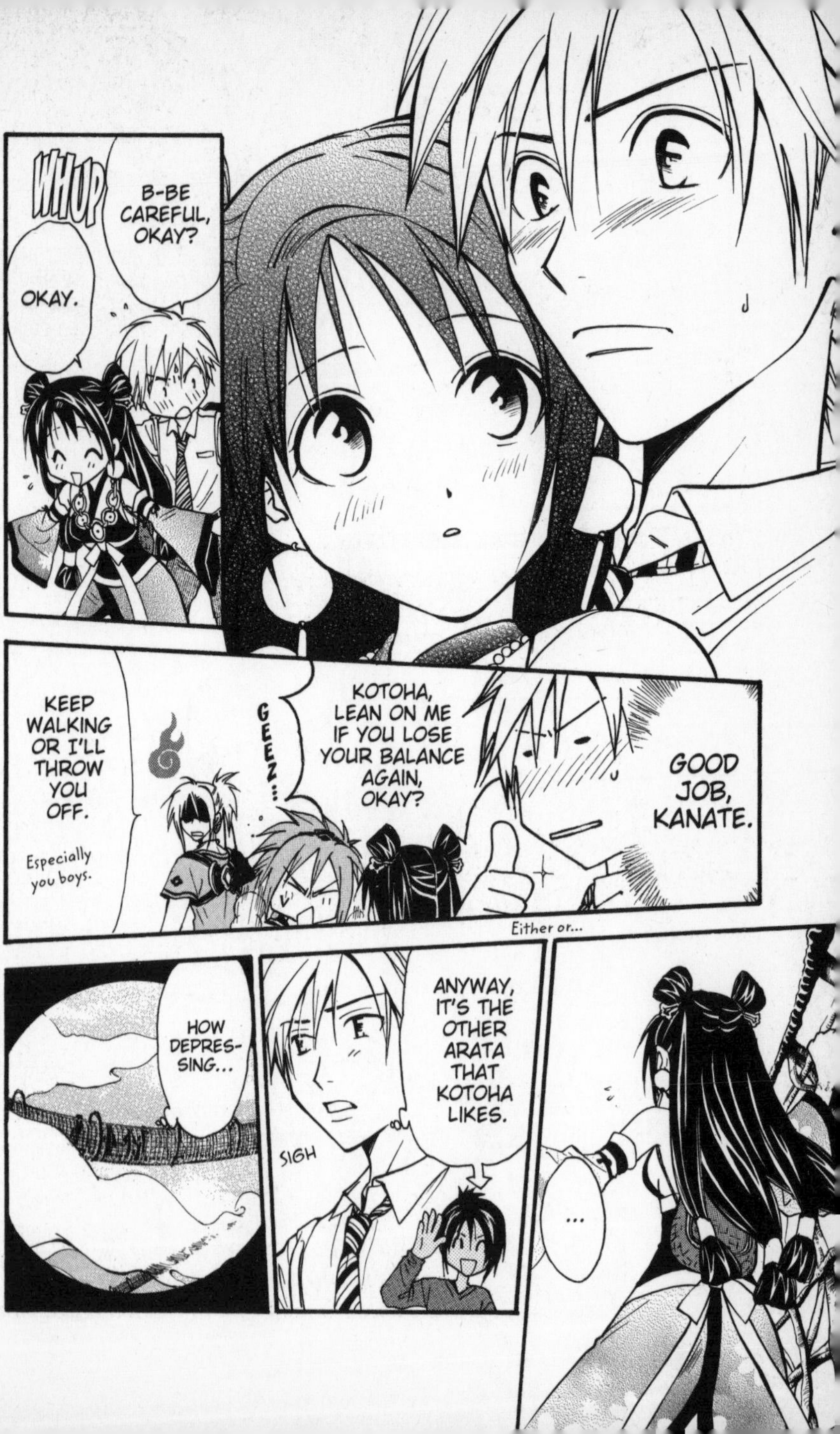
B-BE CAREFUL, OKAY?
WHUP
OKAY.
GOOD JOB, KANATE.
KOTOHA, LEAN ON ME IF YOU LOSE YOUR BALANCE AGAIN, OKAY?
GEEZ...
KEEP WALKING OR I'LL THROW YOU OFF.
Especially you boys.
Either or...
...
ANYWAY, IT'S THE OTHER ARATA THAT KOTOHA LIKES.
SIGH
HOW DEPRES-SING...

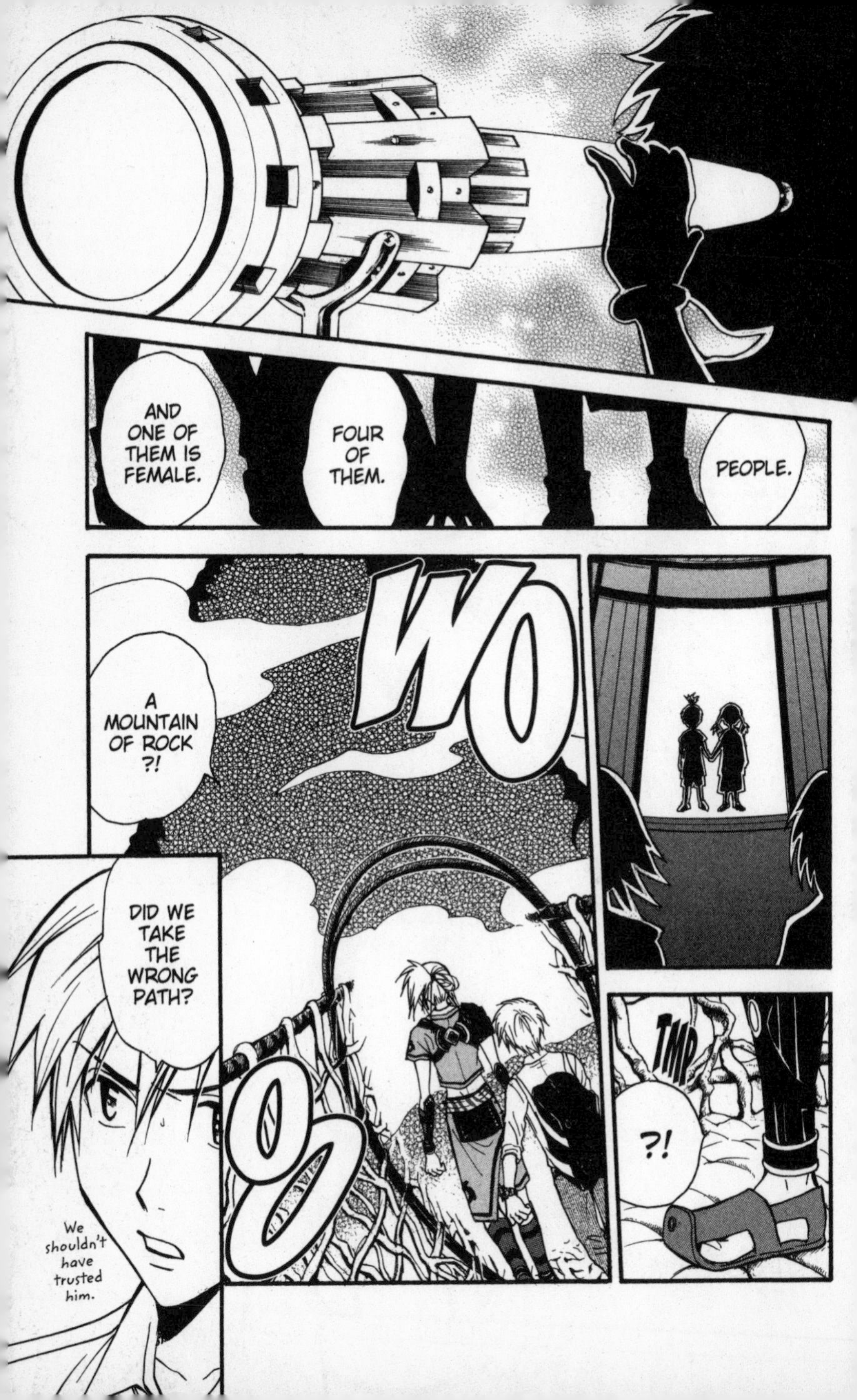
PEOPLE.
FOUR OF THEM.
AND ONE OF THEM IS FEMALE.
TMP
?!
WO
A MOUNTAIN OF ROCK ?!
DID WE TAKE THE WRONG PATH?
We shouldn't have trusted him.

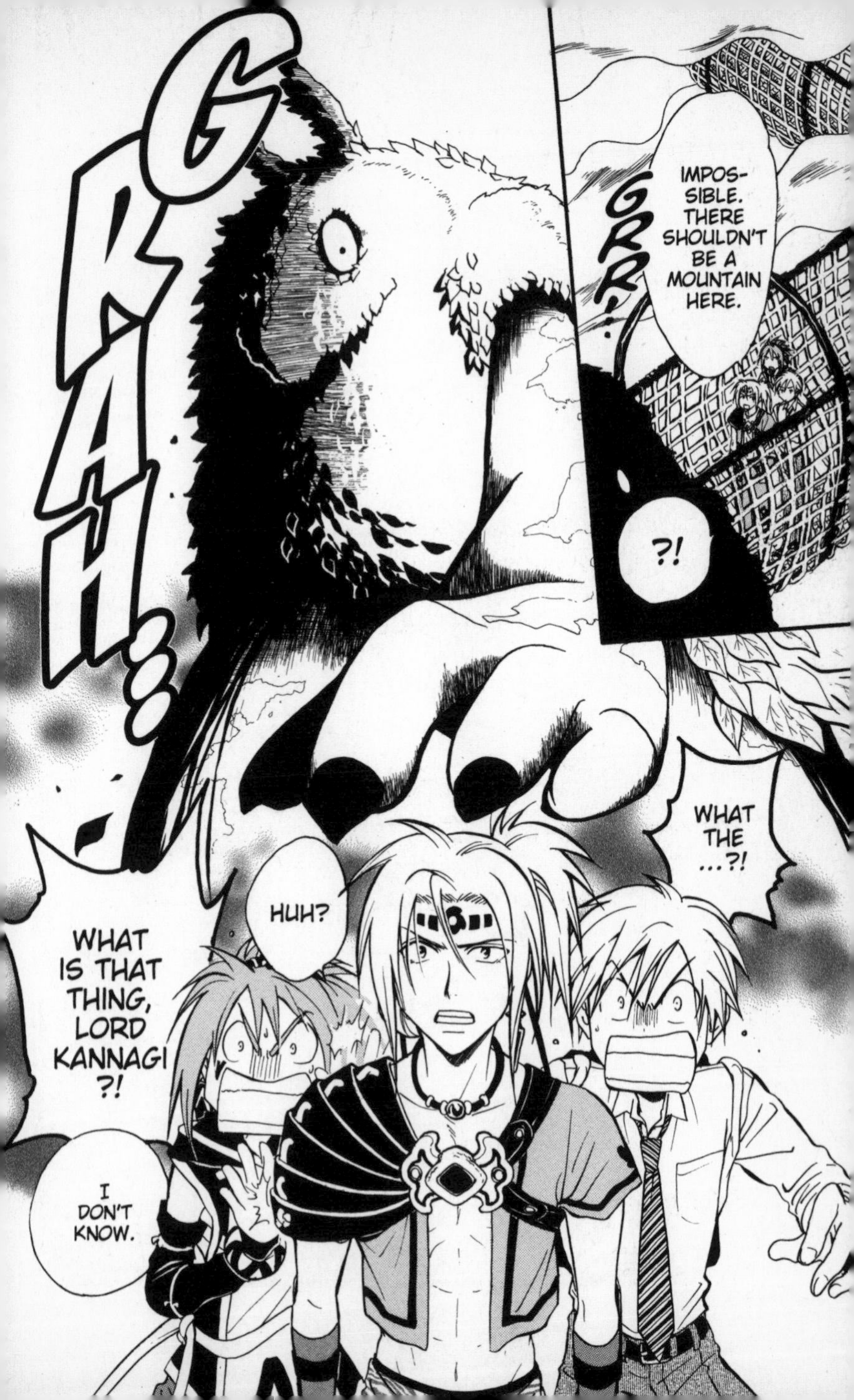
GRR!
IMPOSSIBLE. THERE SHOULDN'T BE A MOUNTAIN HERE.
?!
GRKAH...
WHAT THE ...?!
HUH?
WHAT IS THAT THING, LORD KANNAGI ?!
I DON'T KNOW.

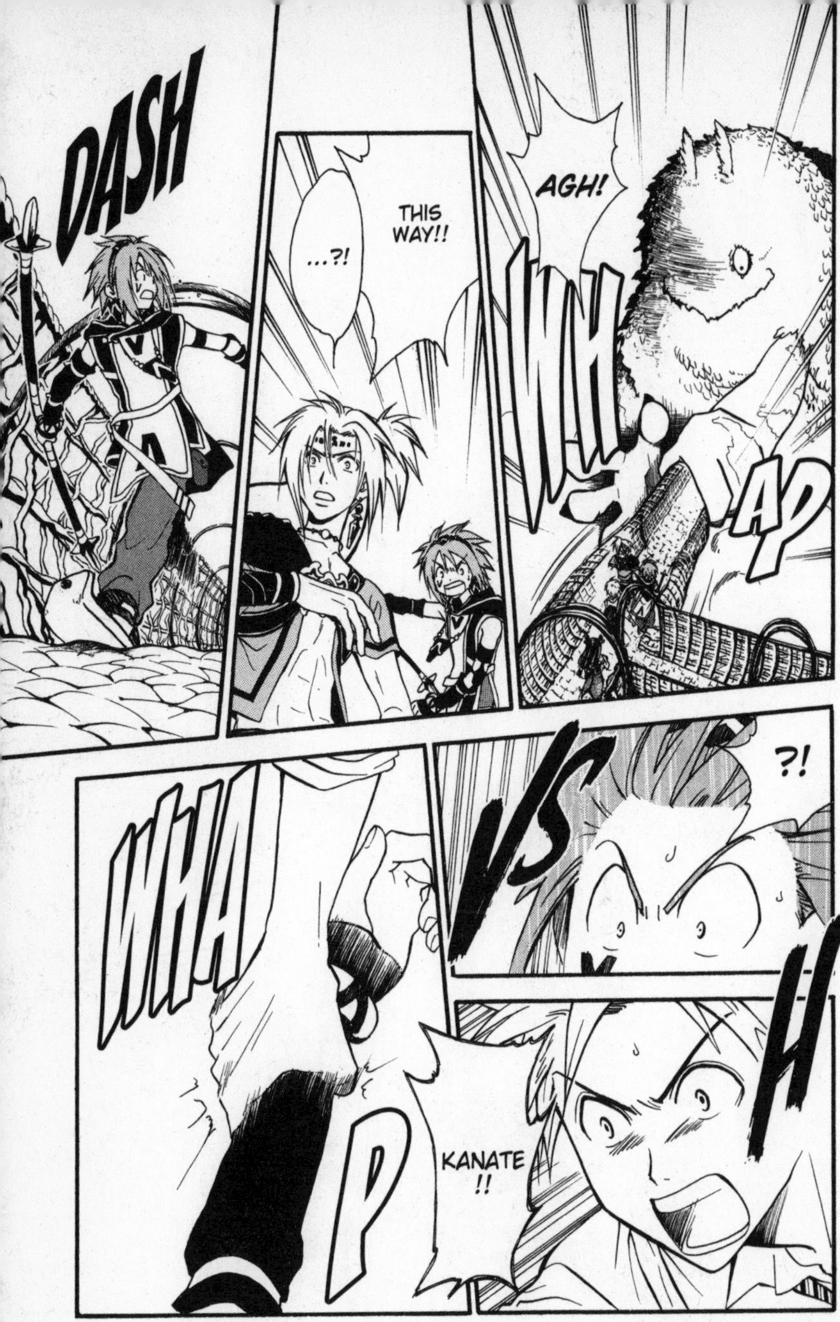
AGH!
WH
AP
THIS WAY!!
...?!
DASH
?!
VS
H
KANATE !!
WHA
P

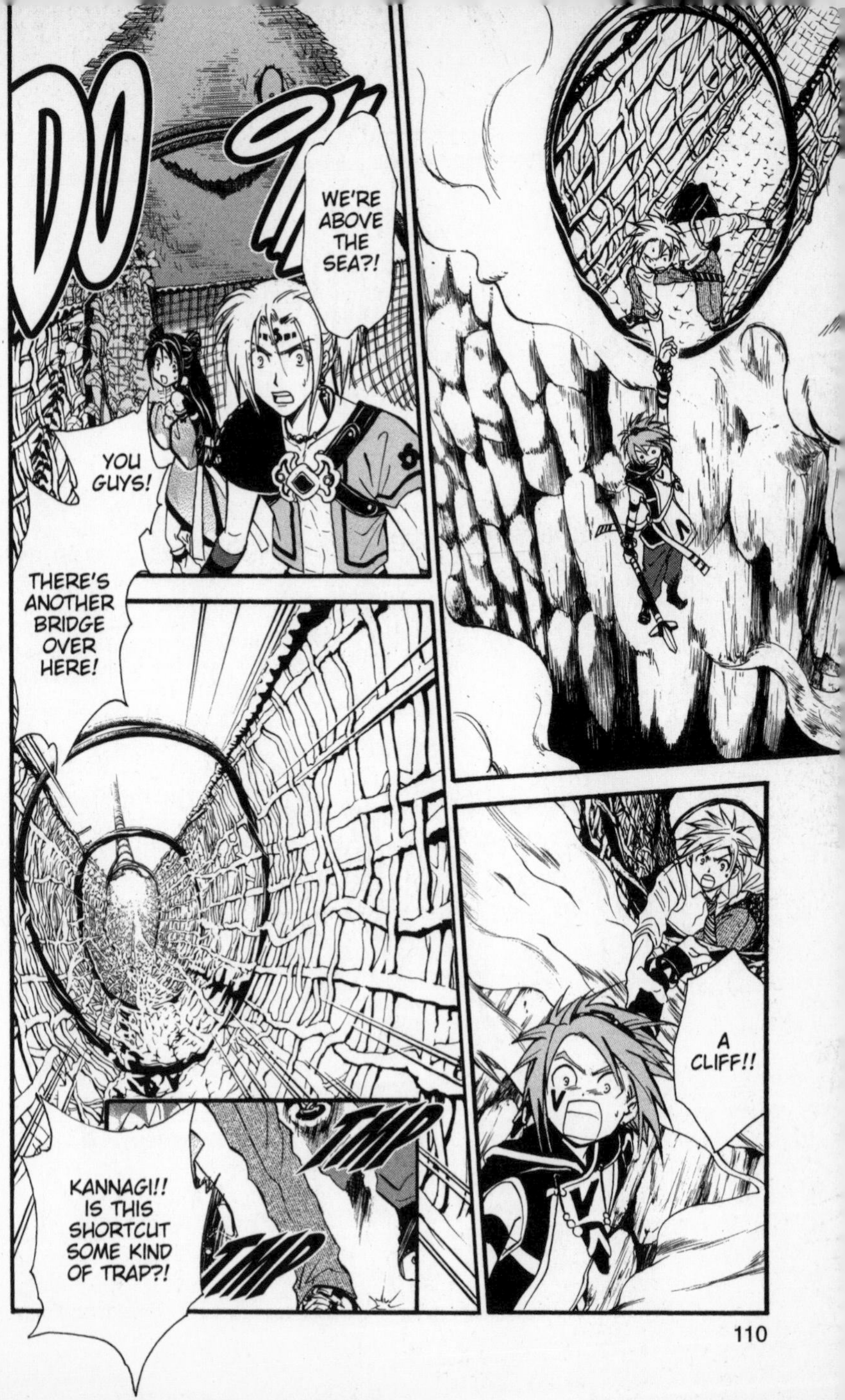
DO
WE'RE ABOVE THE SEA?!
YOU GUYS!
THERE'S ANOTHER BRIDGE OVER HERE!
A CLIFF!!
KANNAGI!! IS THIS SHORTCUT SOME KIND OF TRAP?!

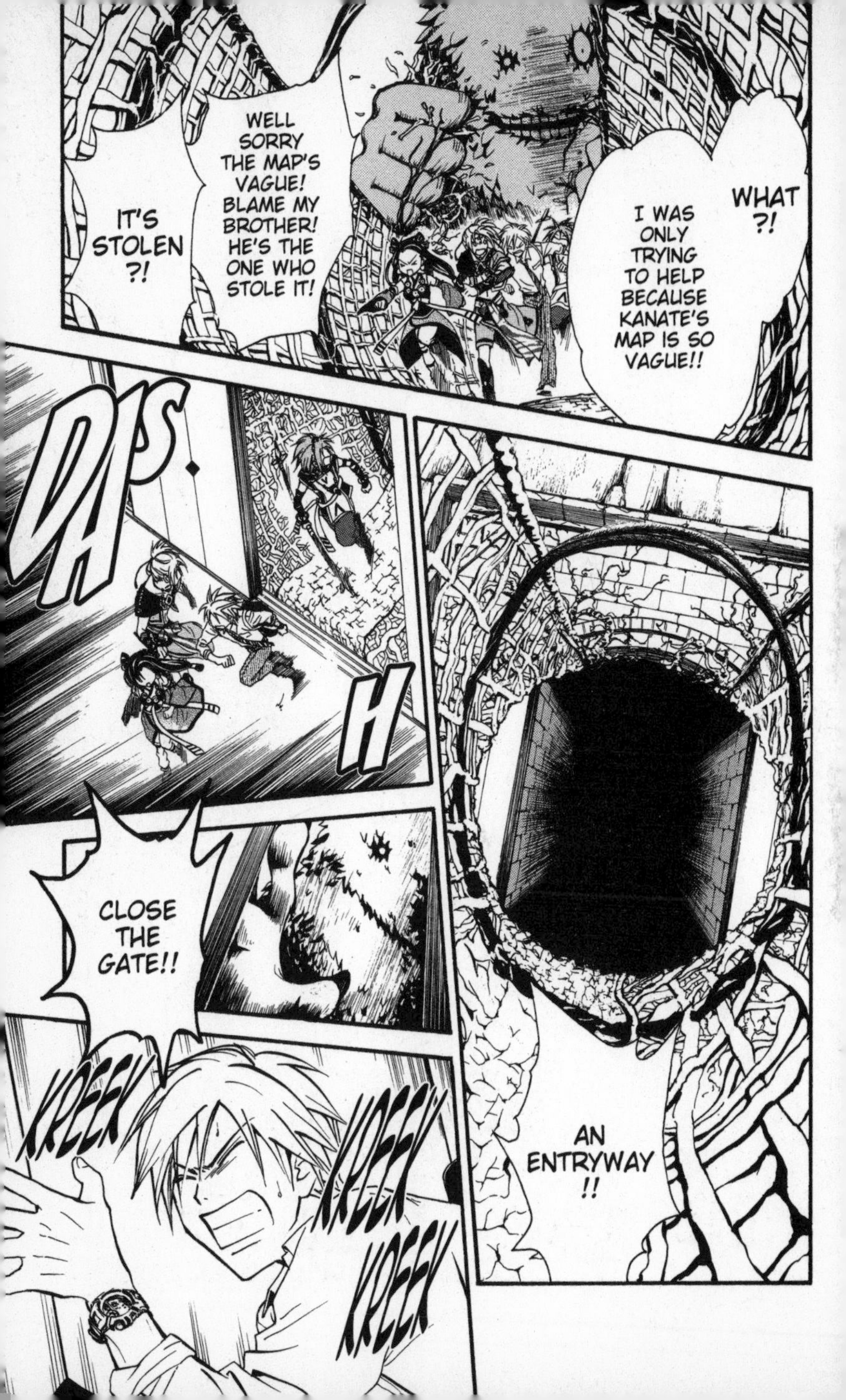
WHAT?!
I WAS ONLY TRYING TO HELP BECAUSE KANATE'S MAP IS SO VAGUE!!
WELL SORRY THE MAP'S VAGUE! BLAME MY BROTHER! HE'S THE ONE WHO STOLE IT!
IT'S STOLEN?!
AN ENTRYWAY!!
DASH
CLOSE THE GATE!!
KREEK
KREEK
KREEK
KREEK

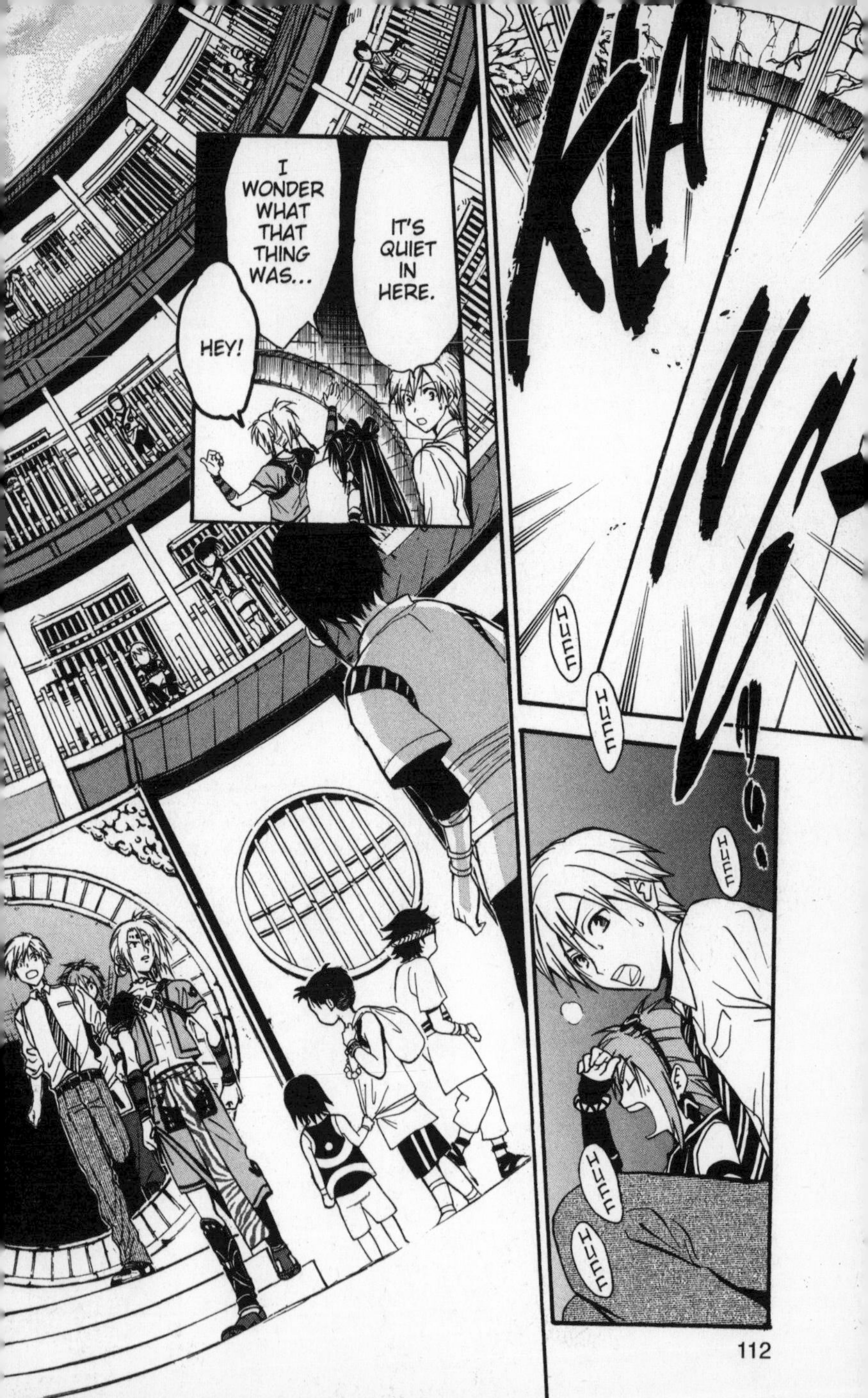
KLANNG!!
HUFF
HUFF
HUFF
HUFF
HUFF
IT'S QUIET IN HERE.
I WONDER WHAT THAT THING WAS...
HEY!

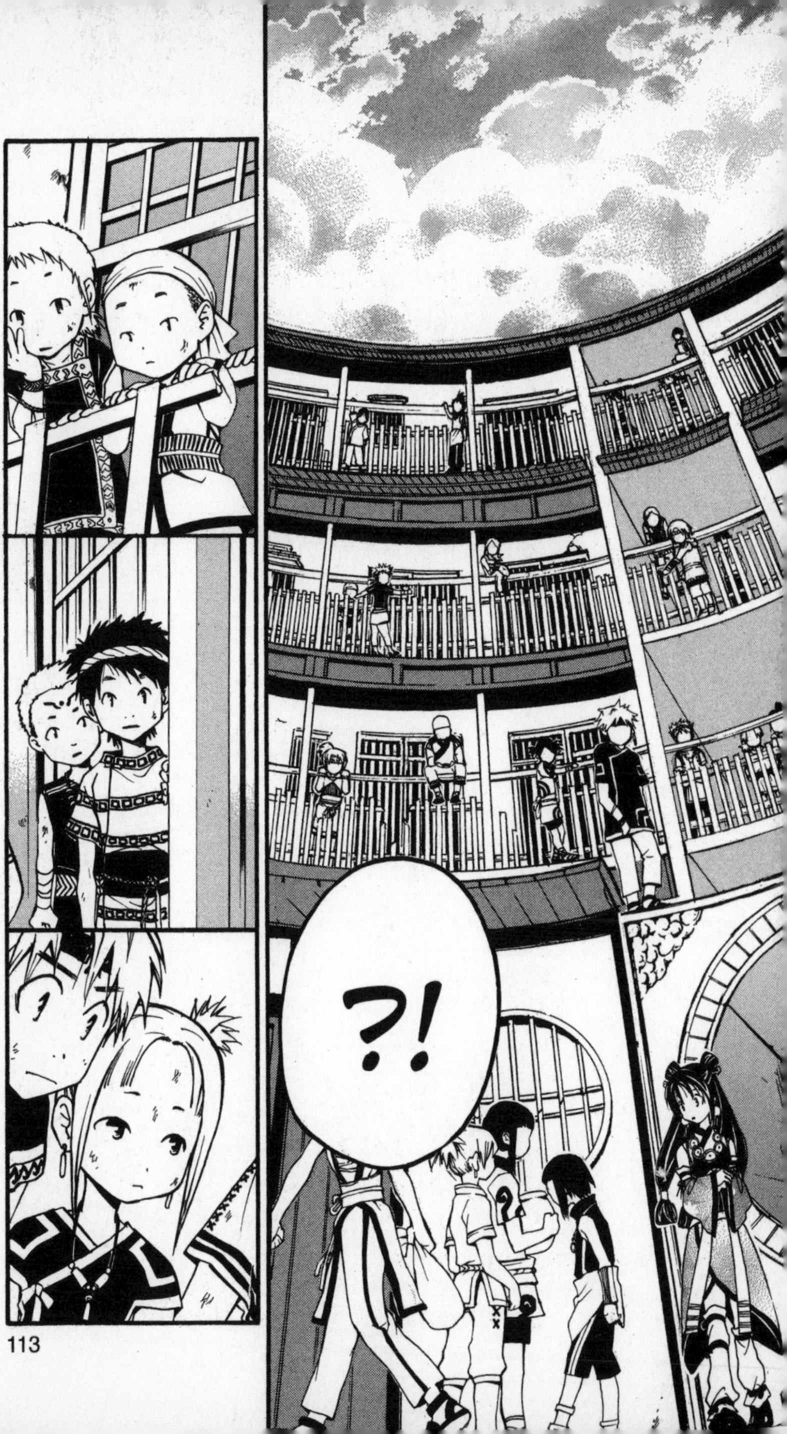
?!

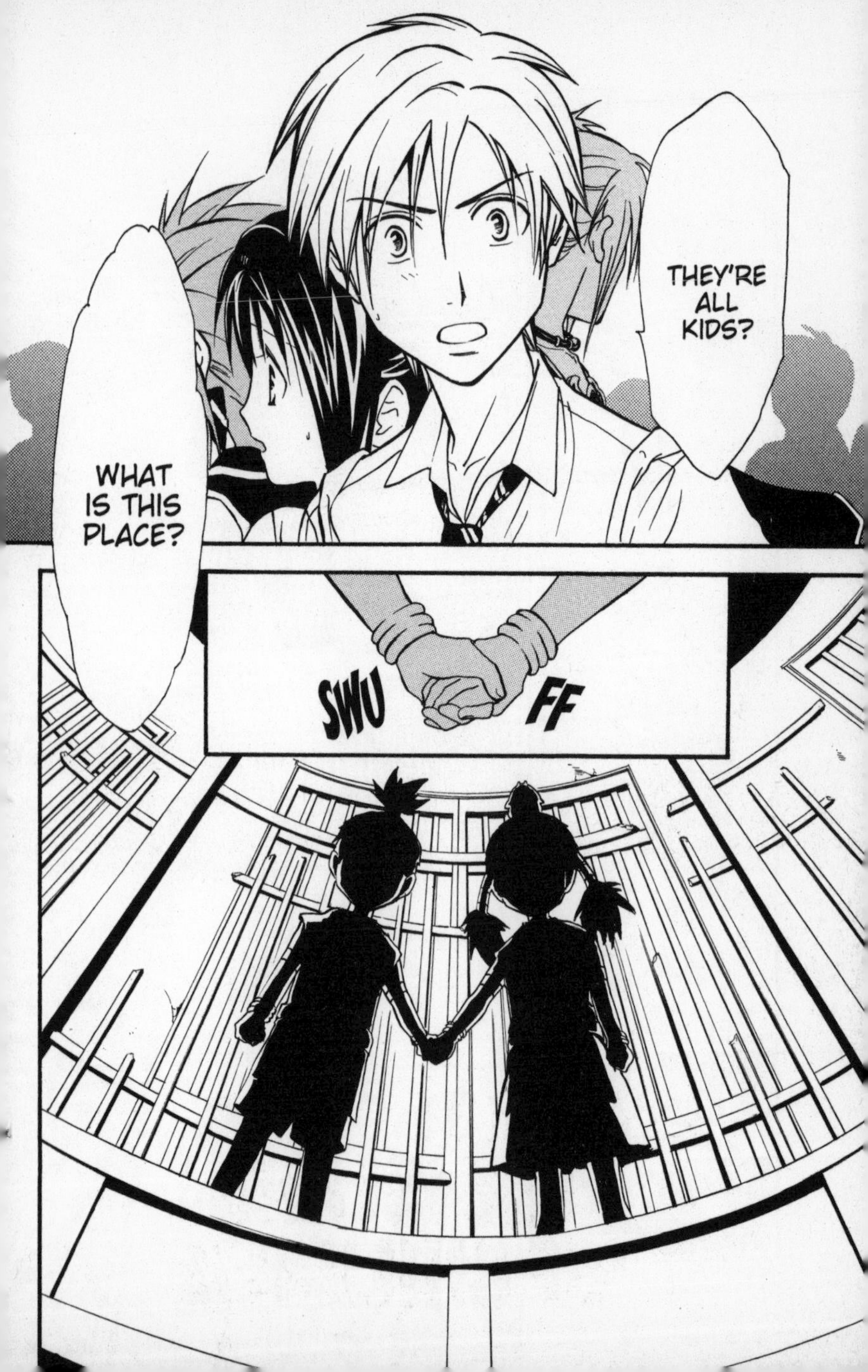
THEY'RE ALL KIDS?
WHAT IS THIS PLACE?
SWUFF

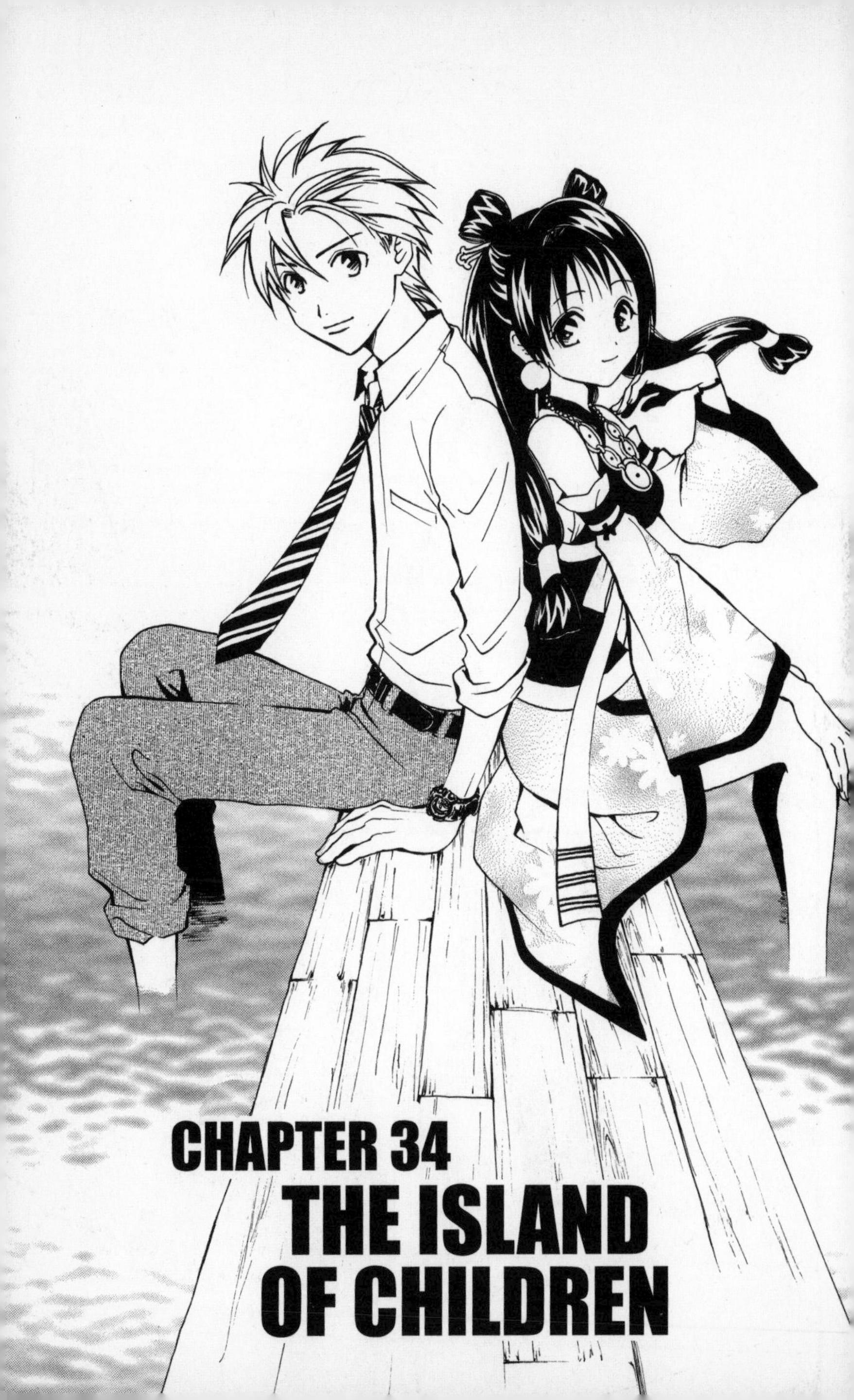
CHAPTER 34
THE ISLAND OF CHILDREN

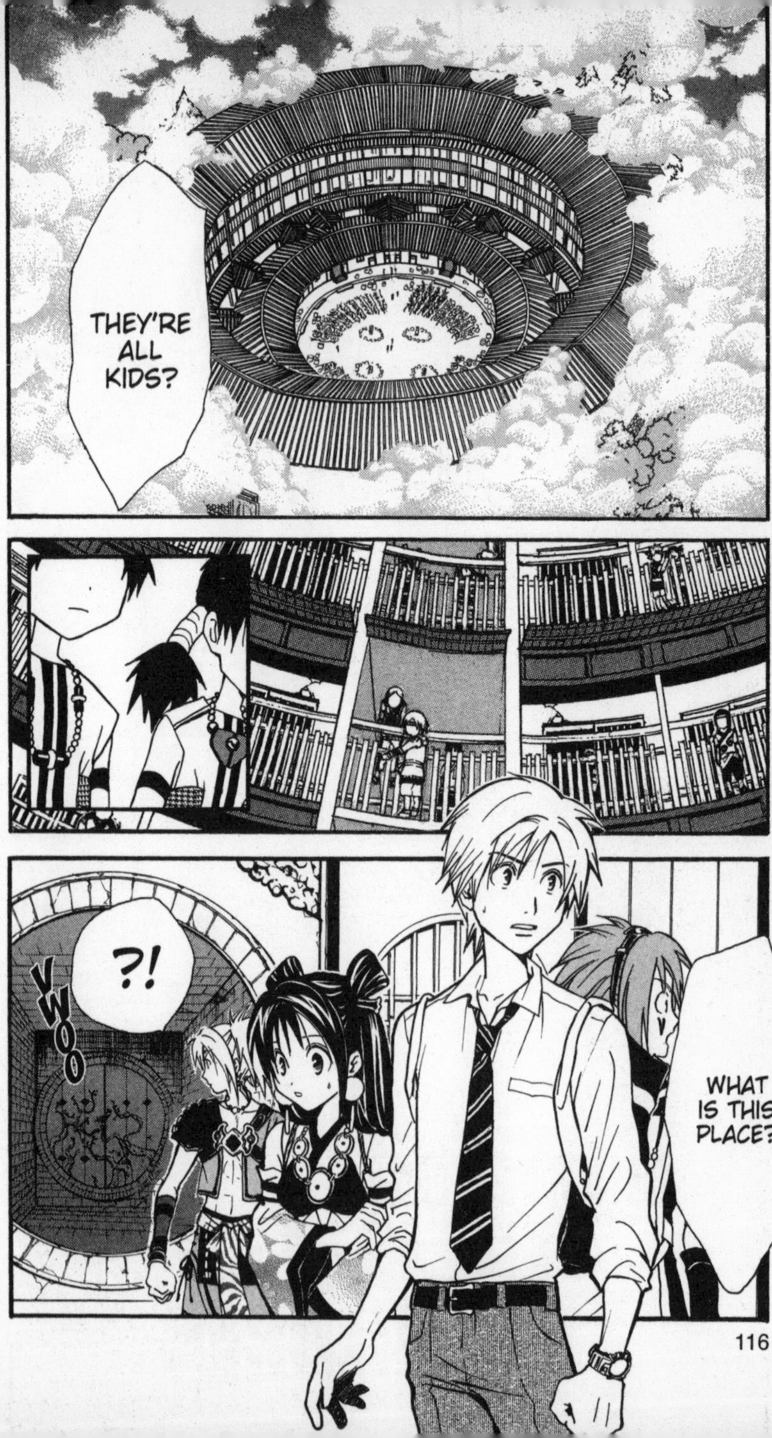
THEY'RE ALL KIDS?
WHAT IS THIS PLACE?
?!
VWOO

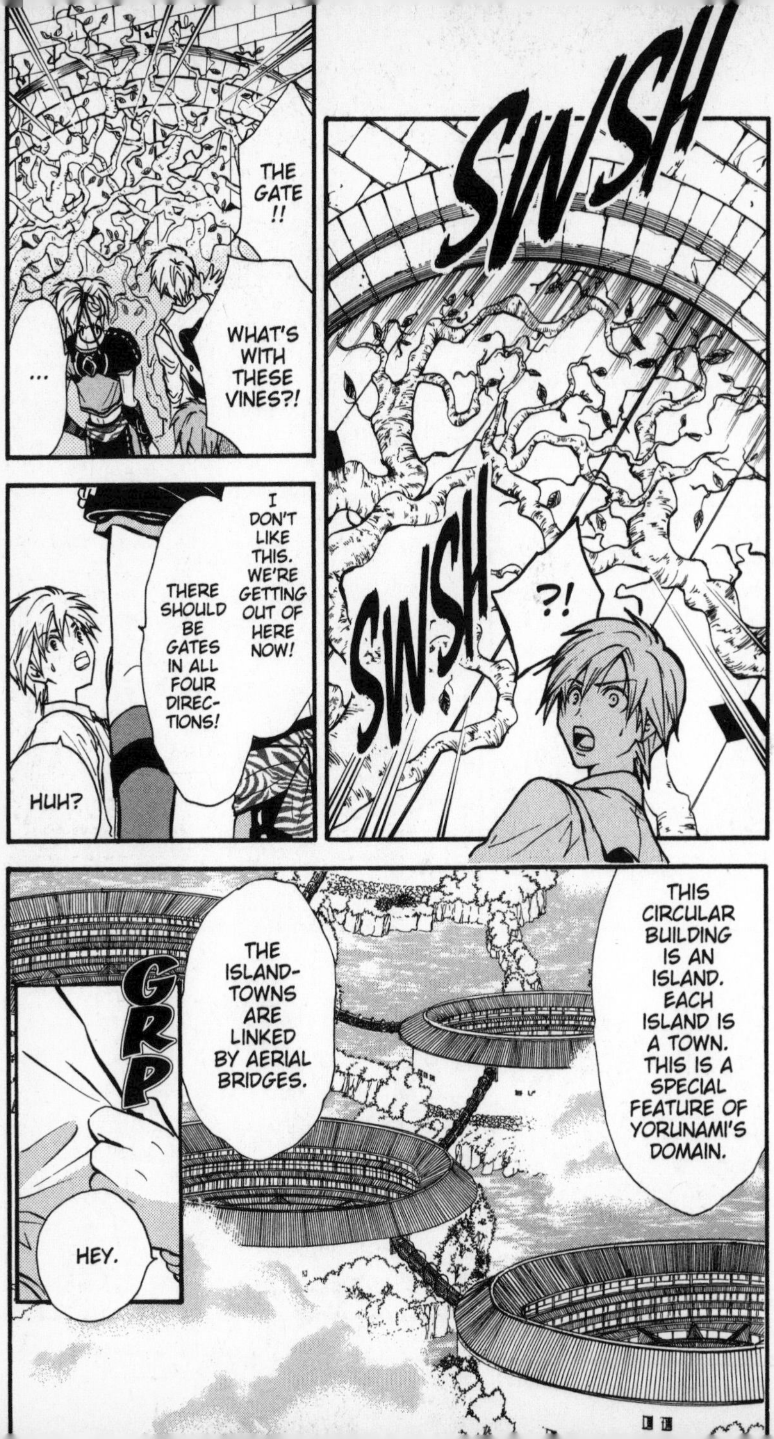
SWISH
SWISH
?!
THE GATE!!
WHAT'S WITH THESE VINES?!
...
I DON'T LIKE THIS. WE'RE GETTING OUT OF HERE NOW!
THERE SHOULD BE GATES IN ALL FOUR DIRECTIONS!
HUH?
THIS CIRCULAR BUILDING IS AN ISLAND. EACH ISLAND IS A TOWN. THIS IS A SPECIAL FEATURE OF YORUNAMI'S DOMAIN.
THE ISLAND-TOWNS ARE LINKED BY AERIAL BRIDGES.
GRP
HEY.

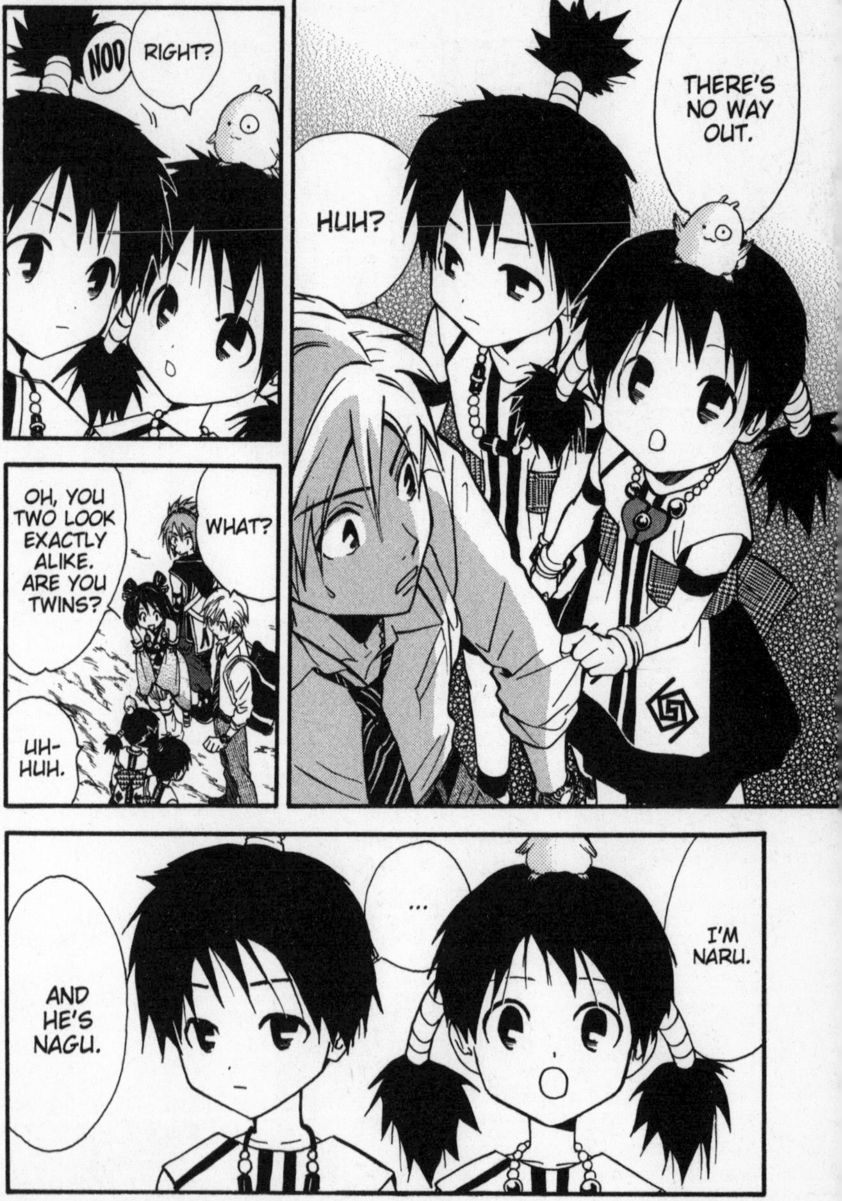
THERE'S NO WAY OUT.
HUH?
RIGHT?
NOD
WHAT?
OH, YOU TWO LOOK EXACTLY ALIKE. ARE YOU TWINS?
UH-HUH.
I'M NARU.
...
AND HE'S NAGU.

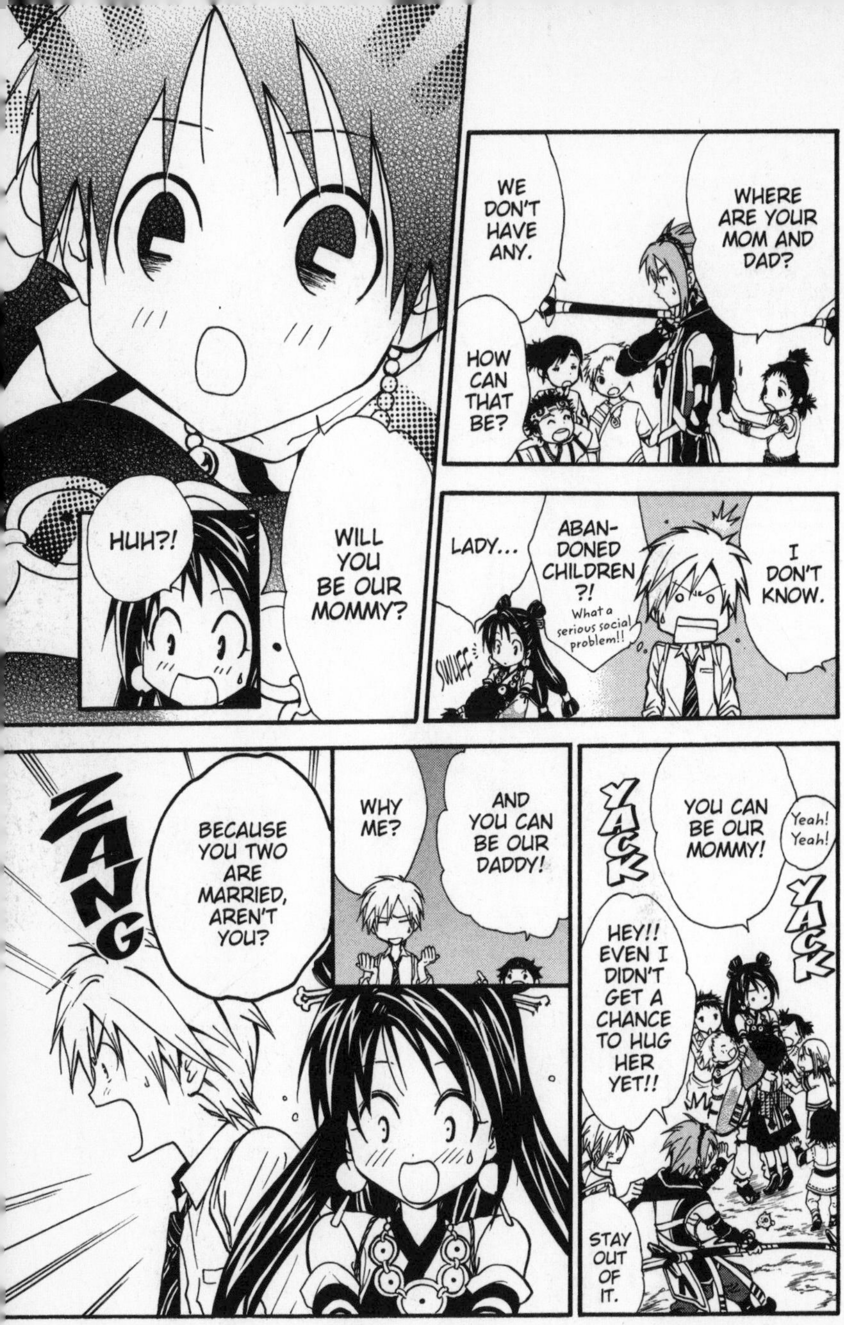
WHERE ARE YOUR MOM AND DAD?
WE DON'T HAVE ANY.
HOW CAN THAT BE?
I DON'T KNOW.
ABAN-DONED CHILDREN ?!
What a serious social problem!!
SWUFF
LADY...
WILL YOU BE OUR MOMMY?
HUH?!
YACK
YOU CAN BE OUR MOMMY!
Yeah! Yeah!
YACK
HEY!! EVEN I DIDN'T GET A CHANCE TO HUG HER YET!!
STAY OUT OF IT.
AND YOU CAN BE OUR DADDY!
WHY ME?
ZANG
BECAUSE YOU TWO ARE MARRIED, AREN'T YOU?

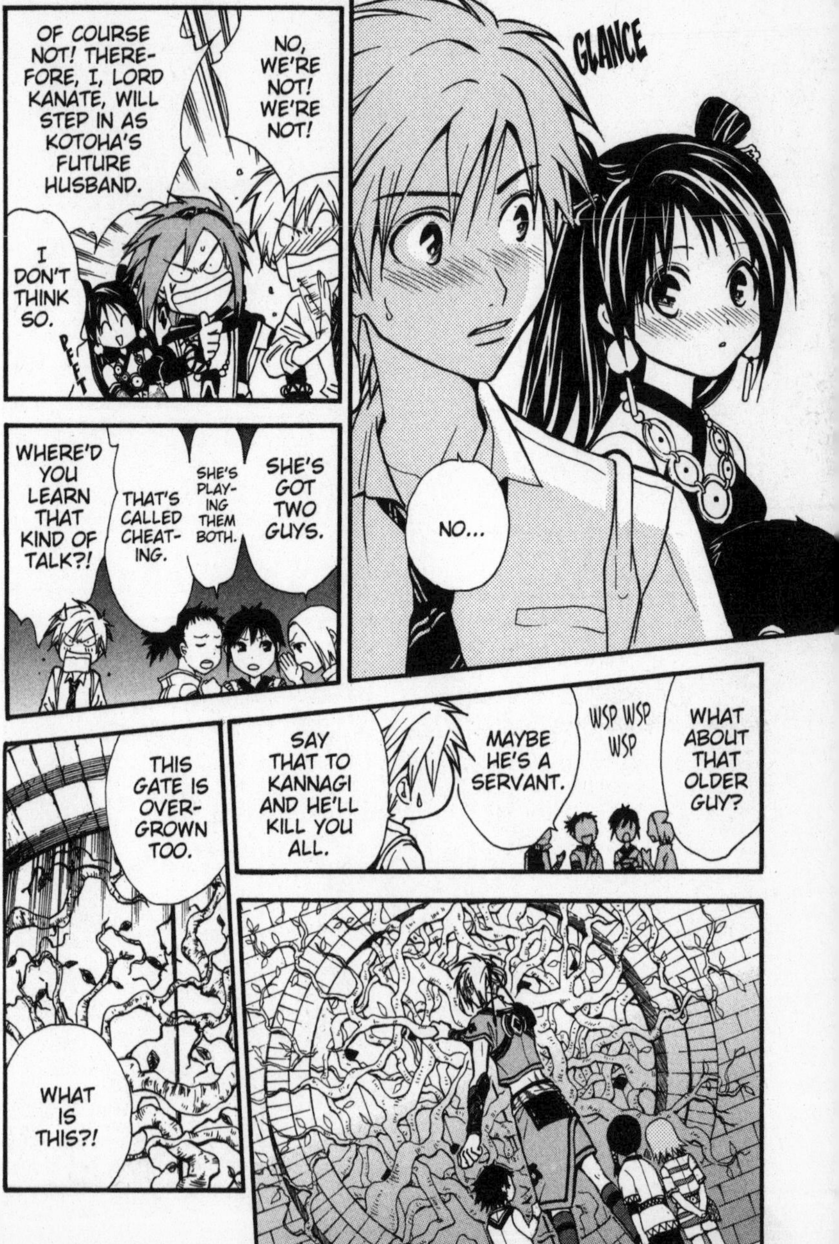
GLANCE
NO...
NO, WE'RE NOT! WE'RE NOT!
OF COURSE NOT! THEREFORE, I, LORD KANATE, WILL STEP IN AS KOTOHA'S FUTURE HUSBAND.
I DON'T THINK SO.
PEET
SHE'S GOT TWO GUYS.
SHE'S PLAYING THEM BOTH.
THAT'S CALLED CHEATING.
WHERE'D YOU LEARN THAT KIND OF TALK?!
WHAT ABOUT THAT OLDER GUY?
WSP WSP WSP
MAYBE HE'S A SERVANT.
SAY THAT TO KANNAGI AND HE'LL KILL YOU ALL.
THIS GATE IS OVERGROWN TOO.
WHAT IS THIS?!

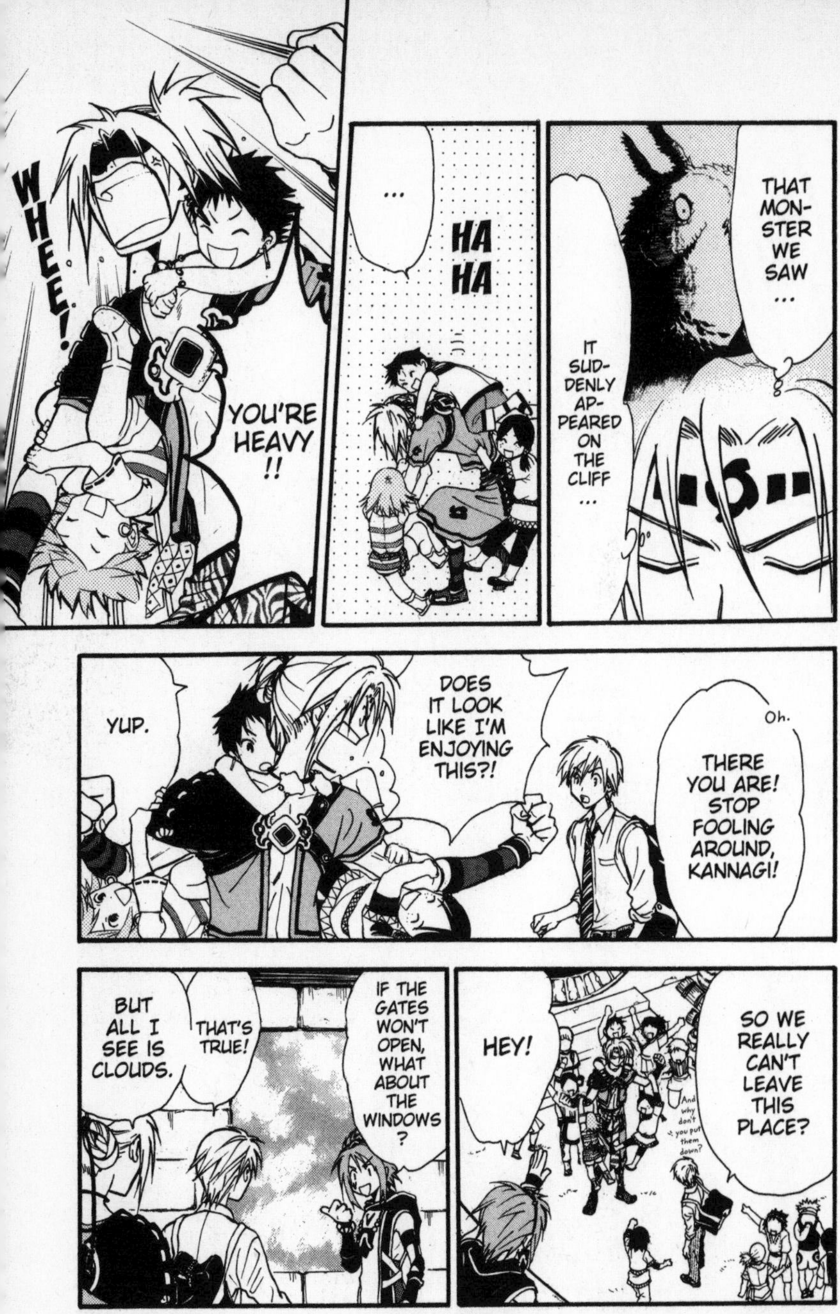
THAT MONSTER WE SAW ...
IT SUDDENLY APPEARED ON THE CLIFF ...
...
HA HA
WHEE!
YOU'RE HEAVY !!
Oh.
THERE YOU ARE! STOP FOOLING AROUND, KANNAGI!
DOES IT LOOK LIKE I'M ENJOYING THIS?!
YUP.
SO WE REALLY CAN'T LEAVE THIS PLACE?
And why don't you put them down?
HEY!
IF THE GATES WON'T OPEN, WHAT ABOUT THE WINDOWS ?
THAT'S TRUE!
BUT ALL I SEE IS CLOUDS.

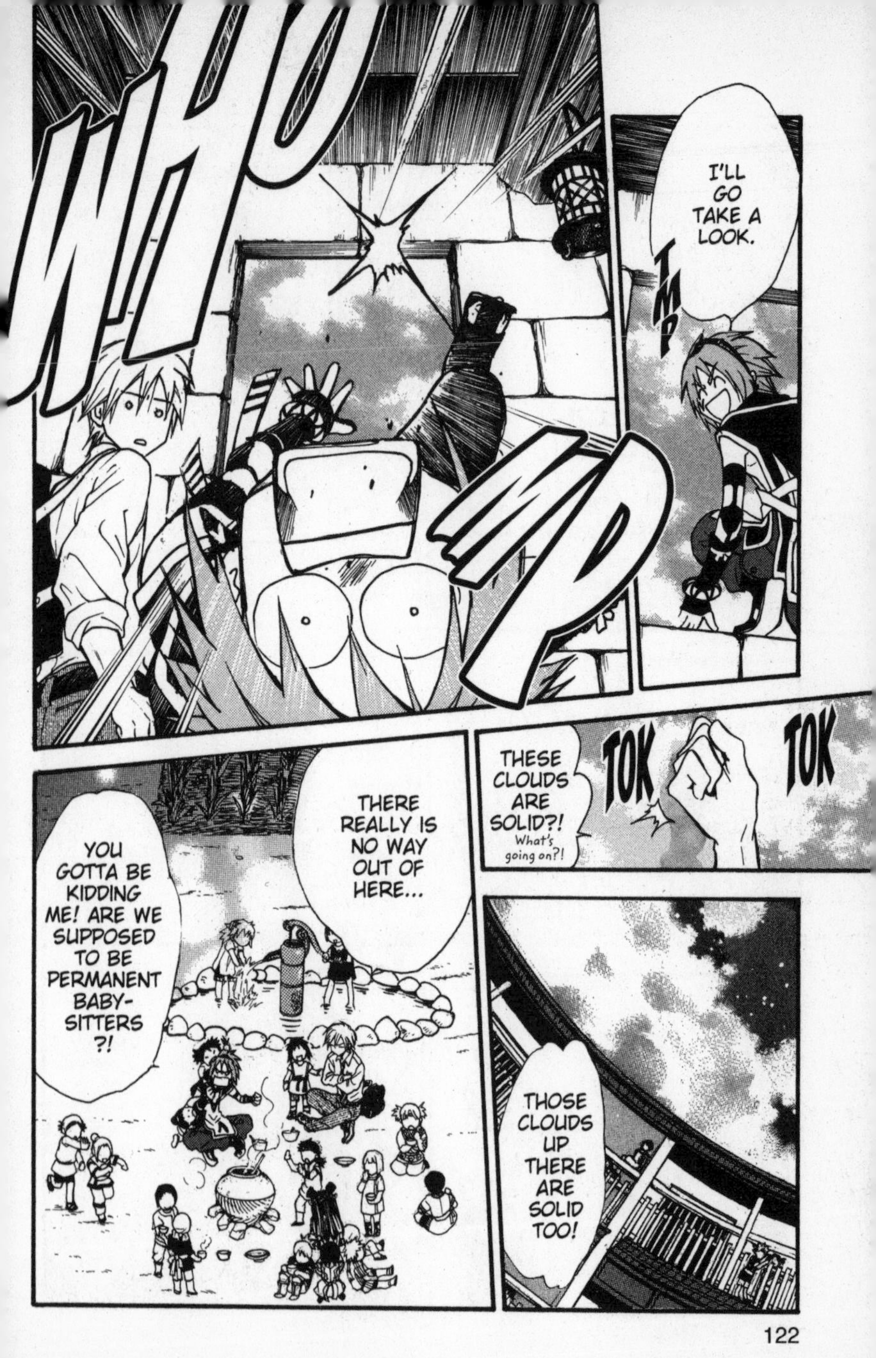
I'LL GO TAKE A LOOK.
TMP
WHU
MP
TOK
TOK
THESE CLOUDS ARE SOLID?!
What's going on?!
THOSE CLOUDS UP THERE ARE SOLID TOO!
THERE REALLY IS NO WAY OUT OF HERE...
YOU GOTTA BE KIDDING ME! ARE WE SUPPOSED TO BE PERMANENT BABY-SITTERS?!

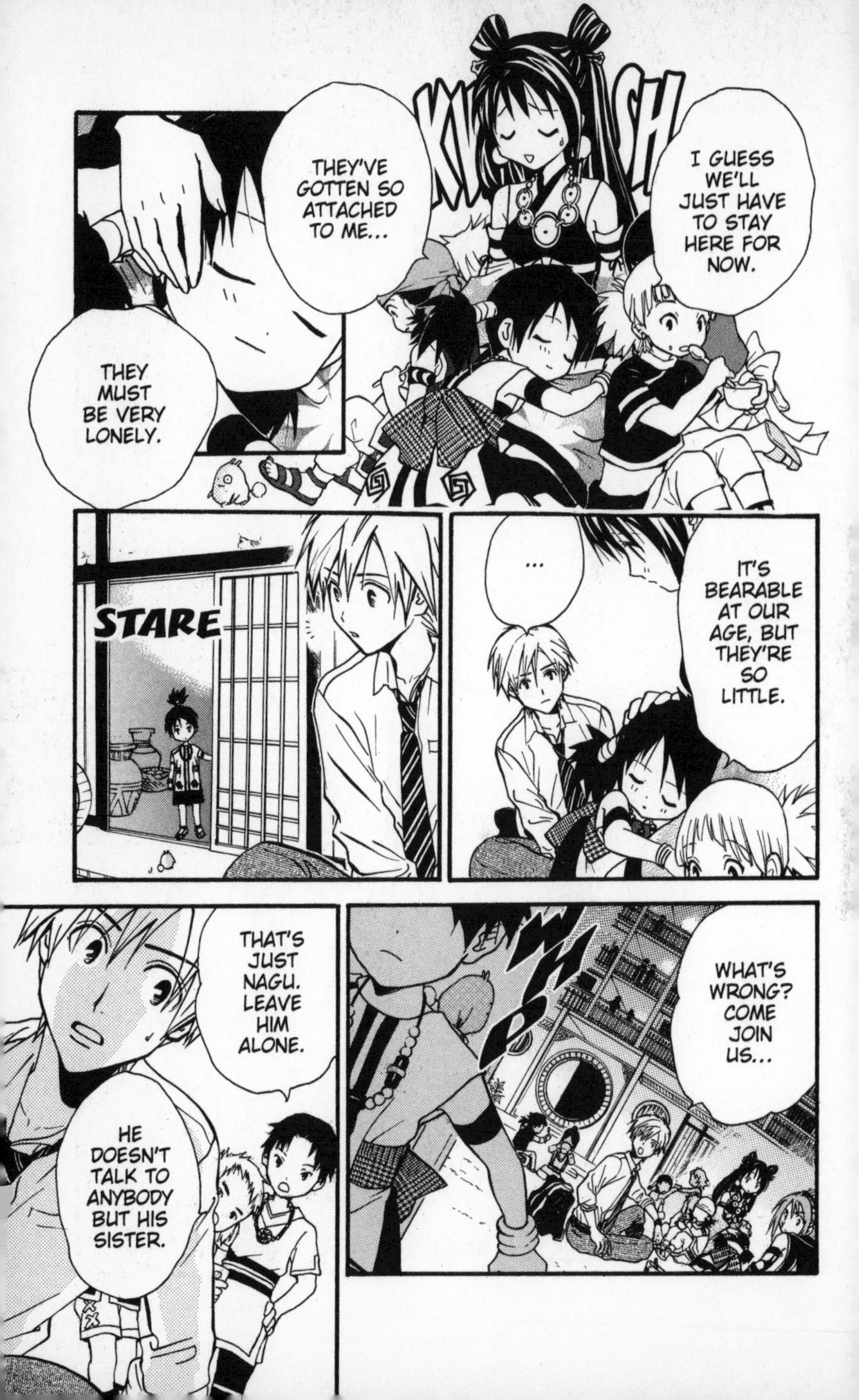
I GUESS WE'LL JUST HAVE TO STAY HERE FOR NOW.
THEY'VE GOTTEN SO ATTACHED TO ME...
THEY MUST BE VERY LONELY.
IT'S BEARABLE AT OUR AGE, BUT THEY'RE SO LITTLE.
...
STARE
WHAT'S WRONG? COME JOIN US...
THAT'S JUST NAGU. LEAVE HIM ALONE.
HE DOESN'T TALK TO ANYBODY BUT HIS SISTER.

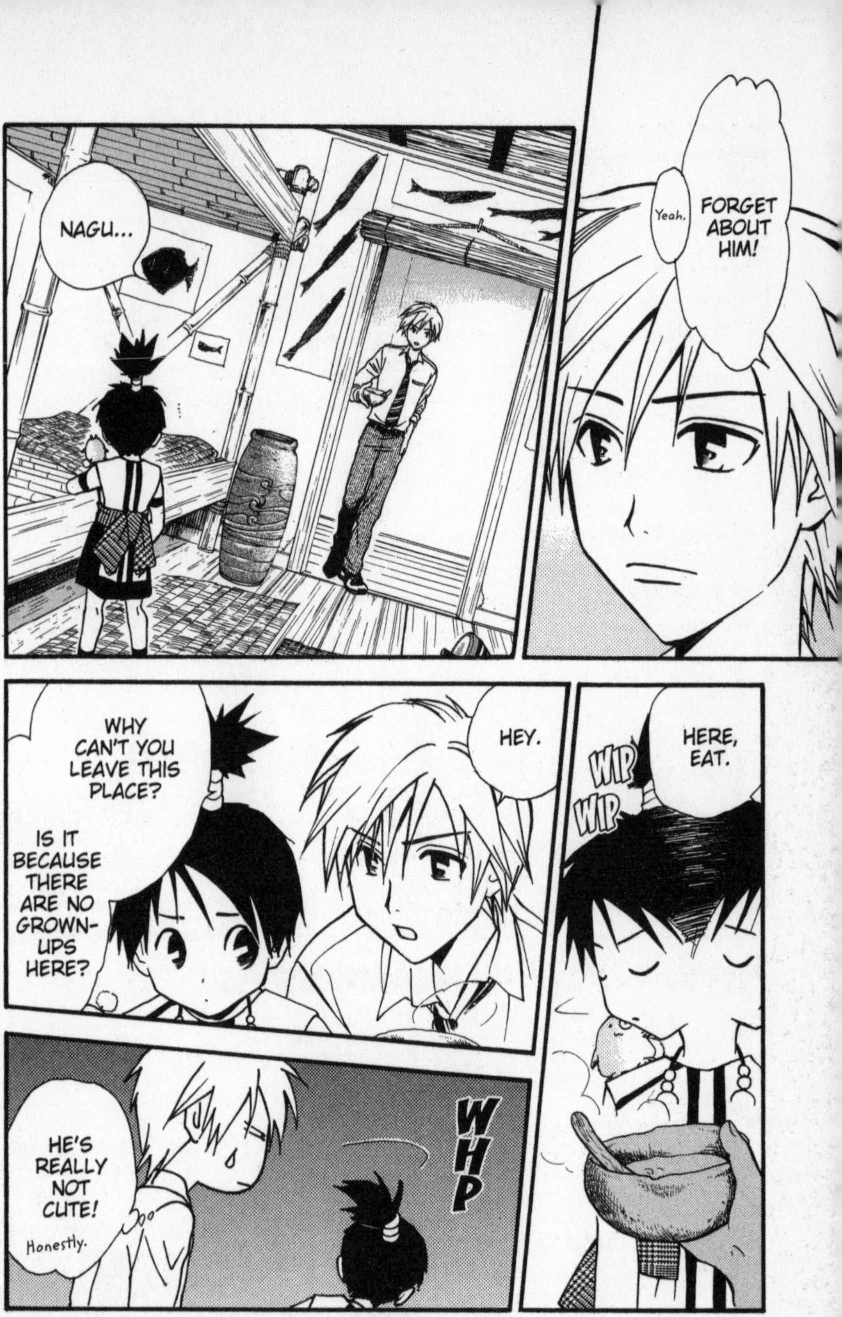
FORGET ABOUT HIM!
Yeah.
NAGU...
HERE, EAT.
WIP WIP
HEY.
WHY CAN'T YOU LEAVE THIS PLACE?
IS IT BECAUSE THERE ARE NO GROWN-UPS HERE?
WHP
HE'S REALLY NOT CUTE!
Honestly.

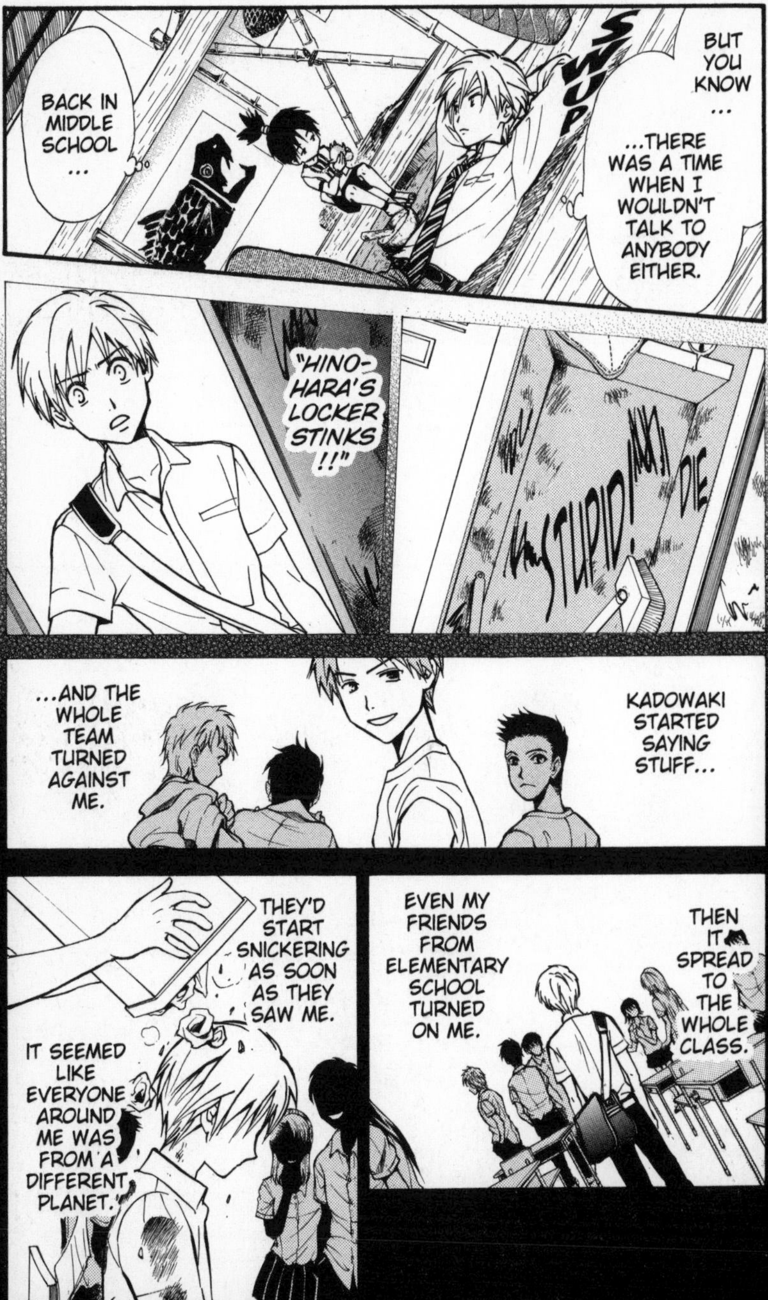
BUT YOU KNOW...
SWUP
...THERE WAS A TIME WHEN I WOULDN'T TALK TO ANYBODY EITHER.
BACK IN MIDDLE SCHOOL...
STUPID!
DIE
"HINO-HARA'S LOCKER STINKS!!"
KADOWAKI STARTED SAYING STUFF...
...AND THE WHOLE TEAM TURNED AGAINST ME.
THEN IT SPREAD TO THE WHOLE CLASS.
EVEN MY FRIENDS FROM ELEMENTARY SCHOOL TURNED ON ME.
THEY'D START SNICKERING AS SOON AS THEY SAW ME.
IT SEEMED LIKE EVERYONE AROUND ME WAS FROM A DIFFERENT PLANET.

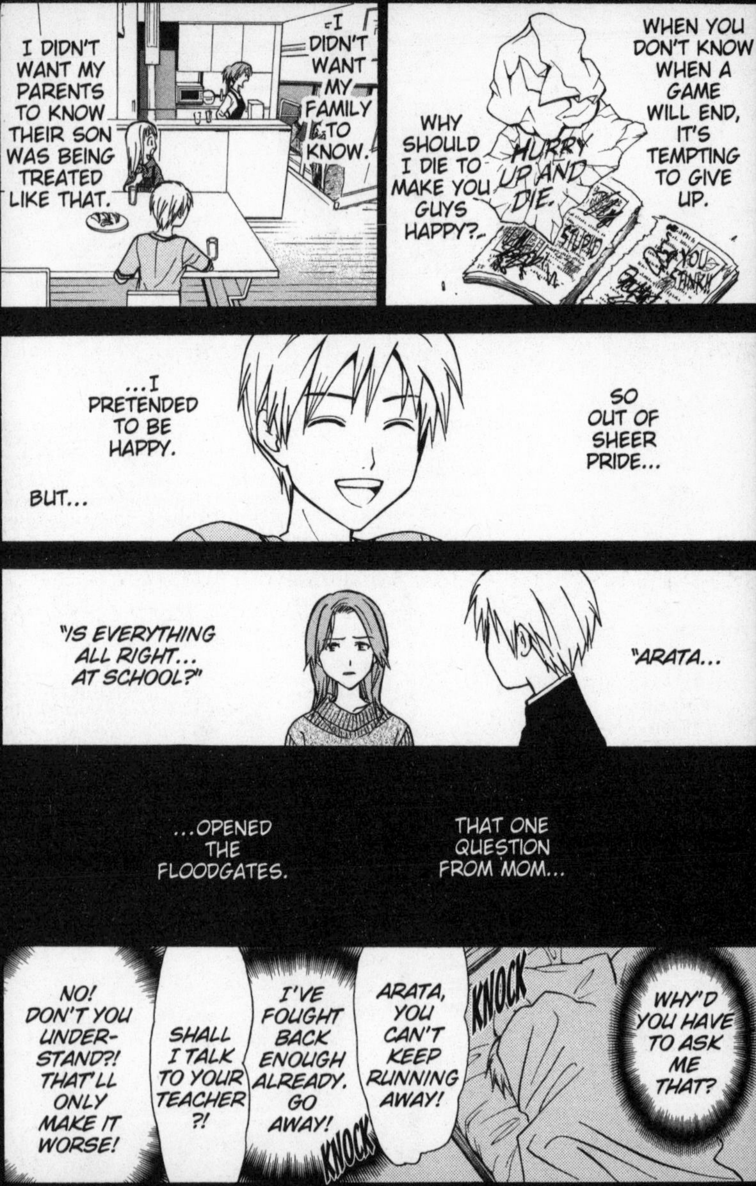
WHEN YOU DON'T KNOW WHEN A GAME WILL END, IT'S TEMPTING TO GIVE UP.
WHY SHOULD I DIE TO MAKE YOU GUYS HAPPY?
HURRY UP AND DIE.
STUPID
I DIDN'T WANT MY FAMILY TO KNOW.
I DIDN'T WANT MY PARENTS TO KNOW THEIR SON WAS BEING TREATED LIKE THAT.
SO OUT OF SHEER PRIDE...
...I PRETENDED TO BE HAPPY.
BUT...
"ARATA...
"IS EVERYTHING ALL RIGHT... AT SCHOOL?"
THAT ONE QUESTION FROM MOM...
...OPENED THE FLOODGATES.
WHY'D YOU HAVE TO ASK ME THAT?
KNOCK
ARATA, YOU CAN'T KEEP RUNNING AWAY!
I'VE FOUGHT BACK ENOUGH ALREADY. GO AWAY!
KNOCK
SHALL I TALK TO YOUR TEACHER?!
NO! DON'T YOU UNDERSTAND?! THAT'LL ONLY MAKE IT WORSE!

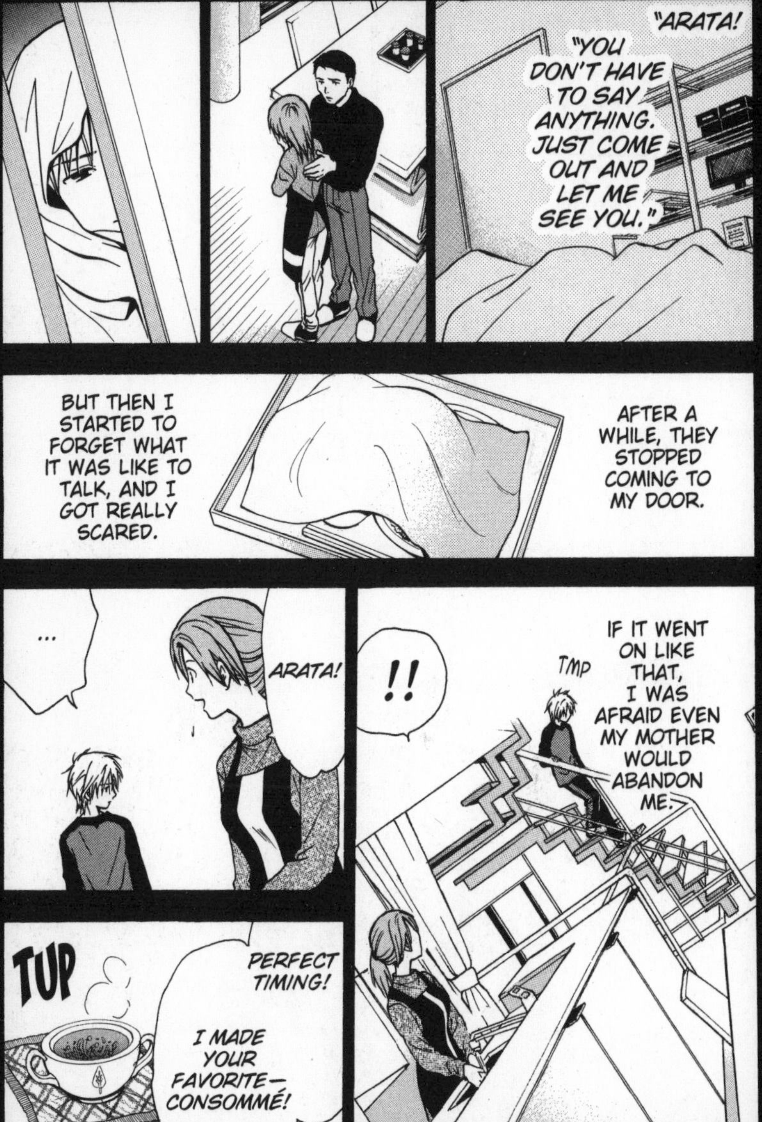
"ARATA!
"YOU DON'T HAVE TO SAY ANYTHING. JUST COME OUT AND LET ME SEE YOU."
AFTER A WHILE, THEY STOPPED COMING TO MY DOOR.
BUT THEN I STARTED TO FORGET WHAT IT WAS LIKE TO TALK, AND I GOT REALLY SCARED.
IF IT WENT ON LIKE THAT, I WAS AFRAID EVEN MY MOTHER WOULD ABANDON ME.
TMP
!!
ARATA!
...
TUP
PERFECT TIMING!
I MADE YOUR FAVORITE—CONSOMMÉ!

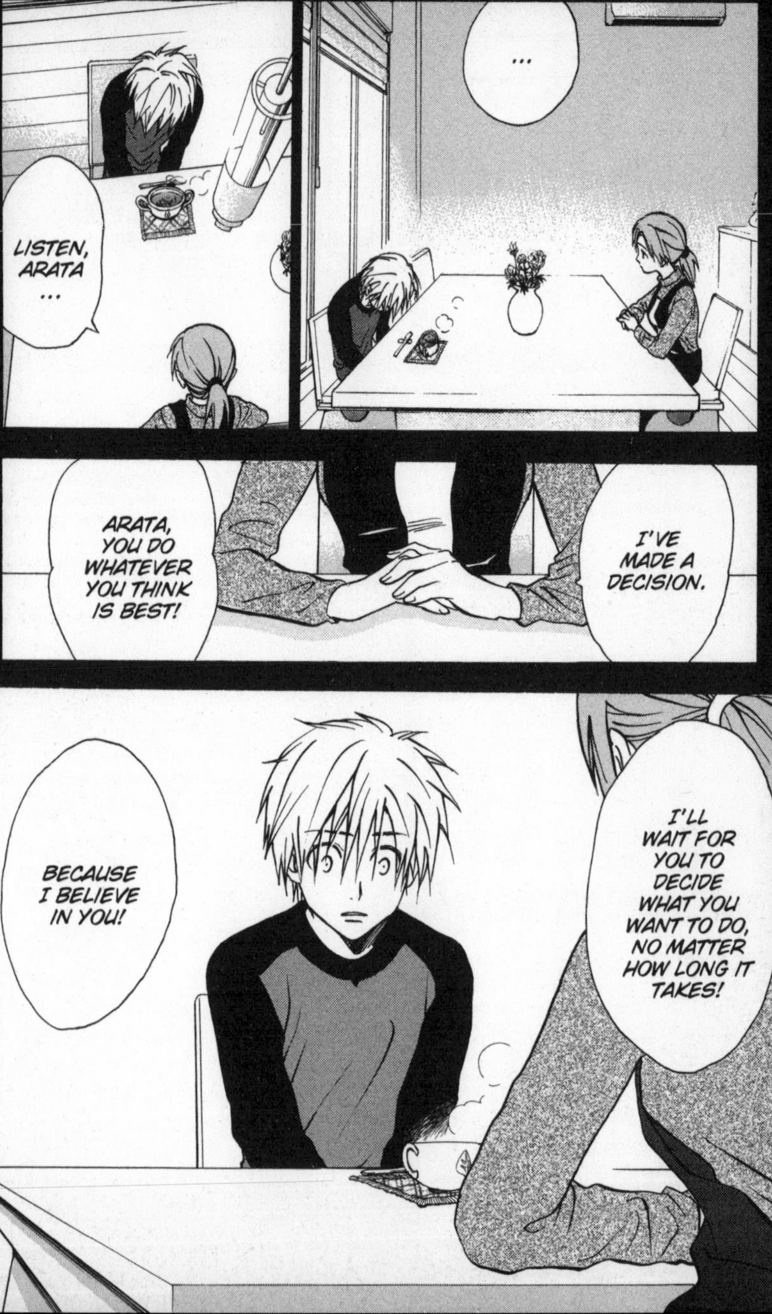
...
LISTEN, ARATA ...
I'VE MADE A DECISION.
ARATA, YOU DO WHATEVER YOU THINK IS BEST!
I'LL WAIT FOR YOU TO DECIDE WHAT YOU WANT TO DO, NO MATTER HOW LONG IT TAKES!
BECAUSE I BELIEVE IN YOU!

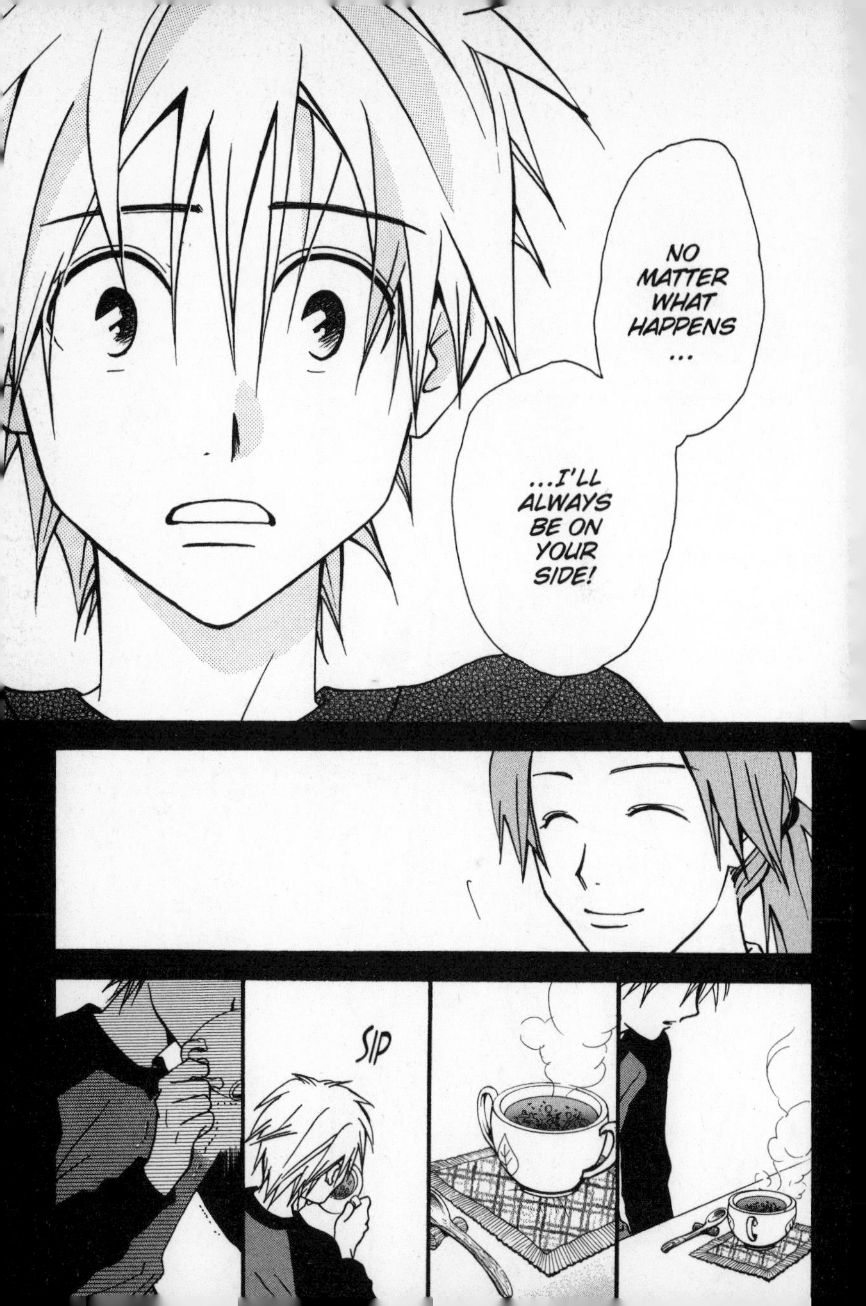
NO MATTER WHAT HAPPENS...
...I'LL ALWAYS BE ON YOUR SIDE!
SIP

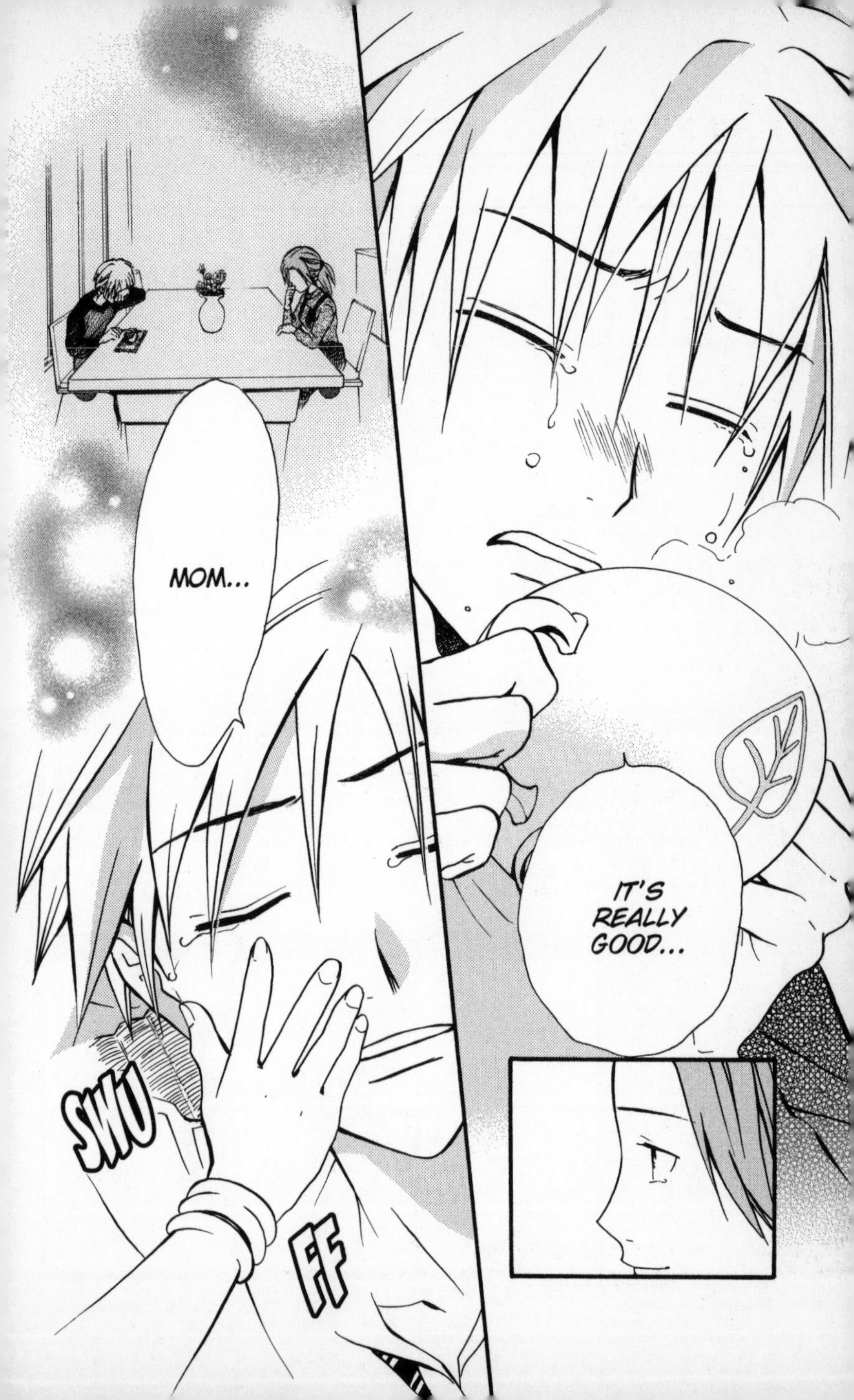
IT'S REALLY GOOD...
MOM...
SWUFF

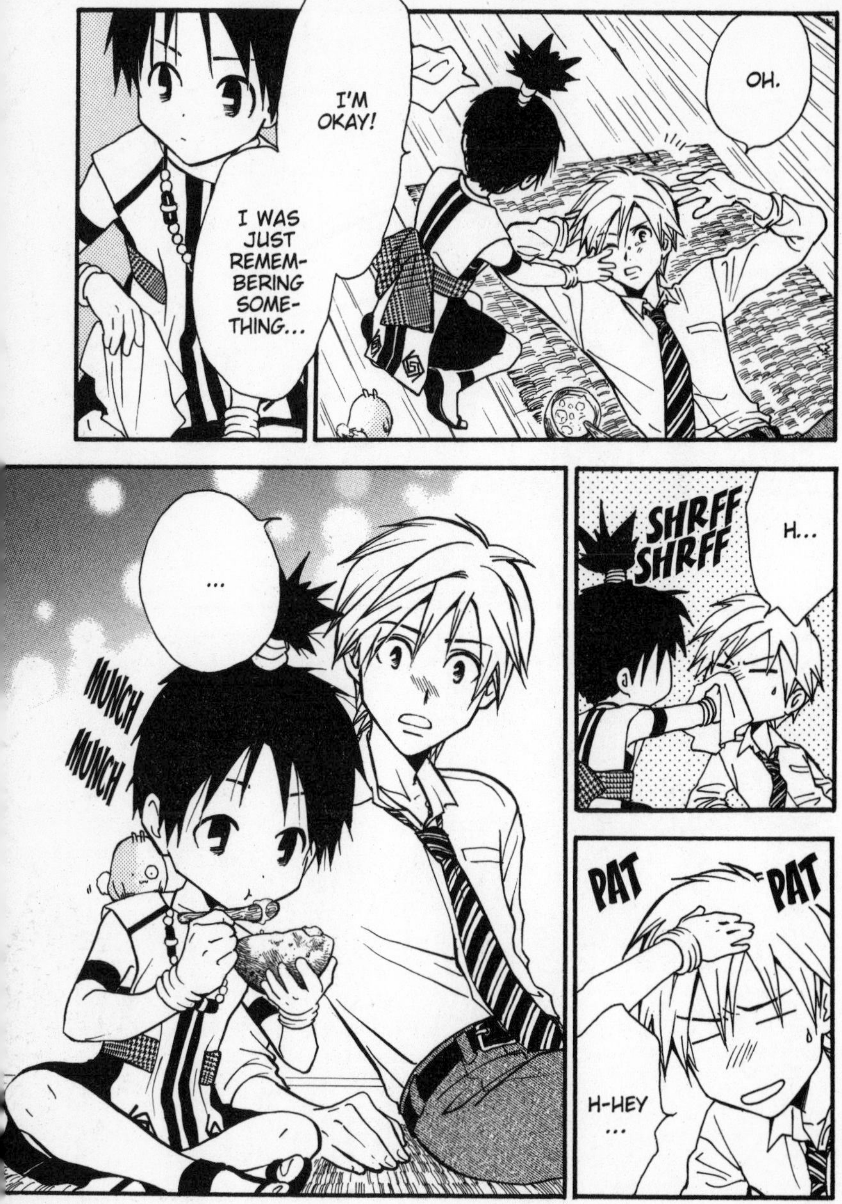
OH.
I'M OKAY!
I WAS JUST REMEMBERING SOMETHING...
SHRFF SHRFF
H...
PAT PAT
H-HEY ...
...
MUNCH MUNCH

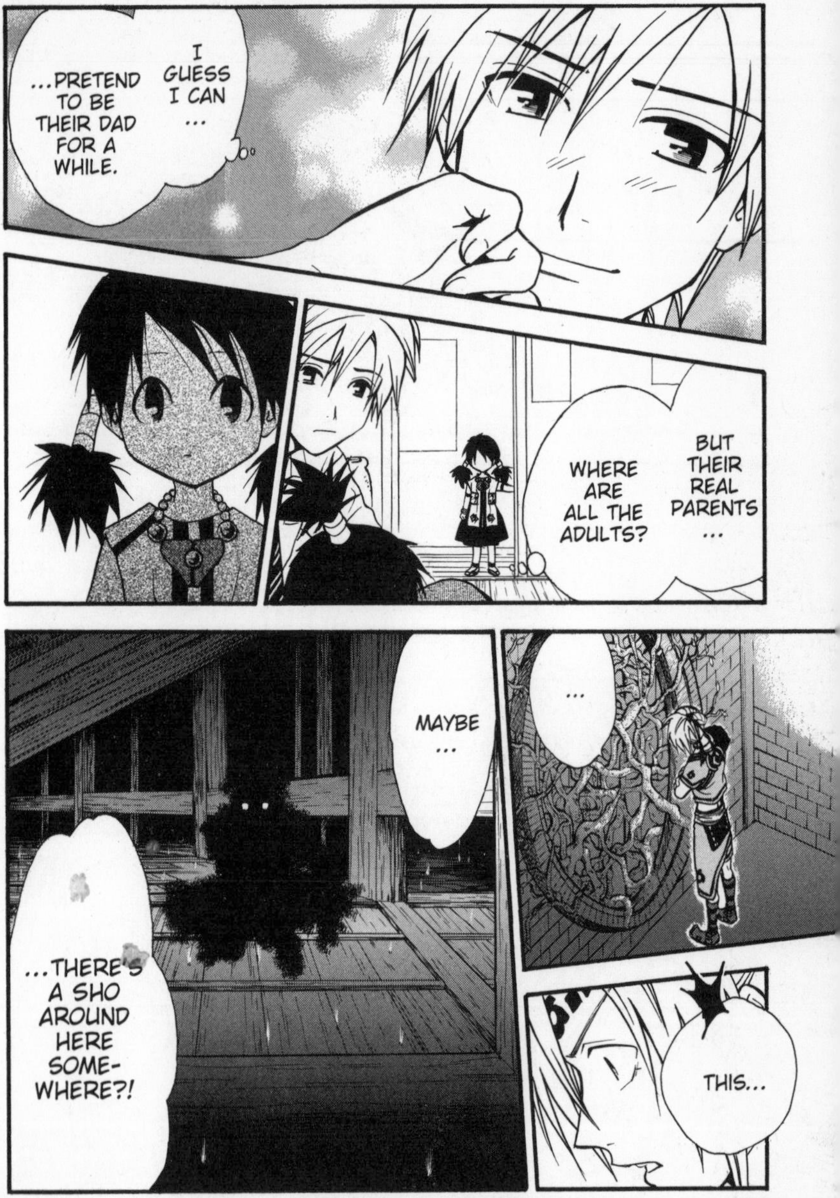
I GUESS I CAN ...
...PRETEND TO BE THEIR DAD FOR A WHILE.
BUT THEIR REAL PARENTS ...
WHERE ARE ALL THE ADULTS?
...
THIS...
MAYBE ...
...THERE'S A SHO AROUND HERE SOME-WHERE?!

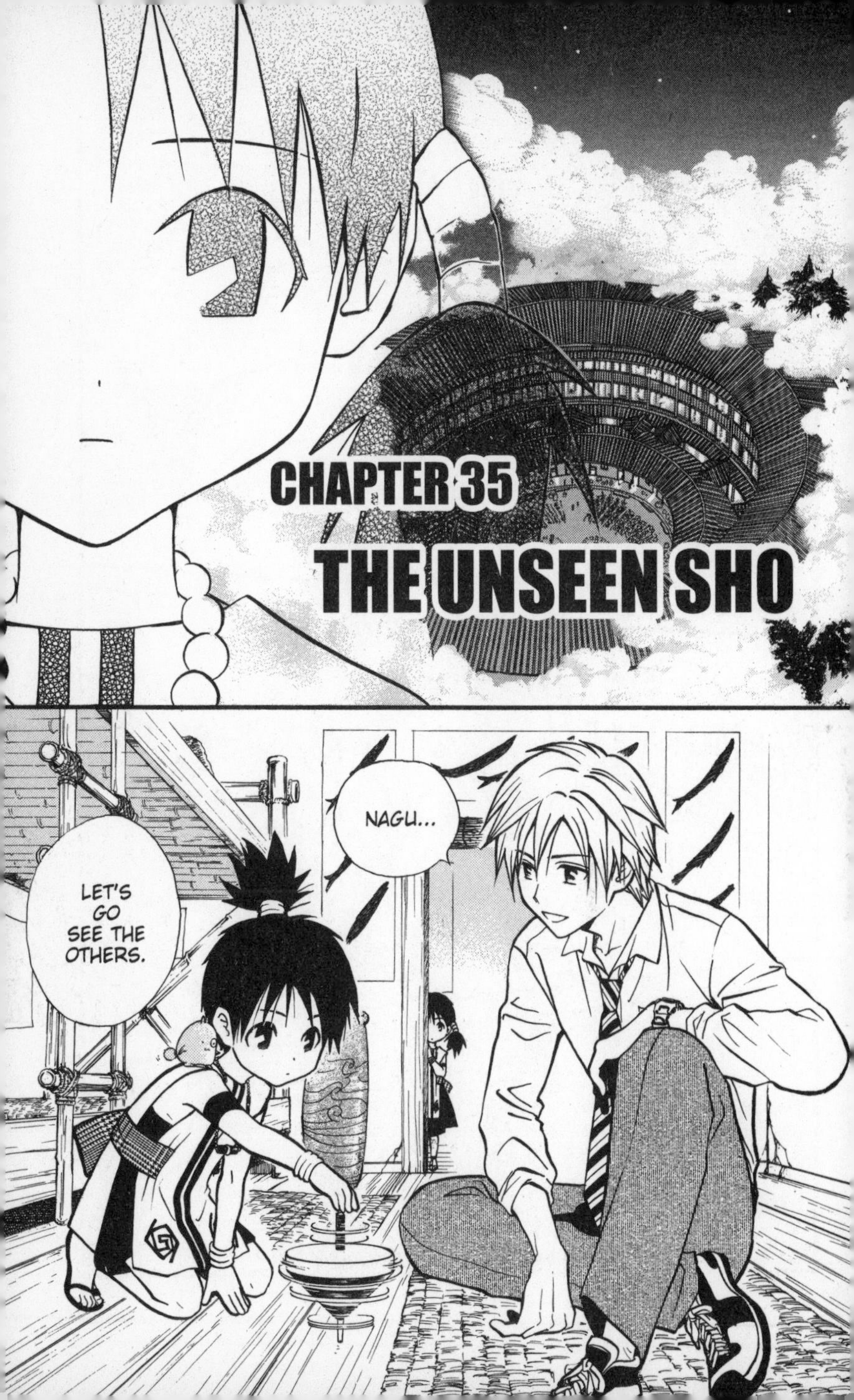
CHAPTER 35
THE UNSEEN SHO
NAGU...
LET'S GO SEE THE OTHERS.

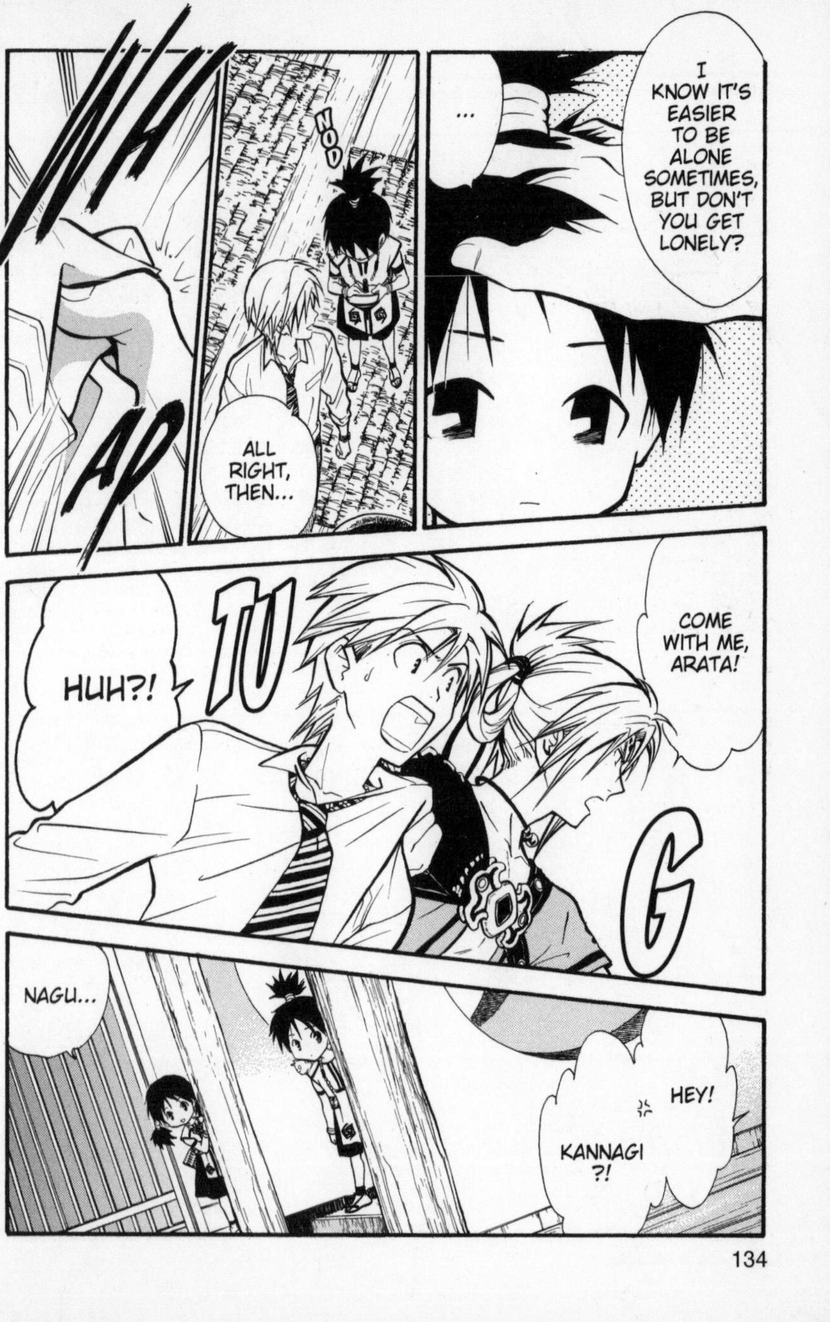
I KNOW IT'S EASIER TO BE ALONE SOMETIMES, BUT DON'T YOU GET LONELY?
...
NOD
ALL RIGHT, THEN...
WHAP
COME WITH ME, ARATA!
TUG
HUH?!
HEY!
KANNAGI?!
NAGU...

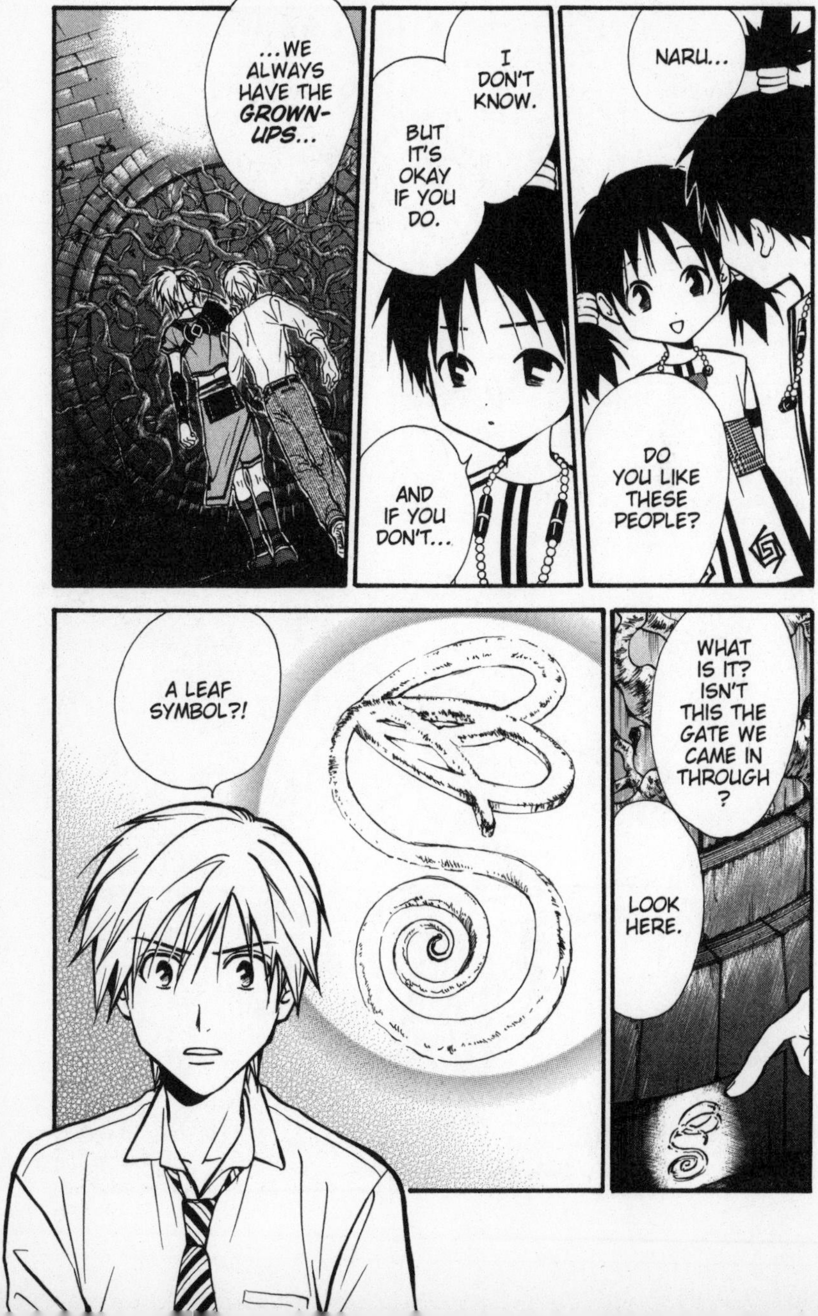
NARU...
DO YOU LIKE THESE PEOPLE?
I DON'T KNOW.
BUT IT'S OKAY IF YOU DO.
AND IF YOU DON'T...
...WE ALWAYS HAVE THE *GROWN-UPS*...
WHAT IS IT? ISN'T THIS THE GATE WE CAME IN THROUGH?
LOOK HERE.
A LEAF SYMBOL?!

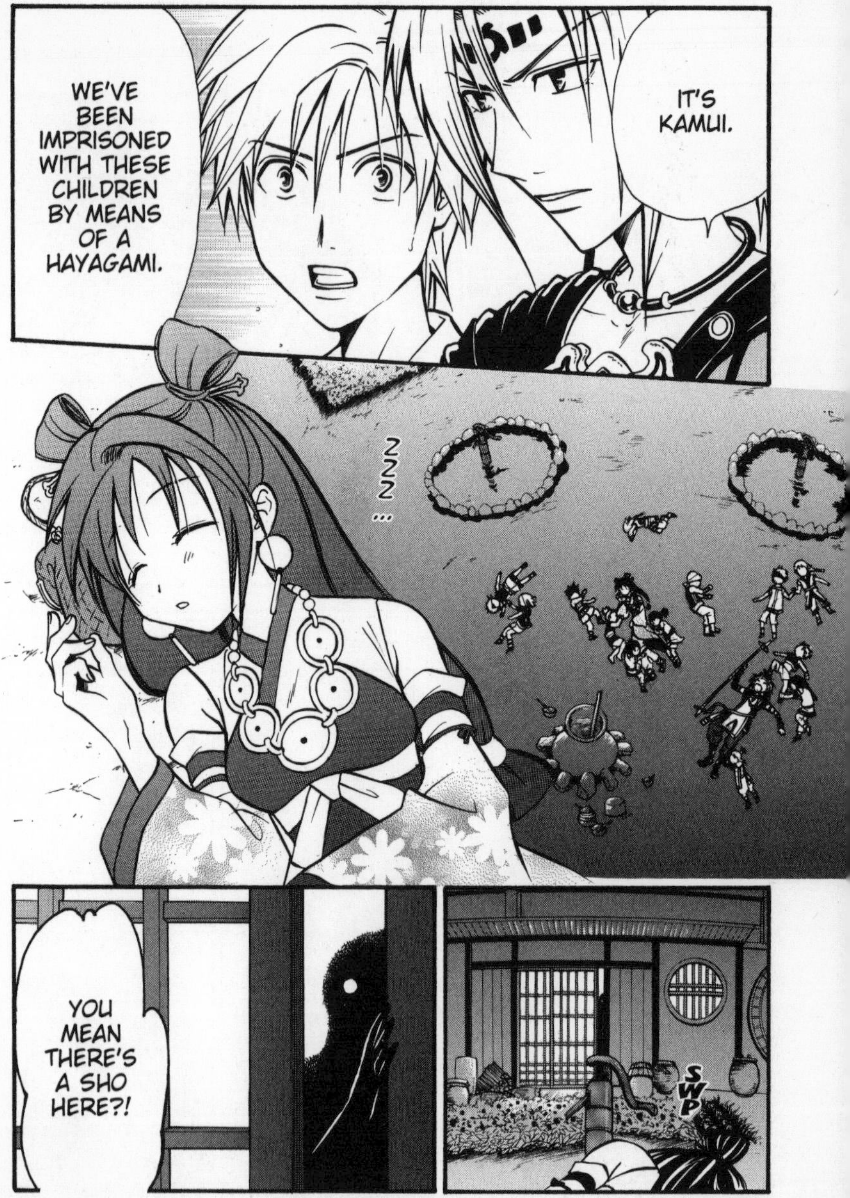
IT'S KAMUI.
WE'VE BEEN IMPRISONED WITH THESE CHILDREN BY MEANS OF A HAYAGAMI.
ZZZ...
SWP
YOU MEAN THERE'S A SHO HERE?!

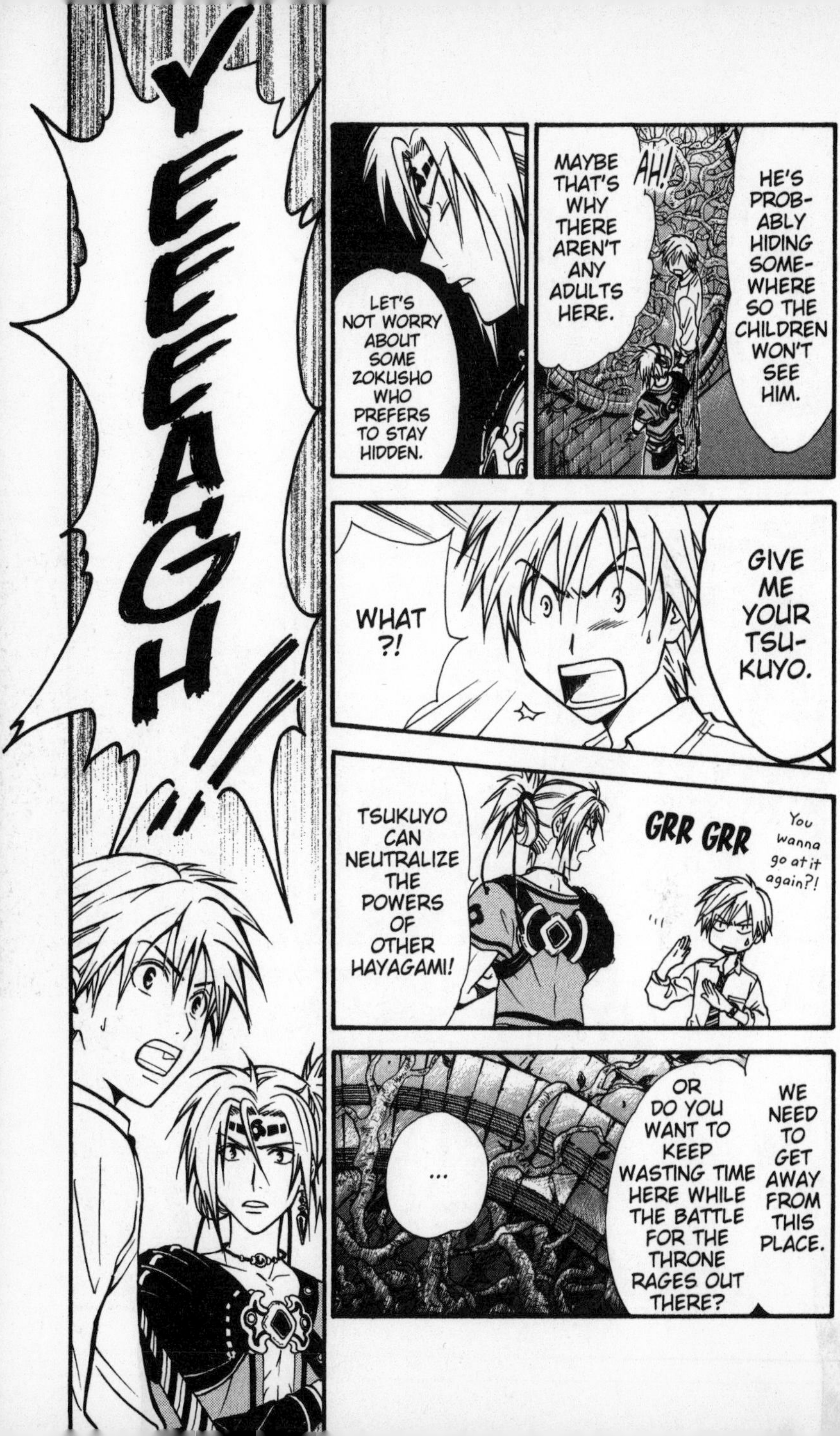
HE'S PROBABLY HIDING SOMEWHERE SO THE CHILDREN WON'T SEE HIM.
AH!
MAYBE THAT'S WHY THERE AREN'T ANY ADULTS HERE.
LET'S NOT WORRY ABOUT SOME ZOKUSHO WHO PREFERS TO STAY HIDDEN.
GIVE ME YOUR TSUKUYO.
WHAT?!
You wanna go at it again?!
GRR GRR
TSUKUYO CAN NEUTRALIZE THE POWERS OF OTHER HAYAGAMI!
WE NEED TO GET AWAY FROM THIS PLACE.
OR DO YOU WANT TO KEEP WASTING TIME HERE WHILE THE BATTLE FOR THE THRONE RAGES OUT THERE?
...
YEEEAGH!!

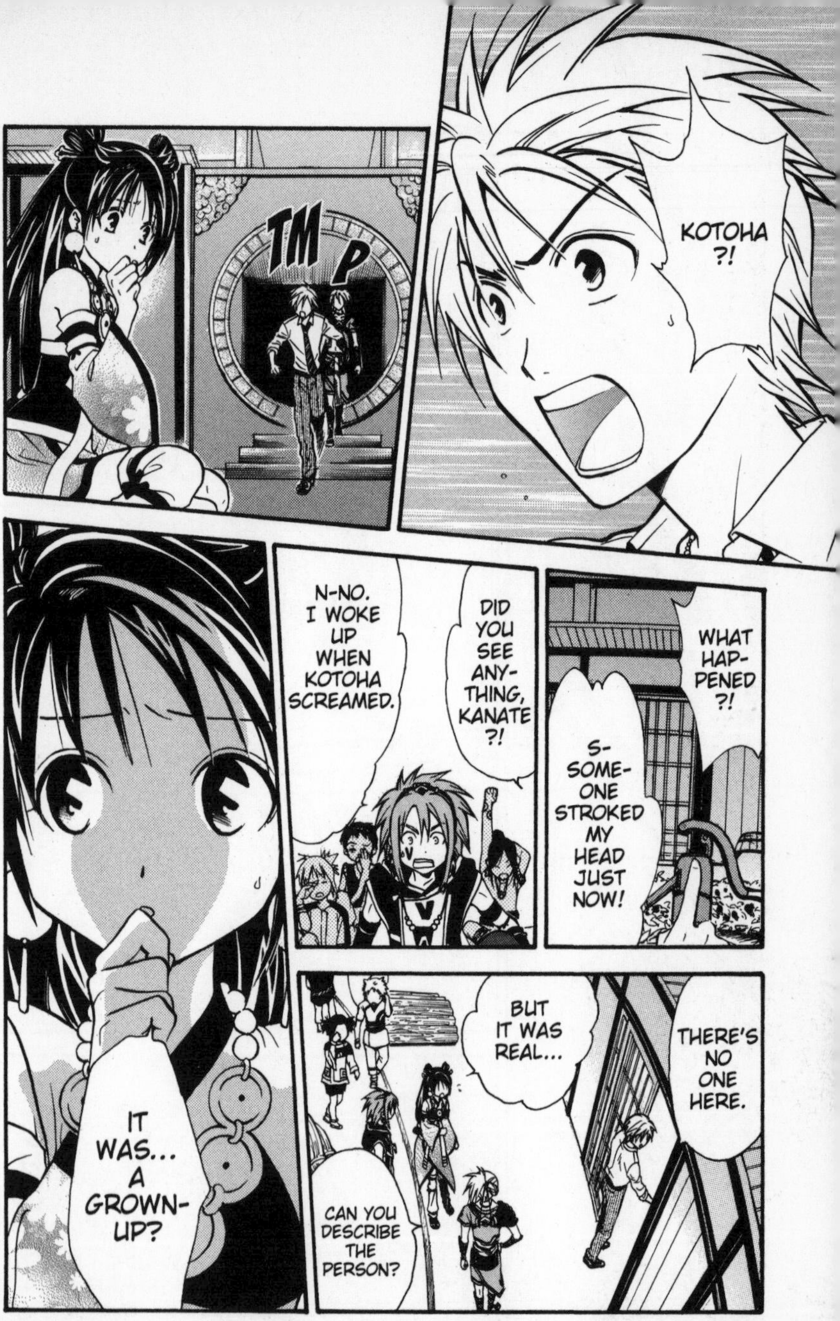
KOTOHA ?!
TMP
WHAT HAP-PENED ?!
S-SOME-ONE STROKED MY HEAD JUST NOW!
DID YOU SEE ANY-THING, KANATE ?!
N-NO. I WOKE UP WHEN KOTOHA SCREAMED.
THERE'S NO ONE HERE.
BUT IT WAS REAL...
CAN YOU DESCRIBE THE PERSON?
IT WAS... A GROWN-UP?

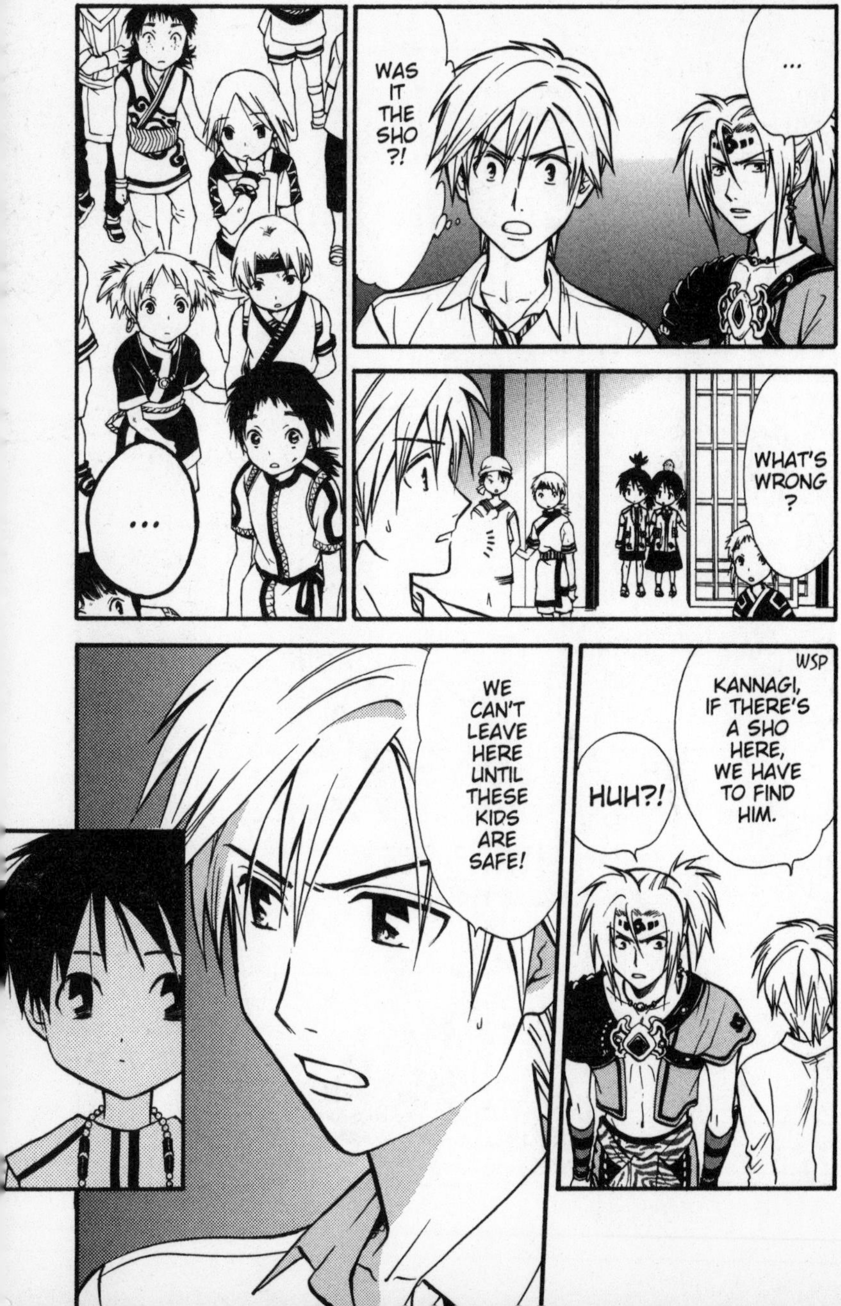
...
WAS IT THE SHO ?!
WHAT'S WRONG ?
...
WSP
KANNAGI, IF THERE'S A SHO HERE, WE HAVE TO FIND HIM.
HUH?!
WE CAN'T LEAVE HERE UNTIL THESE KIDS ARE SAFE!

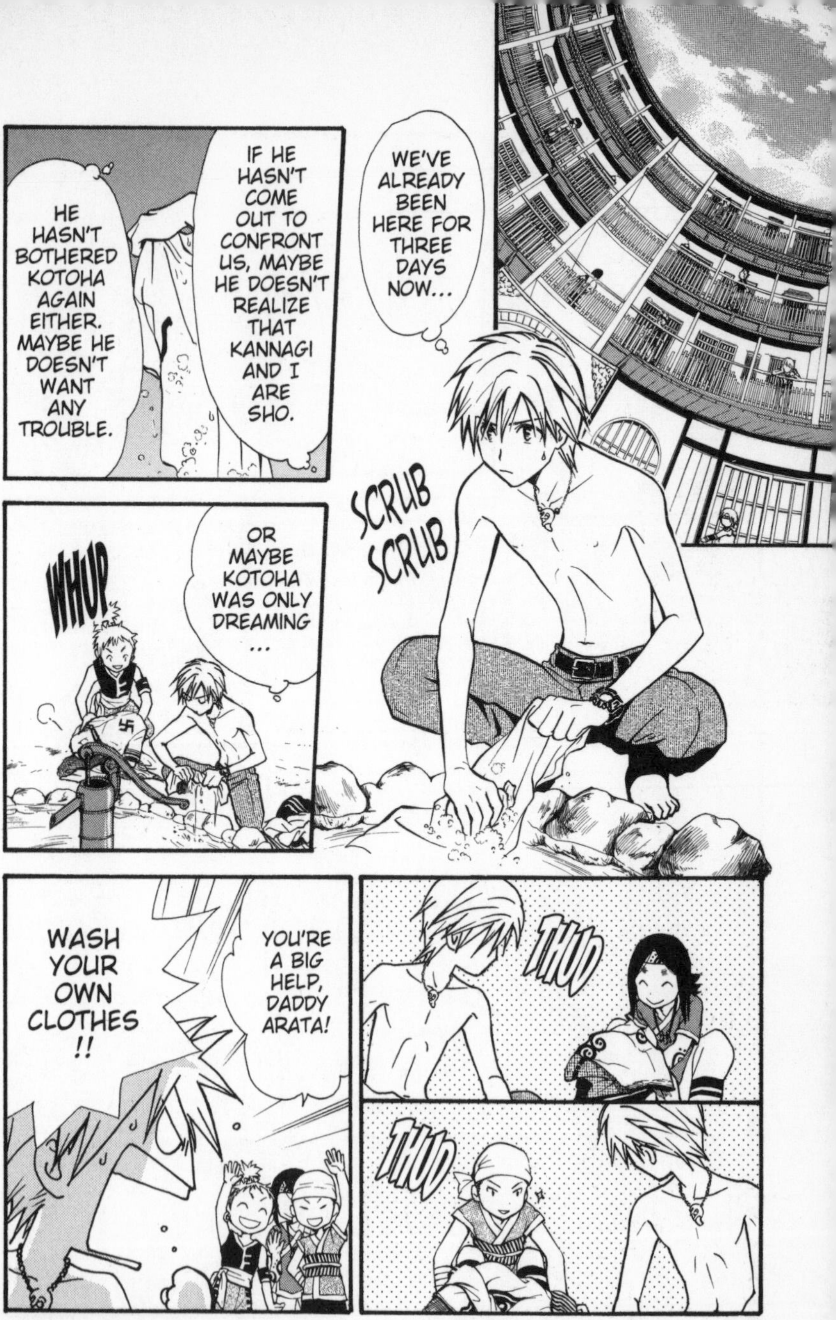
WE'VE ALREADY BEEN HERE FOR THREE DAYS NOW...
SCRUB SCRUB
IF HE HASN'T COME OUT TO CONFRONT US, MAYBE HE DOESN'T REALIZE THAT KANNAGI AND I ARE SHO.
HE HASN'T BOTHERED KOTOHA AGAIN EITHER. MAYBE HE DOESN'T WANT ANY TROUBLE.
OR MAYBE KOTOHA WAS ONLY DREAMING...
WHUP
THUD
THUD
YOU'RE A BIG HELP, DADDY ARATA!
WASH YOUR OWN CLOTHES!!

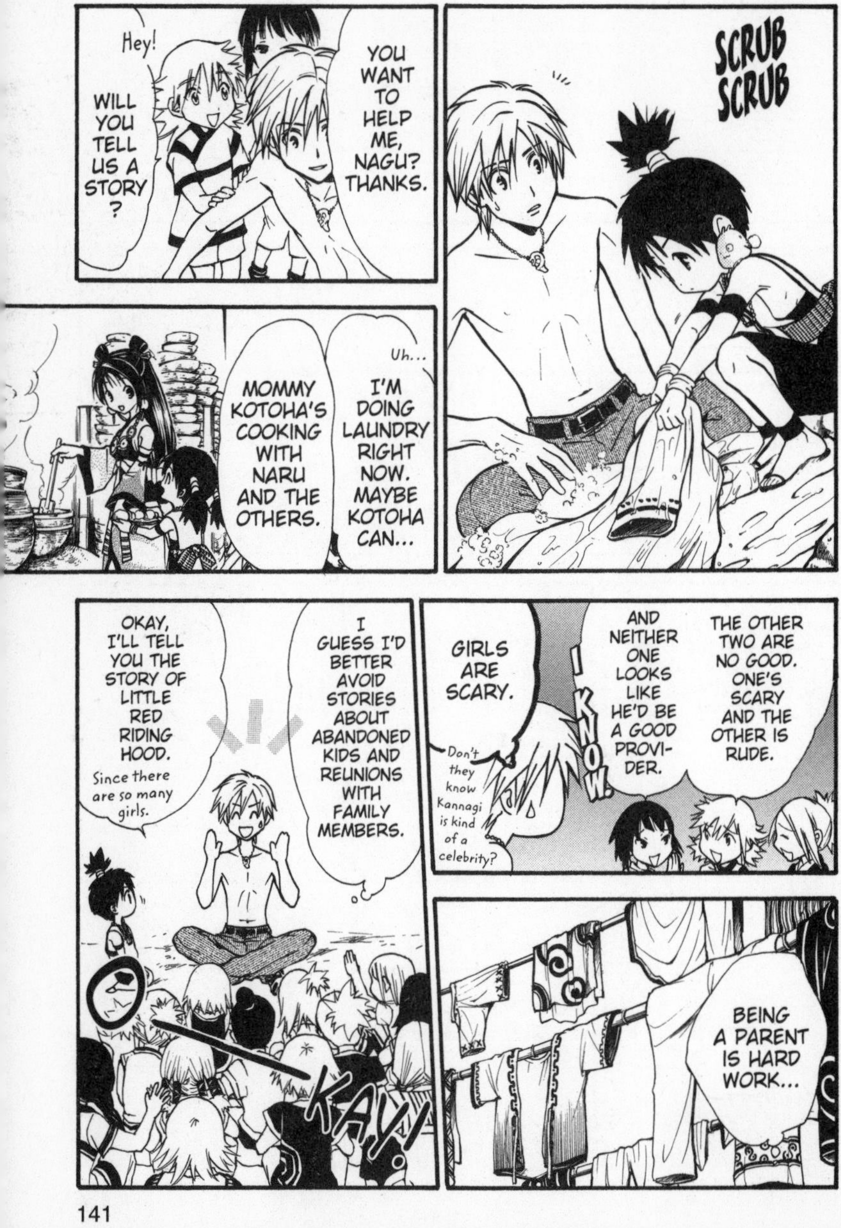
SCRUB SCRUB
YOU WANT TO HELP ME, NAGU? THANKS.
Hey!
WILL YOU TELL US A STORY?
Uh...
I'M DOING LAUNDRY RIGHT NOW. MAYBE KOTOHA CAN...
MOMMY KOTOHA'S COOKING WITH NARU AND THE OTHERS.
THE OTHER TWO ARE NO GOOD. ONE'S SCARY AND THE OTHER IS RUDE.
AND NEITHER ONE LOOKS LIKE HE'D BE A GOOD PROVIDER.
I KNOW.
GIRLS ARE SCARY.
Don't they know Kannagi is kind of a celebrity?
BEING A PARENT IS HARD WORK...
I GUESS I'D BETTER AVOID STORIES ABOUT ABANDONED KIDS AND REUNIONS WITH FAMILY MEMBERS.
OKAY, I'LL TELL YOU THE STORY OF LITTLE RED RIDING HOOD.
Since there are so many girls.
KAY!

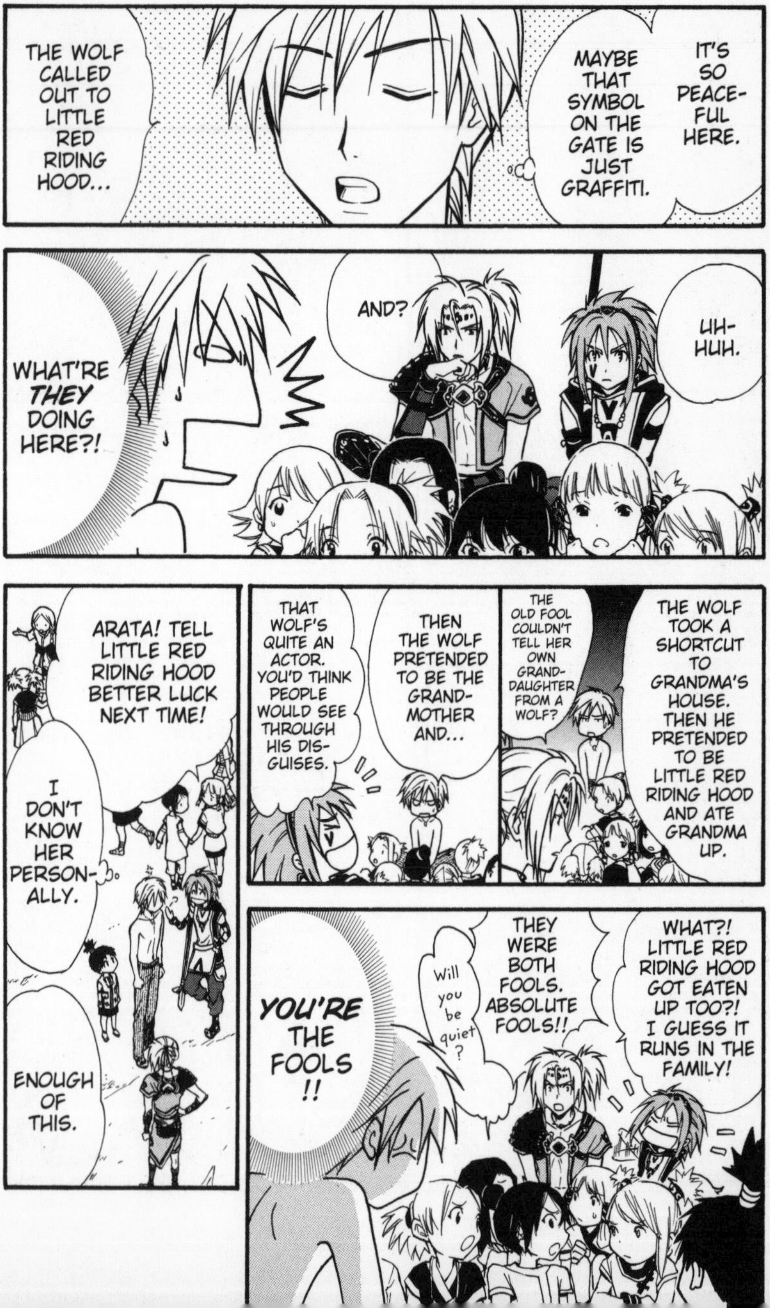
IT'S SO PEACEFUL HERE.
MAYBE THAT SYMBOL ON THE GATE IS JUST GRAFFITI.
THE WOLF CALLED OUT TO LITTLE RED RIDING HOOD...
UH-HUH.
AND?
WHAT'RE *THEY* DOING HERE?!
THE WOLF TOOK A SHORTCUT TO GRANDMA'S HOUSE. THEN HE PRETENDED TO BE LITTLE RED RIDING HOOD AND ATE GRANDMA UP.
THE OLD FOOL COULDN'T TELL HER OWN GRANDDAUGHTER FROM A WOLF?
THEN THE WOLF PRETENDED TO BE THE GRANDMOTHER AND...
THAT WOLF'S QUITE AN ACTOR. YOU'D THINK PEOPLE WOULD SEE THROUGH HIS DISGUISES.
WHAT?! LITTLE RED RIDING HOOD GOT EATEN UP TOO?! I GUESS IT RUNS IN THE FAMILY!
THEY WERE BOTH FOOLS. ABSOLUTE FOOLS!!
Will you be quiet?
YOU'RE THE FOOLS!!
ARATA! TELL LITTLE RED RIDING HOOD BETTER LUCK NEXT TIME!
I DON'T KNOW HER PERSONALLY.
ENOUGH OF THIS.

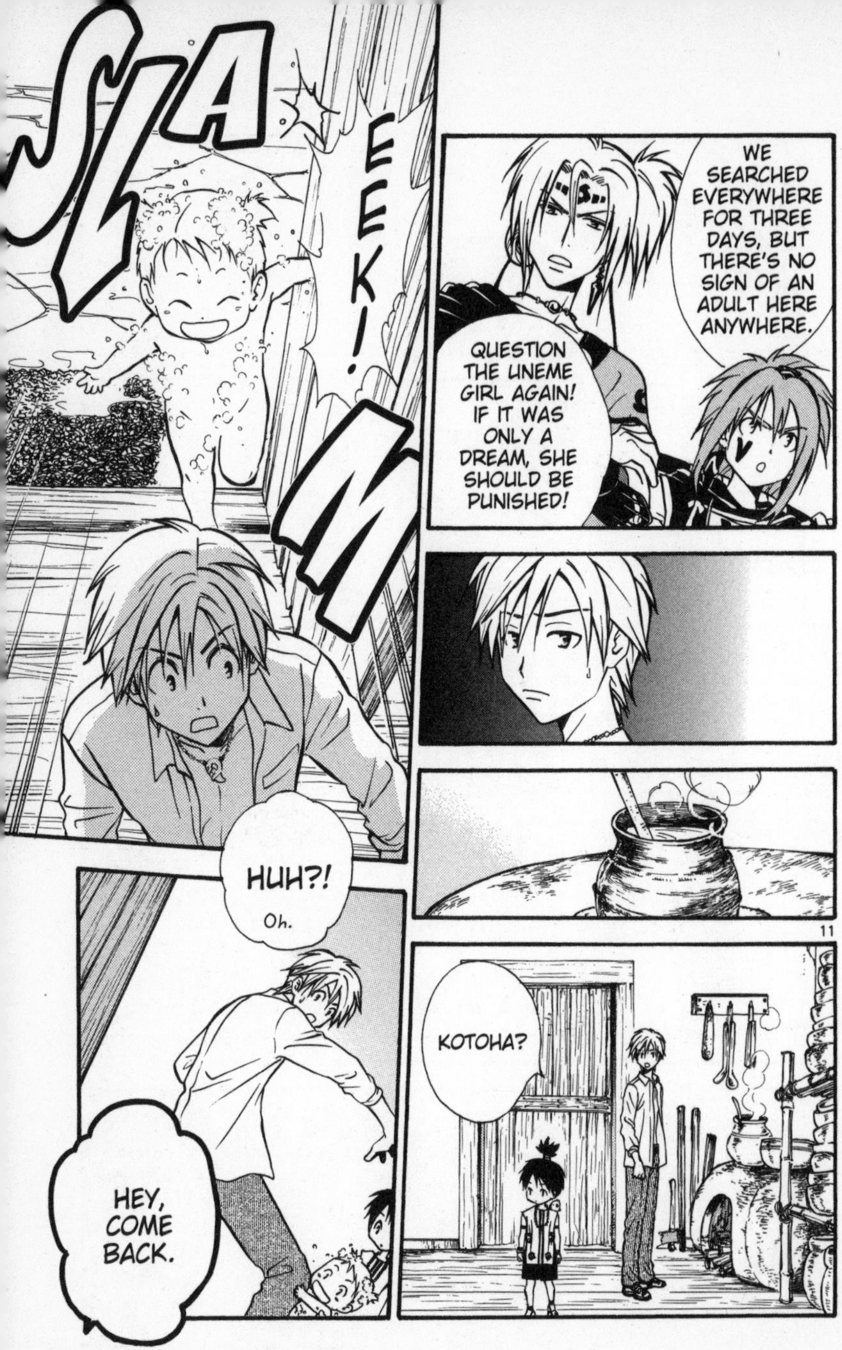
WE SEARCHED EVERYWHERE FOR THREE DAYS, BUT THERE'S NO SIGN OF AN ADULT HERE ANYWHERE.
QUESTION THE UNEME GIRL AGAIN! IF IT WAS ONLY A DREAM, SHE SHOULD BE PUNISHED!
SLAM
EEK!
KOTOHA?
HUH?!
Oh.
HEY, COME BACK.

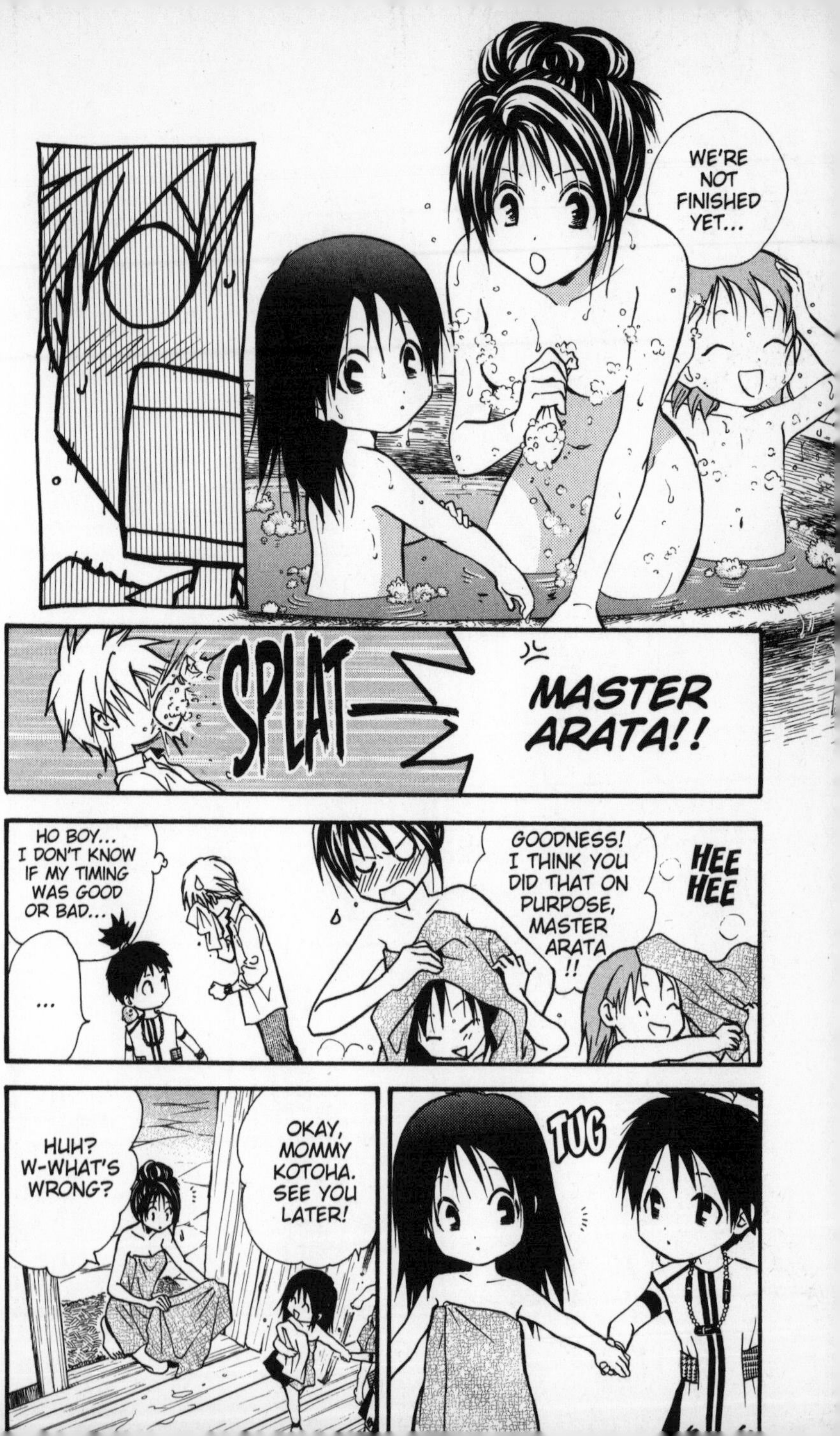
WE'RE NOT FINISHED YET...
MASTER ARATA!!
SPLAT
HEE HEE
GOODNESS! I THINK YOU DID THAT ON PURPOSE, MASTER ARATA!!
HO BOY... I DON'T KNOW IF MY TIMING WAS GOOD OR BAD...
...
TUG
OKAY, MOMMY KOTOHA. SEE YOU LATER!
HUH? W-WHAT'S WRONG?

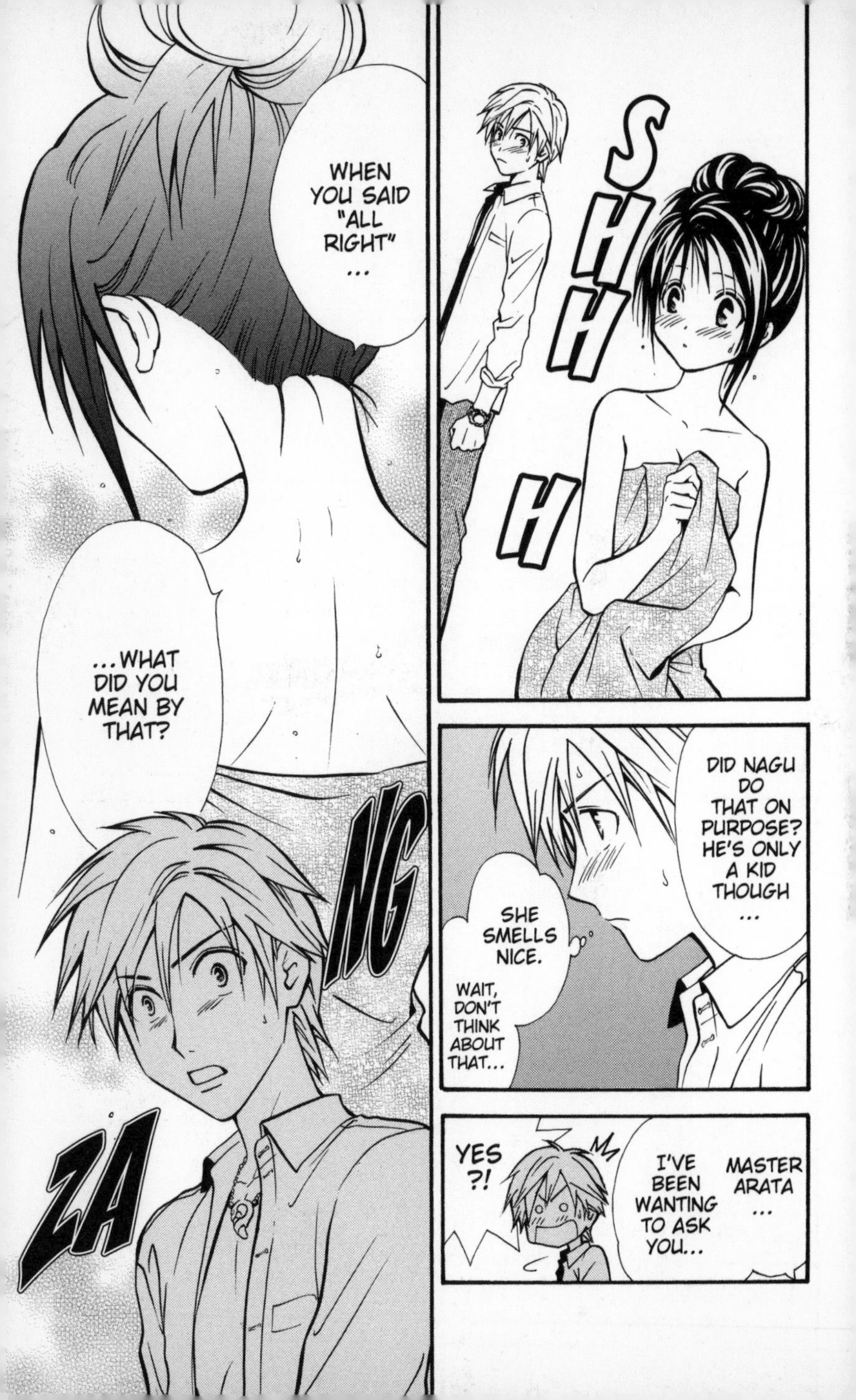
SHHHH
H
DID NAGU DO THAT ON PURPOSE? HE'S ONLY A KID THOUGH ...
SHE SMELLS NICE.
WAIT, DON'T THINK ABOUT THAT...
MASTER ARATA ...
I'VE BEEN WANTING TO ASK YOU...
YES ?!
WHEN YOU SAID "ALL RIGHT" ...
...WHAT DID YOU MEAN BY THAT?
NG
ZA

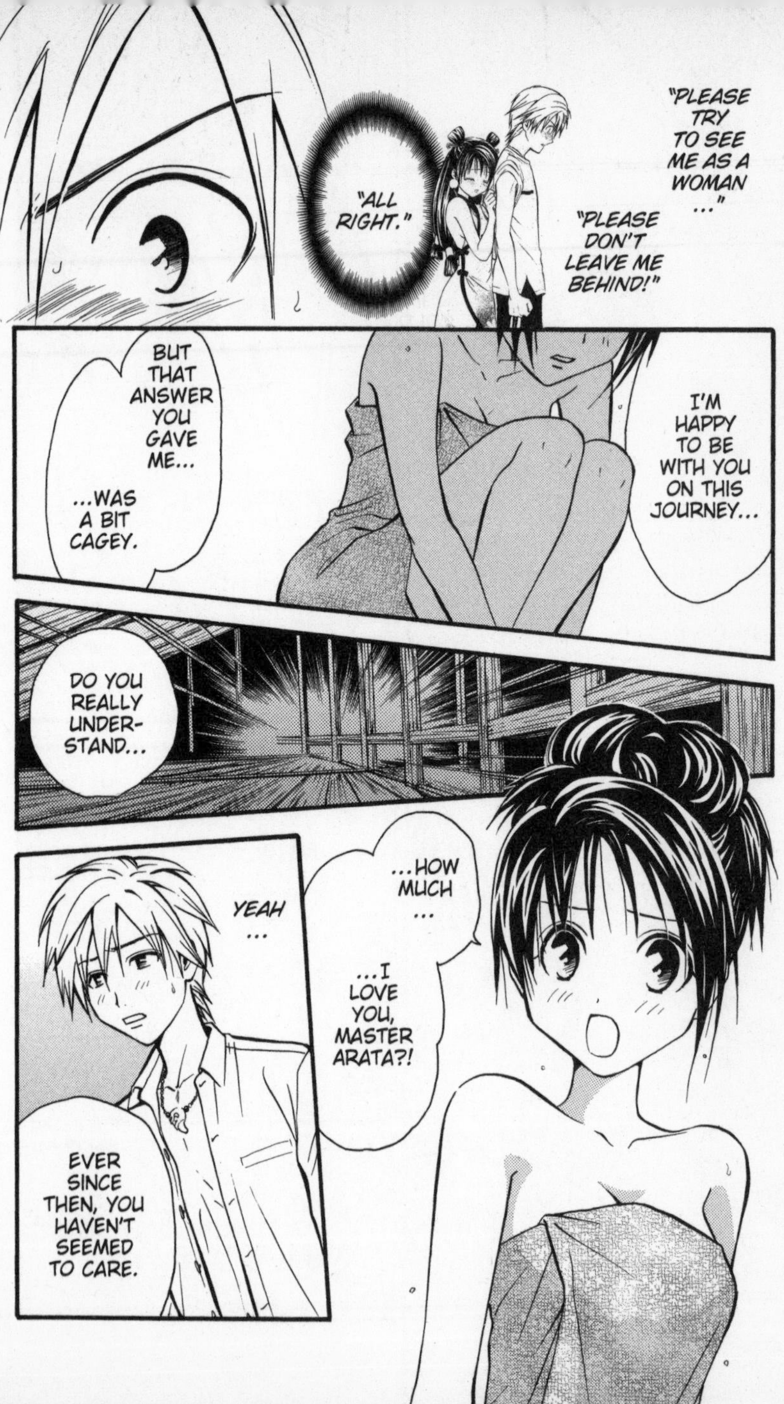
"PLEASE TRY TO SEE ME AS A WOMAN ..."
"PLEASE DON'T LEAVE ME BEHIND!"
"ALL RIGHT."
I'M HAPPY TO BE WITH YOU ON THIS JOURNEY...
BUT THAT ANSWER YOU GAVE ME...
...WAS A BIT CAGEY.
DO YOU REALLY UNDER-STAND...
...HOW MUCH ...
...I LOVE YOU, MASTER ARATA?!
YEAH ...
EVER SINCE THEN, YOU HAVEN'T SEEMED TO CARE.

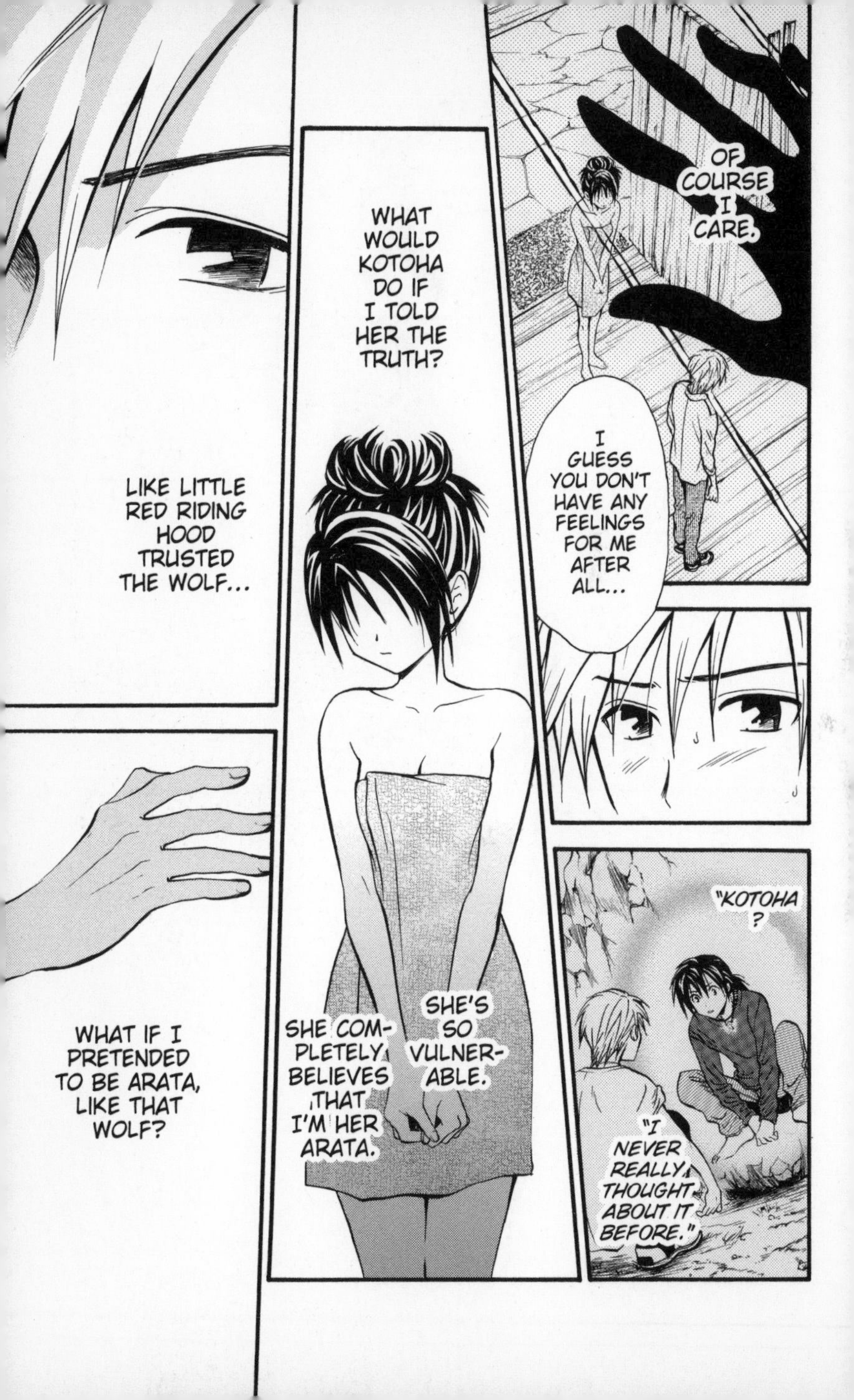
OF COURSE I CARE.
I GUESS YOU DON'T HAVE ANY FEELINGS FOR ME AFTER ALL...
"KOTOHA?
"I NEVER REALLY THOUGHT ABOUT IT BEFORE."
WHAT WOULD KOTOHA DO IF I TOLD HER THE TRUTH?
SHE'S SO VULNERABLE.
SHE COMPLETELY BELIEVES THAT I'M HER ARATA.
LIKE LITTLE RED RIDING HOOD TRUSTED THE WOLF...
WHAT IF I PRETENDED TO BE ARATA, LIKE THAT WOLF?

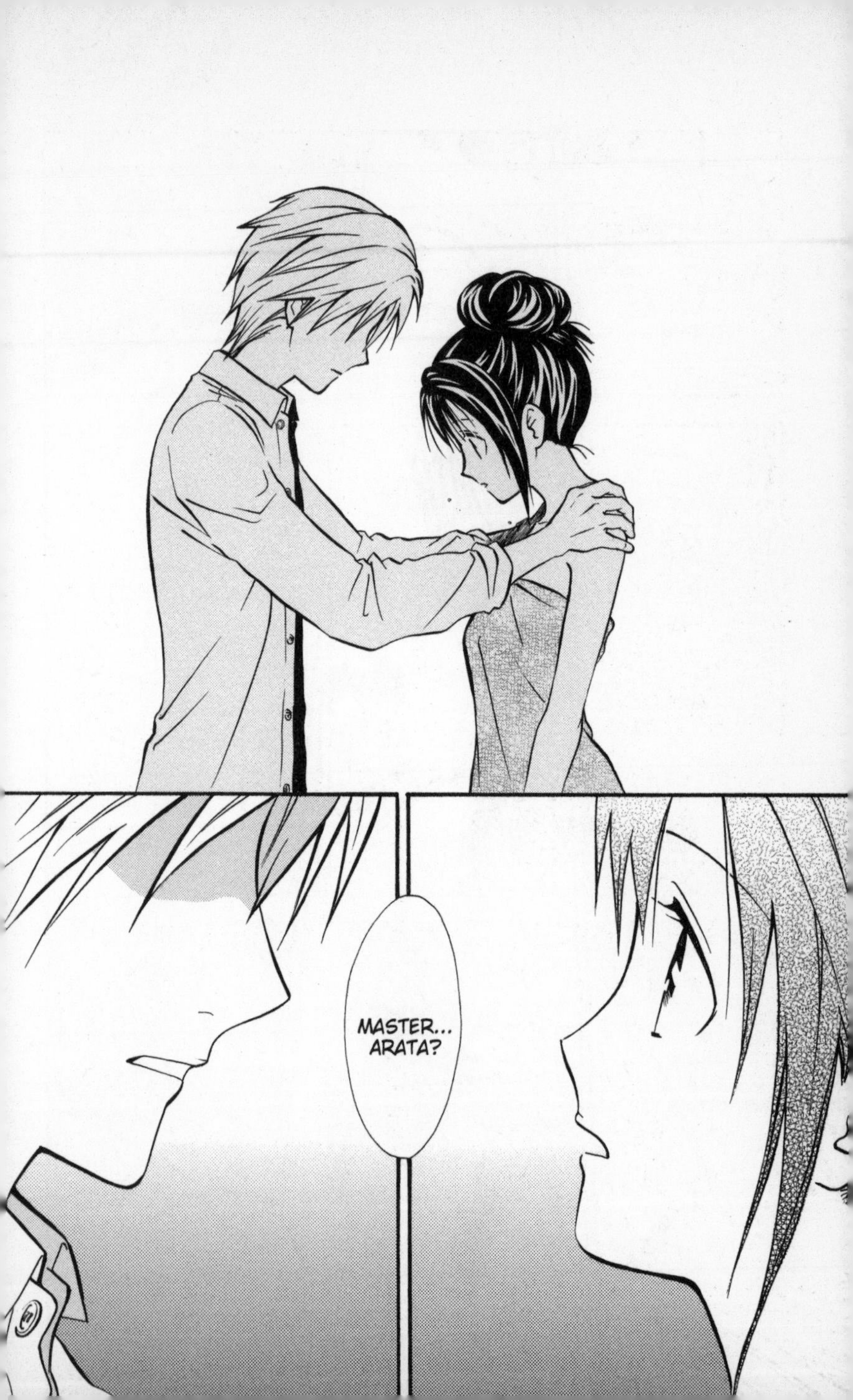
MASTER... ARATA?

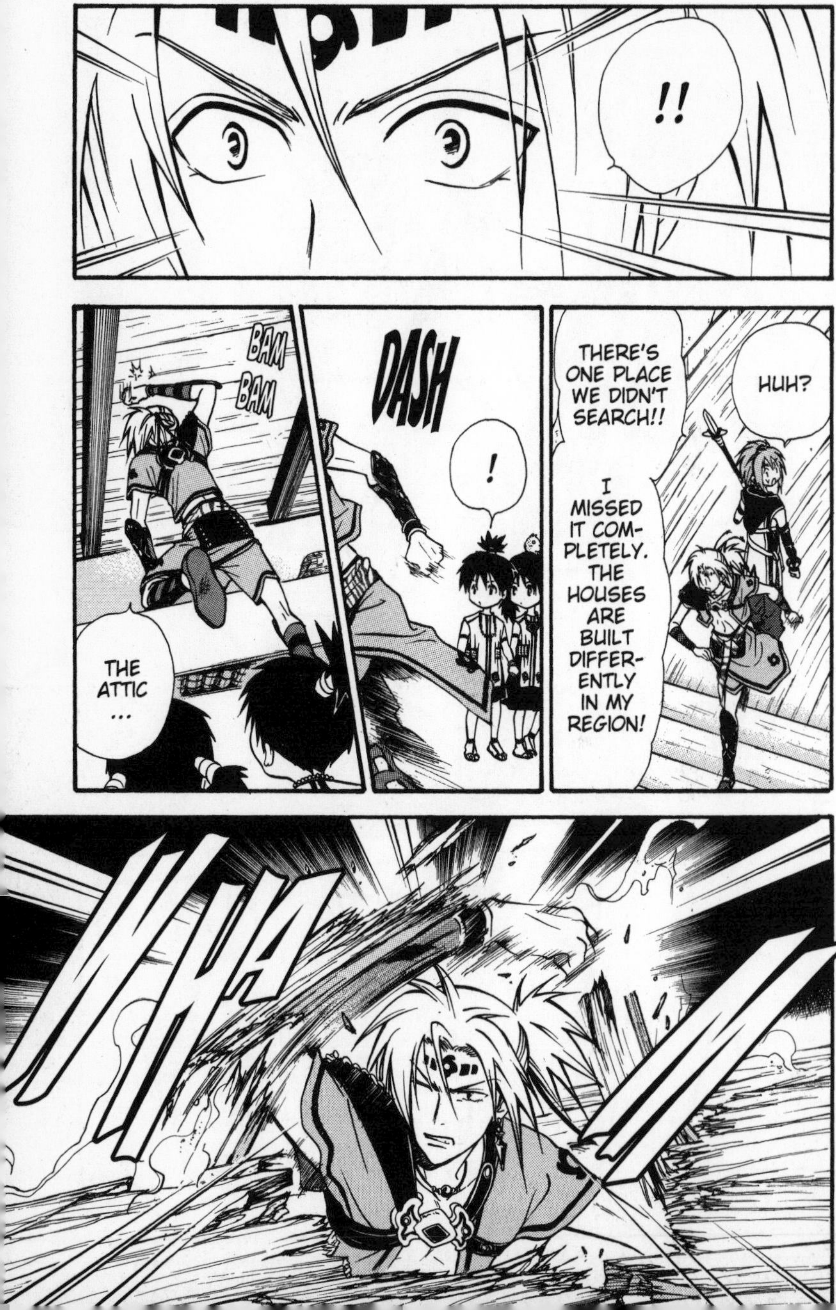
!!
HUH?
THERE'S ONE PLACE WE DIDN'T SEARCH!!
I MISSED IT COM-PLETELY. THE HOUSES ARE BUILT DIFFER-ENTLY IN MY REGION!
DASH
!
BAM BAM
THE ATTIC ...

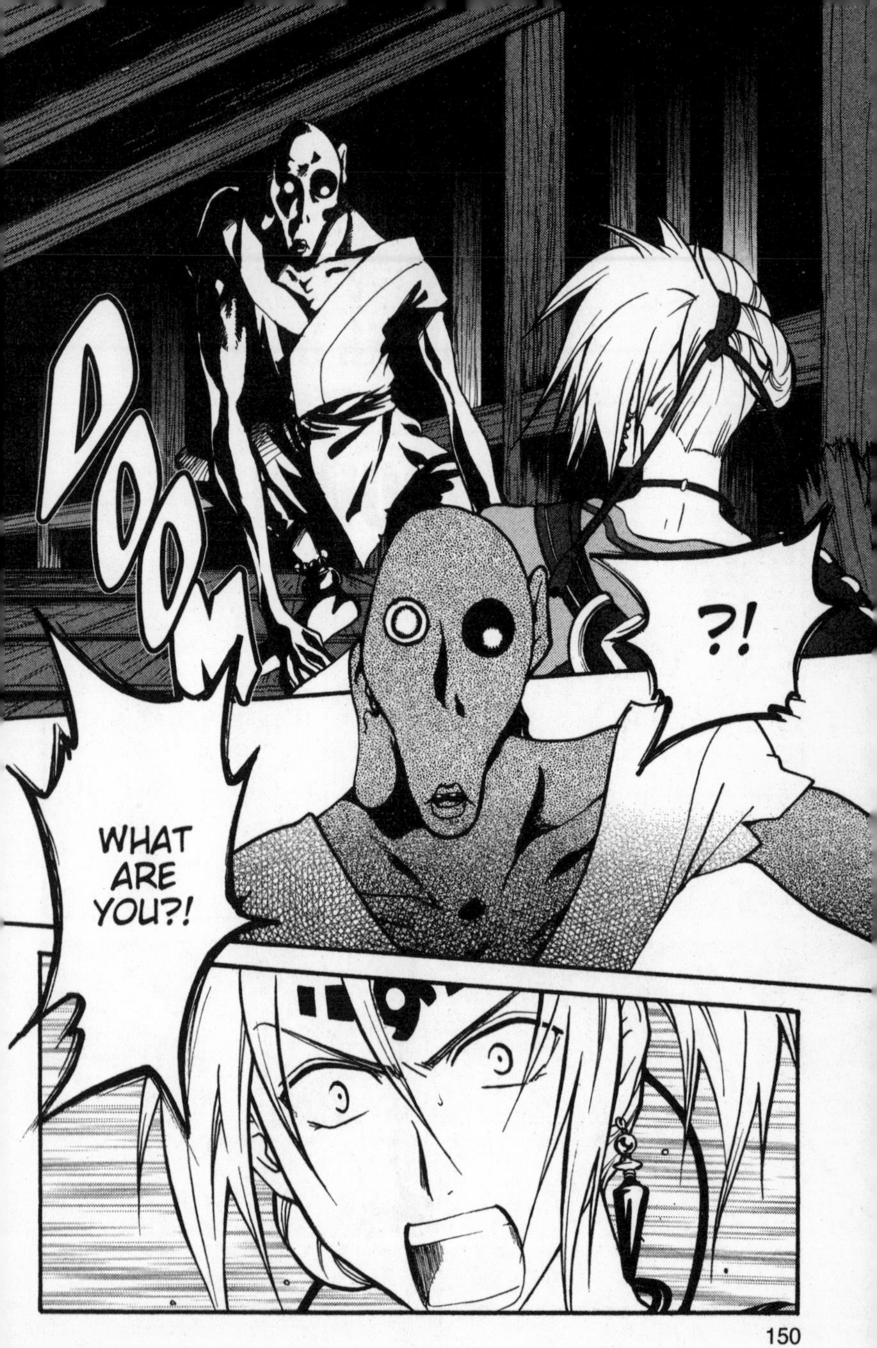
DOOM
?!
WHAT ARE YOU?!

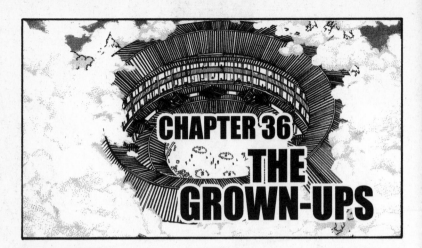

CHAPTER 36
THE GROWN-UPS

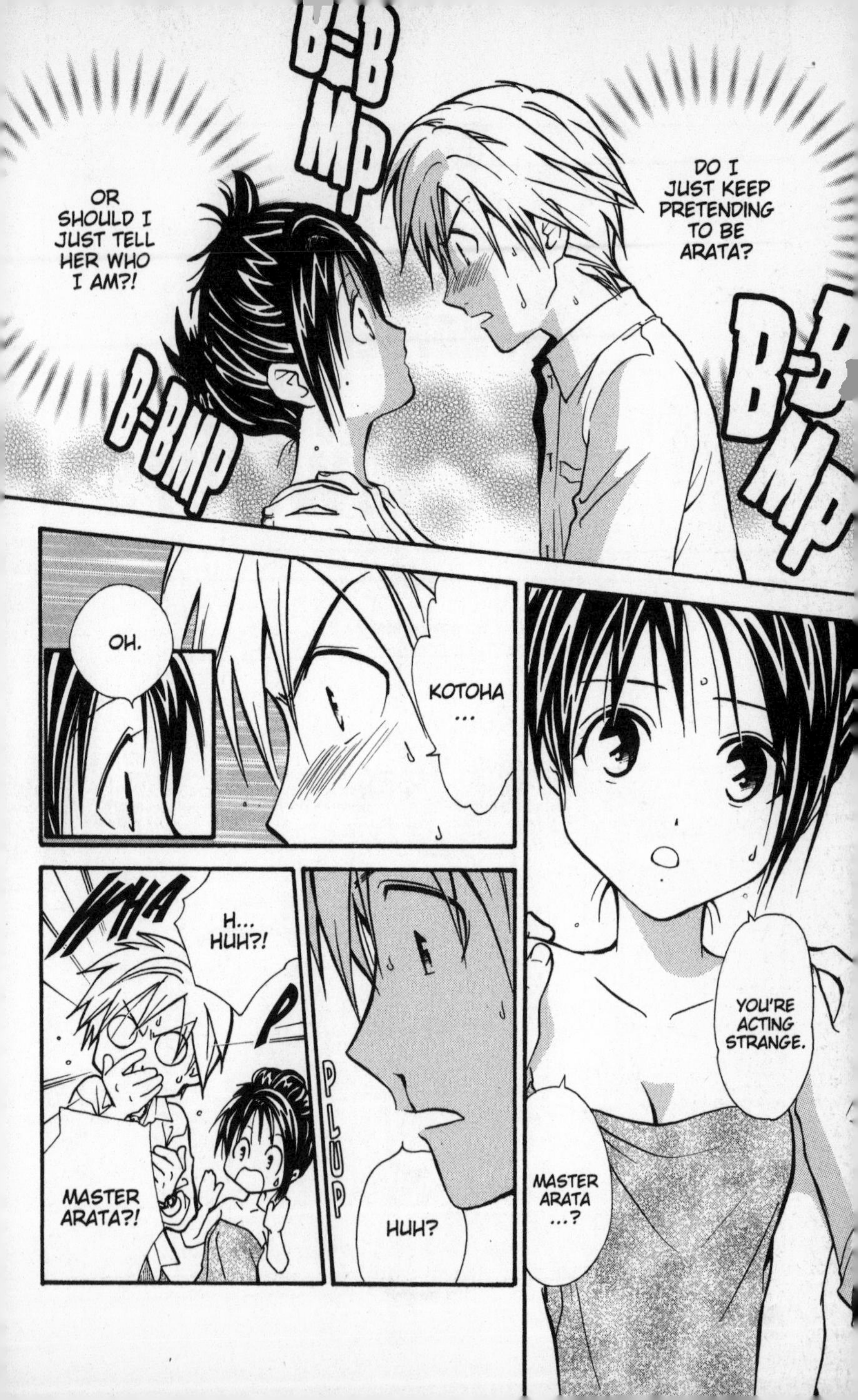
B-BMP
DO I JUST KEEP PRETENDING TO BE ARATA?
B-BMP
OR SHOULD I JUST TELL HER WHO I AM?!
B-BMP
YOU'RE ACTING STRANGE.
MASTER ARATA ...?
KOTOHA ...
OH.
PLUP
HUH?
WHA
H... HUH?!
MASTER ARATA?!

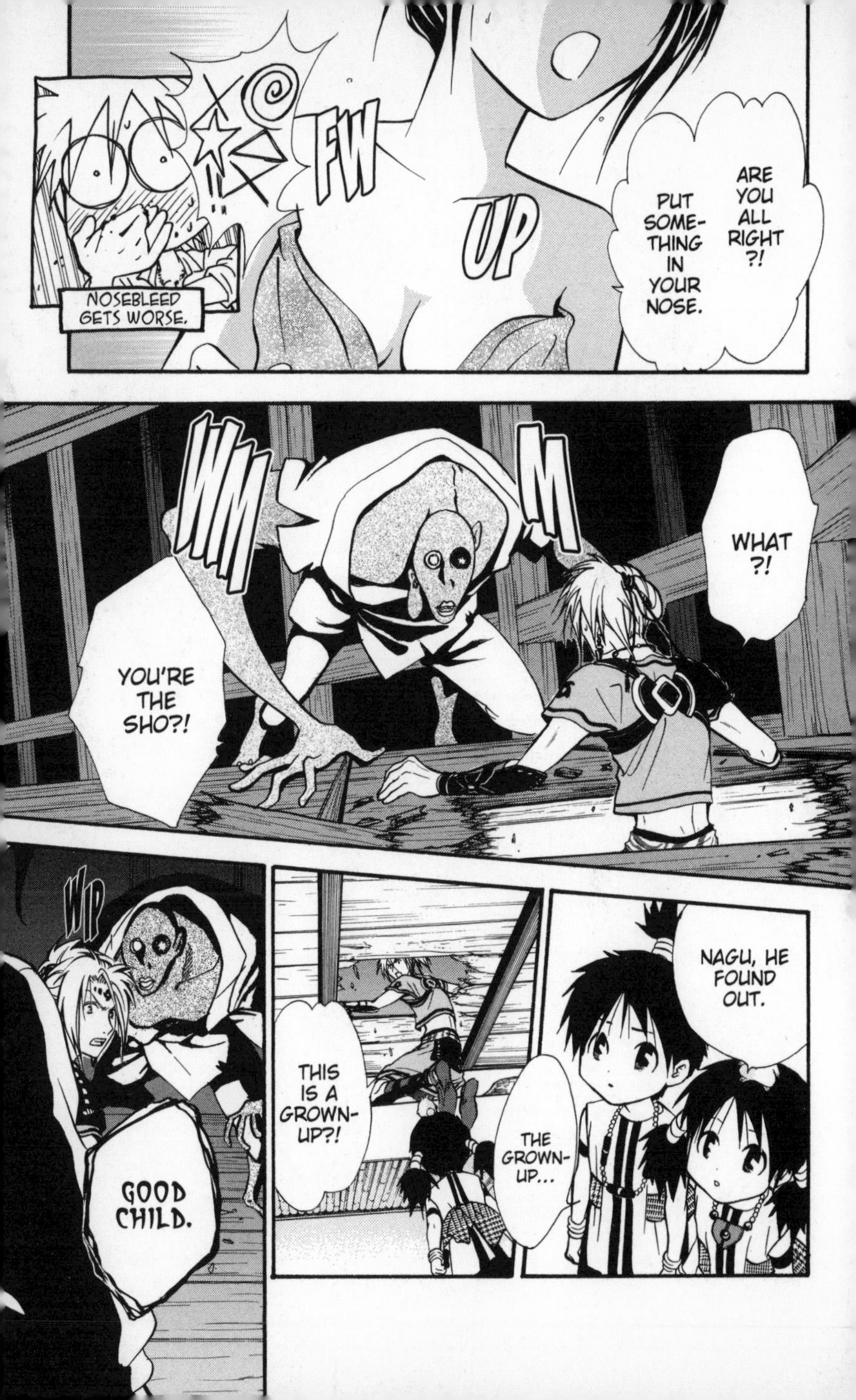
ARE YOU ALL RIGHT?!
PUT SOME-THING IN YOUR NOSE.
FW
UP
NOSEBLEED GETS WORSE.
WHAT?!
M
WM
YOU'RE THE SHO?!
NAGU, HE FOUND OUT.
THE GROWN-UP...
THIS IS A GROWN-UP?!
WIP
GOOD CHILD.

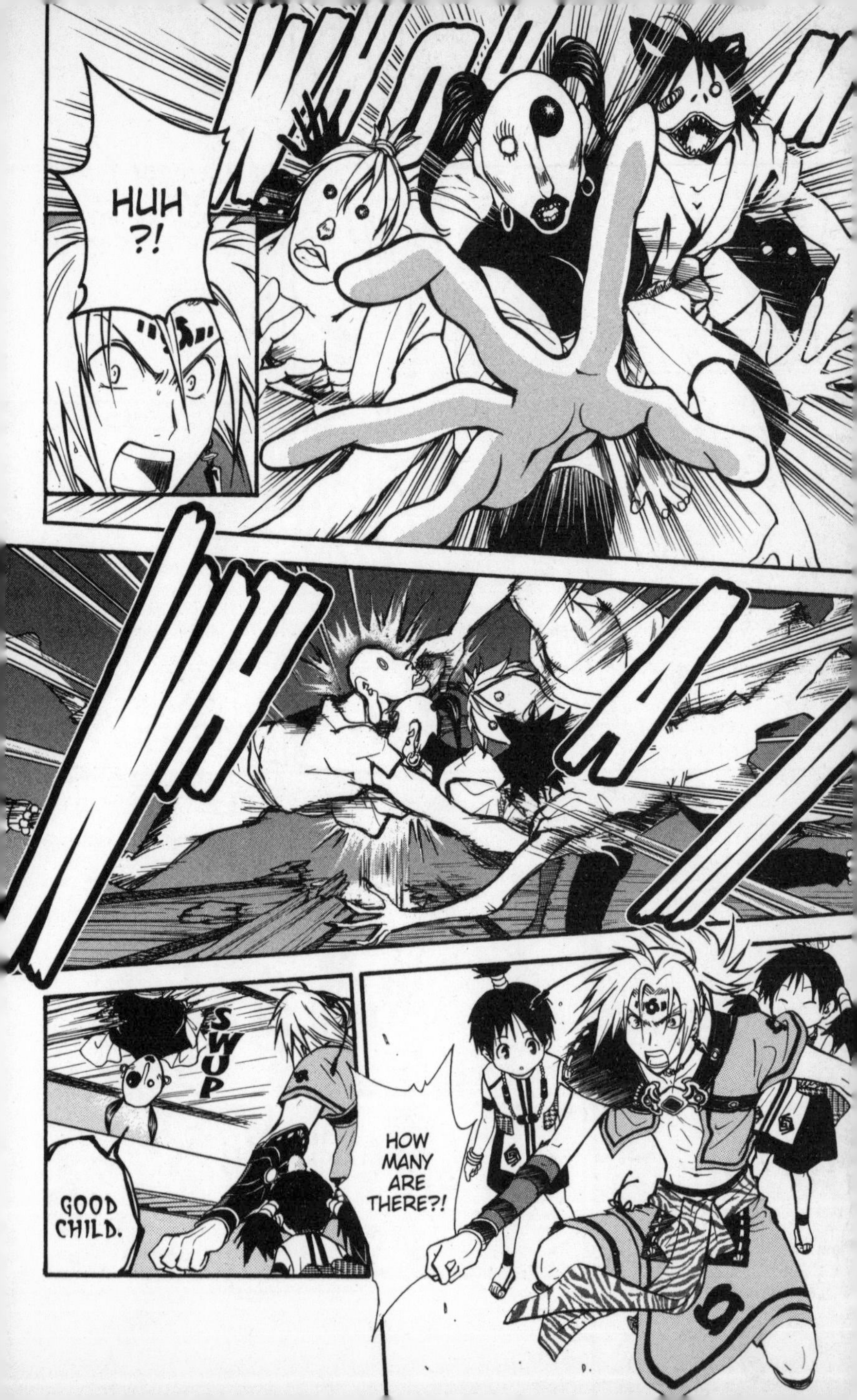
HUH ?!
HOW MANY ARE THERE?!
SWUP
GOOD CHILD.

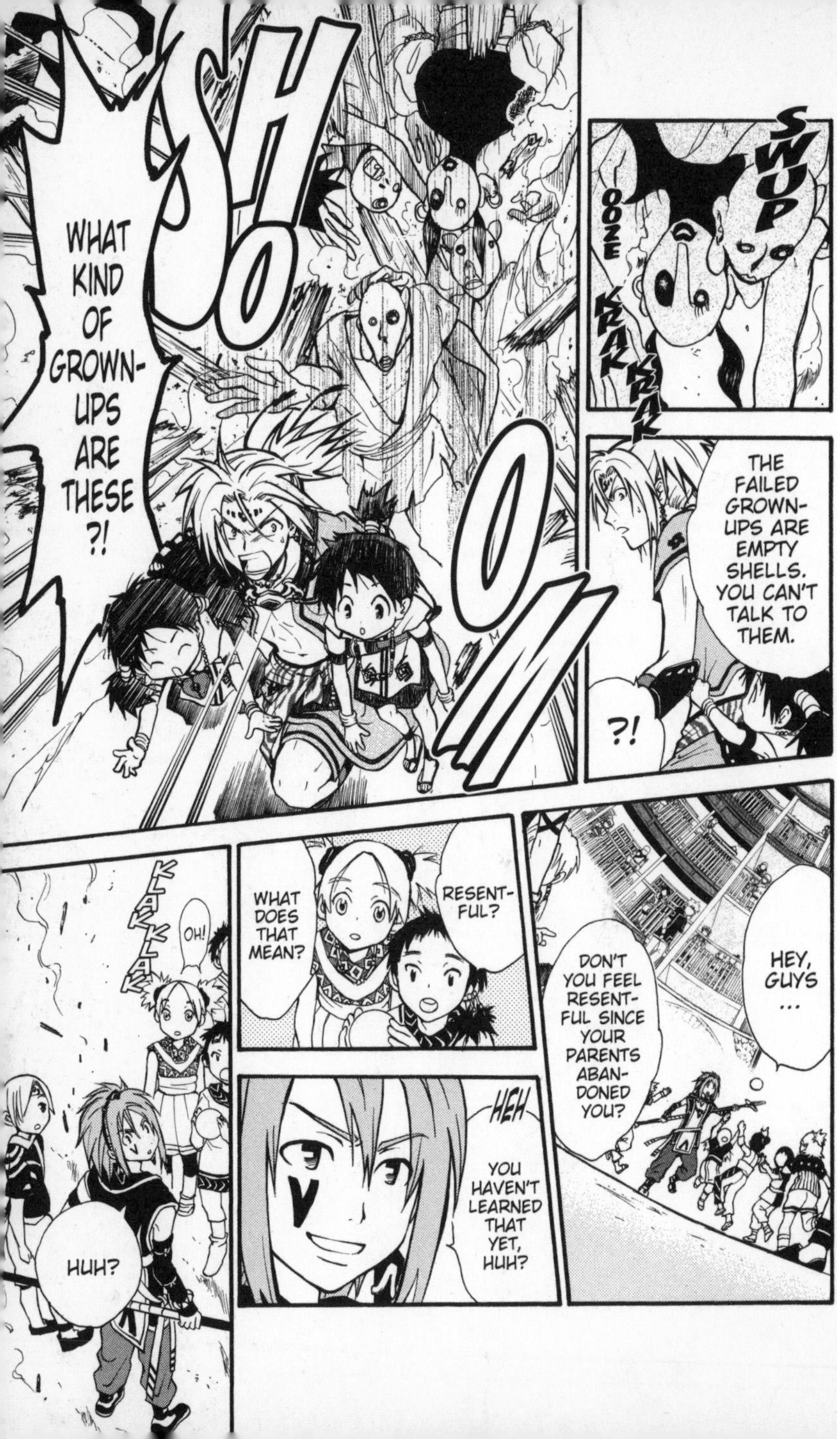
SWUP
OOZE
KRAK KRAK
THE FAILED GROWN-UPS ARE EMPTY SHELLS. YOU CAN'T TALK TO THEM.
?!
SHOOM
WHAT KIND OF GROWN-UPS ARE THESE ?!
HEY, GUYS ...
DON'T YOU FEEL RESENT-FUL SINCE YOUR PARENTS ABAN-DONED YOU?
RESENT-FUL?
WHAT DOES THAT MEAN?
HEH
YOU HAVEN'T LEARNED THAT YET, HUH?
KLAK KLAK
OH!
HUH?

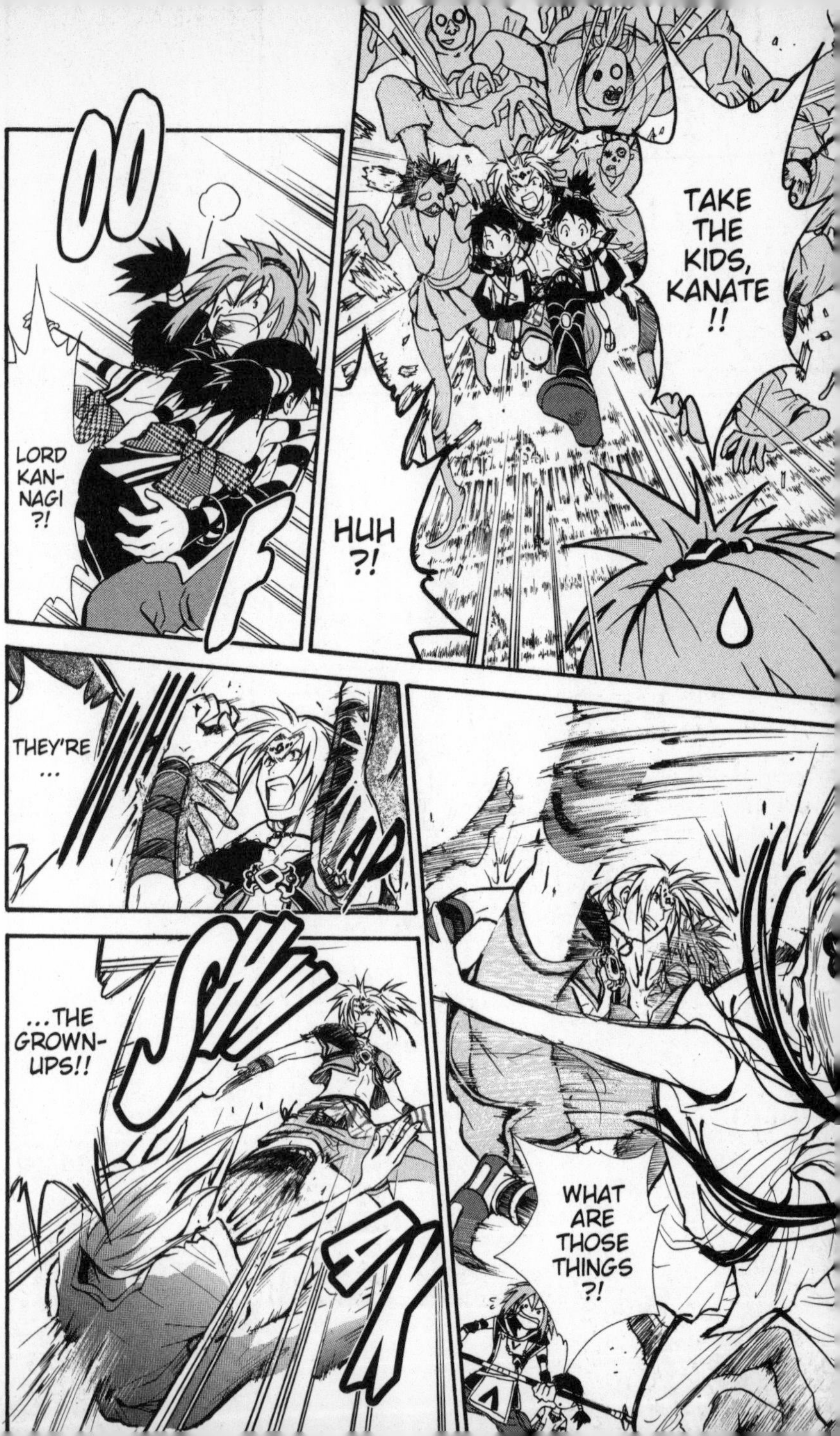
TAKE THE KIDS, KANATE !!
HUH ?!
OO
LORD KAN-NAGI ?!
WHAT ARE THOSE THINGS ?!
THEY'RE ...
...THE GROWN-UPS!!

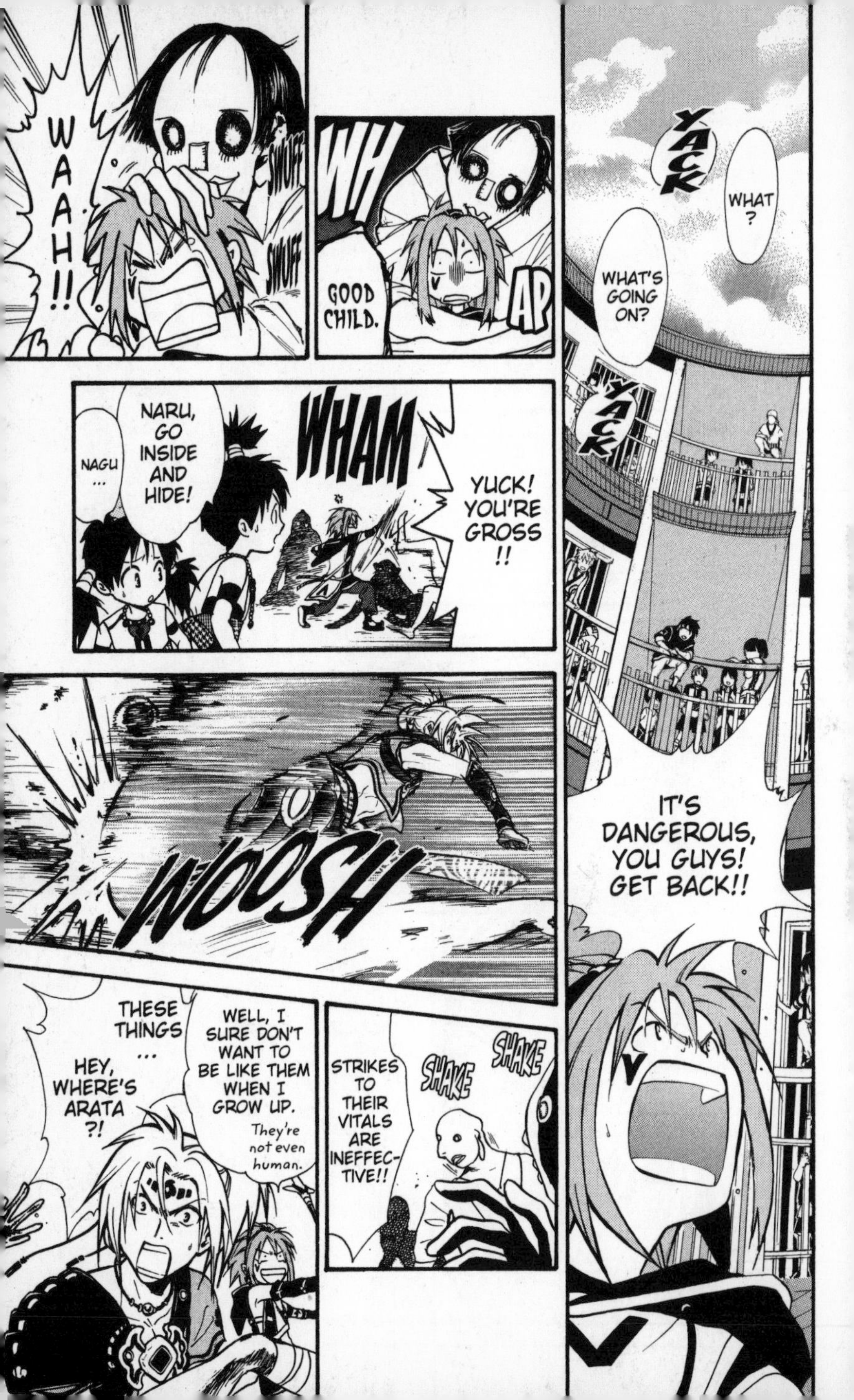
YACK
WHAT?
WHAT'S GOING ON?
YACK
IT'S DANGEROUS, YOU GUYS! GET BACK!!
WH
AP
GOOD CHILD.
SNUFF
SNUFF
WAAAH!!
YUCK! YOU'RE GROSS!!
WHAM
NARU, GO INSIDE AND HIDE!
NAGU...
WOOSH
SHAKE
SHAKE
STRIKES TO THEIR VITALS ARE INEFFECTIVE!!
WELL, I SURE DON'T WANT TO BE LIKE THEM WHEN I GROW UP.
They're not even human.
THESE THINGS...
HEY, WHERE'S ARATA?!

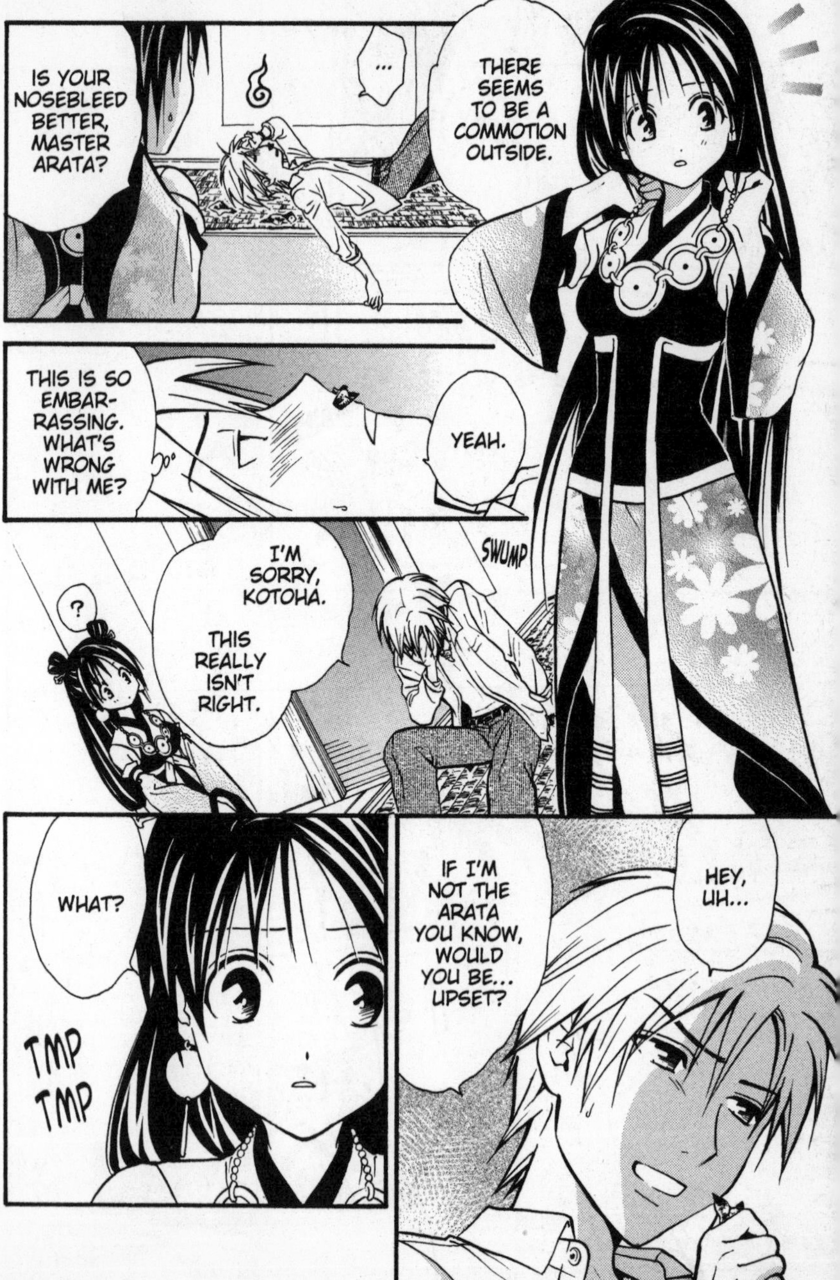
THERE SEEMS TO BE A COMMOTION OUTSIDE.
...
IS YOUR NOSEBLEED BETTER, MASTER ARATA?
YEAH.
THIS IS SO EMBAR-RASSING. WHAT'S WRONG WITH ME?
SWUMP
I'M SORRY, KOTOHA.
THIS REALLY ISN'T RIGHT.
?
HEY, UH...
IF I'M NOT THE ARATA YOU KNOW, WOULD YOU BE... UPSET?
WHAT?
TMP TMP

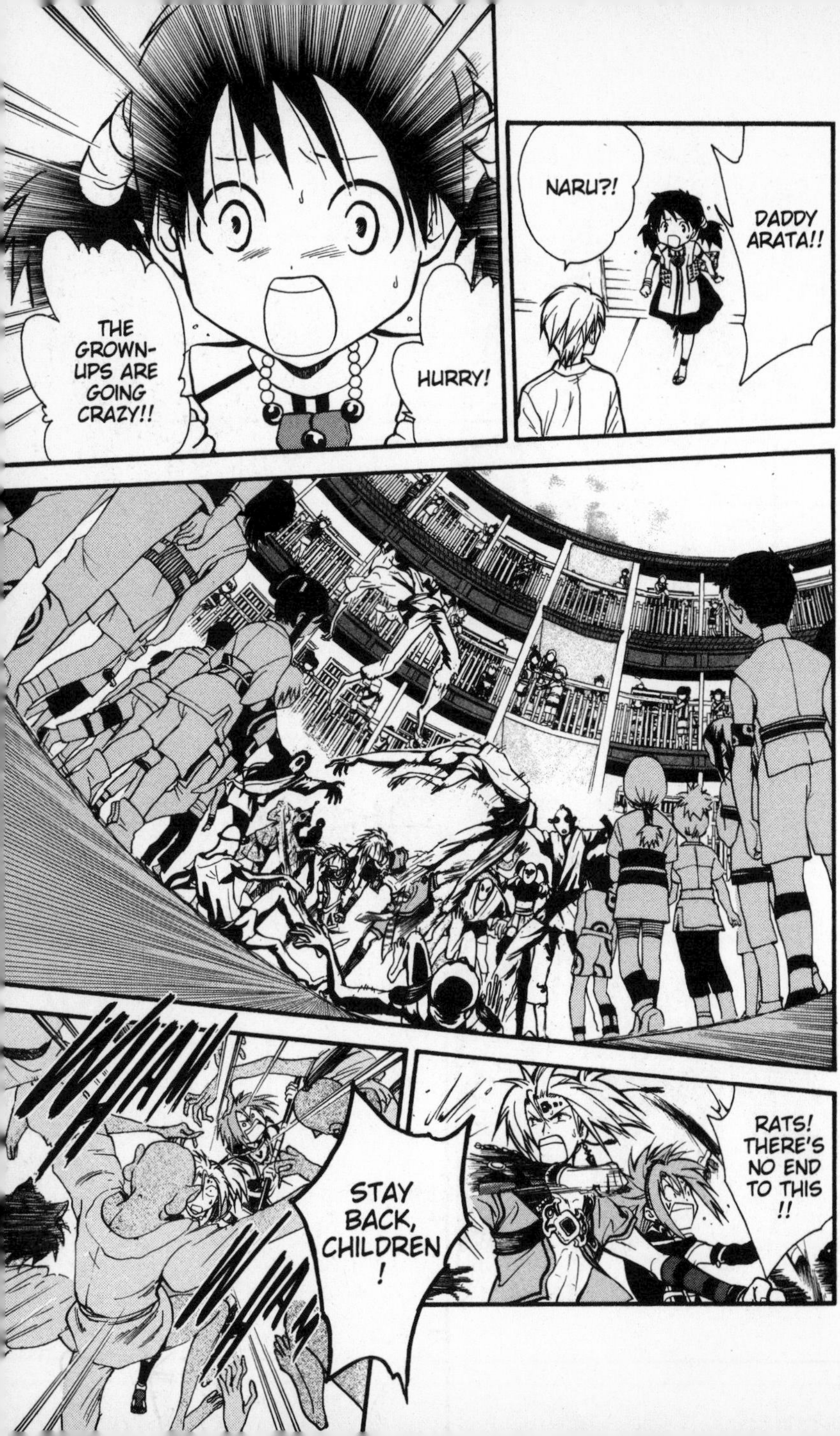
DADDY ARATA!!
NARU?!
HURRY!
THE GROWN-UPS ARE GOING CRAZY!!
RATS! THERE'S NO END TO THIS!!
STAY BACK, CHILDREN!
WHAM
WHAM

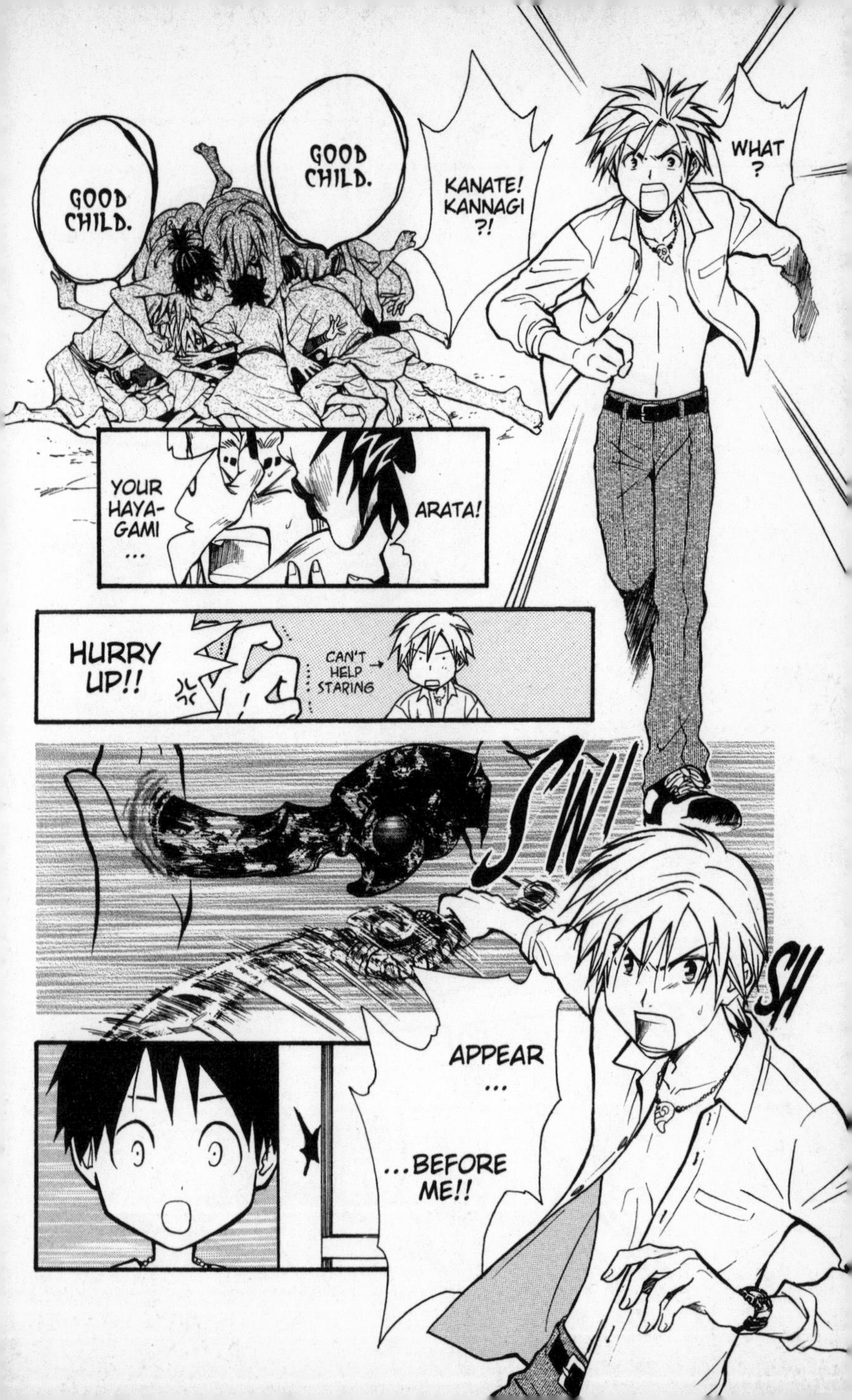
WHAT?
KANATE! KANNAGI?!
GOOD CHILD.
GOOD CHILD.
ARATA!
YOUR HAYA-GAMI...
CAN'T HELP STARING
HURRY UP!!
SWI
SH
APPEAR...
...BEFORE ME!!

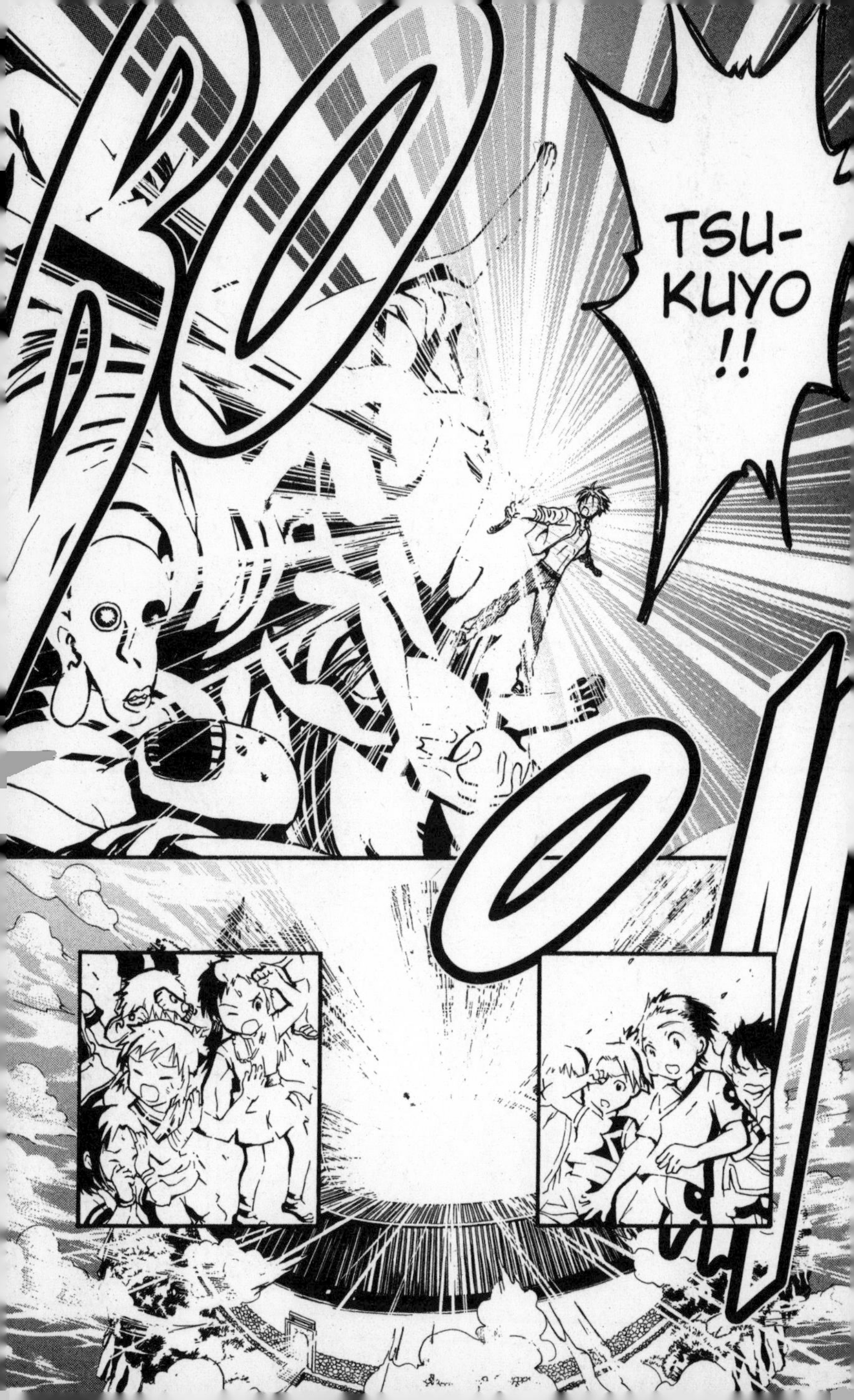
TSU-
KUYO
!!
BOOM!

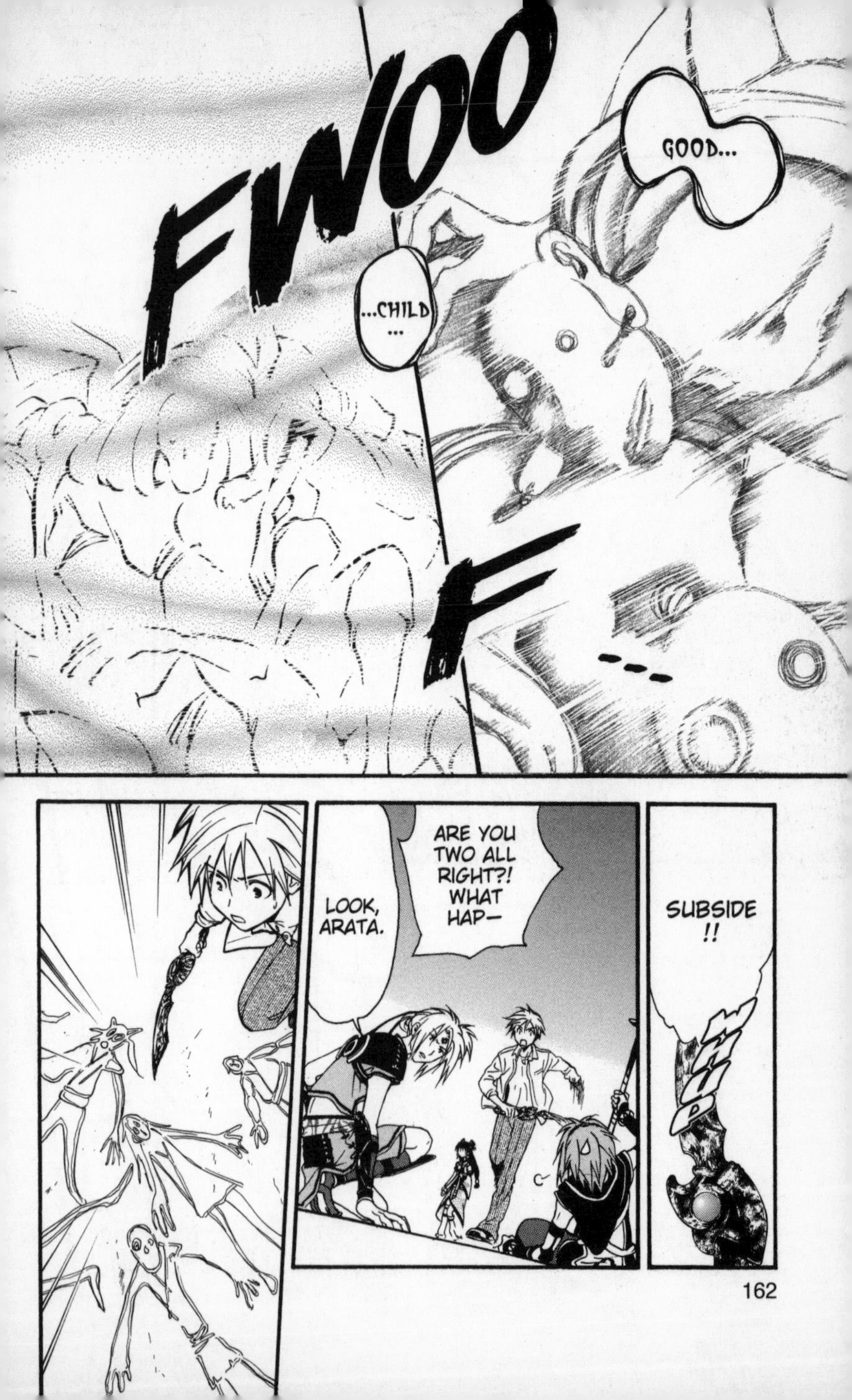
GOOD...
FWOO
...CHILD ...
F
...
SUBSIDE !!
WHIP
ARE YOU TWO ALL RIGHT?! WHAT HAP—
LOOK, ARATA.

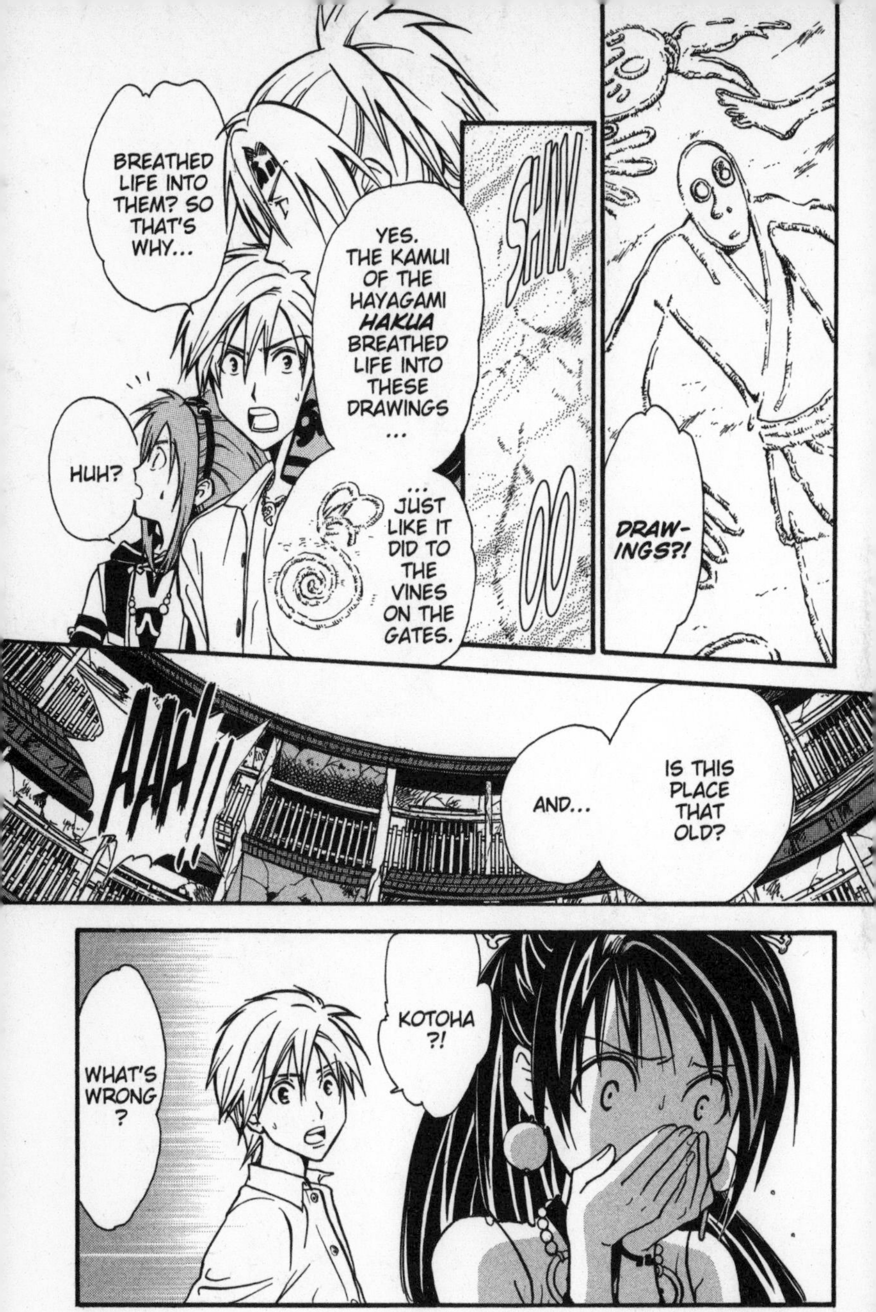
DRAW-INGS?!
SHW
OO
YES. THE KAMUI OF THE HAYAGAMI *HAKUA* BREATHED LIFE INTO THESE DRAWINGS ...
... JUST LIKE IT DID TO THE VINES ON THE GATES.
BREATHED LIFE INTO THEM? SO THAT'S WHY...
HUH?
IS THIS PLACE THAT OLD?
AND...
AAAH!!
KOTOHA ?!
WHAT'S WRONG ?

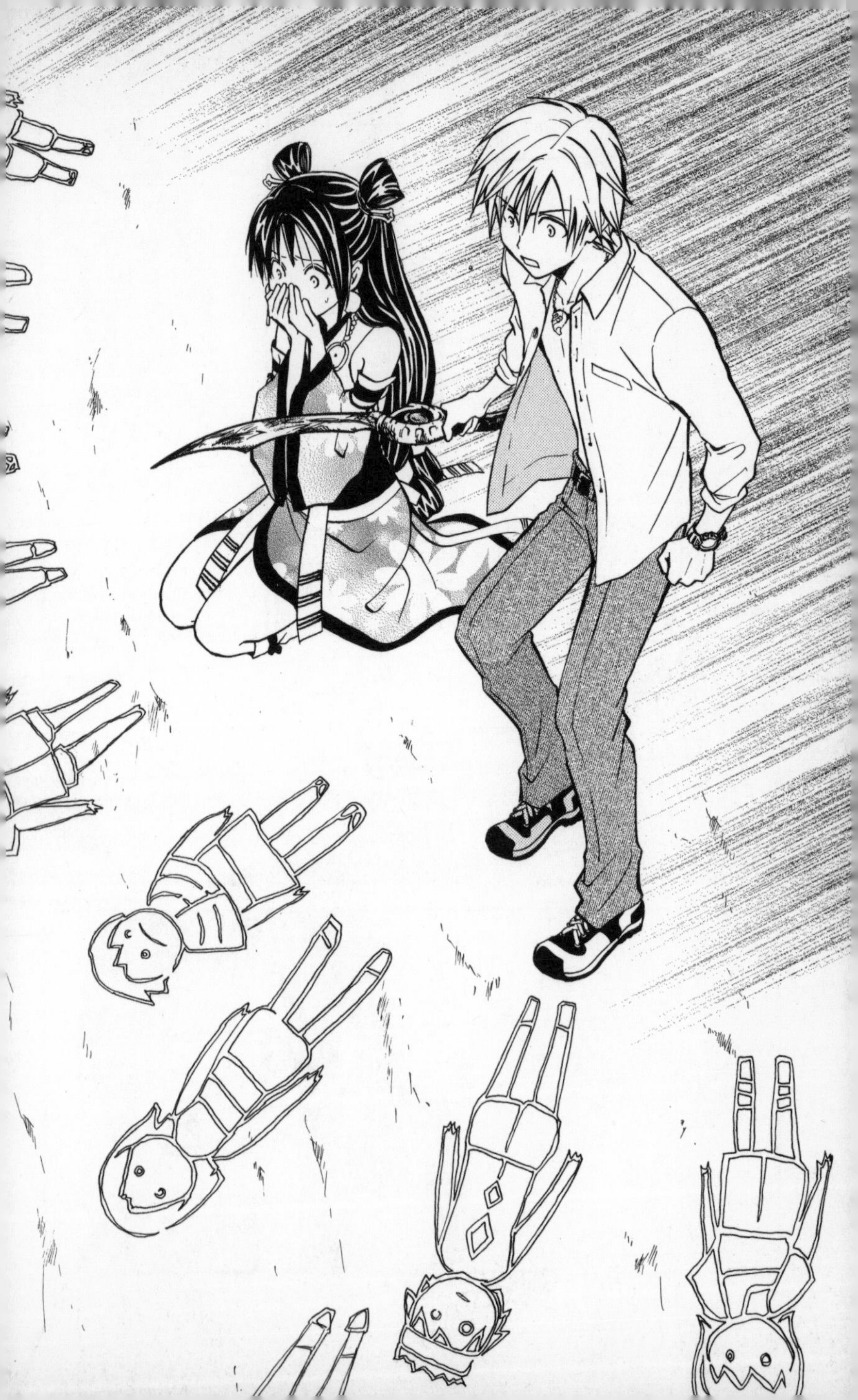

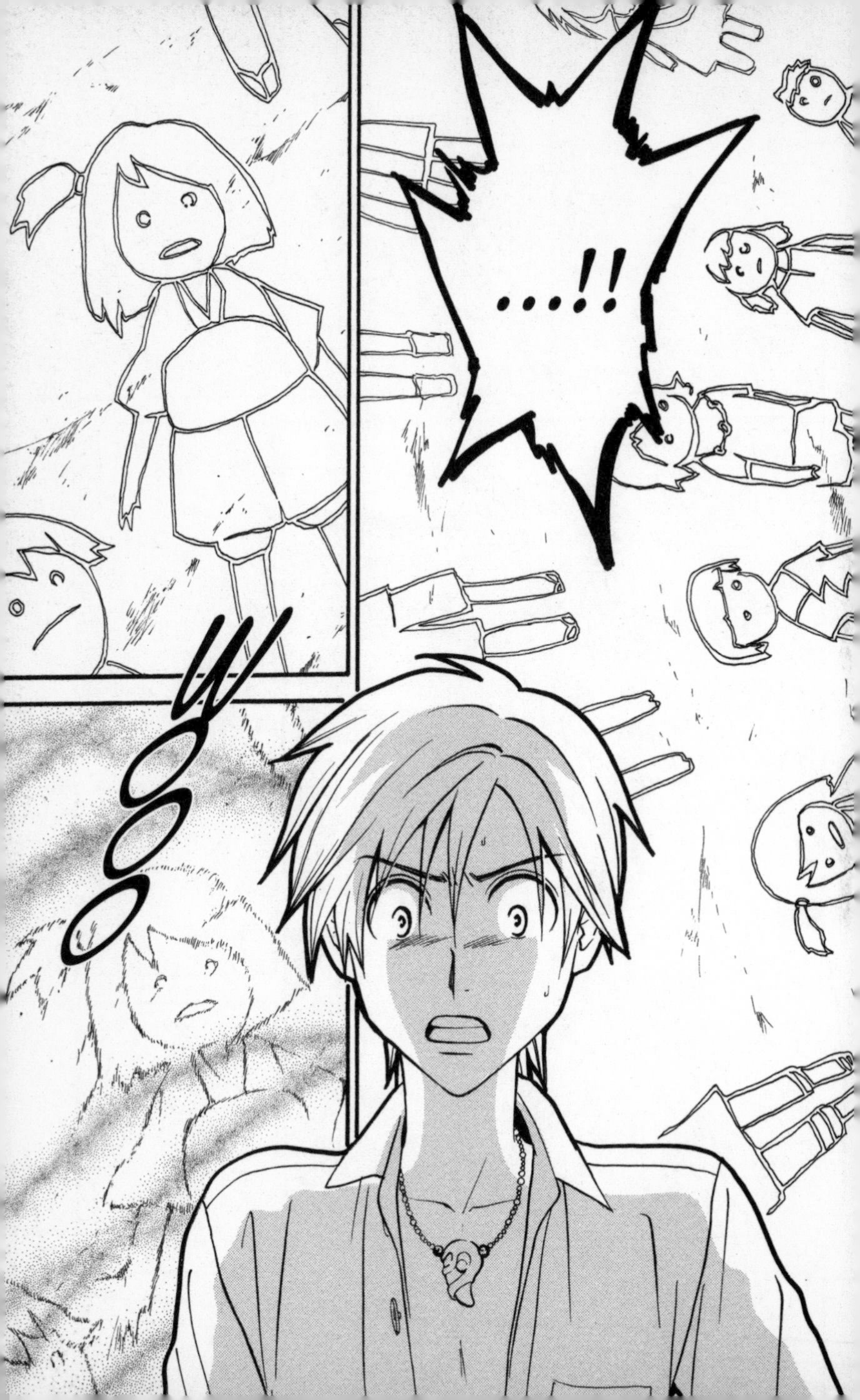
...!!
YOOO

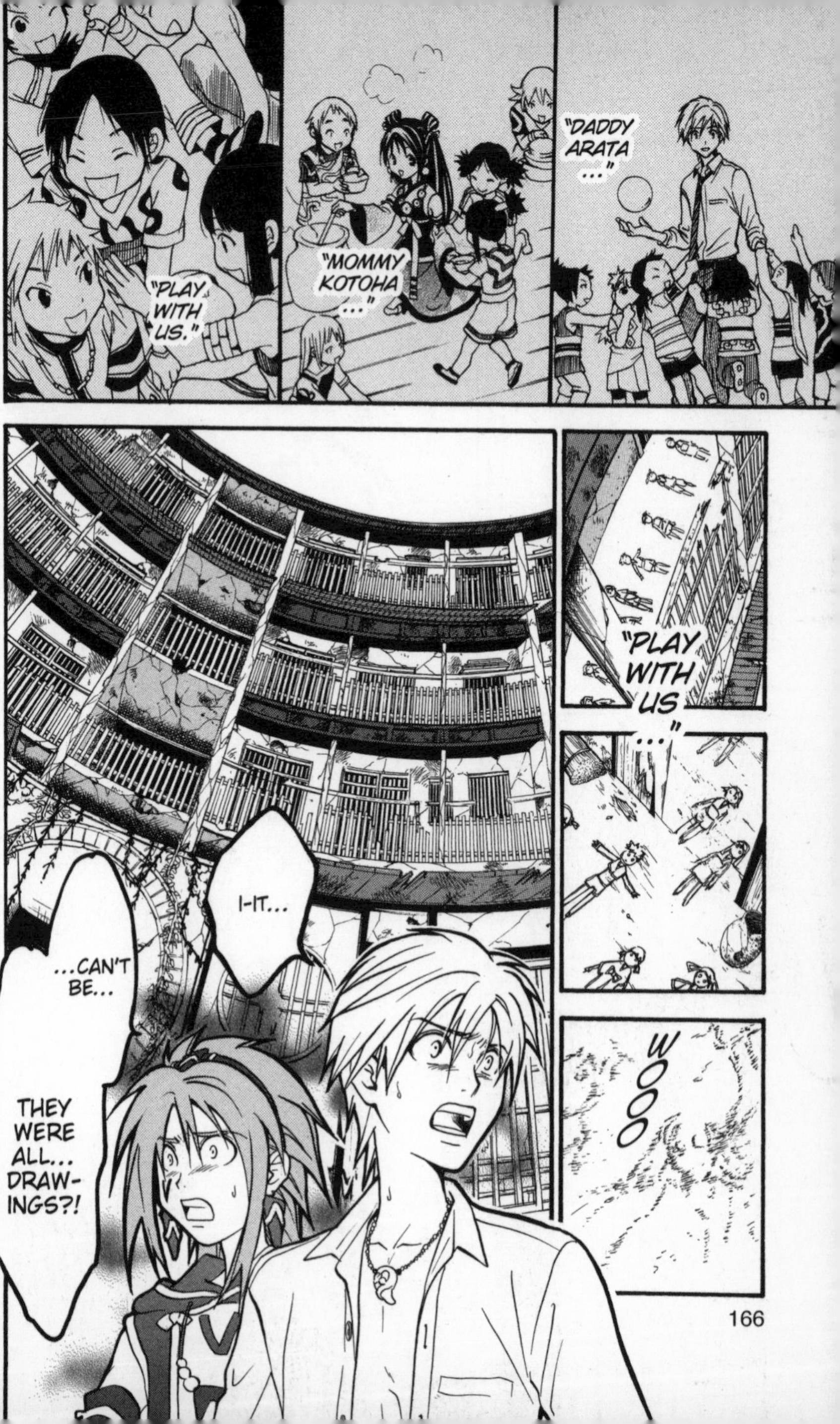
"DADDY ARATA..."
"MOMMY KOTOHA..."
"PLAY WITH US."
"PLAY WITH US..."
WOOOO
I-IT...
...CAN'T BE...
THEY WERE ALL... DRAWINGS?!

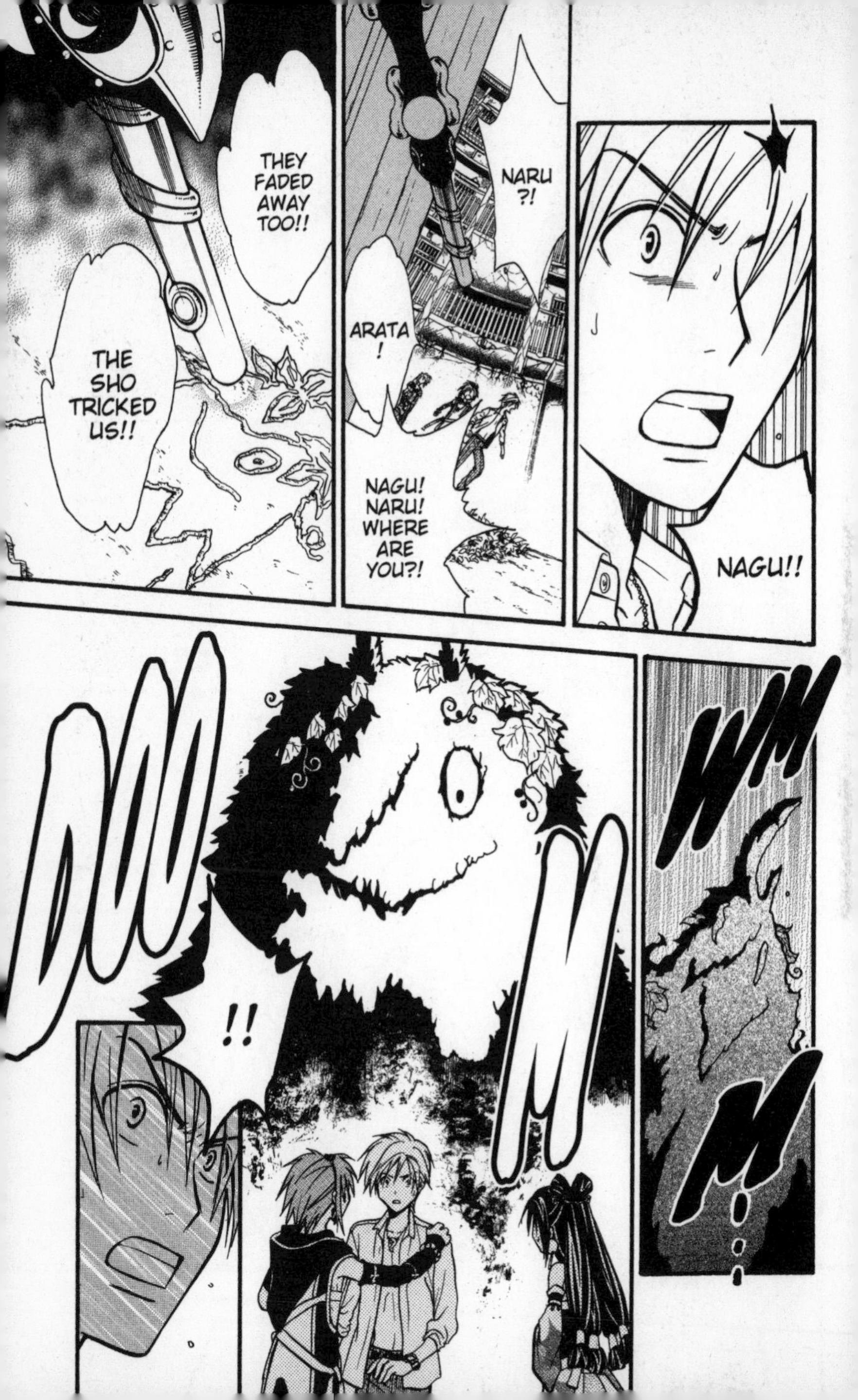
NAGU!!
NARU ?!
ARATA !
NAGU! NARU! WHERE ARE YOU?!
THEY FADED AWAY TOO!!
THE SHO TRICKED US!!
DOOM
!!

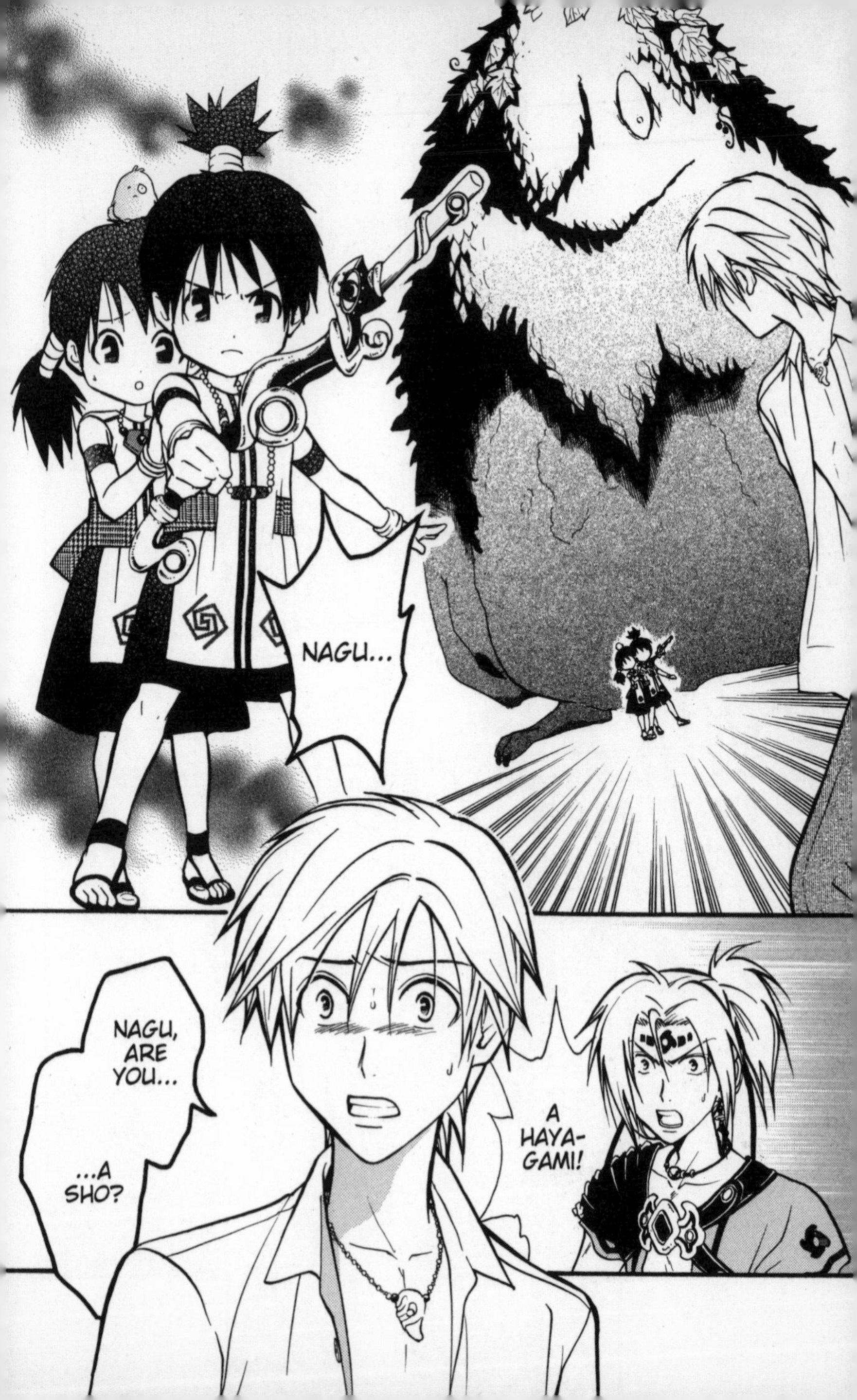
NAGU...
A HAYA-GAMI!
NAGU, ARE YOU...
...A SHO?

CHAPTER 37

NAGU AND NARU

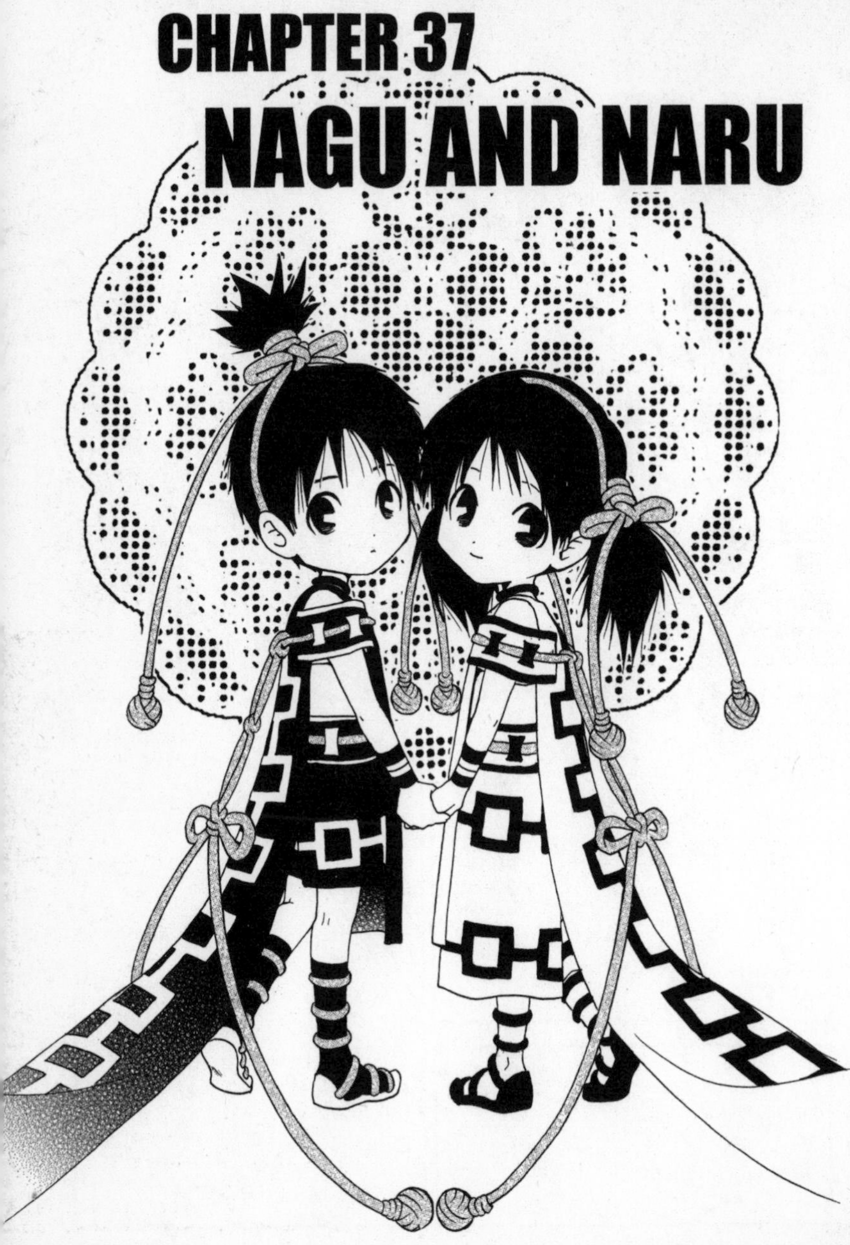

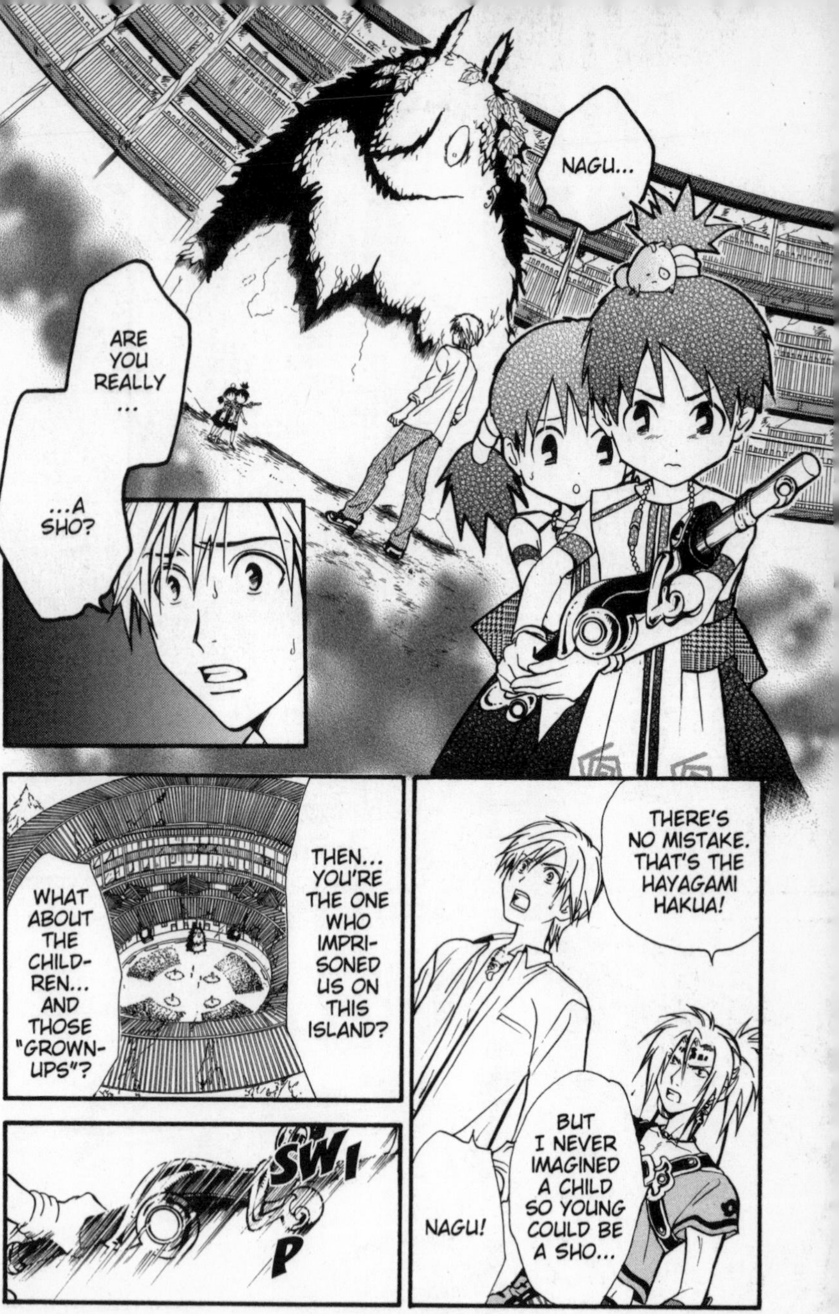
NAGU...
ARE YOU REALLY ... ...A SHO?
THERE'S NO MISTAKE. THAT'S THE HAYAGAMI HAKUA!
BUT I NEVER IMAGINED A CHILD SO YOUNG COULD BE A SHO...
NAGU!
THEN... YOU'RE THE ONE WHO IMPRISONED US ON THIS ISLAND?
WHAT ABOUT THE CHILDREN... AND THOSE "GROWN-UPS"?
SWIP

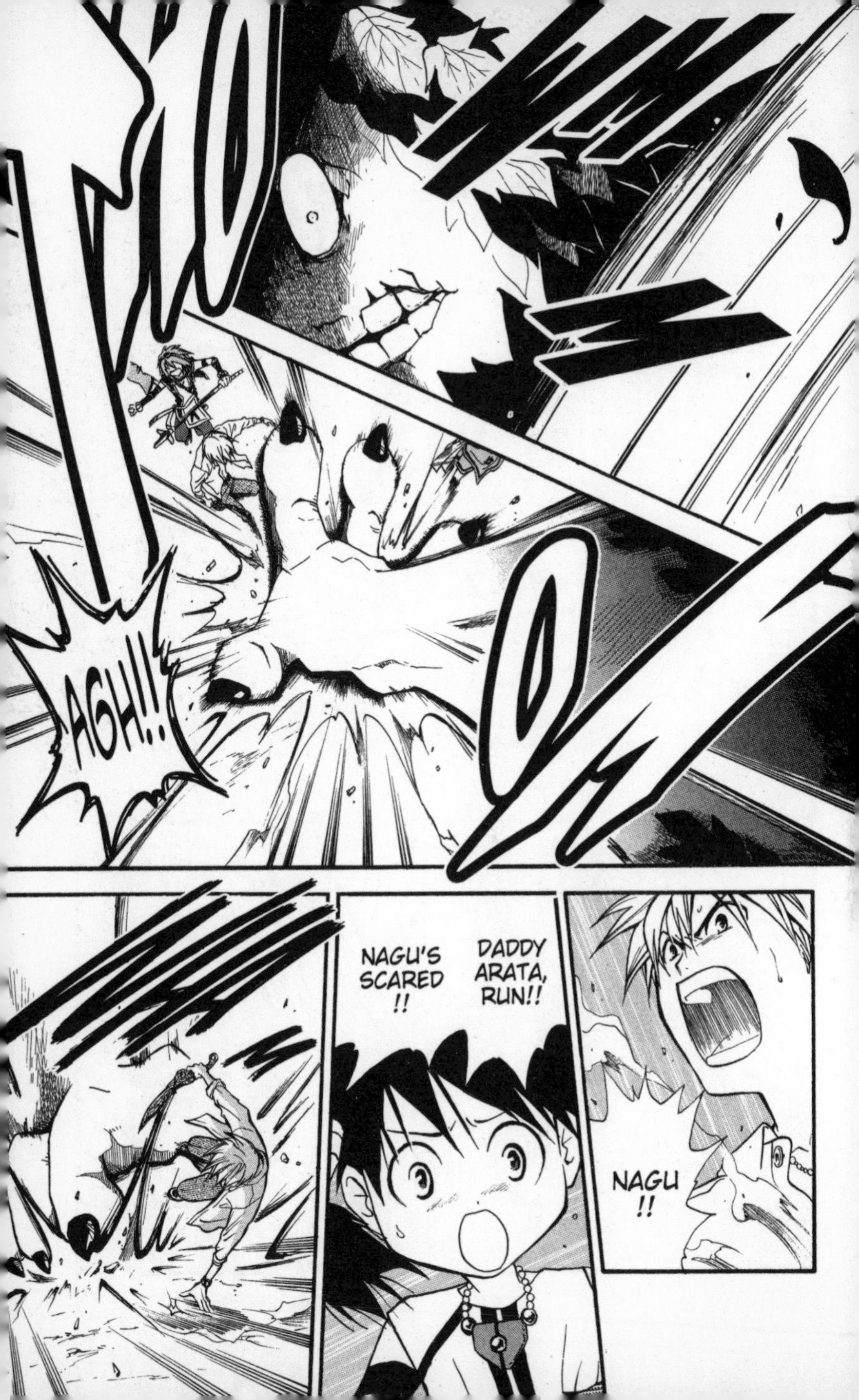
AGH!!
NAGU
!!
DADDY
ARATA,
RUN!!
NAGU'S
SCARED
!!

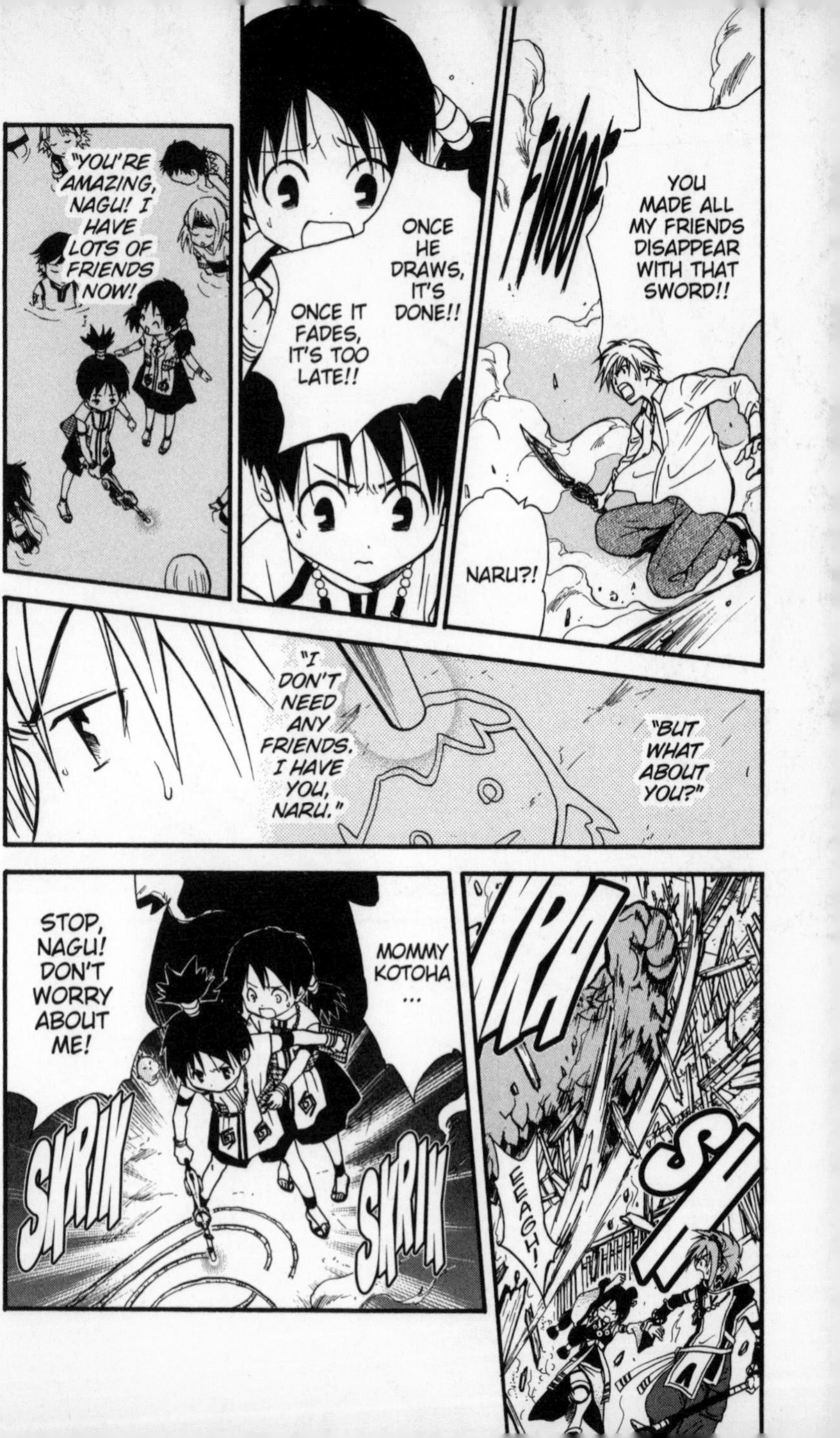
YOU MADE ALL MY FRIENDS DISAPPEAR WITH THAT SWORD!!
NARU?!
ONCE HE DRAWS, IT'S DONE!!
ONCE IT FADES, IT'S TOO LATE!!
"YOU'RE AMAZING, NAGU! I HAVE LOTS OF FRIENDS NOW!
"BUT WHAT ABOUT YOU?"
"I DON'T NEED ANY FRIENDS. I HAVE YOU, NARU."
EEAGH!
MOMMY KOTOHA ...
STOP, NAGU! DON'T WORRY ABOUT ME!
SHRIN
SHRIN

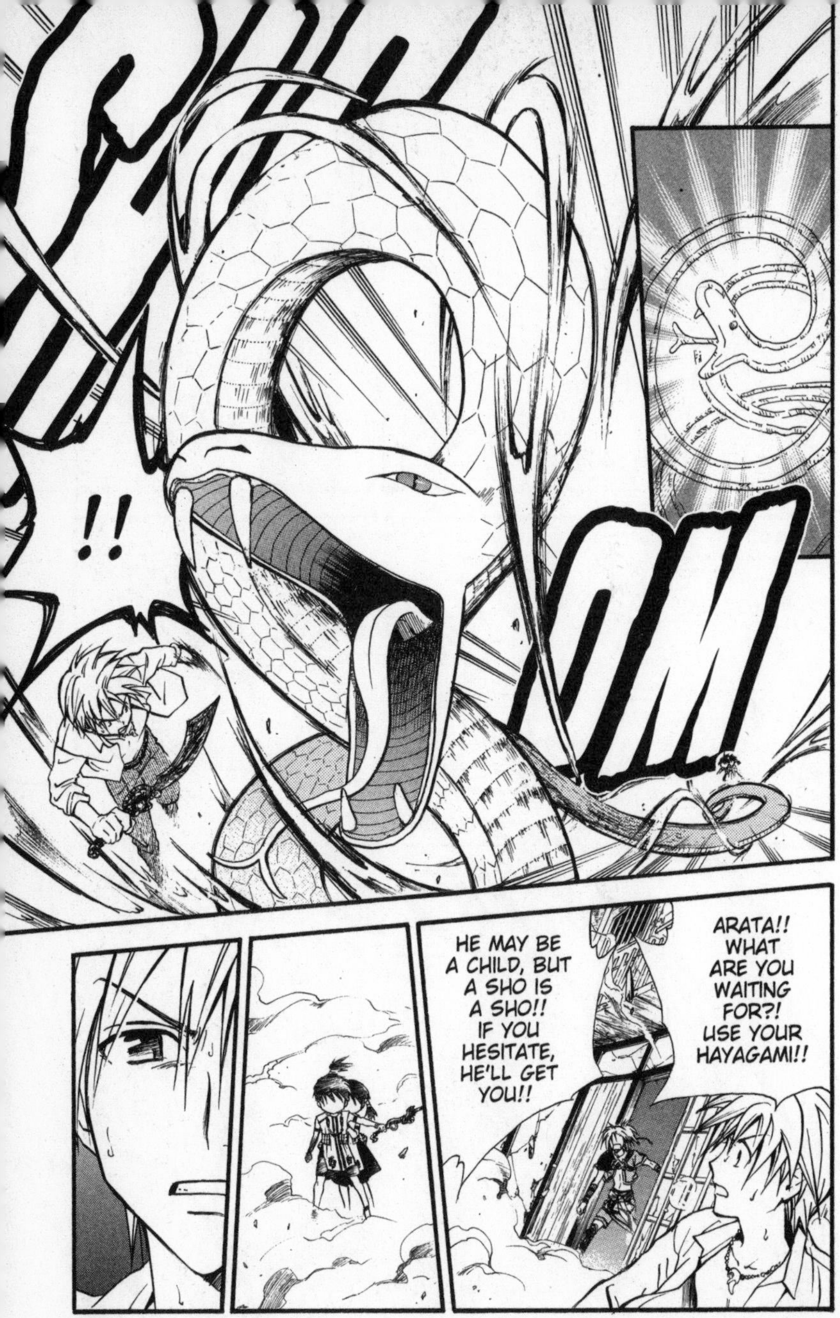
!!
ARATA!! WHAT ARE YOU WAITING FOR?! USE YOUR HAYAGAMI!!
HE MAY BE A CHILD, BUT A SHO IS A SHO!! IF YOU HESITATE, HE'LL GET YOU!!

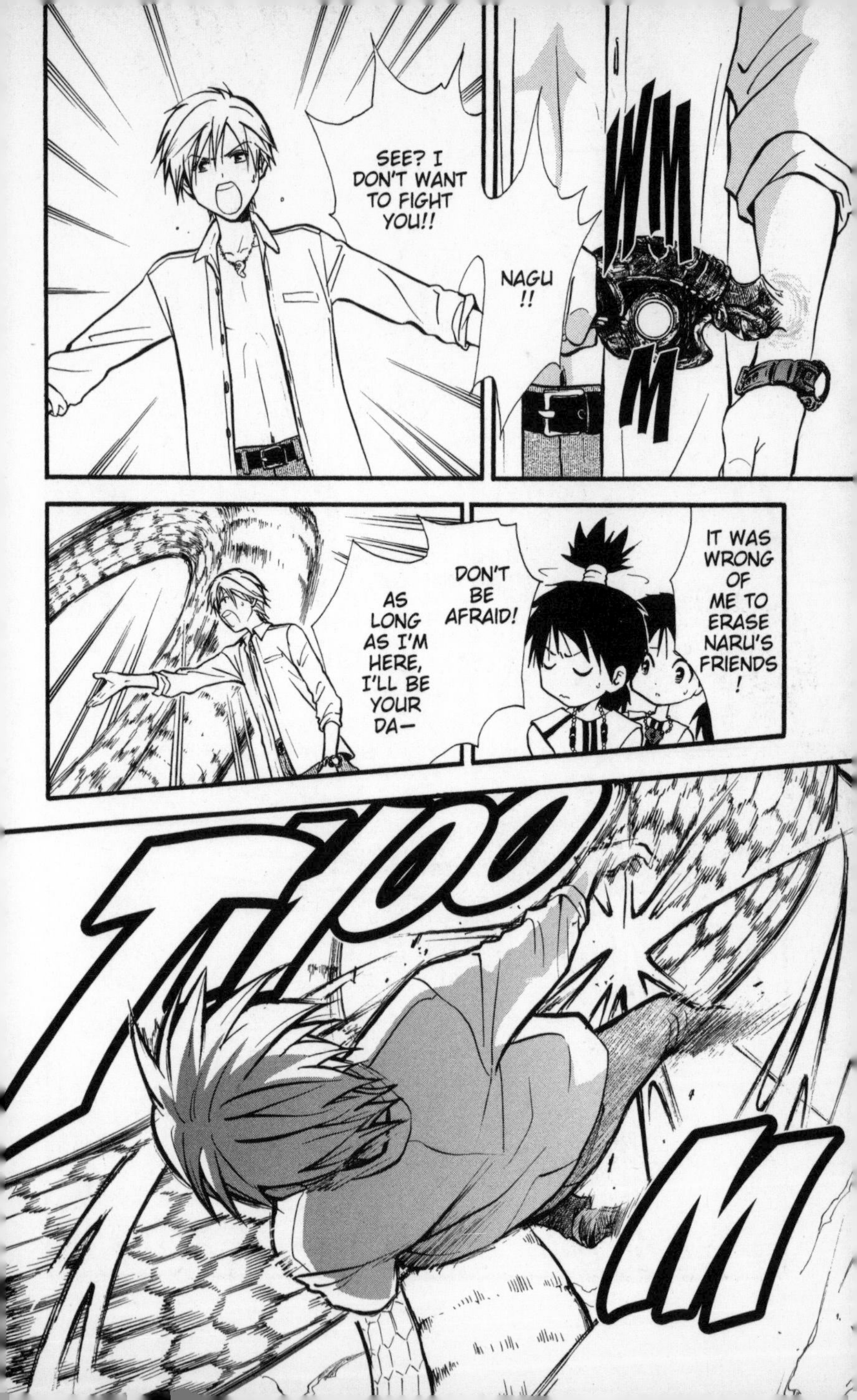
NAGU !!
WMM
SEE? I DON'T WANT TO FIGHT YOU!!
IT WAS WRONG OF ME TO ERASE NARU'S FRIENDS!
DON'T BE AFRAID!
AS LONG AS I'M HERE, I'LL BE YOUR DA—
FOOM

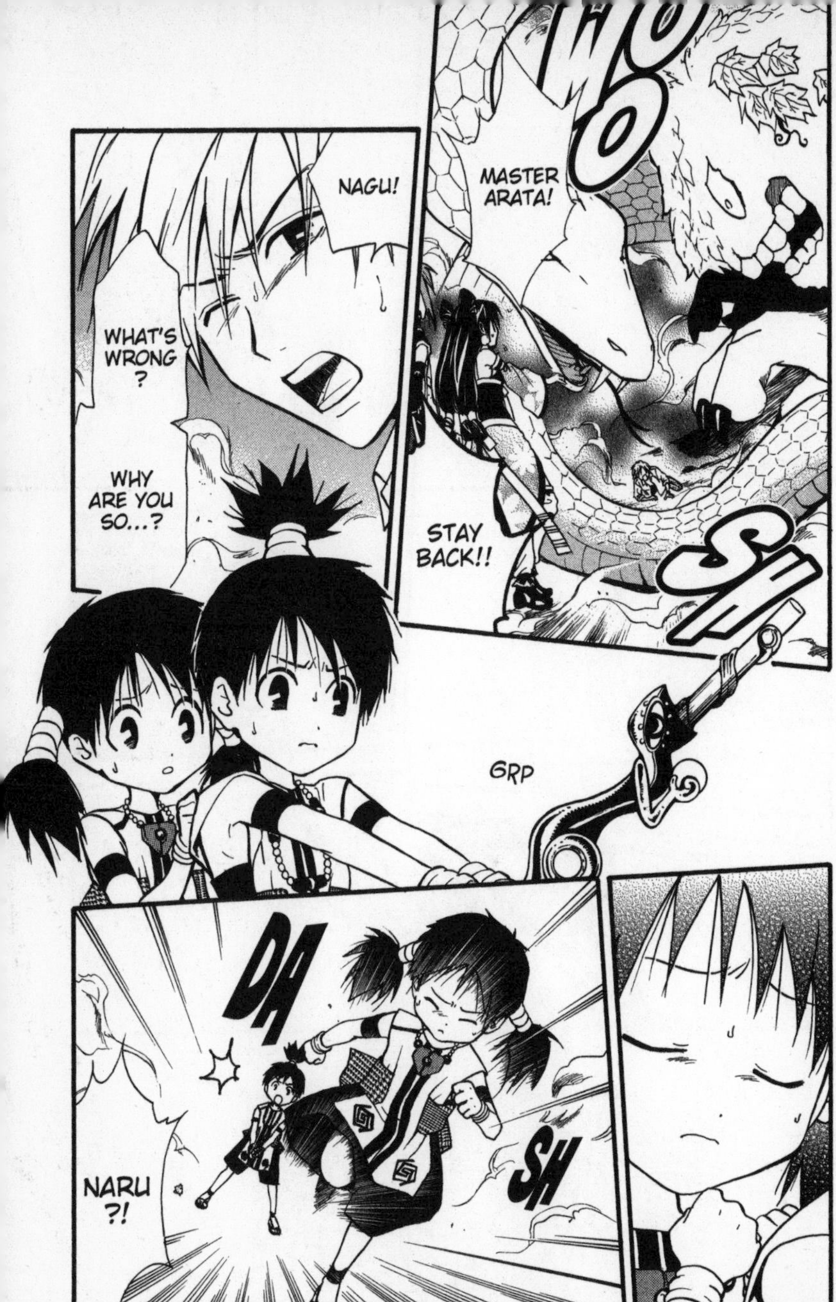
MASTER ARATA!
STAY BACK!!
SH
NAGU!
WHAT'S WRONG?
WHY ARE YOU SO...?
GRP
DA
SH
NARU?!

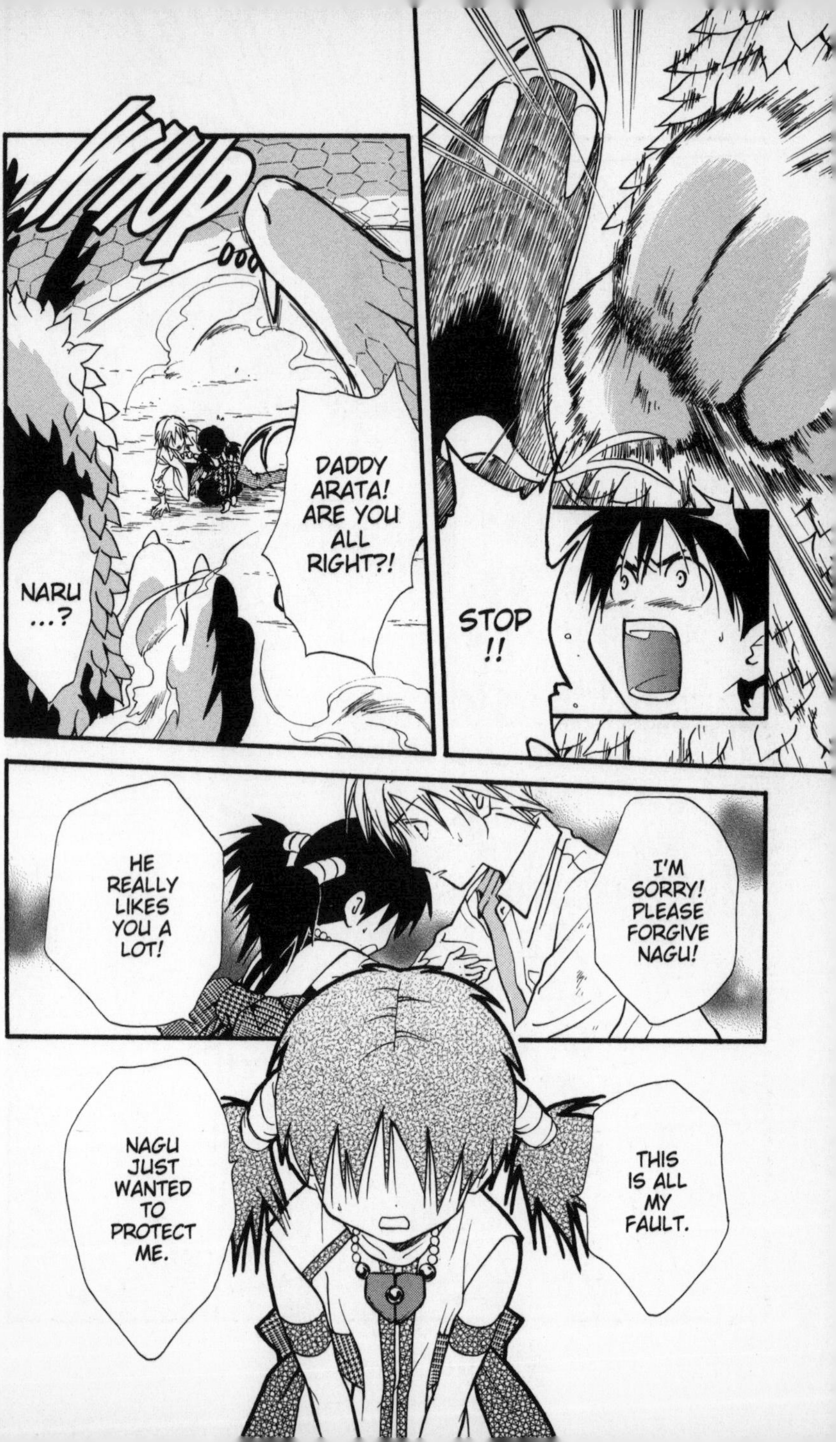
STOP!!
WHUP
OOO
DADDY ARATA! ARE YOU ALL RIGHT?!
NARU...?
I'M SORRY! PLEASE FORGIVE NAGU!
HE REALLY LIKES YOU A LOT!
THIS IS ALL MY FAULT.
NAGU JUST WANTED TO PROTECT ME.

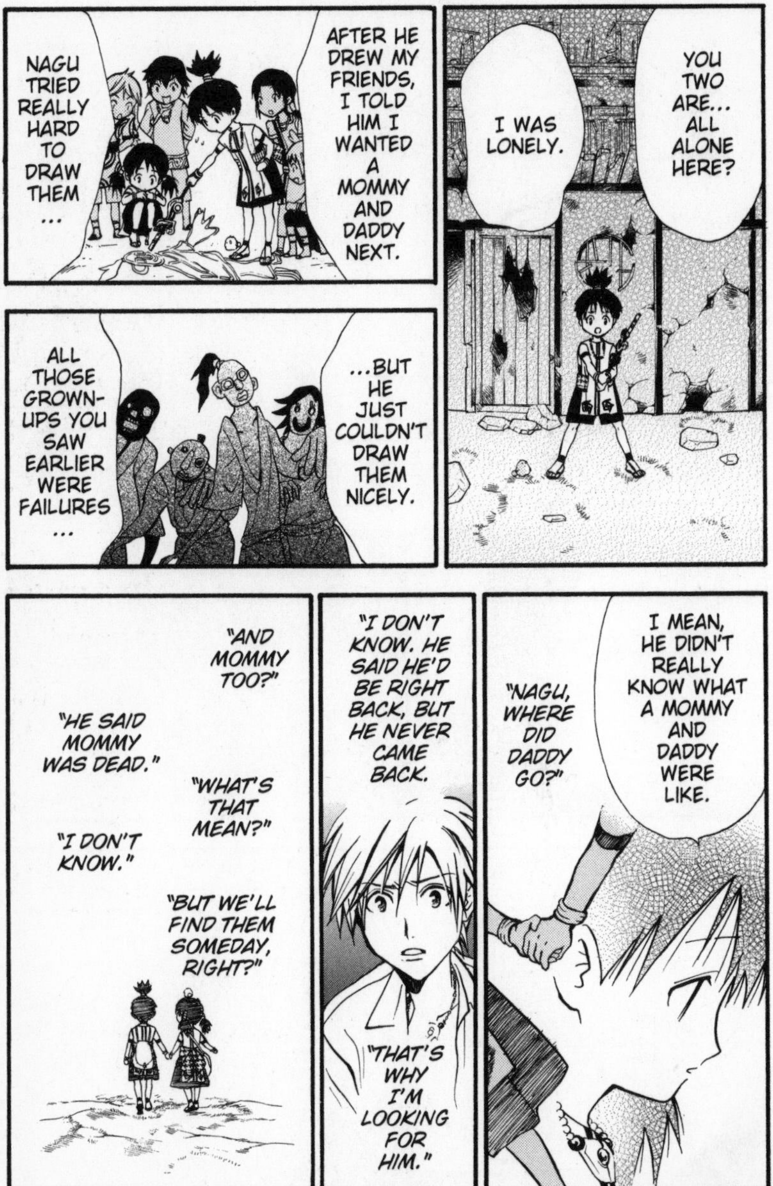
YOU TWO ARE... ALL ALONE HERE?
I WAS LONELY.
AFTER HE DREW MY FRIENDS, I TOLD HIM I WANTED A MOMMY AND DADDY NEXT.
NAGU TRIED REALLY HARD TO DRAW THEM...
...BUT HE JUST COULDN'T DRAW THEM NICELY.
ALL THOSE GROWN-UPS YOU SAW EARLIER WERE FAILURES...
I MEAN, HE DIDN'T REALLY KNOW WHAT A MOMMY AND DADDY WERE LIKE.
"NAGU, WHERE DID DADDY GO?"
"I DON'T KNOW. HE SAID HE'D BE RIGHT BACK, BUT HE NEVER CAME BACK.
"THAT'S WHY I'M LOOKING FOR HIM."
"AND MOMMY TOO?"
"HE SAID MOMMY WAS DEAD."
"WHAT'S THAT MEAN?"
"I DON'T KNOW."
"BUT WE'LL FIND THEM SOMEDAY, RIGHT?"

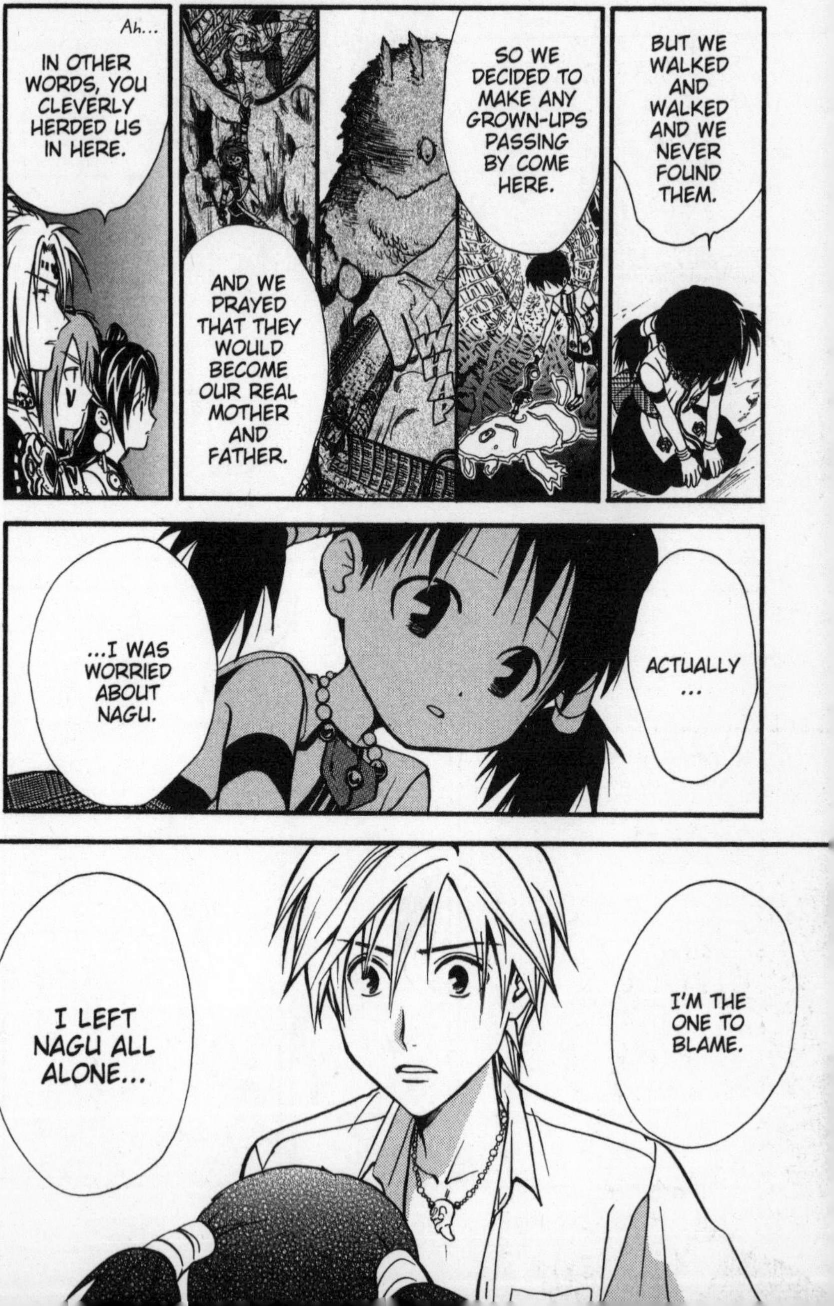
BUT WE WALKED AND WALKED AND WE NEVER FOUND THEM.
SO WE DECIDED TO MAKE ANY GROWN-UPS PASSING BY COME HERE.
AND WE PRAYED THAT THEY WOULD BECOME OUR REAL MOTHER AND FATHER.
Ah...
IN OTHER WORDS, YOU CLEVERLY HERDED US IN HERE.
ACTUALLY...
...I WAS WORRIED ABOUT NAGU.
I'M THE ONE TO BLAME.
I LEFT NAGU ALL ALONE...

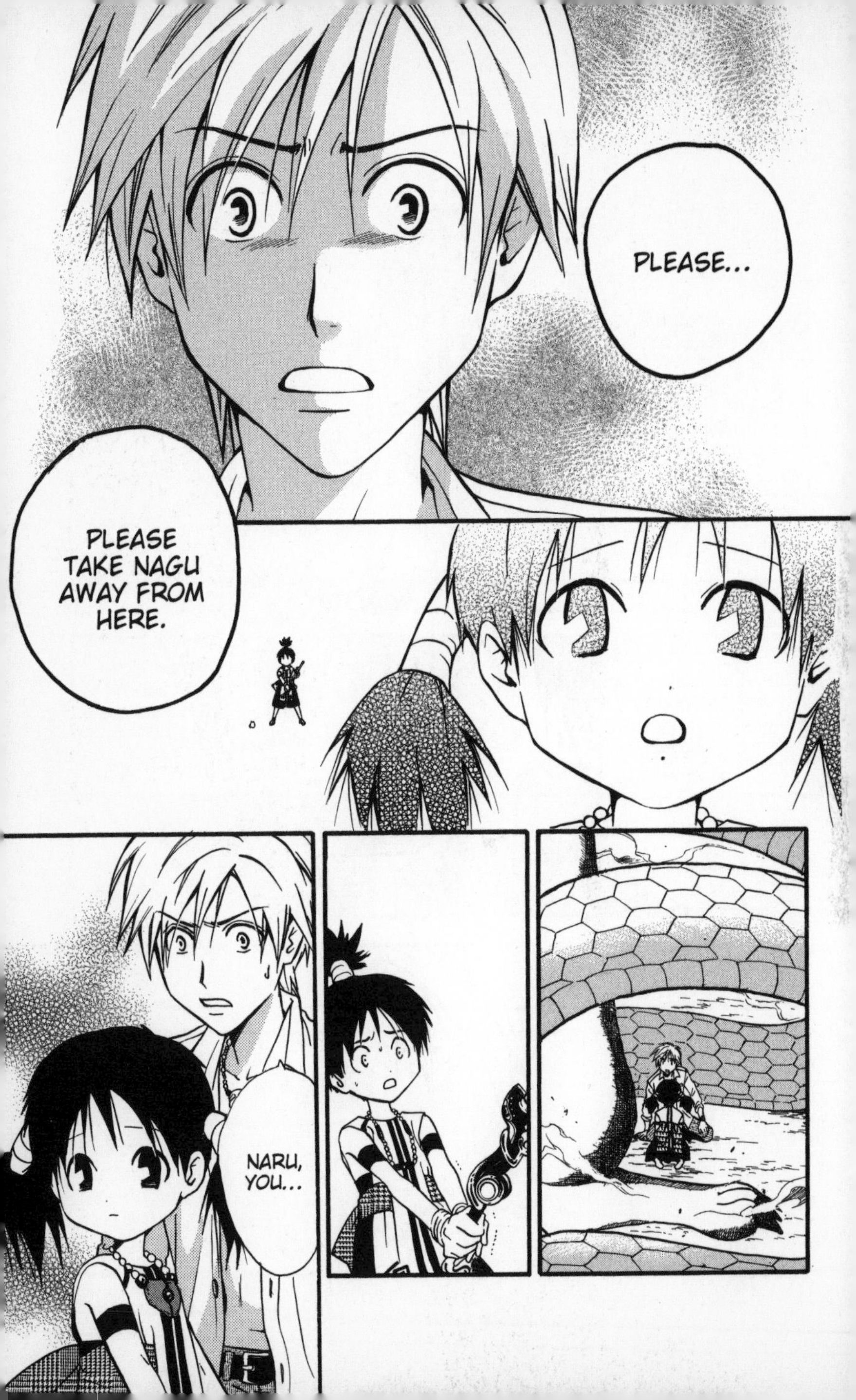
PLEASE...
PLEASE TAKE NAGU AWAY FROM HERE.
NARU, YOU...

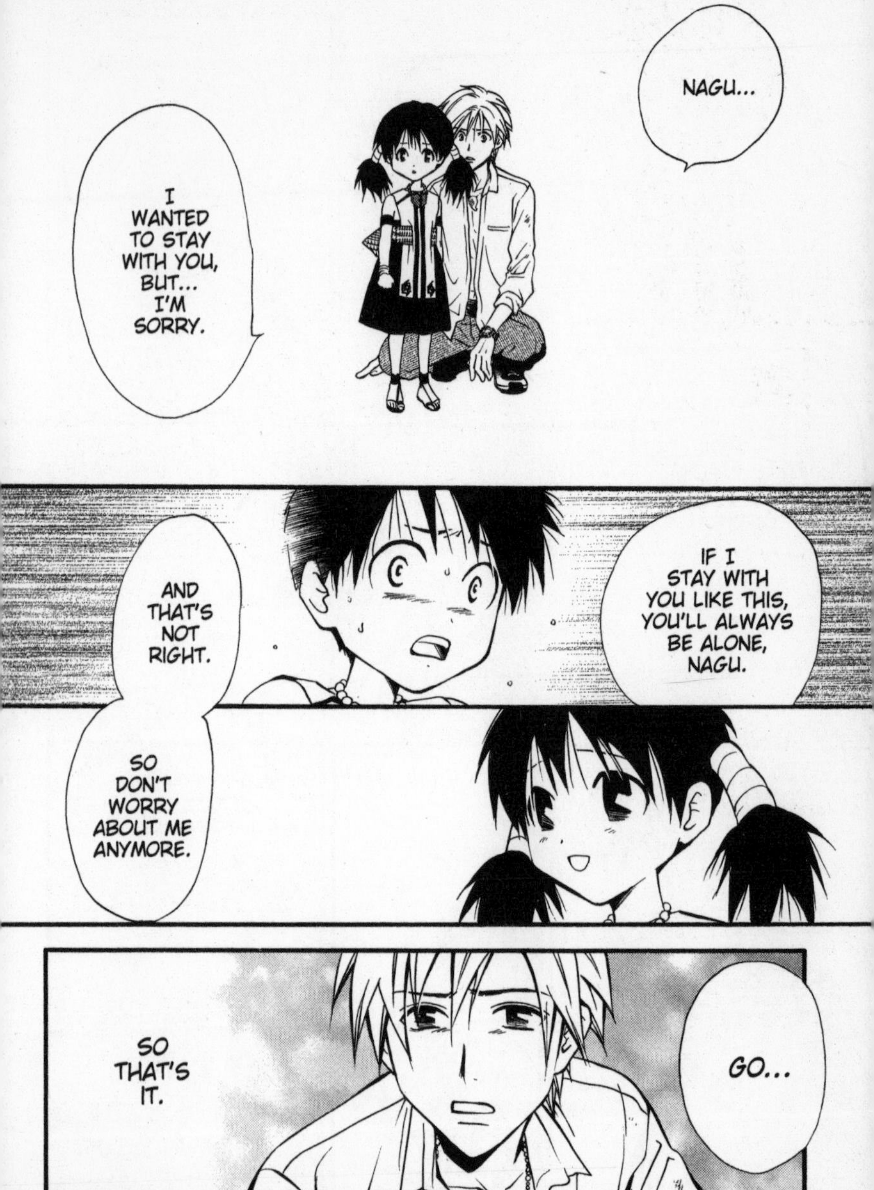
NAGU...
I WANTED TO STAY WITH YOU, BUT... I'M SORRY.
IF I STAY WITH YOU LIKE THIS, YOU'LL ALWAYS BE ALONE, NAGU.
AND THAT'S NOT RIGHT.
SO DON'T WORRY ABOUT ME ANYMORE.
GO...
SO THAT'S IT.

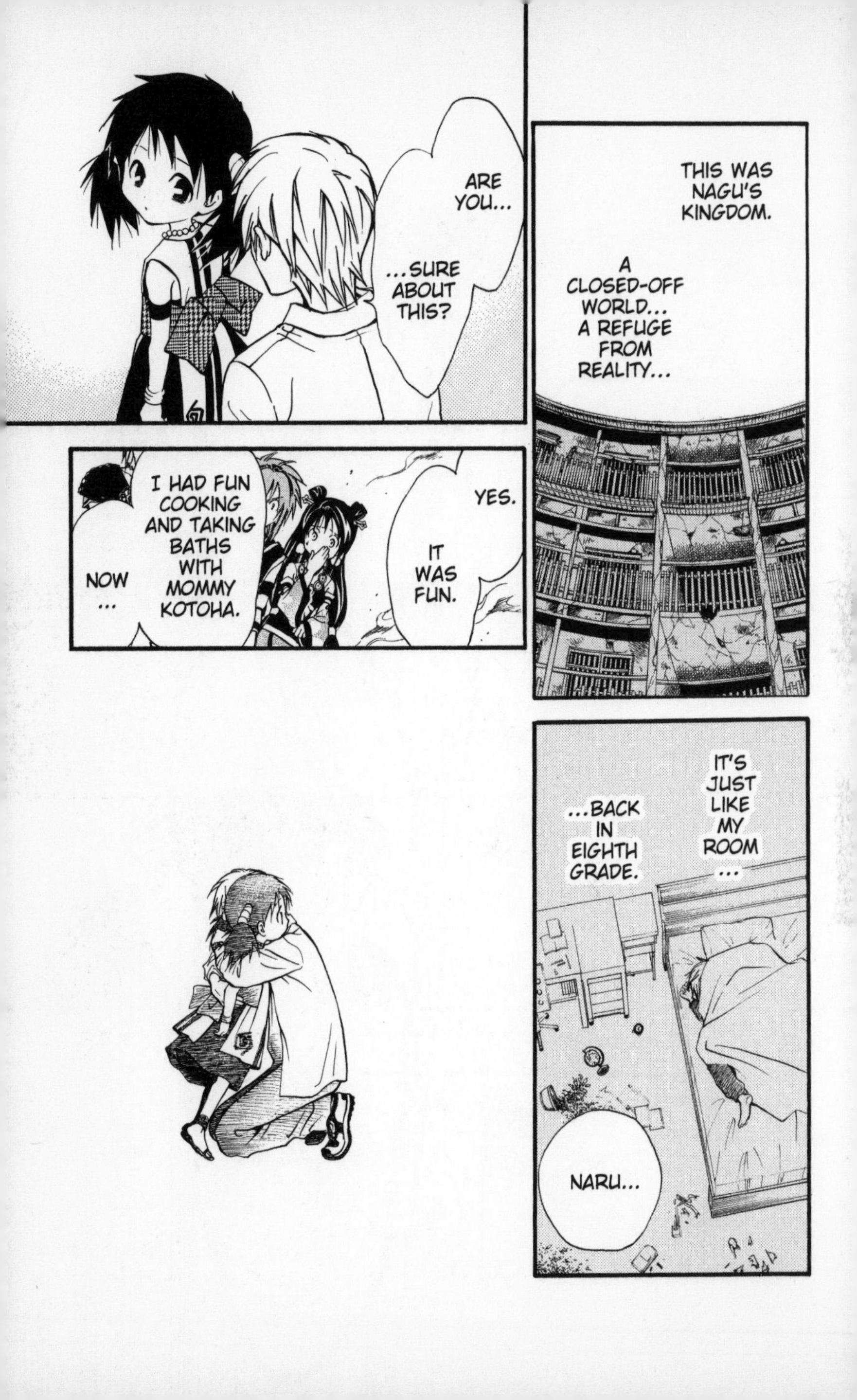
THIS WAS NAGU'S KINGDOM.
A CLOSED-OFF WORLD... A REFUGE FROM REALITY...
ARE YOU...
...SURE ABOUT THIS?
YES.
IT WAS FUN.
I HAD FUN COOKING AND TAKING BATHS WITH MOMMY KOTOHA.
NOW ...
IT'S JUST LIKE MY ROOM ...
...BACK IN EIGHTH GRADE.
NARU...

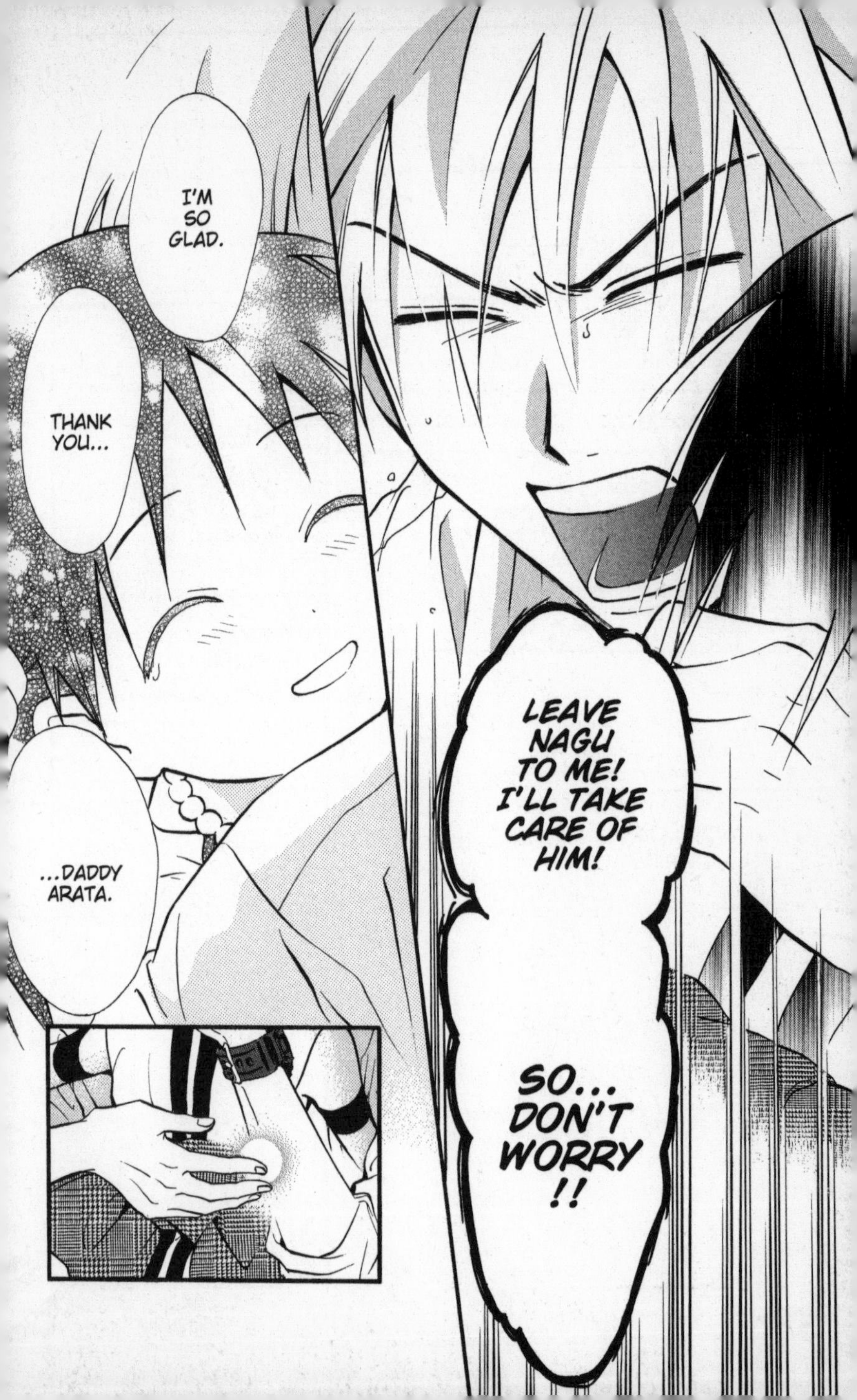
LEAVE NAGU TO ME! I'LL TAKE CARE OF HIM!
SO... DON'T WORRY!!
I'M SO GLAD.
THANK YOU...
...DADDY ARATA.

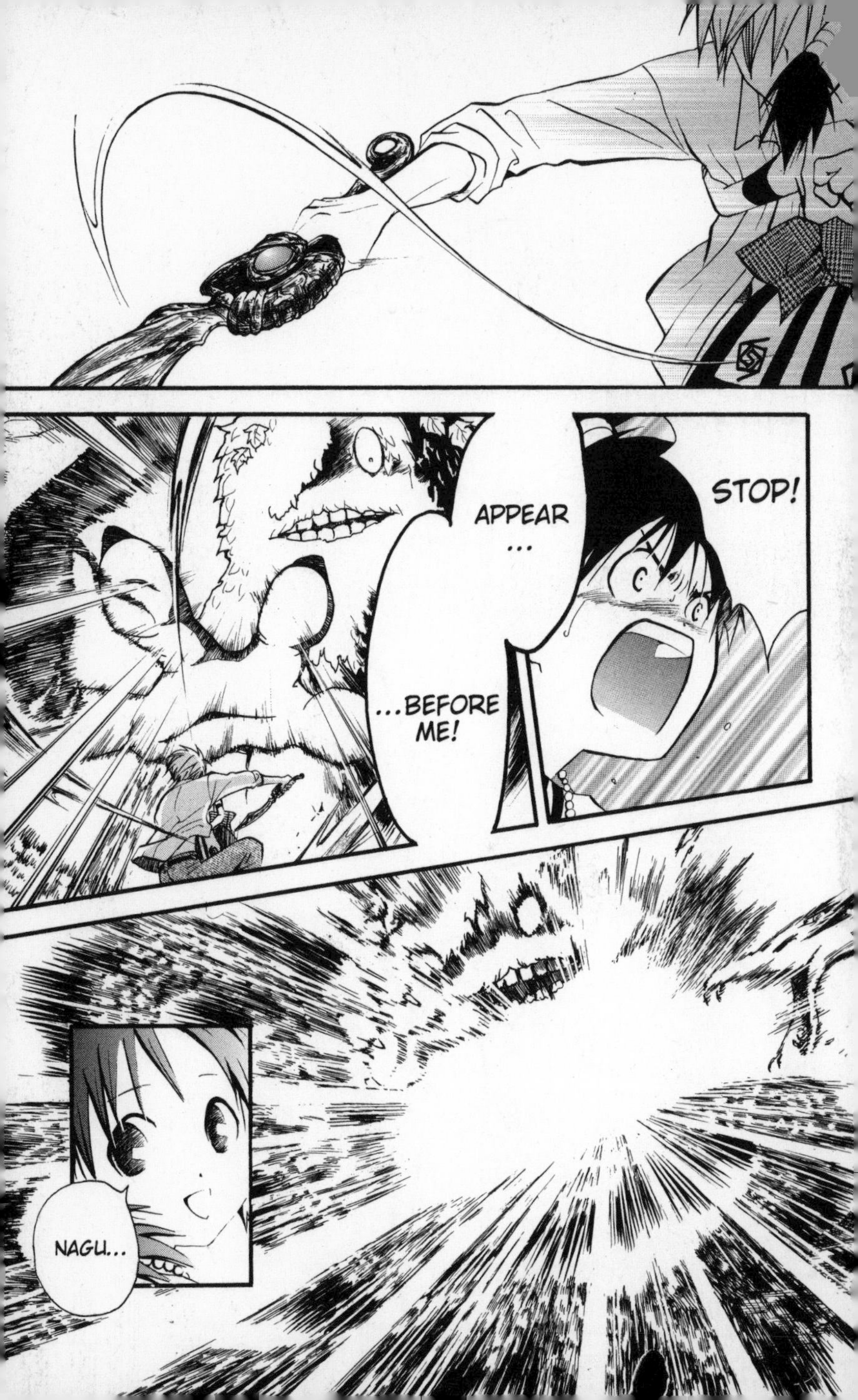
STOP!
APPEAR ...
...BEFORE ME!
NAGU...

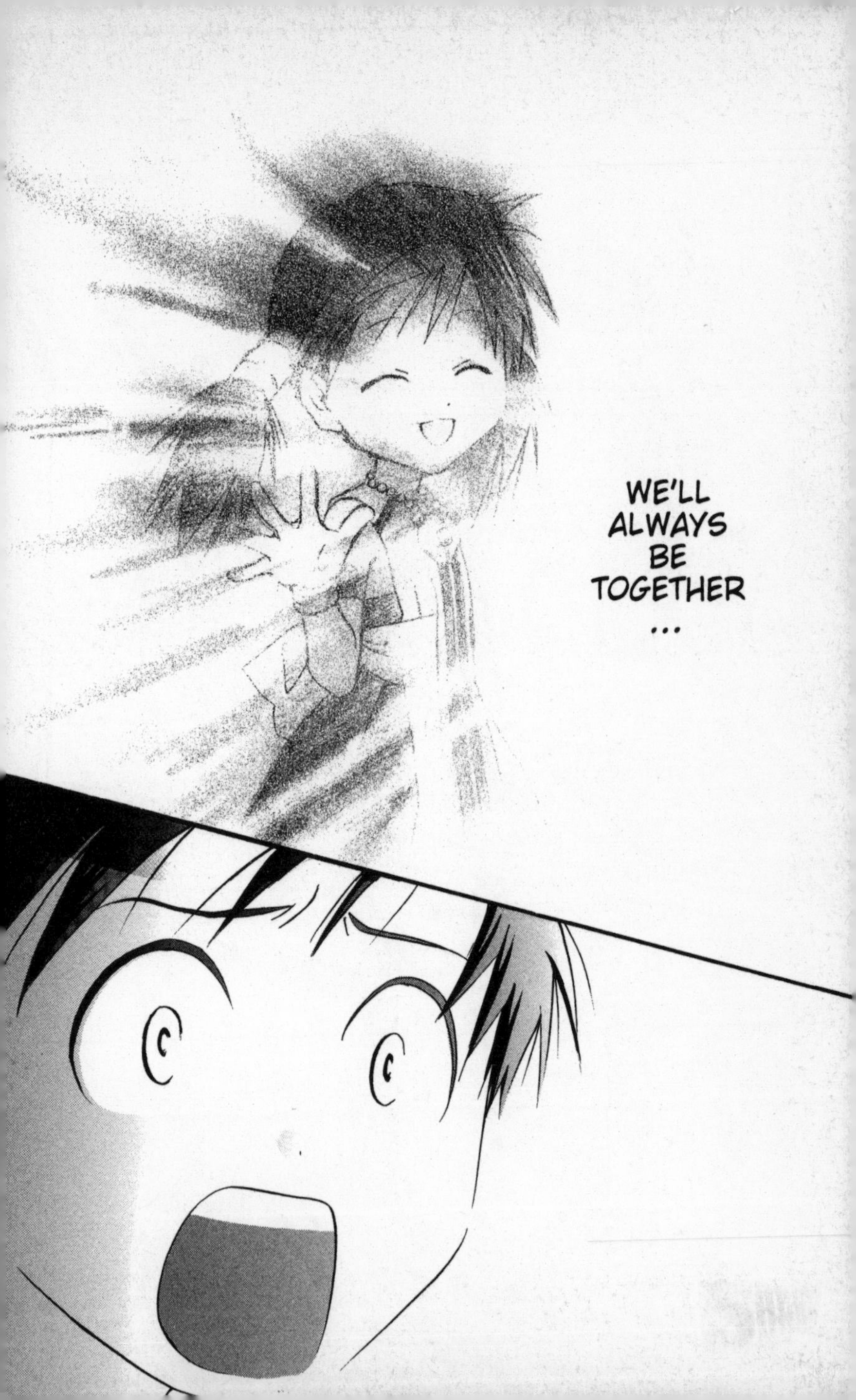
WE'LL ALWAYS BE TOGETHER ...

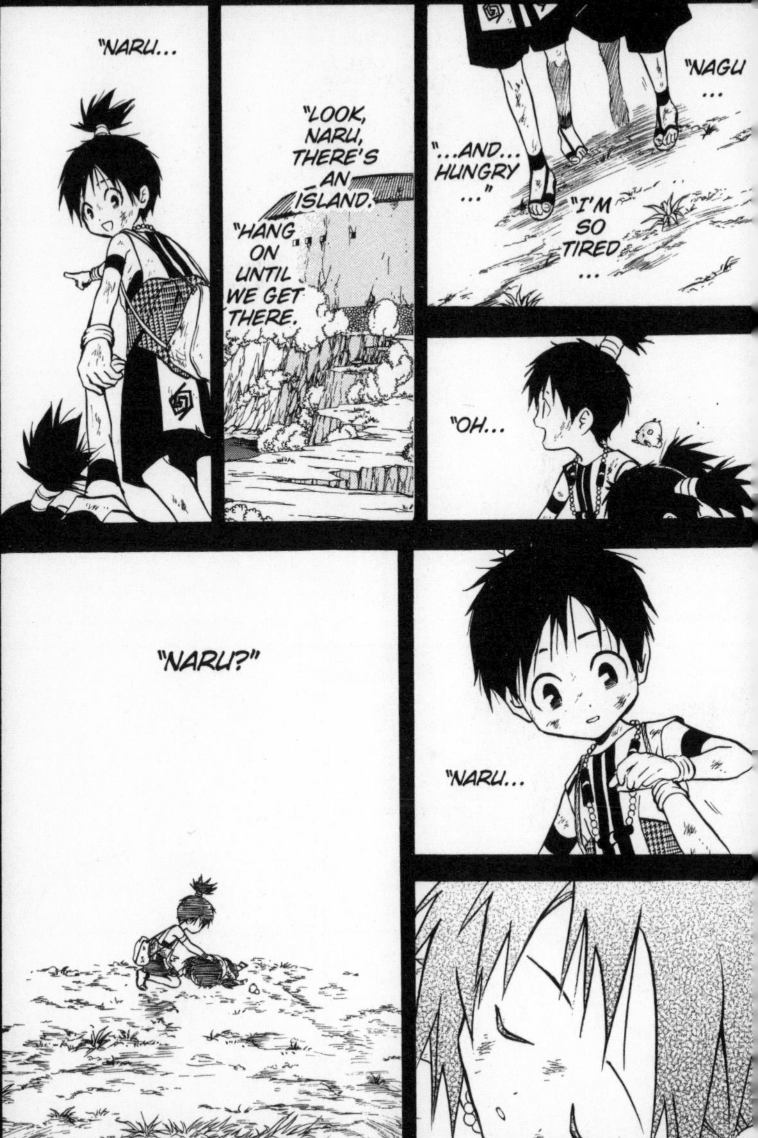
"NAGU ...
"I'M SO TIRED ...
"...AND... HUNGRY ..."
"OH...
"LOOK, NARU, THERE'S AN ISLAND.
"HANG ON UNTIL WE GET THERE.
"NARU...
"NARU...
"NARU?"

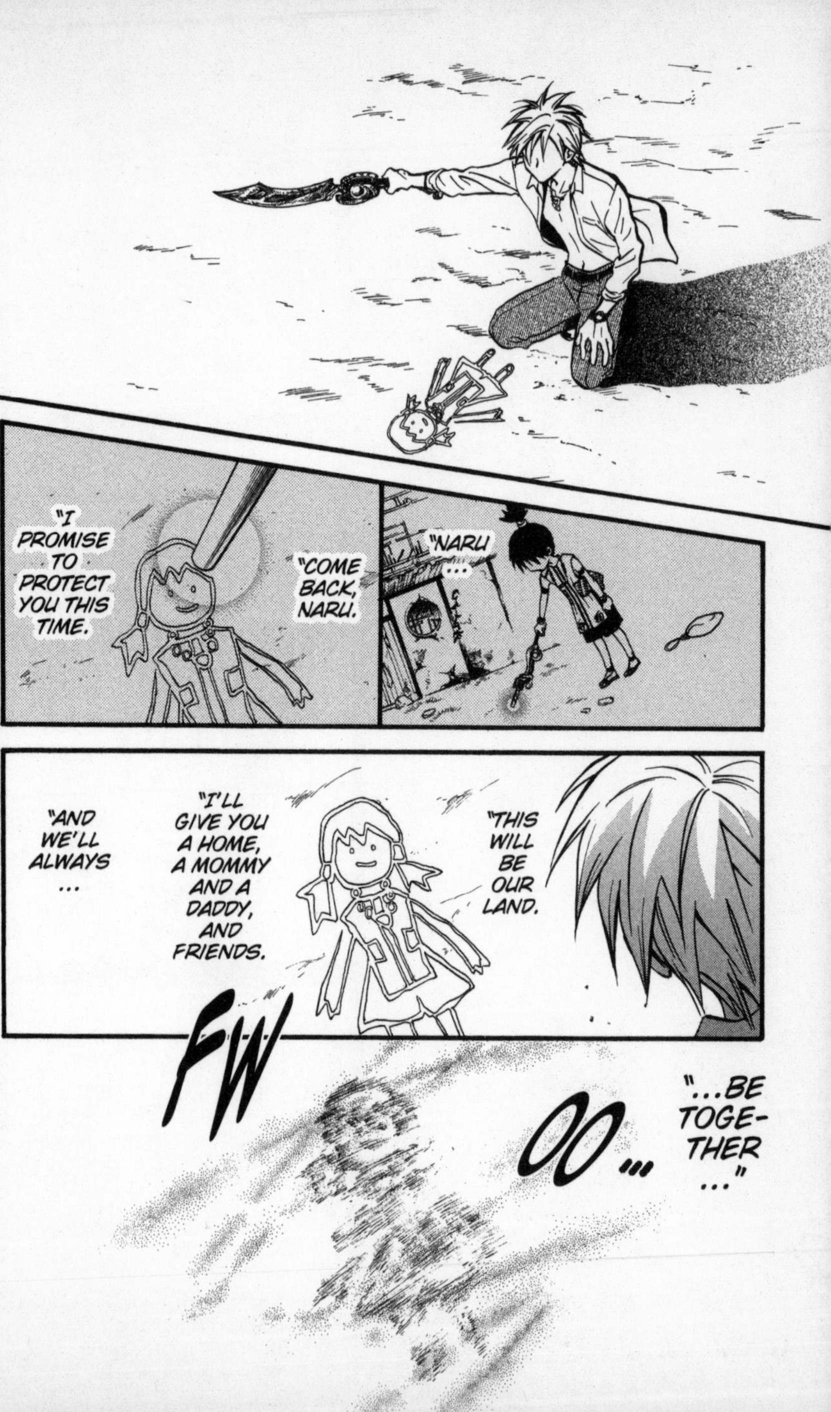
"NARU ...
"COME BACK, NARU.
"I PROMISE TO PROTECT YOU THIS TIME.
"THIS WILL BE OUR LAND.
"I'LL GIVE YOU A HOME, A MOMMY AND A DADDY, AND FRIENDS.
"AND WE'LL ALWAYS ...
FWOO...
"...BE TOGE-THER ..."

ARATA: THE LEGEND 4 (THE END)

ARATA: THE LEGEND

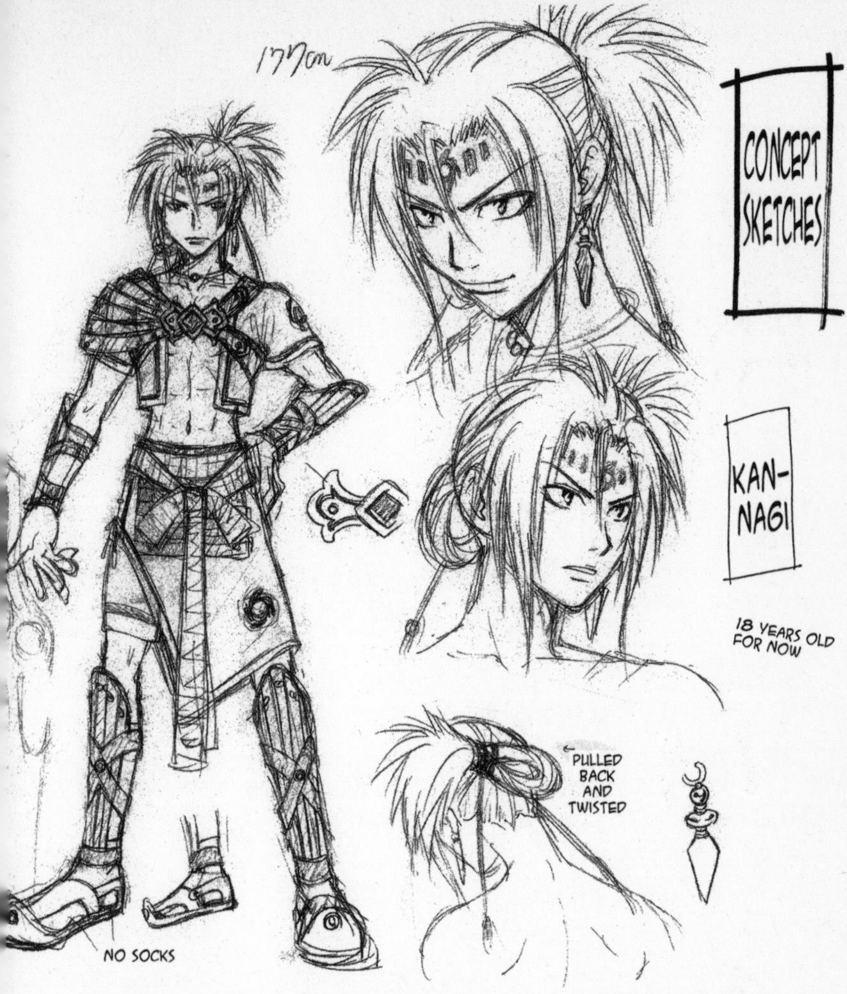

177cm
CONCEPT SKETCHES
KAN-NAGI
18 YEARS OLD FOR NOW
PULLED BACK AND TWISTED
NO SOCKS

HE WAS THE FIRST OF THE TWELVE SHINSHO TO APPEAR, SO THIS WAS A ROUGH DESIGN. I WAS THINKING, "IT'S A WEEKLY SERIES, SO I DON'T WANT TOO MANY DETAILS." BUT IT WAS HARDER TO KEEP TO THIS IDEA THAN I THOUGHT! AND I KNEW I COULDN'T JUST SLAP THINGS TOGETHER...

THE WAISTLINE IS SLUNG LOW BECAUSE, WELL, HE'S YOUNG. (HA!) BUT DOES IT STILL QUALIFY AS ARMOR?! ANYWAY, I LIKE HIS HAIRSTYLE. I MADE HIM LOOK SORT OF LIKE A VILLAIN, BUT WHAT IF HE TURNS INTO A GOOD GUY? HE WAS AN EASY CHARACTER TO CREATE. ISN'T A CHARACTER THIS MANLY A FIRST FOR ME?

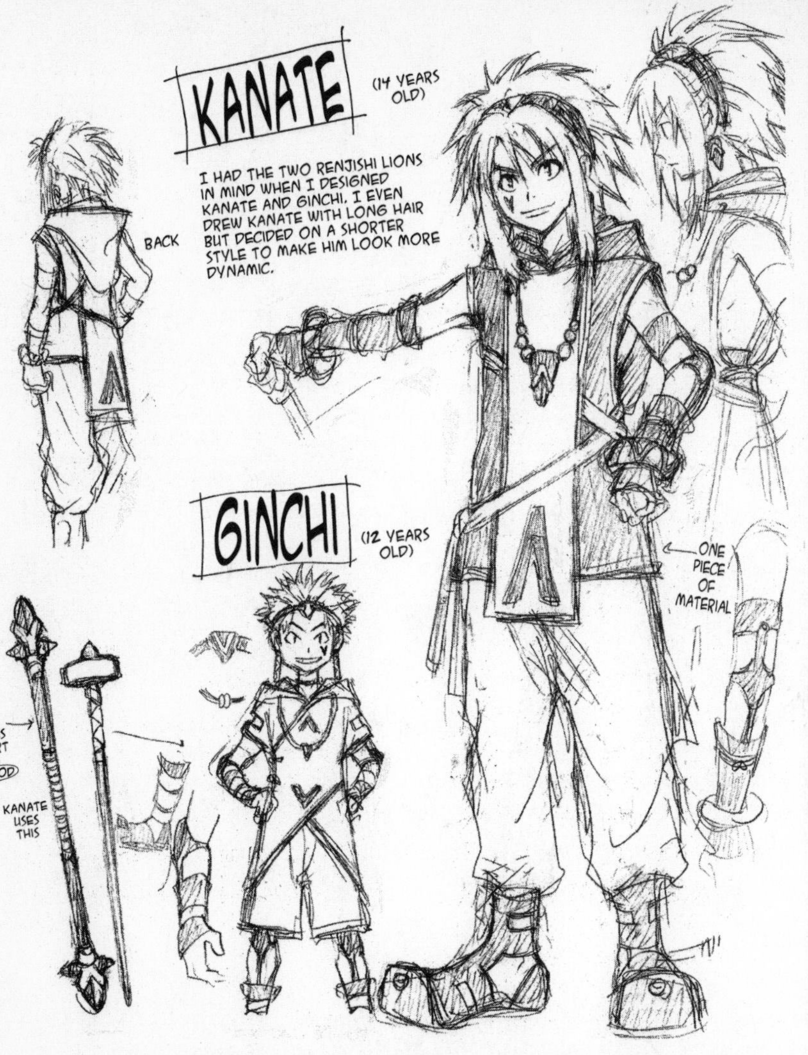
KANATE
(14 YEARS OLD)
I HAD THE TWO RENJISHI LIONS IN MIND WHEN I DESIGNED KANATE AND GINCHI. I EVEN DREW KANATE WITH LONG HAIR BUT DECIDED ON A SHORTER STYLE TO MAKE HIM LOOK MORE DYNAMIC.
BACK
ONE PIECE OF MATERIAL
GINCHI
(12 YEARS OLD)
THIS PART IS WOOD
KANATE USES THIS

AT FIRST, I PICTURED KANATE AS A YOUNG PUNK-TYPE, BUT HE DEVELOPED INTO SOMEONE CUTER. AFTER ALL, HE'S A YEAR YOUNGER THAN ARATA. RIGHT NOW HE'S BASICALLY A HAPPY-GO-LUCKY COMEDIC CHARACTER, BUT HE'LL BE INVOLVED IN SOME MAJOR DRAMA EVENTUALLY. MAYBE HE'LL EVEN BE REUNITED WITH GINCHI.

EVERYONE, *ARATA: THE LEGEND* IS ACTUALLY A DRAMA ABOUT BEING HUMAN. THAT, AND IT'S FILLED WITH BATTLES, ADVENTURE AND FANTASY STUFF. (WHAT STUFF?) SO PLEASE LOOK FORWARD TO VOLUME 5 IN WHICH HUMAN RELATIONSHIPS ARE GOING TO TAKE CENTER STAGE.

Then I'm going to take a month-long vacation. 8/09

I'm sure you've begun to notice that the covers of this graphic novel can be lined up sideways to create a picture scroll. I'm coloring the drawings analog-style and so the parts that join are... Well, I tend to get a bit obsessive. If worst comes to worst, I can always rely on the designer's modern-day convenience (the computer), but I want to color by hand as much as possible. I'm going to do this with my own two hands! In any case, it might be fun to line up all the covers in your room as the volumes pile up.

–Yuu Watase

AUTHOR BIO

Born March 5 in Osaka, Yuu Watase debuted in the *Shôjo Comic* manga anthology in 1989. She won the 43rd Shogakukan Manga Award with *Ceres: Celestial Legend*. One of her most famous works is *Fushigi Yûgi*, a series that has inspired the prequel *Fushigi Yûgi: Genbu Kaiden*. In 2008, *Arata: The Legend* started serialization in *Shonen Sunday*.

Arata THE LEGEND

ARATA: THE LEGEND
Volume 4
Shonen Sunday Edition

Story and Art by YUU WATASE

English Adaptation: Lance Caselman
Translation: JN Productions
Touch-up Art & Lettering: Rina Mapa
Cover Design: Frances O. Liddell
Interior Design: Ronnie Casson
Editor: Amy Yu

Printed in the U.S.A.

Published by VIZ Media, LLC
P.O. Box 77010
San Francisco, CA 94107

10 9 8 7 6 5 4 3 2 1
First printing, December 2010

RATED T FOR TEEN

PARENTAL ADVISORY
ARATA: THE LEGEND is rated T for Teen and is recommended for ages 13 and up. This volume contains fantasy violence.
ratings.viz.com

www.viz.com

MANGA STARTS ON SUNDAY
WWW.SHONENSUNDAY.COM

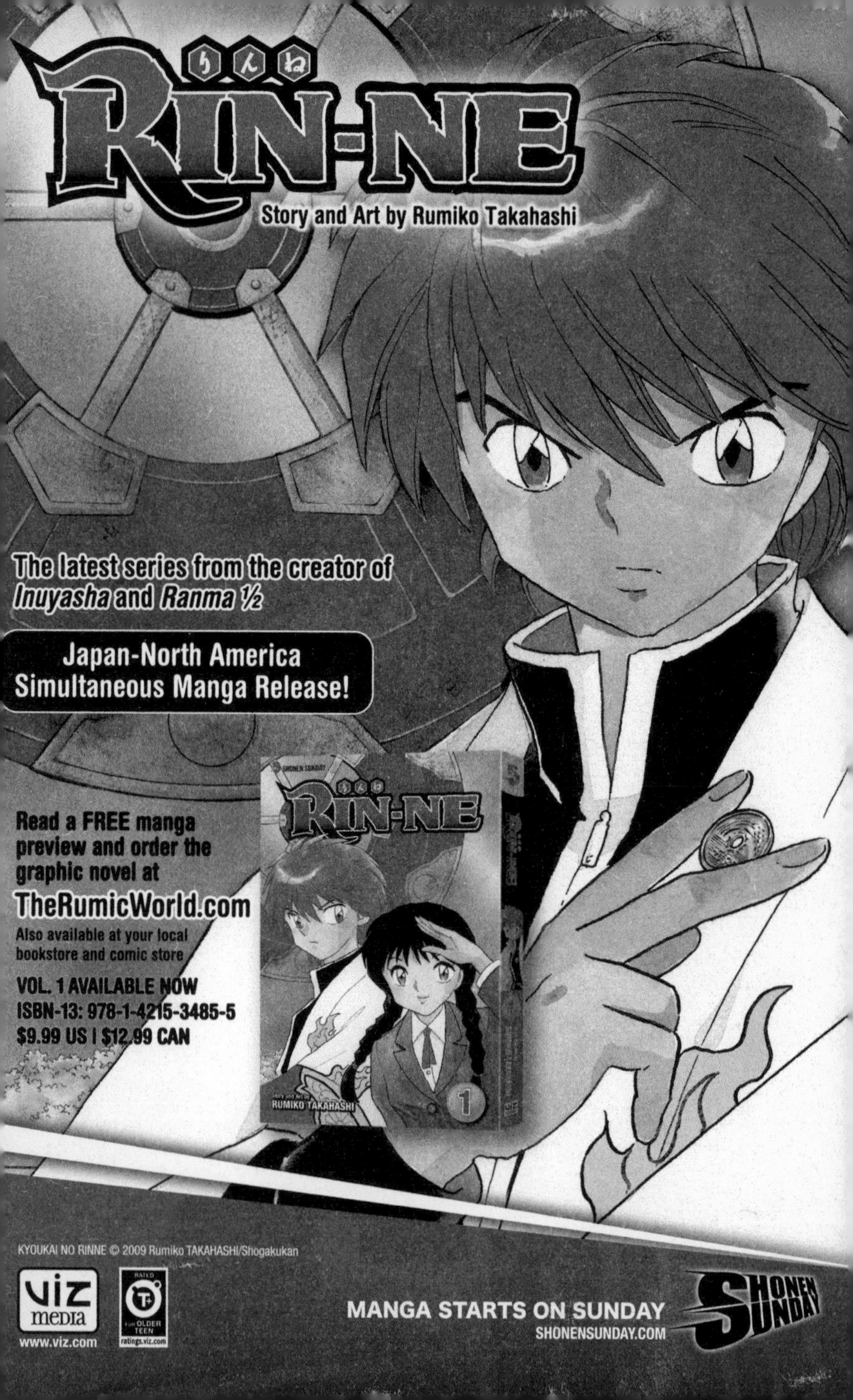
りんね
RIN-NE
Story and Art by Rumiko Takahashi
The latest series from the creator of
Inuyasha and Ranma ½
Japan-North America
Simultaneous Manga Release!
SHONEN SUNDAY
RIN-NE
Story and Art by
RUMIKO TAKAHASHI
1
Read a FREE manga
preview and order the
graphic novel at
TheRumicWorld.com
Also available at your local
bookstore and comic store
VOL. 1 AVAILABLE NOW
ISBN-13: 978-1-4215-3485-5
$9.99 US | $12.99 CAN
KYOUKAI NO RINNE © 2009 Rumiko TAKAHASHI/Shogakukan
viz media
www.viz.com
RATED T+ FOR OLDER TEEN
ratings.viz.com
MANGA STARTS ON SUNDAY
SHONENSUNDAY.COM
SHONEN SUNDAY